A BIKER'S PILGRIMAGE

Sabya Sachi Ghosh is a visual artist and a Master of English at the Doon School, Dehradun. He is also an ardent history enthusiast and a biker, who rides to far-flung places in India to document ancient ruins, monuments and archaeological sites. He is a contributing author of the book *Muslims and Media Images: News vs Views* and has written a few travel articles for the Delhi edition of the *Deccan Herald* newspaper.

A BIKER'S PILGRIMAGE
Forgotten Edifices, Unfortunate Histories

SABYA SACHI GHOSH

RUPA

Published by
Rupa Publications India Pvt. Ltd 2025
7/16, Ansari Road, Daryaganj
New Delhi 110002

Sales centres:
Bengaluru Chennai
Hyderabad Jaipur Kathmandu
Kolkata Mumbai Prayagraj

Copyright © Sabya Sachi Ghosh 2025

The views and opinions expressed in this book are the author's own and the facts are as reported by him which have been verified to the extent possible, and the publishers are not in any way liable for the same.

All rights reserved.

No part of this publication may be reproduced, transmitted, or stored in a retrieval system, in any form or by any means, electronic, mechanical, photocopying, recording or otherwise, without the prior permission of the publisher.

P-ISBN: 978-93-6156-025-5
E-ISBN: 978-93-6156-103-0

First impression 2025

10 9 8 7 6 5 4 3 2 1

The moral right of the author has been asserted.

Printed in India

This book is sold subject to the condition that it shall not, by way of trade or otherwise, be lent, resold, hired out, or otherwise circulated, without the publisher's prior consent, in any form of binding or cover other than that in which it is published.

To my father who taught me how to ride the difficult cast-iron-engine-wrong-side-gear Royal Enfield motorcycle. To my mother who allowed him to do so. To my mother-in-law, who loves me as the son she never had. To my father-in-law, who I wish were with us to see the publication of this book. To my wife, who is my greatest pillar of support and strength...without her approval, my solo rides across India to see its countless historical monuments would have only lasted as far as the corner shop.

Contents

Preface		*ix*
Introduction		*xi*
1.	Ravages of Kashmir	1
2.	Haridwar: The Spiritual Gateway	20
3.	In Krishna's Cradle	41
4.	The Ruins of Kannauj	90
5.	Lord Rama's Janmabhoomi	127
6.	Prayagraj: The Immortal Tree and the Invisible Saraswati of the Sangam	160
7.	Eternal Banaras	189
8.	The Lost Treasures of Sarnath	240
Acknowledgements		261
Notes		263

Preface

Earlier I would just ride to a historical place, click photos of the ruins, and post them up on Facebook. Seeing the photos and the number of places, most of which were unknown, my wife recommended that I make a website and include in it my travel documentation, along with pictures of my paintings. I did that but was not happy with the outcome. It was then that the idea of writing a book was given to me by my friend Waswo X Waswo, an American artist residing in Udaipur.

At first, I intended for it to be a coffee table book, but then I realized that if I had to write, why not do exhaustive research on the history of those places? Once I began researching, particularly studying primary sources, my trajectory changed from the drawing room table to the bookshelf of a collector's library. In this regard, I have tried to incorporate the history and geography of, and the stories of my travel to, those places in a continued narrative.

Regarding the information that has helped me write the history of those places: I have mostly used primary sources like translated manuscripts, ancient literary and mythological texts, archaeological reports, inscriptional records from *Epigraphia Indica* and other such books, gazetteers compiled during colonial times, my field visits, and conversations with locals about the oral history of the place. This book tries to understand the complex layers of India's past, which I believe is mankind's modern link to the ancient world vis-à-vis its destruction and regeneration.

Introduction

The Geography of India

Like the socio-religious and cultural aspects of India, its geography is also complicated and varied. Laid out as a quadrilateral on the southern end of Asia, the world's seventh largest country, with the second largest population, is a heterogeneous block. Hemmed in by two seas, an ocean, the Himalayas and a desert, the country is also called a subcontinent in geographical terms. Within the landmass are found mountain and hill ranges, plateaus, forests, plains, hot and cold deserts, arid landscapes, glaciers, rivers and lakes. Outside its landmass are two clusters of islands that belong to it, in the western and the eastern seas, one named after Arabia and the other after Bengal. The vast ocean south of the tip of the peninsula is named after India.

What's in a Name?

Oddly, the ancients decided to bring all these varied landforms with their various flora and fauna under the shade of one tree, the Indian blackberry, i.e. *jamun*, whose scientific name, *Syzygium cumini*, just like the imagination of the ancients, makes no sense at all. They then named the subcontinent Jambudwipa, or 'the island of the Jamun tree', as if this was the only tree that grew aplenty there. It's perhaps as if they disliked the prospect of naming their homeland after the neem tree, which, though a more sensible choice, is rather unpalatable for its bitterness; even though the neem is considered a *kalpavriksha*.

On its name: India, or rather the western part of it, where flourished the Indus–Saraswati Civilization, was called Meluha by the Sumerians 1,600 years before the birth of Herodotus. By the time Herodotus wrote his *Histories* in the fifth century BCE, Jambudwipa to the Greeks was known as 'Indoi', after Indus River, whose Sanskrit name is Sindhu. A century after Herodotus, Alexander invaded the subcontinent and marched as far as the Jhelum in the Punjab. By then the name Indoi began to be used to denote all the other land and peoples who lived to the east of the Indus River, and the word 'Indica', from Megasthenes' book of the same name, denoted everything belonging to the subcontinent.

Since then, the name gained currency. This is a classic example of an exonym, just like the name 'Greece', derived from the Latin 'Graecia'. The Greeks call themselves 'Hellada', derived from 'Hellas', while we Indians call them 'Yavana' after the Ionians, who, ironically, dwelt in the west of Turkey. And just like the Greeks, we also have an endonym for our country, i.e. Bharat. From the Mahabharata we get the legend of Bharat, the son of Shakuntala and Dushyant. This prince went on to become an emperor, giving his name, 'Bharat', to India. This is an alternative name used by every Indian and is also the constitutional name of the country.

The Chinese used several versions of the names of India, one being 'Tianzu', and the Japanese used 'Tenjiku'. The seventh century CE Chinese pilgrim Hieun Tsang does not mention anything specific for India but calls the country 'Wu-Tien' (Five Indies), denoting an amalgamation of several kingdoms within Jambudwipa.

A few years after Hieun Tsang left the subcontinent, another pilgrim named I-Tsing arrived from China. It is speculated that the grand funeral of Hieun Tsang was witnessed by I-Tsing, who was in the western capital during that time. I-Tsing, whose records have come down to us like Hieun Tsang's, mentions that the people of the 'northern tribes', i.e. the Mongols, called the subcontinent 'Hindu'.[1] He goes on to state that the people of India themselves did not know this name by which they were called. They, in turn, referred to the Great Chau (China) as 'Cina'. The various names with which he addresses the subcontinent are 'Si-Fang' (West), 'Wu-Tien' (Five Countries of India), 'Aliya-Tisha' (Aryadesa), 'Moti-Tisha' (Madhyadesha),

'Polo-Men-Kuo' (Brahmarashtra), 'Chan-Pu-Chou' (Jambudwipa), 'Hsin-Tu' (Hindu) and 'Yin-Tu' (Indu). The word 'Indu', as I-Tsing states, is derived from the word for the moon and is not a proper name.[2]

India, as a culturally integrated landmass, is as old as time, preceding even the Buddha, who went about preaching his doctrine in the Gangetic plains of the east. Two centuries after him, the Sanskrit grammarian Panini, who was from the western extremity of the subcontinent, through his works on grammar gave us the names of many known places in the India of those days, covering nearly every corner of the present country. In the final compilation of the Mahabharata in its present written form, which happened during the third and fourth centuries CE, the great epic included names of places in the subcontinent that if placed on a map, correspond to not only the present country, whose landmass ends at Kanyakumari, but beyond its borders, including Central Asia, Afghanistan, Tibet and China. These last four places were not a part of India but the epic claims that their rulers sided with the Kauravas during the great battle of Kurukshetra.

Was the knowledge of India's geography only limited to the mention of places in old Sanskrit literature? Did Indians travel outside as much as India received outsiders? We know for certain that Indians were travellers just like the Arabs, the Persians or the Greeks and Romans. Greek/Roman works of astronomy/astrology, like the *Yavanajataka*, were greatly influential among the known pandits of that time, around the second century CE. The sixth century CE astronomer/astrologer Varahamihira's encyclopaedic work, the *Brihat Samhita*, mentions that for an astronomer/astrologer to be great, he must know, among other Indian texts on the subject, the *Paulisa Siddhanta* and the *Romaka Siddhanta*. These two books are believed to have been authored by Paul of Alexandria in the fourth century BCE or by Paulus, a Greek astronomer, and by an unknown Roman astronomer, respectively. The *Brihat Samhita* is replete with names of places and peoples in India and outside, which, like the great epic, can be used to form a clear idea about the known extent of the subcontinent that corresponds to the political map of India today.

It is definite that there was a vigorous exchange of knowledge between the two poles of the ancient world. This is contrary to what Brahminical ideas, which say that the flow of knowledge was only export-oriented, would have us believe. Confirming and countering this fallacy, Megasthenes tells us: 'India neither received a colony from abroad nor sent out a colony to any other nation.'[3]

Is India a State?

While studying political science during my intermediate, I encountered an interesting question in a chapter related to statehood. If the modern definition of a state relies on the unity of a people based on religion, culture, language, racial ethnicity or geographical factors, then in what way is India a state? It does not check any of the boxes mentioned above. This question is best answered by a rather metaphysical proposition about India's statehood based on people's experience of the concept of India. However vague this may sound, it is as real as China's unitarian dictatorship or America's federalism. The best way to understand this in the context of India is through the understanding of an oxymoronic but oft-used phrase: 'unity in diversity'.

The concept of a unified entity, which is best described in modern parlance by the expression 'unity in diversity', existed before the British brought the various parts of Jambudwipa under their rule for the last time. Did this concept exist during ancient times? The answer is yes and no. Despite the nature of the subcontinent's polity at the time before the Buddha, statehood as we know it revolved around the person of the monarch and his ability to mobilize a feeling of unity among his subjects. Simultaneously, there existed many republics, called *janapada*s, which, during the lifetime of the Tathagata, numbered sixteen.

Kautilya's ideas of nation-building and statecraft as envisioned in his *Arthashastra* do tell us that even during such times in the hoary past, attempts were made to foster a sense of patriotism based on loyalty to the king, whose moral and political duty was to consider all his subjects as his children.[4] At present, this loyalty is not to the government but to the sovereign nature of the state, of which the government is a part and the prime minister the chief executive, exercising power in the name of the president.

The Idea of India through Pilgrimage

Here a doubt arises—a landmass cannot be claimed to be united just by the mere mention of places on a map, at least politically. This doubt is best answered not through the prism of geopolitics but through the socio-religious aspects of the lives of the people of Jambudwipa.

Over aeons, India experienced inter-religious cohesion in the many ancient centres of pilgrimage that are to be found across the length and breadth of this country. And sometimes, there were religious flare-ups between them. However ironic the previous sentence is, despite the differences between India's religions, namely Jainism, Buddhism and Hinduism, before the coming of Islam and the birth of Sikhism in its soil, people did indulge in long-distance travel to visit remote holy places, some of which catered to pilgrims belonging to all of the first three faiths.

Ancient holy cities like Banaras, Prayag, Ayodhya, Mathura and Thaneshwar are great examples of such centres of pilgrimage. The Mahabharata and some Puranas give us detailed lists of holy places in the subcontinent, called *tirtha*s, which, if visited, brought great spiritual merit to the pilgrims.[5] And the holiest among the holy places in the Mahabharata was a place called Samanta-Panchaka, which is Thaneshwar in Kurukshetra.

Parasurama, the sixth avatar of Vishnu, had emptied the blood absorbed by his axe at Kurukshetra, and five lakes were formed due to this, giving the place the name Samanta-Panchaka. It was at Samanta-Panchaka that the battle of Kurukshetra is believed to have been fought, making it even more venerated till other places gained an equal amount of prominence. The sanctity of the place was such that it was accorded the name 'Brahmavarta' by the law-giver Manu, as the land of Brahma. It was through Brahmavarta that the rivers Saraswati and Drishadvati flowed.[6]

Apart from the shared places of pilgrimage, Jains visited their exclusive centres in different parts of the country, as far south as Shravanbelgola in Karnataka and the Parasnath Hill in the east, to the Shatrunjaya Hill of Palitana in the west and Hastinapur in the north. The Buddhists, during the heyday of their existence in India, likewise visited stupas that are to be found across the length and breadth of the subcontinent. Among them were foreign pilgrims, who specifically visited India to pay their respects to the many stupas that contained the bodily remains of various teachers of the Buddha's doctrine.

The Hindus, even though not a homogeneous unit like the Jains or the Buddhists, had/have more centres of pilgrimage than the other two religions combined. Theirs extended to every nook and cranny of the subcontinent—these were found on the banks of every stream, in the depth of every cave, on the trunk of every oddly shaped tree,[7] and in every direction, with India's northernmost pilgrimage site being the holy Mount Kailash in Tibet. The religious landmass of the subcontinent traversed by pilgrims was the basis of its nationhood, even though divided by political compulsions under the suzerainty of different monarchs.

Did this loyalty extend beyond the king and spill onto the land? That, once again, cannot be simplistically answered with a yes or a no. On the one hand, one must keep in mind that the common people of the bygone era were not the pleasure tourists of today, and had no love for Kanyakumari or desire to visit it the way a Bengali from the furthest corner of the state may do today. On the other hand, one must also keep in mind the religious tourist who braved the perils of the journey and visited far-flung places in the subcontinent, which included Kanyakumari. Imagine it to be something like a Muslim pilgrim's love for Mecca. Even though their loyalties lie with the different countries that they are the citizens of, the concentrated focus as the basis of the unity of their *deen* (the way of life that Muslims follow to comply with the divine law of Islam) is that city in Saudi Arabia towards which they direct their prayers.

Another question arises: did the ancient Indians do something about their desire to visit far-flung centres of pilgrimage throughout the subcontinent? If they did, then how did they accomplish that? The answer to the first question is a definite yes. Those unable to travel listened to stories about those places and brought them close to where they lived by replicating their names in local tirthas. These stories were told in the form of fantastic tales associated with sages, gods and goddesses, and their affinity to certain places all across the geography of the land.

The Conceptualization of the Idea of India, the Land of the Jamun Tree

The ancients, with their limited worldly knowledge,[8] envisioned a fantastic map of the subcontinent that, to a geographer, is nightmarish. The authors of the various Puranas conceptualized Jambudwipa as a divine island surrounded by seven concentric islands, between which existed seven oceans. The *Markandeya Purana* by Sage Markandeya, which is one of the oldest Puranas, possibly composed in the third century CE, gives a vivid imaginary description of the geographic extent of Jambudwipa.

The Jambudwipa of *Markandeya* was envisioned as a circular island stretching 100,000 *yojanas* (one yojana being between 3.5 and 15 km) in length and breadth, containing seven lofty mountain ranges named Himavat, Hemakuta, Nishadha, Meru, Nila, Sveta and Sringin.[9] The venerable sage then tells us that one country of Jambudwipa was named Bharat after the son of Shakuntala and Dushyant. It was divided into nine parts called Indradwipa, Kserumata, Tamravarna, Ghavistimata, Nagadwipa, Saumya, Gandharva and Varuna.[10] To the south of Varuna is a sea that surrounds it (the peninsular portion of South India).

In Bharat dwelt Brahmins, Kshatriyas, Vaishyas and Sudras. To the east of Bharat were the Kiratas (forest people) and to the west were Yavanas (foreigners like Greeks, Persians, and others). The land of Bharat had in it several mountains and rivers that arose from the Himavat (Himalayas).

Aeons before *Markandeya*, the Rig Veda named a few rivers of North India as well, in its 'Nadi Stuti Sukta', composed by Rishi Priyamedha. Starting with the Ganga, the hymn mentions the Yamuna, the Saraswati (now dead but identified with the Ghaggar), the Satadru (Sutlej), the Parushini (Ravi), the Asikli (Chenab), the Marudvridha (unidentified but its name means an old river flowing through the desert or a feeble stream), the Vitasta (Jhelum), the Sushoma (another name for the Indus) and the Arjikiya, identified with the Haro.

The Tangible Past of the Past

The vast expanse of the land in the subcontinent has seen continuous occupation from well before the Ice Age. Our earliest ancestors have left behind the marks of their presence in the forms of not only stone tools and complex paintings on the walls of rock shelters, but also flat bronze anthropomorphic figurines, some of which are pretty large, their purpose as mystifying as their existence. As recently as 2022, a large cache of copper swords, spear heads and four such anthropomorphic figurines were unearthed by a farmer from his field in Ganeshpur village in the Mainpuri district of Uttar Pradesh.[11]

A decade or so ago, Sanauli in the Bagpat district of Uttar Pradesh gave us several similar copper weapons, including a chariot.[12] Swords, spears, daggers, shields, chariots, and skeletal remains of the people who used them are easy to understand, but the strange nature of those flat copper figurines baffles my comprehension and makes them rather mysterious.

Talking of mystery, the Indus Valley Civilization, also called the Harappan Culture, vis-à-vis the Vedic conundrum is a binary that puzzles me. The question is not only which among them came first, but also about the missing keystone used to join these two arms of India's historical arch. The Indus script is yet to be deciphered satisfactorily. Its many seals with hieroglyphics hold a key to unravelling the connection between the two limbs of India's prehistory. Well, I am eagerly waiting for the day when a Rosetta Stone is discovered for the Indus script.

It is a fact that the earliest material signs of urban civilization in India are the ancient foundational ruins of close to 1,400 sites belonging to what is known as the Indus Valley Civilization (nowadays it is broadly called the Indus-Saraswati Civilization). Its people knew the art of writing and building cities, with indoor toilets, covered drains, right-angular streets, and advanced methods of water harvesting. They used uniform weights and measures for their vast commercial enterprise that spread as far as Mesopotamia. All of these are the hallmarks of a 'modern' society.

It is also an established fact that the subcontinent's earliest signs of spiritual advancement, from nomadic life to settled agriculture, come down to us in the form of the Vedic texts. Vedic Indians were a nomadic group of people and pastoralists. Being verily termed as the Aryans, they are believed to have migrated into India from Central Asia and Persia during the declining phase of the Indus-Saraswati Civilization, sometime around 1700 BCE.

Some scholars have even attributed the downfall of some Indus sites to attacks by these nomadic hordes, giving linguistic examples such as the name of the primary Vedic god Indra, who is also called Purandar, or 'the one who destroys a *pur* or a city'. The hypothesis of the existence of two different peoples, i.e. the urban indigenous group versus the nomadic Aryan outsiders, began during colonial times and is still a raging debate. It is the longest bone of contention amongst the two primary schools of Indian historiographers, and I don't see any confluence of ideas between them in the near future.

Here, I have no desire to wade into this controversy, but want to analyse the logic put forward by both the schools: the left and the right. Clarifying my stance, I would like to state that I am not a historian or an archaeologist, but an artist and an English teacher, who loves riding to different historical destinations in the country. I am doing this for my own understanding and trying to demystify the cluttered and overlapping imagery of the subcontinent's ancient past.

While the Indus–Saraswati sites were flourishing, neolithic sites in Kashmir, namely Burzahom and Gufkral, began their civilizational journey unmindful of what was going on down in the plains. These two sites have been dated back to 3000 BCE and they continued till 1500 BCE.[13] Neolithic sites like Ror, Dera-Gopipur, Baroli, Basawal, and the river banks below the Kangra Fort in the Kangra district of Himachal Pradesh are yet to be properly excavated and documented.

In the valley between Nalagarh and Pinjore near Chandigarh, several neolithic tools were found. These all testify to an emerging culture that began independently of influences from the Indus–Saraswati sites. About 22 km southwest of Nalagarh is Ropar (now Rupnagar), on the banks of the Sutlej. This is a celebrated site of the Indus–Saraswati Civilization that has seen continuous occupation beginning from 2000 BCE to medieval times.

Predating the existence of the neolithic peoples in Kashmir and Himachal is a site in the uppermost part of the Himalayas called Gaik in Ladakh. This site has been dated back to 4700 BCE.[14] The excavation of another Indus–Saraswati site in the village of Bhirrana in the Fatehabad district of Haryana was conducted in 2003–04. The dig has pushed back the dates of the Indus–Saraswati Civilization by at least 2,000 years. Bhirrana's earliest phase of settlement is dated between 7500 BCE and 6000 BCE, making the site 9,000 years old.[15]

And even before that—before any recorded memory, be it via potsherds or myths—were the ancient Indians living in the area that is now referred to as the Potwar Plateau region of northern Punjab (undivided Punjab) by archaeologists, adjacent to the foothills of the Himalayas. These palaeolithic peoples in the north shared the subcontinent's geography with their southern cousins at Bhimbetka in Madhya Pradesh. The time span of these ancient hunter-gatherers of the subcontinent is much greater than the Indus–Saraswati or the Aryan peoples, which also includes the continuous occupation of Jambudwipa to the modern age. Basically, I am of the opinion that the ancients of the Potwar Plateau and Bhimbetka are the ancestors of the Indus–Saraswati peoples.

The Raging Controversy and Understanding Its For and Against

If I were a proponent of the Aryan Migration Theory into India, I would ask: Did the Vedic people establish the Indus–Saraswati sites? If they did, then why do we not find mention of their doing so in the Vedas? Why are Vedic gods and the religious practice of *yagna*s similar to those of the ancient people of Persia and the Hittites of ancient Turkey? Why are there so many mentions of indigenous peoples being compared to uncivilized demons, and being destroyed by the fair-skinned mythological *aryaputra*s (Sanskrit for 'sons of noble beings') and Vedic gods, in Brahminical literature? Why do the facial features of the few human sculptures excavated from Indus sites match those of the Dravidians and not the generic description of the classical aryaputras, with their long noses? If the ancient Indus Civilization was called Meluha by the Sumerians, did the word *mlechchha* originate from Meluha? After all, non-Aryans were classified under the term 'mlechchha'.

Not to mention that the word 'Iran' comes from Aryan, and the ancient name of the land where Zarathustra revealed the gospel of Ahura Mazda was Airyanem Vaejah, which corresponds to northern Iran. And just like the sages of ancient India, Zarathustra, after taking a purifying dip in the river Daitya (Oxus/Amu Darya), offered a sacrifice of *haoma* (the *soma* drink) and meat to Mazda and had the god come down to him. Another point to note is that the vital ingredient of any form of Hindu worship is the darbha grass, which is postulated to be a reminder of the grasslands of Central Asia, whence the Aryans are believed to have migrated.[16]

One more vital aspect of the logic of Aryan migration is that Alexander had to battle the native tribes of the Mallois, who dwelt on the banks of the Indus. During one such skirmish, he was badly wounded by several arrows.[17] Were the Mallois, whose descendants in the Punjab go by the surnames of Malhi and Mallas of North India, a caste associated with plying ferry boats across rivers, the Meluhans? After all, ancient historians who have told the tale of Alexander's conquests and subsequent return via the Indus, state that the Mallois had walled cities on the banks of the river.[18] Doesn't this ring a bell about the Indus–Saraswati urban centres excavated beside rivers?

Horses were the mainstay of the Aryans, so why is there such a paucity of horse remains in the Indus–Saraswati sites? And out of so many different animals, why are horses not depicted in any of the 3,500-odd steatite Indus–Saraswati seals? The tiger is another animal that is often depicted in the Indus seals and not a lion, which, in the Brahminical religion, is a symbol of prowess.[19] The former is a lonely ambush predator of thick jungles, while the latter is a creature of grasslands such as those in Central Asia.

Another question arises that concerns India's many indigenous tribes whose marginal existence is out of the ambit of Brahminism even today. These tribal people still cling on to their hunter-gatherer lifestyle, worship gods that have not yet found a place in the pantheon of the 33 crore divinities of Hinduism, and speak a language that is not influenced by Sanskrit; some even wear ceremonial headgear that looks like the horned helmet of a meditating yogi from an Indus seal.

Talking of language, the close affinity of Sanskrit to some European languages is speculated to be due to a common place of origin, somewhere in Central Asia.[20] This linguistic group, called the Indo-European family, of which modern North Indian languages are an intrinsic part, shares common root words with Latin, Greek, German, English, and so on. It is strange that within the subcontinent, North Indian languages differ so drastically from South Indian tongues, classified as the Dravidian group.

With new archaeological discoveries like the burial site of Sanauli and DNA analysis of skeletons from the Indus–Saraswati site of Rakhigarhi, the binary in the Aryan debate is slowly being erased. The ancient DNA from two of the forty-six skeletons excavated from the necropolis of Rakhigarhi in the Hisar district of Haryana, dating back to 2500 BCE, has yielded an interesting result. The analysis convincingly proves that the people of Rakhigarhi are closely related to the Dravidians or the group of people who have the Ancestral South Indian DNA.[21] Ironically, Haryana, a North Indian state, is believed to be a cradle of Aryandom, the home of the Kauravas and the Pandavas.

Also, a vast number of people north of Maharashtra are classified as part of the Ancestral North Indian DNA group, whose DNA has a greater affinity with the Iranians than with the Tamils.[22] And the further north one goes, the more the traces of Ancestral South Indian DNA diminish—unlike the physical features of the people, which get sharper, their heads getting longer and skin fairer. Corresponding to this is the family of languages spoken of earlier.

If I were a proponent of the Out of India Theory, this would be my reply: The dating of the earliest layer of Bhirrana and other pre-Harappan sites like Kalibangan, Sothi, Banawali, Balu, Rakhigarhi, Kunal, Padri, Bagor, Balathal, Gilund, Baror, Girawar and Lotheswar in Haryana, Rajasthan and Gujarat makes it amply clear that civilization most probably started from the Indus–Saraswati Valley and radiated westwards. One valid argument put forward is the advent of 'zero', or rather, the mathematical concept thereof. Could so many cities have been built on grids based on the principles of geometry without the concept of a zero angle? In the impossible computations of the sheer number of Aryan gods that multiplied as time moved towards the modern age, the early evidence of zero is apparent. How else would one even conceive of the number crore, which has seven zeroes?

The cities conquered by Alexander in the Punjab and on the banks of the Indus were none other than the urban centres of the Indus–Saraswati Civilization that were witnessing continuous occupation. The presence of fire altars in Indus–Saraswati sites that have been excavated, the continuing practice of shell bangles being worn by married Hindu ladies (particularly Bengali women) just like by the Indus dames, the recurring imagery in the likeliness of a seated yogi, the prevalence of the bull imagery in Indus seals, and the discovery of small votive phallic objects are a few pieces of evidence that can be used to convincingly prove the Vedic origin of the Indus sites.

The mention of the various rivers of the subcontinent in the Rig Veda can also be cited as further evidence that the Vedic Aryans were indigenous peoples. Another compelling proof that can be cited is the flora and fauna mentioned in the Vedic texts, from which one can infer that the Vedic peoples were indigenous to the subcontinent. Of the trees and their products referred to in the Vedas, all are native to the subcontinent.[23]

Famed archaeologist the late B.B. Lal, often referred to as an archaeo-mythologist, in his essay titled 'The Rig Vedic Flora and Fauna: What Light do These Throw on the "Aryan Invasion" Debate?' gives us the names of the native plants. These are asvattha (*Ficus religiosa*), kimsuka/flame of the forest/palash (*Butea monosperma*), khadira (*Acacia catechu*), nyagrodha (*Ficus benghalensis*), vibhidaka (tropical almond), salmali (silk cotton tree), simsapa (Indian rose wood), urvaruka (*Cucumis melo*), darbha, pakada, munja grass, sipala (*Blyxaoctandra*), and the famed soma, whose intoxicating juice was a sought-after Vedic drink.[24] This plant has not yet been correctly identified and is still a mystery. However, in his *Harshacharita*, written in the seventh century CE, Bana has mentioned beds of this plant growing in the courtyard of his cousins' house, beside drying sacrificial rice cakes spread out on the skins of black antelopes.[25]

The excavation of a necropolis in Sanauli has yielded the remains of a solid-wheeled chariot, with a narrow yoke meant for horses.[26] The site also yielded several skeletons in coffins and bronze double-edged swords, bows, arrows and other objects. These have been dated between 2000 BCE and 1800 BCE, which corresponds to the declining phase of the Indus–Saraswati Civilization. The discovery of such an important burial site is one of the greatest archaeological discoveries of the twenty-first century, and it lays to rest the speculation about the unavailability of horses in mainland India.

This discovery can be hailed as another missing link that connects the Indus–Saraswati Civilization with the Vedic people. However, dampening the exultation, it can also be seen as a sign of their presence during the later phase of the Indus–Saraswati Civilization, indicative of the migration by Aryans and the replacement of the indigenous peoples by sword-wielding chariot-borne conquerors, as described in the epics. At present, I am watching this space and awaiting the result of the DNA analysis of the warriors of Sanauli...

My Common Theory

So, what is going on here, between the north and the south? And why have so many burials been discovered so far, but not cremations, as is the regular and traditional practice in ancient Hinduism? A point to keep in mind here is that ancient Hindus also buried their dead, a practice that was uncommon among the commoners but reserved for the heads of tirthas and children.[27]

So many questions, and each question is a controversy. It appears that the more one searches for answers, the more zeros one encounters—which brings me to state that the Babylonians knew the concept of zero 4,000 years ago and represented it as a mere blank space in their cuneiform tablets. This, once again, begs the question of the possibility of the concept travelling to the west from the east, which confirmedly happened when the Arabs took the Hindu numerals and inadvertently introduced them to the West.

In the bazaars of Béjaïa in Algeria, Leonardo Fibonacci came across decimal calculations and compiled them in his book *Liber Abaci* in 1202 CE, which then popularized Indian numerals and revolutionized calculation.[28] Come to think of it, this was so recent that it coincided with the destruction of the Nalanda University by Bakhtiyar Khilji.

My understanding of the two polarities is best explained with the example of Delhi, the metropolis that has been the centre of North Indian politics for the past 800 years. It is home to a cosmopolitan potpourri of peoples. Delhi had its indigenous occupants and then became the home of conquering peoples and economic migrants alike. The same was true for most of the Indus–Saraswati urban centres. Some were compelled to die out on account of the drying of the Saraswati and the Drisadvati, while others did not.

Do we not see a gigantic Buddhist stupa on the topmost part of

Mohenjo-daro? Or the continuous settlements on the ancient mound of Ropar? Or the present village beside the inhospitable Kalibangan and the verdurous locality of Rakhigarhi that exists adjacent to the Indus–Saraswati mound? Are such sites not glaring examples of continuous occupation? Once again, so many questions and each a controversy.

Here I will argue that a land exists irrespective of its timeline but that is not so for its occupants. However, the overlapping layers of various phases that succeed each other in a continuum tell us less about supplantation than they do about changes in the lifestyle of the people that made them different from their ancestors. This change is often mistaken as a break in a civilization's timeline... Take the case of the Indian converts to Islam and Christianity or a westerner's conversion to Hinduism, and a Hindu's conversion to Buddhism. New cultural traits are adopted and made their own, while those of their forefathers are forgotten. Here I am citing the examples of the Coptic Christians of Egypt, the Orthodox Greek Christians and the Catholics of Rome, or the Persians, for that matter. The Copts trace their ancestry to the Pharaonic peoples of Egypt, the Greeks to the Homeric peoples, and the Persians to the Zoroastrians. The culture of each one of these peoples changed or was compelled to change, causing them to remain in an amnesic stupor about their past.

Civilizations Are Born Irrespective of Migration

Away in the east, far from Mohenjo-daro, Kalibangan, Rakhigarhi and Sanauli, a civilization that coexisted with the mature phase of the Indus–Saraswati settlements was unearthed in West Bengal. The mound, called the Pandu Rajar Dhibi in Panduk village in Burdwan district, has yielded a civilization hitherto unknown to historians. Situated on the banks of the Ajay, the ancient settlement had all the traits of an urban culture. The excavation at the mound, carried out by the Archaeological Survey of India (ASI), was done over three years in 1962, 1963 and 1964. The lowest level of the site belonged to the Copper Age, making these finds the earliest evidence of civilization in eastern India.[29] The finds have been radiocarbon dated to 3000 BCE, which is contemporaneous with the Indus–Saraswati Civilization. The independent existence of this civilization, which also saw continuous growth and occupation till the Pala era in Bengal, is another reminder of people's cultural evolution, whose initial and later stages are not reflective of each other. Did this civilization in its early phase interact with its counterpart in the river valleys of the Indus and the Saraswati? So far, the evidence of any such exchange is lacking, so one cannot conclude anything.

The Polity of the Wheel Turner

At what point of time in the ancient past the country became politically unified is difficult to say. Mythology supplies us with the knowledge of several kingdoms spread out in the subcontinent. We know that in the sixth century BCE, northern India was divided between a medley of sixteen mahajanapadas. Similarly, there were kingdoms in the south. Different religious texts written in different periods of time give us different names for the kingdoms that existed in the subcontinent. On some occasions, there are certain kingdom names that are common to the different books, which informs us of their continuous existence. Here I can cite the example of the Trigarta kingdom in Kangra, among others. However, no two books are unanimous in their mention of the time when the first unification of the country occurred.

Even the rather imaginary map of Jambudwipa, whose centre was topped by the heaven-dwarfing Mount Meru, differs in terms of the various descriptions offered by its three native religions. However, what is common between these religions in their conceptualization of the land is that every other kingdom and republic existed within it, and that the person who conquered or united them under his umbrella was called the *chakravarti* (the wheel-turning monarch). The person with the title of chakravarti, whose English meaning is 'emperor', later became known as the *samrat*.

According to legends, the earliest-known person to be given

credit for being Jambudwipa's first samrat was Bharat. However, in historical records, the first samrats of India were Chandragupta Maurya and his grandson Ashoka. The Satavahana rulers lorded over the Deccan as samrats, immediately after the Mauryas. The third samrat after the Mauryas was an outsider named Kanishka. This Scythian emperor had conquered large swathes of northern India up to Bihar and united the land with his realm that stretched from Central Asia. The Gupta monarchs of Magadha, who came about 400 years after Kanishka, were also samrats because of their vast conquests.

After the eclipse of the imperial Guptas, an important samrat from ancient India was Harshavardhan. The last major Hindu king of North India, Prithviraj Chauhan III, was not a samrat, though he is addressed as such. However, the imperialism associated with the word 'samrat' can be truly applied to the Chola monarchs of Tamil Nadu, who extended their political influence as far as Java and Sumatra in the eleventh and twelfth centuries CE. Ironically, the Chola conquests in mainland India were limited to the kingdoms on its eastern shores and parts of Bengal.

During the medieval phase of India's history post the Islamic conquest, the first Muslim samrat of northern India per se was Alauddin Khilji. Despite his vast conquest of the subcontinent, he was not addressed by the Persian equivalent of 'samrat' as such, which is *padishah/badshah*, but by the relatively humble title of 'sultan'. The last Hindu ruler to have held the status of an emperor was Krishnadevaraya of the Vijayanagar Empire in the Deccan, which lasted between 1336 CE and 1646 CE.

After the end of the Delhi Sultanate, the title of padishah was accorded to the Mughal rulers, starting with Babur, whose conquests were rather paltry when compared to Alauddin Khilji's. Babur's grandson Akbar was a true samrat, in the true spirit of the term, having consolidated Babur's gains and added new territories of his own. His great grandson—the last great Mughal—the infamous Aurangzeb bulldozed his way through the other realms of Hindustan and mindlessly swelled the Mughal Empire to its largest extent. His conduct was the least like a samrat's, alienating the Hindus of his empire, who comprised the majority of his subjects. Even though, from what I have observed, this puritanical character is much loved by one section of India's population, Hindus have nothing good to say about him.

After the decline of the Mughals, the Marathas managed to subjugate most of the subcontinent and earned the right to be called an empire. Their end too, like that of the Mughals, happened rather unceremoniously, and in their stead the political vacuum so created was once again filled by outsiders. The English, over the span of a century post their arrival in the subcontinent, gained political paramountcy in 1757 CE, after the Battle of Plassey, and began the process of conquest, either through force or through clever ploys. By the nineteenth century CE, the subcontinent once again came under a single political unit headed by the British Empire, only to be divided when they left in 1947.

The Charm of Water

Why is it that the subcontinent was such a major draw for migrants, conquerors, traders and pilgrims? Why don't we, in the same vein, hear of similar ancient mass migrations into China, Central Asia, Russia or, for that matter, Europe, stretching over such a great length of time? To understand this, one must consider the subcontinent's geography.

Broadly, the region that lies between India, Central Asia and Europe is the inhospitable Arabia and the arid lands of Greater Persia, which included Afghanistan. At the end of Greater Persia is the Punjab, the first truly green tract of land irrigated by its five rivers, sandwiched between the Himalayas in the north and a desert in the south. Connecting this green tract with the alluvial plains of the Yamuna and the Ganga was the Saraswati, which once flowed in all her glory through Haryana and Rajasthan and merged with the Arabian Sea via the Rann of Kutch. This entire landmass, characterized by fertile soils and unparalleled verdure, stretched for nearly 2,000 km, till the riverine plains ended at the foothills of the mountains of Tripura, Mizoram and the Arakan.

Say an ancient immigrant, along with his kin, manages to traverse the rugged mountains and deserts of Baluchistan or Afghanistan with great difficulty and arrive in the valley of the Indus at Larkana or Multan—from then on, there is nothing much to deter him from venturing inland. The land is green and takes on a deeper hue the farther east he travels. What I am trying to get at here is that if I were an ancient farmer living somewhere in Larkana, I would prefer travelling east into India's heartland rather than braving the inhospitable qualities of the land in the waterless regions of West Asia to find a better life for myself and my family. It was the magnetism of water that drew the first migrants into India.

Here, I must pause and remind the reader not to see any sort of conspiracy that is fed on the binary understanding of either the 'Out of India' Theory or its antithesis, the Aryan Invasion Theory.[30] I fundamentally believe that people come into and go out of a land based on their needs. And the lands that can provide the best resources are the obvious choice for people to visit and populate. This is the first prerequisite for survival and the growth of civilization. So, with India's fertility due to its easily accessible sources of water, it was akin to a honeypot...and this migration into India continued throughout prehistory, up to the recorded time of Darius I's conquest of the plains around the Indus.

Honeypot

Alexander was next. After conquering the empire of Darius III, he reached the Jhelum, battled the son of Poros, and was wounded. In the same battle, he lost his beloved horse, Bucephalus.[31] Then he battled Poros and defeated him, restored his kingdom, and built two cities in the Punjab: one at the site of his victory over Poros and another in memory of his beloved horse. These were named Nikaia and Bucephala, respectively.[32] It was in Bucephala and at a place called Kuropolis[33] that many Macedonians settled among the natives.[34]

In India, Alexander captured ten religious mendicants and had a long discourse with one of them, named Kalanos—the ubiquitous Indian guru, so strongly associated with the land that even in 325 BCE it was considered rather exotic.

Two centuries after him followed the Sakas, who were followed by the Scythians, then the Hunas, and then came the Tibetans from across the Himalayan borders. From the eastern Himalayan borders, the Khen people and other tribes migrated into the northeast. The migration of these tribes continued over centuries.

After the advent of Islam, the Arabs got a toehold in Sindh, with the conquest of Muhammad Bin Qasim in the seventh century CE. The Zoroastrians from a vanquished Persia made India their home a century after that, and along with them also arrived the Sakadwipi Brahmins, who introduced the iconographic representation of a knee-length-boot-wearing Surya.

Two centuries after that, Islamic incursions into the heartland began with Mahmud of Ghazni's raids into the holy places of the subcontinent. And along with him went out of the country, particularly from the area around Kannauj, thousands of people, who were captured and enslaved. The descendants of these slaves are the Roma people in Europe and the Americas.[35]

A century and a half after the death of Mahmud of Ghazni, the plundering raids culminated in Muhammad Ghori's attainment of political supremacy in North India, after the Second Battle of Tarain in 1192 CE. Within a few decades of the establishment of the Delhi Sultanate, the subcontinent saw another wave of mass migration in the Brahmaputra River Valley. The Shan people of northern Myanmar, known as the Ahoms, arrived there and made the place their home.

While the Delhi Sultanate was busy swallowing up independent kingdoms, Persian and Arab settlers and mercenaries began pouring into India. Many were compelled to leave their homes due to the fear of the Mongol raids taking place in Central Asia and nearby places. Baghdad had fallen to the Mongols in 1258 CE.

Then arrived the Mongols, who first came as berserkers and began their incursions into the subcontinent. This recurring blight was checked by Alauddin Khilji, who stood as a bulwark between the berserkers from Mongolia and the rest of India. A few thousand captured Mongols made Delhi their home after accepting Islam.

About eighty years after Alauddin Khilji, an offshoot of the Mongols arrived as a scourge once again and ravaged North India, including Delhi; they were led by Timur the Lame, one of the ancestors of Babur. And then the Mughals arrived, and then arrived the Europeans, who, unlike the others, never called India their home but colonized the subcontinent nevertheless...

Wanderlust and Avarice

Peoples travel and so do people. India not only attracted violent migrants but also those afflicted with wanderlust. There are those who came from outside and those who travelled within. The seventh century CE author Banabhatta[36] too had set out wandering for years outside his native place, which was somewhere on the banks of Sone River in the Chapra district of Bihar. He did so in the company of some colourful characters.[37] Another great 'domestic' traveller was Shankaracharya in the eighth century CE. He traversed the length and breadth of the country, starting from his native Kerala.

I like this phrase by J.R.R. Tolkien: 'Not all those who wander are lost.' Applying this here, I can say that not all visitors to the subcontinent came with the sole aim of conquest. Some came for personal reasons, to fulfil their cravings for seeing new worlds; some came to learn; and most just came, saw, and left no record for us to ponder over their reasons for visiting.

However, the earliest record of a visit that has come down to us is by Megasthenes, who was a political traveller, an ambassador specifically. Even though his book, the *Indica*, is lost, it has survived as a quoted text in the works of classical Greek and Roman historians.

Within a few years after Christ's death, one of his disciples named Didymos, who is known as St Thomas, arrived in India. He came not only to escape the persecution of the early Christians but also to propagate the new faith. The Syrian Christian tradition of

Kerala states that St Thomas arrived at Muziris in Kerala in 52 CE, and was speared to death on 3 July 72 CE, at what is now the St Thomas Mount near Chennai. The route taken by this Apostle is interesting, for he sailed across the Arabian Sea with the aid of the monsoon winds and made landfall in the southern part of the Indian peninsula.

The unknown author of the *Periplus of the Erythraean Sea*, written sometime in the first century CE, credits the discovery of the monsoon winds to a certain Hippalus in the first century BCE. Since then, Roman ships avoided the indirect route via the Persian Gulf, and began their journey from Red Sea ports like Berenice on the southern coast of Egypt to reach India. The monsoon winds made their journey towards their destination of the pepper-growing lands easier and faster. The craze for this spice was phenomenal, which, due to its demand among the Romans, was respectfully known as *yavanpriya* (beloved of the foreigners). This route was used for trade even during the European domination of the Arabian Sea by the Portuguese, after the pioneer Vasco da Gama's arrival at Kozhikode on 20 May 1498 CE.

In the meantime, people in the north of the subcontinent traded with the Romans via Arab and Persian merchants, which, despite the cut in profits, still managed to help great commercial cities like Agroha in Haryana flourish. At the same time, the peninsula saw the establishment of several seaports, which the *Periplus* details. The merchants of these ports imported Roman bullion,[38] silver coins, female slaves, horses and amphoras of wine, and exported spices, ivory, wootz steel and fine cotton fabric, among other items, to Rome. This flourishing trade continued from the first century BCE to the seventh century CE, a good 800 years.[39] Here I find it most strange that during this phase, written records of such activity by either the merchants, sea captains or travellers are conspicuously absent. However, evidence of this trade has been acquired from archaeological excavations.[40] Literary and religious works that were composed during the heyday of Indo-Roman trade and the Gupta Era detail the geographical story of the subcontinent and its international trade. This period is also documented in records of Chinese pilgrims visiting India.

The First Islamic Conquest of the Subcontinent and the Chroniclers

After the establishment of Islam in the Arab peninsula by Muhammad in the sixth century CE, the first Muslims reached India during his lifetime. They arrived as traders and left evidence of their presence in the form of the Barwada Masjid of Ghogha in the Bhavnagar district of Gujarat, and the Cheraman Masjid in Thrissur in Kerala.[41]

In the years between the seventh and twelfth centuries CE, several powerful dynasties were founded in India. These were the Gurjara-Pratiharas, the Rashtrakutas, the Palas, the later Cholas, the Chalukyas of Vatapi, the Kalyani Chalukyas, the Chandelas, the Kalachuris, the Chauhans, the Parmars, the Gahadavalas, the Kashmiri dynasties (Karkota, Utpala and Lohara), the Somavamsis of Odisha, and the Senas of Bengal, to name a few. This period saw the greatest examples of temple architecture that were built all over the subcontinent, of which only a fraction remain intact.

After Islam overwhelmed Arabia, Egypt and Persia, Muslim Arabs began arriving in the subcontinent as conquerors. During Al Hajjaj's governorship of Iraq and Iran under the Umayyad Caliphs in the seventh century CE, Sindh fell to the forces led by Muhammad Bin Qasim, who hailed from the western city of Taif in the Hejaz province of Saudi Arabia. This young commander, as mentioned in the *Chachnama*, defeated Raja Dahir and conquered his kingdom sometime between 708 and 711 CE, which was just seventy-nine years after the death of Muhammad.[42]

After the conquest of Sindh and Multan, Arab and Persian traders began arriving in large caravans. They have left behind some records of their venture into the country. The Arab merchant from whom we get the earliest account of its kind was Sulaiman. He visited India in the ninth century CE,[43] during the hegemony of the

Gurjara-Pratiharas and the Palas in Bengal. His book, titled *Silsilat al-Tawarikh*, is in two parts. The first part was written by him and the second by Abu Zayd Hasan ibn Yazid Sirafi, who did not visit the subcontinent but took some of the accounts by other merchants and added them to Sulaiman's book.

The second such book, titled *Kitab al-Masalikwa-l-Mamalik*, was authored by Ibn Khurdadba, whose grandfather was a Zoroastrian.[44] Khurdadba was a second-generation convert to Islam and held a high office in Baghdad under the Caliph. In his spare time, he studied books by travellers and eventually compiled one. He died in 912 CE.

The next account of India comes down to us in the form of an authoritative work titled *Murujul-Zahab* by Al Masudi, who had extensively traversed the length and breadth of Islamdom and reached India in the tenth century CE, around 940 CE.

The next record mentioning India is to be found in a book titled *Kitabu-al-Alkalim* by Abu Ishak. This author also travelled to India and compiled his work around 951 CE. Another traveller who had reached India was Ibn Haukal.[45] Abu Ishak had met Ibn Haukal near the Indus and these two exchanged notes.

The greatest among all the early Muslim chroniclers to visit India was undoubtedly Al Biruni, who arrived in 1017 CE. He lived in several places in the subcontinent for the purpose of study. His book, titled *Tahqiq Ma Li-l-Hind* (or *Kitab al-Hind*, or *Al Biruni's India*), gives us detailed geographical descriptions of the various places, rivers and mountains of India, as well as its religion, philosophy and sciences.[46] For my research on the history of the places mentioned in this book, I have, at several points, relied on the authority of this learned personality.

This polymath was a contemporary and an employee of one of the worst genocidal maniacs to have ever set foot in the country, Mahmud of Ghazni. While Al Biruni was busy studying ancient texts in Banaras, Mathura, Ujjain and other places, Mahmud of Ghazni was busy conducting raids on and plundering various cities and temples of the subcontinent.

While giving us a detailed record of Mahmud's plundering raids, Al Utbi, his biographer, inadvertently wrote about the polity of the country and its religious sites.

The Second Islamic Conquest of the Subcontinent

Mahmud's incursions began with the conquest of the domains of the Hindu Shahi ruler Jayapal in Kabul in 1001 CE. Jayapal was captured and released. In 1006 CE, Mahmud invaded Multan, which was then ruled by Abul Futah of the Ismaili sect of Islam.[47] Contrary to popular belief, the ancient Sun temple of Multan was not destroyed by Mahmud of Ghazni but by the Ismaili ruler Jalam bin Shayban; some years before his death, he built his mosque and a palace on the site. Al Biruni tells us that the famous idol of the sun at Multan was made from wood and covered with stretched horse skin. For eyes the idol had two rubies. En route to Multan from Ghazni, Mahmud ousted the Hindu Shahi ruler Jayapal and his son Anangpal from Peshawar, who sought shelter in Kashmir.[48]

In 1009 CE, the impregnable Kangra Fort in Himachal Pradesh was invaded by Mahmud. In 1013 CE, the holy city of Thaneshwar in Kurukshetra was sacked. After that, he made two attempts to invade Kashmir and succeeded.[49] Between 1017 CE and 1020 CE, Mathura and Kannauj were sacked and all their ancient temples destroyed. Thousands were enslaved and taken to Ghazni. In 1023 CE, he captured the Gwalior and Kalinjar forts. In the meantime, Anangpal succeeded to the Hindu Shahi throne after Jayapal's suicide and tried to recover their lost domain with the aid of the Sakambari Chauhans from Ajmer.[50]

In 1025 CE, Mahmud attacked Ajmer (Pushkar) and sacked the city. After Ajmer, Mahmud then attacked Gujarat and plundered the famous Somnath Temple. While he was returning to his capital in Ghazni after the completion of his raids through Sindh in 1026 CE, the Chauhans, along with the ruler of Gujarat, having joined forces, met him in battle somewhere in the Thar Desert.[51] In 1030 CE, Mahmud of Ghazni died in his capital.

In 1144 CE was born Muhammad Bin Sam, better known as Muhammad Ghori.

The Third Islamic Conquest

In the intervening period between the death of Mahmud of Ghazni and the rise of Muhammad Ghori, the Chauhan dynasty gained prominence in the northern part of India. In this period, North India witnessed a few sporadic invasions by the Muslim armies of the descendants of Mahmud of Ghazni. The last great ruler of the Chauhan dynasty, Prithviraj Chauhan III, had furthered his territorial conquests up to the western extremities of the Punjab, Kannauj in the east, and Mahoba in the southeast. This eastward expansion was at the cost of other kingdoms belonging to the Chandelas and the Gahadavalas. And then he clashed with Muhammad Ghori.

The First Battle of Tarain, fought about 16 km north of Karnal at a place called Taraori in 1191 CE, ended with the defeat of Ghori. A year later in 1192 CE, the Second Battle of Tarain was fought in the same place. In this, Ghori routed the Rajput forces and killed Prithviraj Chauhan III, thereby establishing Muslim rule in India proper.[52] Following the death of Prithviraj Chauhan III, the conquering army marched down to Ajmer and destroyed the city and its many temples.[53] With the building of the Adhai Din Ka Jhonpra Masjid in the Chauhan capital by Ghori's general Qutbuddin Aibak, political Islam was established in India. The sultanate that was formed because of this conquest came to be known as the Delhi Sultanate, which, between 1206 and 1526 CE, was ruled by kings belonging to the Mamluk, Khilji, Tughlaq, Sayyid and Lodhi dynasties.

More Travellers

During the reign of Muhammad Bin Tughlaq, there arrived in India a young Berber named Abdullah Muhammad Ibn Battuta from Tangiers in Morocco, in the year 1333 CE. By the age of twenty-nine, he had crossed the Indus after extensively travelling across the length and breadth of the north and east African coastlines, Arabia, Turkey and Persia. His valuable documentation of Tughlaq's craziness is a precious contribution to the study of India's history.

Marco Polo visited the peninsular tract of the subcontinent in the thirteenth century CE; so did his countryman Niccolò Dei Conti in the fifteenth century CE. Sometime during the brief rule of the Sayyid Dynasty in the first half of the fifteenth century CE, the great Chinese mariner Zheng He reached the coast of Kerala. That century also saw visits from Abdur Razzaq of Iran and Athanasius Nikitin from Russia. Vasco da Gama arrived at the fag-end of the fifteenth century CE, when Sikandar Lodhi was the Sultan of Delhi. He is credited with the discovery of the direct sea route from Europe to India via the Cape of Good Hope. Duarte Barbosa, Domingo Paes, Nuniz and Monserrate were the Portuguese travellers who visited India in the sixteenth century CE.

After the death of the last Lodhi sultan, Ibrahim, in the battlefield in Panipat in 1526 CE, Babur established the Mughal Empire in India, ending the Delhi Sultanate. The largest number of foreign visitors during the medieval age was during the Mughal period. Travellers such as Monserrate, Ralph Fitch, Caesar Fredriseh, John Linschoten, Captain Hawkins, William Fisch, John Jurdan, Nicholas Doughton, Withurgton, Thomas Coryat, Thomas Roe, Paul Canning, Edward Terry, Paelsert, Della Velle, Loyatt, Fryer, Mundy, Tavernier, Bernier, Ali Reis, Manucci, Thevenot and Careri have left behind accounts of their travel to the subcontinent during the Mughal epoch.

Demographic Changes

With the establishment of Islamic rule and the consolidation of its territorial conquests, several abrupt changes came about in India. Demographic changes were the first and the most important. With the settlement of Muslims who came from outside India and the large-scale conversion of the local Hindus, a drastic alteration happened in the urban society of the day. Since the places targeted for conquest were obviously urban centres, a massive upheaval occurred among those who survived the onslaught. Urban landscapes changed with the wanton demolition of places of worship, which resulted in the transformation of not only the skyline but the ground too—massacres, deportation, fleeing refugees, empty cities whose hollow alleyways were occupied by the conquerors. Those who could make their way to safety reached Odisha in the east or sought shelter in the defiles of the Himalayas. And this was an oft-repeated occurrence, taking place with the fall of every city over several centuries. Even as late as the time of the so-called benevolent Akbar in the sixteenth century CE, more than 30,000 inhabitants of Chittor were put to death, emptying the Mewar metropolis for good.[54]

The first two generations of Muslims in the Delhi Sultanate never called this land their home but behaved like conquerors. A generation or so after them, particularly those born in the land began to see themselves as separate from their brethren in Persia and Arabia. By the time of the Khiljis and the Tughlaqs, 'Indian Muslims' had become an established demographic entity.

With the lure of greater prospects, economic migration from Persia and Arabia to the metropolis of Delhi continued, as it surpassed Baghdad and other urban centres in the northern and eastern parts of the subcontinent in its splendour. It was during this phase that, in spite of all the differences, a new composite culture was being born—languages were being enriched, new music and art were being composed, new types of clothes were being designed, new culinary delights were being formulated—what we know today as the distinctive Indian Culture.

Mindless Iconoclasm

The entire span of Muslim rule and the first hundred years of the Bengal Sultanate saw the overall destruction of splendidly constructed temples in India. This happened at such a scale that all the way from the Punjab to the foothills of Tripura, barring a handful of ancient temples, not a single edifice stands as it was originally envisaged. In places in North India—like Chamba in Himachal Pradesh—where

Islamic armies never set foot, ancient temples have remained intact.

The scale at which this destruction was carried out over time by different monarchs is mindboggling. During my rides to many ancient places, I have come across countless destroyed temples that find no mention in the pages of mainstream history.

Unlike the rest of India, where the majority of the population has still remained non-Muslim, Kashmir had it the worst, after the advent of the Shah Miri Dynasty that began from the first half of the fourteenth century CE. The valley's demographic was turned on its head and of the thousands of temples that once dotted the Himalayan heaven, as reported by Kalhan[55] and Mirza Haidar Dughlat,[56] only a handful remain in their ruinous state.

Frank Questions or Islamophobia?

What I find annoying is the taboo around talking about the barbarism experienced by the non-Muslims of those days. I am on the threshold of being termed an Islamophobe. What I also fail to understand is how disagreeing with the barbaric act of destroying a work of art can be termed as an aversion towards a particular religion.

Even for the sake of debate and general understanding of the genocides faced by Indians at the hands of various conquerors, some of us mimic the action of an indolent ostrich. Why can't we talk about it? Why can't there be a reformation in the historiography of the country? Here, I am not talking about a superficial change in the history syllabus, which is done every time a different political dispensation occupies Delhi.

When are we going to call a spade a spade? Presently, a school opposed to Nehruvian historians, who are decried as 'left-leaning intellectuals', is trying to bring to the fore what the latter had avoided.[57] These scholars are decried by the latter as 'right-leaning non-intellectuals', and these days as 'WhatsApp University graduates' for their shoddy method of historiography.[58]

To be truthful, reading some of the works of rightist authors is a tad boring for me, and some are utterly infantile. Such works are often guided by emotion rather than by factual reporting of original sources, and almost always clouded by hearsay from the pages of legends. Any serious lover of history can easily conclude that these works are glaring examples of cheap counter-propaganda to the subtle subversion of history perfected by the polished scholars from the Nehruvian school.

Many historians who shaped the study of Indian historiography post-Independence strangely never addressed the Muslim influx as the Islamic conquest, but used the rather ambiguous term 'the Turkish rule'...whatever that means. Apparently, they were afraid to call a spade a spade and went about whitewashing the method of conquest used by these Islamic forces, often rubbing out the horrendous acts of wanton iconoclasm and genocide, omitting them from the pages of school history books. One such example from my student days that I am taking the liberty of citing is the dedication of an entire paragraph to the piety of Babur and his prayer to exchange his life for the ailing Humayun,[59] without mentioning a word about his destruction of the gigantic rock-cut Jain monolithic statues on the cliff side below the Gwalior Fort.[60] These colossi are the largest collection of such rock giants in India and a wonder to behold even in their damaged state.

India's polity as a secular democratic nation has a direct bearing on this lopsided rendering of India's history. Understandably, history writers 'tried' to strengthen the secular ethos of India and not disturb it. This paradigm backfired, because it was based on manipulation of the truth that is palpable whenever one visits any ancient monument ravaged by Islamic forces.

With changes in political ideology, changes in history writing are often encouraged, and these may be clouded with emotion rather than based on facts. This has spawned the rise of the two monolithic schools of Indian history. The outcome of such historiography is the seed of distrust that has been sown in the minds of India's two major communities, the Hindus and the Muslims. And those genuinely interested in India's past are basically in the no-man's-land between these two warring factions.

The Book

This book is an attempt to document the history of a few places that were unfortunate enough to face the destructive aspect of Muslim conquerors. This is not the first book of its kind, for there exist several about which I know. The first such comprehensive attempt was made by Sir Alexander Cunningham when, after his visit to Ladakh, he wrote the book *Ladakh: Physical, Statistical, and Historical*, and published it in 1854 CE. Even before him there were Europeans who had begun to document ancient sites in India, but Cunningham's exhaustive writings in several volumes are specific to historical documentation and are rather mindboggling.[61] In the process, he began archaeological excavations, inspired by Jean Baptiste Ventura, the French mercenary in Maharaja Ranjit Singh's army. Cunningham's contribution to India's historiography is immense, for he was the first archaeological surveyor of the Government of India, a post created for him in 1861 CE, which he held till 1865 CE. This was the practical wing of the Asiatic Society and the precursor to the Archaeological Survey of India.

Just like Cunningham, his assistant, the Dhaka-born Indo-Armenian Joseph David Beglar, visited several ancient sites in Delhi, Agra, Bundelkhand, the Central Provinces, the Southeastern Provinces and the Bengal Provinces, and wrote extensively about them in several volumes. He is also the earliest documenter to have used a camera to click pictures of the ruins.[62]

Generally, the writing of history is personality-specific and revolves around epochs surrounding an individual or a group of individuals. In this book, I have tried to reconsider history from the perspective of a place or a monument and the events that happened in and around it. I have selected eight places to discuss in the book on the basis of their unfortunate history, i.e. those that have been victims of conquest and destruction, particularly the temples there. While doing this, I have included the overall history of the place through the passage of time and interspersed it with my personal narratives about riding to those places.

Personal Narrative

Talking of rides, I visit historical sites on my Royal Enfield motorcycle. Two reasons why I do this are: I love to ride and have been doing so ever since graduating from tenth standard, and secondly, I suffer from wanderlust, and riding to lesser-known destinations across rural roads is more convenient. I am often asked about the dangerous aspects of such solo ventures, to which I reply that I am a careful rider and don't think about the mishaps that might dampen my enthusiasm for adventure. So far, I have traversed the length and breadth of the country on my bike, completing my sojourn through all its states and union territories, except the islands of Lakshadweep and the Andamans. Often, I have crisscrossed through several states and visited the same site multiple times, and sometimes I have driven to far-flung historical places in the company of my wife. On some of these visits, I have availed public transport, and I once visited an ancient mound (Karnasubarna near Baharampur in West Bengal) on a bicycle, covering a to-and-fro distance of more than 100 km.

In all my rides, I have met with three minor accidents so far: one somewhere near Longewala in the Thar Desert of Rajasthan; another caused by a person on a bike who braked hard, somewhere near Rekong Peo in Himachal Pradesh; and the last somewhere along the forest road en route to the Champhai district of Mizoram. All these mishaps were skids. I have faced only a single tyre puncture, somewhere near the Sabalgarh Fort in the Morena district of Madhya Pradesh. Of mechanical failures, I have experienced none, except when the bike's battery drained out once, somewhere near the Indo-Nepal border in Bihar, while I was on my way to the northeastern states from Shimla. Here I was assisted by a kind person, who took me in his car to the nearest town, Forbesganj, to procure a battery, while my luggage-laden bike was left under the care of some villagers.

In all my lonely sojourns to remote places, I have experienced only two threatening incidents that could have led to kidnapping or waylaying. The first incident was very tactfully avoided in a place called Pahargarh in the Morena district. In the company of a few other bikers from Agra, I had gone to see the rock shelters of Likhichhaj near Pahargarh. The caves of Likhichhaj are obscure and situated inside the northern part of the Palpur Kuno forest. At Pahargarh, one of the riders was offered help by two suspicious characters, who were more than eager to take us to the caves. In their eagerness I sensed something wrong, particularly when they began calling someone with great urgency. This was in 2013 and not the '90s, when travelling to places in the Morena district was avoided like the plague due to its bad reputation as a haven for dacoits. However, Morena still retained the reputation of being a hub of kidnapping, and that is what we suspected those two characters were about to do after they led us into the forest. No sooner did the two go on ahead on their bike towards Likhichhaj than we did an about-turn from near the small Pahargarh Fort and sped away.

The other incident happened when I was riding solo to see the Gohad Fort in the Bhind district of Madhya Pradesh. After my visit to the fort, I wanted to take the interior road and reach the Ater Fort near the Chambal, from where I would cross the pontoon bridge and reach Bah in Uttar Pradesh. I had visited Ater a few months ago and fallen in love with the place and its innumerable ravines. Wanting to experience riding through them once again, I got lost on one of the rural roads. At one point in this stretch, three youngsters stopped me, and one of them rushed at me with the intention of taking out the key from my bike. I immediately accelerated and rode over his foot, nearly falling off the bike in the process…

Here I must state that I have met largely helpful people throughout my journey across the country. Some have shared their lunch with me, like an elderly couple inside the Vellore Fort in Tamil Nadu. Some have invited me to their homes and fed this dusty rider, which happened several times, the most memorable being in Mehsana in Gujarat. A person took me to his house and put me up for the night, which happened near the rock-cut temple of Masroor in Himachal Pradesh. Many have offered tea, and some even liquor, which I respectfully declined because I don't drink and ride.

During my rides I have met people from all walks of life, from all sorts of cultures and religions, speaking different languages, and wearing different kinds of clothes, all belonging to different worlds. Often, I have been surrounded by youngsters, who would click selfies with me, and once on the bank of the Brahmaputra in Tezpur I was mobbed by a group of college boys, who had all sorts of questions about me and my motorcycle...

1
Ravages of Kashmir

My first ride to Kashmir was in the summer of 2014, with five riders from Agra. During that ride I merely touched a few places of historical interest in a cursory manner and quickly moved on towards our destination: Ladakh. My second and third rides to Jammu and Kashmir had me going there specifically in order to document the places that had seen only a quick visit earlier and those that I did not see, particularly the famed Martand Sun Temple. In this regard, I still left out the mysterious horses-with-riders sculptures of Ghora Gali near Gool village in the Ramban district.[1] I was deterred from going to Gool, which is about 45 km from Ramban, due to a landslide that had taken place. Owing to the paucity of time on my hands, I was forced to move on ahead. Hopefully, I will visit Gool during my fourth ride to Kashmir and see those enigmatic sculptures, two of which are displayed in the compound of the Sri Pratap Singh (SPS) Museum in Srinagar.

The Ancient History of the Kashmir Valley

I will begin the story of Kashmir with a brief discussion of its early history. Ancient Kashmir is best metaphorized through the ruins of the Martand Sun temple. If stones could speak, they would sing the ballad of blood and gore. If stones could bleed, they would colour the Jhelum red. Stones can only break, like crumbled pieces of the valley's history stolen by weekly screams from rabid mobs enthused by the carrot offered from heaven. The exterior of Kashmir, suffused with the pleasant colours of the seasons, hides within it the contents of a grave. The untold story of the masses turned foreigners in their own land by occupation is one of the greatest tragedies of the millennium.[2] It is etched so well on the stones of Martand that it does not require any special skill to read, except a deep sense of truth and a head unclouded by the convenient blight of amnesia.

The earliest narrative about the history of Kashmir is found in the voluminous work titled *Rajatarangini* (River of Kings), written by Kalhan, the son of Kanpaka, 'the great Kasmiri minister',[3] in the twelfth century CE.

Regarding Kalhan's ancestry, we know nothing except his father's name and profession, which the son verily mentioned. Here we don't know what portfolio his father held and under which specific monarch he served—perhaps there was more than one. We know of a certain Kanpaka, during the reign of the Kashmiri king Harsha, but we cannot be sure whether he was Kalhan's father or grandfather. We know that Kalhan was a boy during the troubled period of Harsha's rule and he also witnessed the reign of Jayasimha,[4] between 1128 and 1148 CE. Jonaraja, in his own *Rajatarangini*, mentions that Kalhan belonged to a Brahmin family.[5]

After Kalhan, the River of Kings once again began flowing through the narration of Jonaraja in the fifteenth century CE, during the reign of Zainul Abidin. The history of Kashmiri kings by Jonaraja is called the *Dvitiya Rajatarangini* (Second River of Kings). In 1459 CE, Jonaraja died in the thirty-fifth regnal year of his patron, Zainul Abidin, and the chronicle of Kashmiri kings kept flowing through the pen of his pupil, Srivara Pandita.[6]

This worthy pupil titled his work *Tritiya Rajatarangini* (Third River of Kings) and covered the period between 1459 and 1486 CE. He makes a quick mention of the fact that he was brought up by King Zainul Abidin like his son and received various gifts of wealth and villages, 'and the privilege of performing the *Homa* sacrifice', calling the *Rajatarangini* of his master the *Zainatarangini* after Zainul Abidin.[7] Srivara ends his River of Kings with the crowning of Fateh Shah in the year 1486 CE. After a gap of twenty-seven years, Shuka, the son of Buddhyashraya, begins his narration of another chronicle of the kings of Kashmir. Shuka informs us that after Jonaraja, Prajyabhatta composed a book named *Rajavalipataka* starting with the reign of Fateh Shah[8] in 1486 CE and ending in 1507 CE.

The Legendary Account of the Valley

Let us now look back, way before the first *Rajatarangini* was written, to find Kashmir in the pages of ancient manuscripts. Traditional Hindu beliefs among the Kashmiri Pundit community posit that Kashmir derived its name from Rishi Kashyap, the son of Marichi, the mind-born son of Brahma and Kala. The first among the seven immortal sages, Kashyap, the composer of Vedic hymns, is credited with draining a large lake called Sati Sarovar, named after Sati, the wife of Shiva and the daughter of Daksha, and reclaiming the land. The act of draining a lake has also been attributed to the tenth century CE Buddhist *mahasiddha* Naropa, who founded the Lamayuru Monastery in Ladakh by draining a lake there.

One of the theories of the origin of the name Kashmir is that it is the shortened version of Kashyap Mira (the waters/mountains of Kashyap). The *Nilamata Purana* categorically mentions the name of the valley as Kashmir and so does the *Rajatarangini*. Other sources provide different etymological accounts of the word, one example of which is *ka* (water) and *shimir* (desiccate), leading to the meaning 'the land removed from water'.[9] Interestingly, Dr Ved Kumari, the author of the book titled *The Nilamata Purana: Cultural and Literary Study of a Kashmiri Purana*, mentions that Babur too gave a 'suggestion' regarding the origin of the name Kashmir, saying it was derived from Kas (a hilly tribe).[10] Well, I have not yet come across any such suggestion by the founder of the Mughal Dynasty in his autobiography, the *Baburnama*.

About 19 km from the SPS Museum in Srinagar is Burzahom. This place is famous for housing an archaeological site that has yielded the earliest remains of settlements in the valley, dated to 3300 BCE. It is also home to the pit-dwelling culture and has several large menhirs erected by the ancients. I visited the site while riding towards Sonmarg en route to Ladakh. The finds from this site are in various museums across India, including the SPS Museum. The primary attraction of the place is its monoliths, some leaning on their side and some lying on the ground. This site is the earliest archaeologically recorded evidence of settlement in Kashmir, which is contemporaneous with the mature phase of Kalibangan from the Indus–Saraswati Civilization.

Historically, this region in the Himalayas was settled by the clans of Uttar Kurus, and after them, the Kambojas, who are mentioned in the Mahabharata. The fourth century BCE Sanskrit grammarian from Salatura near Lahore, Daksiputra Panini,[11] also called Salaturya, mentions in his *Astadhyayi* the Kambojas and Kasmira, and so does his commentator, Patanjali.[12] Claudius Ptolemy, the second century CE geographer, refers to Kashmir as Kaspeiria. He also mentions the rivers Bidaspes (Vitasta/Jhelum), Sandabal (Chandrabhaga/Chenab) and Adris (Iravati/Ravi). He states that Kashmir is situated between the Daradas on the Indus and the Kylindrine (Kulindas) on the river Hyphasis (Beas). Varahamihira, in his *Brihat Samhita*, written in the sixth century CE, also mentions Kashmir,[13] along with the Daradas of Kashmir, who are mentioned quite frequently in the *Rajatarangini*.

The *Nilamata Purana*, used as a reference by Kalhan for the mythical aspect of Kashmir's history, provides a legendary account of the valley. This Purana, which spans a great length of time, was composed in the sixth–seventh century CE.[14] The story of Kashmir in the Purana begins with a large lake called Sati Sarovar. During the seventh *manvantara* (Hindu cyclic period of time and the era started by Manu), Vishnu killed the water-dwelling demon, Jalodbhava, after Ananta (another aspect of Balarama) drained the lake with the help of his plough, for Jalodbhava was invincible in the water. The land that was reclaimed was settled by Rishi Kashyap alongside the Nagas (dragons), who were the original inhabitants of the region.[15]

The *Mahavamsa* and even Hieun Tsang talks about this legend. Of the birth of Kashmir, Hieun Tsang, the seventh century CE Chinese pilgrim, who had visited the valley and resided at the Jayandra Vihara built by King Jayandra for a night,[16] mentions the Buddhist version of the story. The country was once a 'dragon lake'. While crossing over the lake, the Buddha, who was flying back to the 'middle kingdom' (India) from Udyana (Swat) after subduing 'a wicked spirit', predicted to Ananda that after his death the Arhat Madhyantika would found a kingdom in this land, civilize the people, and by his own effort spread the law of the Buddha. Fifty years after the *Mahaparinirvana* of the Buddha (the death of the Buddha), Arhat Madhyantika, with the help of his spiritual powers, tricked the Naga who lived in the lake and wrested the land from him.[17]

It is interesting to note that the origin of the legend can hold water, as the structure of the valley, shaped like a basin, indicates that there could have been a large lake there that got drained due to natural factors.

Another Chinese pilgrim who visited Kashmir in 759 CE and left behind an account was Wu Kong.[18] He lived in Gandhara for four years. This pilgrim also visited other places associated with Buddhism in India.

A Persian scholar from Khiva and an employee of Mahmud of Ghazni, Al Biruni, the Indologist who visited India in the eleventh century CE, left behind a detailed account of the subcontinent. In his monumental work, titled *Kitab al-Hind* (translated as *Al Biruni's India*), he names Vasukara, a famous Brahmin from Kashmir, who wrote a commentary on the Vedas.[19] According to him, the Siddhamatrika script was believed by some to have originated from Kashmir, and it was thought that Kashmir and Varanasi were the 'high schools of Hindu sciences'. He states that the people in Kashmir worshipped a wooden idol of Sarada/Saraswati, the goddess of learning and speech.[20]

We don't know whether this polymath visited Kashmir or not, but he mentions that one can reach Kashmir from Kannauj via Billawar in present-day Jammu.[21] He also gives an alternate route, which, according to him, was the best-known entrance to the valley, beginning from the town of Babrahan (I am unable to identify this town on the map), between the Indus and the Jhelum. He states that Adisthan (Srinagar) was the capital of Kashmir, which was built on both the banks of the Jhelum,[22] and names two other places in

Kashmir: Ushkara (in Baramulla) and Rajaouri with the fortress of Rajagiri.

Regarding the people, he writes that they were much troubled by periodic invasions by the Turkish-speaking armies of a king titled Bhatta Shah, who ruled Gilgit, Aswira (Hasor) and Shiltas (Chilas).[23]

Of the periodic invasion of India by his patron Mahmud, Al Biruni notes that due to the utter ruin of the 'prosperity of the country' caused by him:

> Hindus became like atoms of dust scattered in all directions, and like the tale of old in the mouth of the people. Their scattered remains cherish, of course, the most inveterate aversion towards all Muslims. This is the reason, too, why Hindu sciences have retired faraway from those parts of the country conquered by us and have fled to places which our hand cannot yet reach, to Kashmir, Banaras, and other places. And there the antagonism between them and all foreigners receives more and more nourishment both from political and religious sources.[24]

The credit for the wanton obliteration of religious buildings belonging to the Hindus of Kashmir goes to Sikandar Shah Miri, aka Sikandar Butshikan (1389–1413 CE). Collective memory as well as the history of Kashmir by Jonaraja testify to this tragic history of this Himalayan kingdom.[25]

Three-hundred-and-ten years before Sikandar Shah, there existed another king named Harsha, the son of Kalasha from the Lohara Dynasty. This eleventh century CE Hindu monarch is described by Kalhan as an iconoclast. He was responsible for the destruction of many idols made up of precious metals. From these temples he looted their accumulated wealth and used it for his own needs.[26] Kalhan also calls him 'Turk King Harsha', addressing him derogatorily as a Muslim monarch, and says that he had appointed one Udayraja as an 'officer for uprooting the gods'.[27] However, those temples continued to function as structures, albeit with newly established idols made up of cheaper metals.

The Earliest Muslim Rulers of the Valley and Its Last Hindu Ruler, Queen Kota

The earliest Muslim ruler to have occupied Kashmir was one mercenary named Kajjala. We don't know much about him, but Jonaraja mentions that this *Turushka* (old term used by Indians for Muslims, derived from the Turkic peoples of Central Asia) murdered the king Lakshmanadeva of the Lohara Dynasty in 1286 CE.[28] Kajjala assumed power in Srinagar, for Jonaraja says that a certain Simhadeva became the king of only Ledari. Ruling a diminished state, he built a *math* (a residence for monks adjacent to a temple) in Ledari and installed an image of Narasimha at Dhyanoddara. After reigning for fourteen years, five months and twenty-seven days, Simhadeva was murdered by the husband of his lover.[29] By then, Islam had established itself well in the valley to start converting people.

The second Muslim ruler of Kashmir was an initially Buddhist prince named Rinchen. It was during the reign of Simhadeva (1286–1301 CE) that Rinchen escaped to Kashmir from the Waka Valley in Ladakh (known in the ancient times as Vakatanya)[30] to flee from the wrath of his uncle, and he sought to serve Simhadeva.[31] Later on, Rinchen became the king after the death of Simhadeva's brother Suhadeva, who had succeeded the former in 1301 CE. Lankar Chak, the ruler of the Daradas, also sought shelter in Kashmir around this time. He was deposed by his kinsmen and entered the service of Simhadeva.[32] Lankar Chak's descendants ruled Kashmir for a brief while until the valley was annexed to the Mughal Empire under Akbar. Along with Lankar Chak also came his people the Chak Daradas, and they made Kashmir their homeland.

Suhadeva's reign was filled with bloodshed on account of an invasion by the Mongol Dalcha, aka Zulfi Kadir Khan,[33] a descendant of Genghis Khan. The Mongol invasion of Kashmir is vividly described by Jonaraja, who says that Dalcha invaded Kashmir with 60,000 horsemen. In order to prevent the invasion, Suhadeva tried to pay off the raiders by imposing a tax on all people irrespective of their caste. The Brahmins of Kashmir refused to pay such a tax and went on a hunger strike.[34]

Rinchen, in league with Dalcha, began the plunder of Srinagar. Many able-bodied men were enslaved by Rinchen and Dalcha and were sold to fatten them on the misery of their victims. Dalcha plundered many temples and desecrated them, and just before winter set in, he left a devastated land at the mercy of Rinchen. Kashmir, devoid of able-bodied men, '...became almost like a region before the creation, a vast field with few men, without food, and full of grass.'[35] Ramachandra, the commander-in-chief of Suhadeva, had tried to save Srinagar but failed miserably. Leaving the people to their fate, he had run for safety to the Lohara Fort, where he bided his time and waited for the catastrophe to end. The Lohara Fort was invaded by Rinchen, and Ramachandra soon went to the netherworld. Rinchen had taken the princess Kota as his bride, whom Jonaraja calls 'a kalpa creeper in the garden of Ramachandra's household'.[36] Here, it is not clear whether Kota, who became the fourth sovereign queen to rule Kashmir, was Ramachandra's daughter or wife...

During the reign of Suhadeva, there arrived in the valley an adventurer named Shah Mir, from Swat. Jonaraja mentions that Shah Mir was the founder of the first Muslim dynasty of Kashmir, to which his patron, the famous Zainul Abidin, belonged. Jonaraja names Kuru Shah as the grandfather and Taharaja as the father of Shah Mir. Shah Mir settled in Kashmir with his family and relatives, and King Suhadeva '...greatly favoured him by giving him a salary'.[37] His arrival coincided with the invasion of Dalcha.

King Suhadeva died in 1320 CE, and Rinchen became king. Initially, Rinchen had wanted to become a Hindu, and approached a certain Brahmin named Devaswami for the same. But since he was a Bhotta (Tibetan), Devaswami refused his request; out of disgust, Rinchen converted to Islam. The person who converted him was Bulbul Shah, aka Abdul Rahman Shah, who had entered Kashmir during Rinchen's brief reign. His *dargah* (burial place) is in Srinagar. Jonaraja mentions his name as being 'Vyalaraja'.[38]

During Rinchen's reign, Udayandeva, a brother of Simhadeva, returned from Gandhara and attacked Rinchen. In a battle fought in Vimshaprastha, Rinchen received a sword wound to his head, which festered and caused his death in 1323 CE. Before Rinchen died, he placed his infant son, Haidara (Haidar), and his queen, Lady Kota, under the care of Shah Mir.[39]

After the death of Rinchen, Shah Mir did not install Haidar to the throne, and since he '...did not have the necessary strength, he did not himself rule the kingdom.' Instead, he sided with the Lohara prince Udayandeva, and '...bestowed on Udayandeva the country of Kashmira, together with Queen Shri Kota who was like the goddess of victory incarnate.'[40] Udayandeva, in turn, bestowed on the two sons of Shah Mir, namely Jayamshara (Jamshed) and Allesha (Ali Sher), the governorship of Kramarajya (Northern Kashmir).[41]

Queen Kota was a powerful personality and was the de facto ruler of the kingdom. Her orders were duly followed by Udayandeva. King Udayandeva spent his time 'in bathing, in penance, and in prayer [...] [he] dressed himself like a hermit, [...] tied bells in the neck of his horses, through fear lest worms should be crushed to death.'[42] He did not trouble the Lavanyas (Damaras), or anybody for that matter. Another Mongol/Turk invader, Achala, entered Kashmir in a reiteration of Dalcha's invasion. Udayandeva fled Srinagar for Ladakh, leaving the valley to be defended by Shah Mir and Queen Kota, who tricked Achala by offering him the throne in the absence of Udayandeva, by sending him a letter stating that he could have the throne since the king had fled, and that he should stop harassing the common people on account of that.[43] Jonaraja notes that '...during the dreadful time of the troubles caused by Achala, the people, in fear, had taken shelter of Shahmera [Shah Mir].' He also adds, 'Strange that this believer in Alla became the saviour of the people.'[44]

After Achala's exit from Kashmir, Udayandeva returned, and there he remained a king in name only, for Shah Mir kept him in check by propping up Haidar, Rinchen's son, threatening to install him as the king.[45] While Udayandeva was busy with his rituals, Shah Mir consolidated his hold on Kashmir, fortified the Chakradhara Hill, and effectively turned the king into a puppet. Soon, he was dead 'with the touch of Shah Mir,'[46] and the chess board was thrown open to a struggle between a queen and her knight.

Queen Kota had two sons and she hid them from Shah Mir. She also hid the death of Udayandeva from him for four days. Then, supported by the Lavanayas and a prominent person named Bhatta Bhikshana, she assumed the role of a sovereign. Everybody including Shah Mir bowed down to her. 'As the summer rain allays dust and heat, and nourishes plants, even so she brought back prosperity to the subjects,'[47] says Jonaraja, who, like Kalhan, rarely has a kind word to say about independent and powerful women.

Queen Kota was under the shadow of Shah Mir and feared that she would be overthrown by him. In order to consolidate her power and keep in check the rising powers of Shah Mir, she appointed Bhatta Bhikshana as her prime minister. Bhatta Bhikshana was soon murdered by Shah Mir. Jonaraja tells us how the deed was carried out. Feigning a fatal illness, Shah Mir confined himself to his quarters, and when Bhikshana came to see him, he was overpowered and stabbed by Shah Mir.[48]

With Bhikshana out of the way, Shah Mir was the sole source of power apart from the queen, who marched against a certain lord of Kampana in order to punish him. There, she was captured by the lord of Kampana and incarcerated. She soon escaped from her prison with the help of her courtier Kumarbhatta in a clever manner.[49] After her return to Srinagar, she ruled alongside Shah Mir, who dangled his own power over her as the sword of Damocles. Soon, the queen had to go to Jayapidapura for some business, and in her absence, Shah Mir took the opportunity and '...possessed himself of the capital'.[50]

The queen then took shelter in the fort of Kotta, which was besieged. She capitulated after receiving assurance from Shah Mir that she could share her throne with him by marrying him. We don't know whether she agreed to the marriage proposal, but Jonaraja informs us that Shah Mir spent a night with her, and the very next day, he had his guards imprison her. Soon, he had her murdered, in 1339 CE, in the month of Shravana (July/August), and imprisoned her sons. Regarding her sons Jonaraja is silent, but the logic of statecraft dictates that they were removed from the realm of life. After becoming king, Shah Mir assumed the name Sultan Shamsuddin.[51] He was effectively the third Muslim monarch of Kashmir and the progenitor of the Shah Mir Dynasty.

It is well known that post the death of Queen Kota and the subsequent capture of Kashmir's throne by Shah Mir, the destruction of its ancient religious structures began. The advent of Sikandar Shah, aka Butshikan ('idol-breaker'), the sixth ruler of the Shah Miri Dynasty, in 1389 CE spelt doom for the temples of Kashmir and its allied territories. This bigot destroyed most religious sites and is still remembered by the Kashmiri Pandits as the devil incarnate. Sikandar Lodhi, who became the sultan of Delhi exactly one hundred years after the enthronement of Sikandar Shah in Kashmir, is also known as Butshikan for his iconoclastic deeds.

Regarding the destruction of temples and idols during the rule of Sikandar Shah, Jonaraja says:

> Of the tree of misgovernment [...] Harshadeva the Turushka [he repeats the epithet used by Kalhan] was the seedling, sinfulness was the root and the terrible devastations caused by the Lavanyas [Lone caste of Kashmir] was the leaves. Its flower was Dalacha the king of the mlechchhas; and its fruits were the daily troubles of the king who broke images at the instigations of the mlechchhas. He [Sikandar Shah] broke the images of Marttanda, Vishaya, Ishana, Chakrabhrit, and Tripureshwara...[52]

It was during Sikandar's reign that another 'king of the mlechchhas' plundered Delhi.[53] This king of the mlechchhas was none other than Timur, who plundered Delhi in 1398 CE after defeating Nasiruddin Tughlaq.

Demographic Changes and Iconoclasm in the Valley under Sikandar Shah

Sikandar Shah's reign was a demographic disaster for Kashmir. This ruler, Jonaraja mentions, invited 'Yavanas' (foreigners, referring here to Muslims) to settle en masse in Kashmir. Jonaraja says, 'The king had a fondness for the Yavanas, even as a boy has a fondness for mud. Many Yavanas left other sovereigns and took shelter under this king.' Sikandar was a devotee of 'Mahammada of Mera' (Mir Syyed Ali Hamdani).[54]

Sikandar single-handedly destroyed the composite culture of Kashmir with his Islamic zeal and iconoclastic acts. He imposed the *jizya* (tax on non-Muslims) and destroyed countless temples, earning him the everlasting hatred of the Kashmiri Pandits.

Jonaraja then continues to name other temples that were desecrated by this monarch, which were 'Shesha, Sureshwari, Varaha and others'. I quote him once again: 'There was no city, no town, no village, no wood [forest], where Suha the Turushka [a converted minister of Sikandar Shah named Suha Bhatta] left the temples of the gods unbroken. Of the images which once had existed, the name alone was left...'[55] Just as Harsha had an agent named Udayraja tasked with the looting of temples, so did Sikandar Shah have the convert named Suha Bhatta. Jonaraja laments that after he destroyed every temple standing, he '...felt the satisfaction which one feels on recovering from illness.'[56]

The narration of this part of the history of Kashmir by Jonaraja is filled with pathos and regret. It is possibly the first recorded lament of any native of a place decrying the arrival of outsiders who destroyed the local culture to impose an alien one on them. He records the arrival of Muslim settlers en masse in Kashmir, encouraged by Sikandar Shah. I quote Jonaraja:

> As the bright moon is among the stars, so was Mahammada of Mera[57] country among those Yavanas; and although he was a boy, he became their chief by learning. The king waited on him daily, humble as a servant, and like a student he daily took his lessons from him. He placed Mahammada before him, and was attentive to him like a slave. As the wind destroys the trees, and the locusts the shali crop, so did the Yavanas destroy the usages of Kashmira. Attracted

by the gifts and honours which the king bestowed, and by his kindness, the mlechchhas entered Kashmira, even as locusts enter a good field of corn.[58]

This Sanskrit poet, member of the court of Zainul Abidin (1418–70 CE), a monarch known to have reversed the intolerant policies of his father Sikandar Shah, did not live long enough to complete the history of Kashmir. Jonaraja died in the thirty-fifth regnal year of Zainul Abidin, and the next *Rajatarangini* was carried forward from where he had left off, by his pupil Srivara.

The Account of Mirza Muhammad Haidar Dughlat

The pages following this paragraph will note the vile story of ancient Kashmir's destruction, beginning with an account of a sixteenth-century Mughal marauder from Kashgarh, Mirza Muhammad Haidar Dughlat. This kinsman of Babur, who also fought alongside his son Humayun in the fateful Battle of Kannauj,[59] conquered the valley in the sixteenth century CE. He ruled Kashmir for ten years till his death in 1550 CE near Srinagar, and is buried in the cemetery where Zainul Abidin's grave is situated.

In his book on the Mughals of Mughlistan, titled *Tarikh-i-Rashidi*,[60] Dughlat has given a detailed account of the valley. Apart from his military and political rendition of the events that unfolded during his conquest of the Himalayan heaven, he also records his observations about the land and its socio-cultural aspects, religion, art and architecture.

About the religion of the Kashmiris, Dughlat tells us that their conversion to Islam '…is a comparatively recent event. The people were all Hindus and professed the faith of Brahma.'[61] He writes that at the time of the arrival of Sultan Shamsuddin (Shah Mir) in the valley disguised as a *kalandar* (mendicant), there was a queen who was ruling the valley (Queen Kota). Shamsuddin entered her service and the queen desired to marry him. Thereafter, he became supreme in the land. Shamsuddin was succeeded by Alauddin and he by Qutbuddin. It was during the reign of Qutbuddin that Syyed Ali Hamdani reached the valley. Less than forty days after the arrival of Hamdani, Qutbuddin died, and he was succeeded by Sultan Sikandar Shah, '...who established the Musalman faith and destroyed all the idol-temples.'[62]

From Dughlat, we also learn about Zainul Abidin and his long and benevolent reign of fifty years, in which '...he devoted himself to embellishing Kashmir with buildings, and in order to humour all the nations [religions] of the world, he paid attention neither to Infidelity nor to Islam.'[63]

While riding towards Srinagar from the historic Verinag Spring, I came across a few gigantic chinar (maple) trees and wondered at the extent of their girth. Dughlat too mentioned a tree in a place called Nagam (presently a town about 20 km south of the Dal Lake) that was so tall that '...if an arrow be shot at the top, it will probably not reach it,'[64] noting that if one shook a small branch of it, the entire tree also quivered. Dughlat's account also notes the springs of Verinag and of Devsar, the Wular Lake and the man-made island that was constructed by Zainul Abidin.[65]

The Martand Sun Temple

Having spelt out the socio-religious landscape of Kashmir, let us now come to that ruin that represents the history of the valley like no other, the Martand Sun Temple, which I reached after visiting the ancient Verinag Spring, which is one of the sources of Jhelum/Vitasta River. The river is of paramount importance in local lore and the culture of the valley, for it is the lifeline of Srinagar and other areas. In fact, the *Nilamata Purana* also calls Kashmir 'Vaitastika' after the river. The Verinag Spring was also called Nilanaga Tirtha,[66] associated with a snake deity of the same name. During ancient times, this spring was one of the holiest sites of the valley and legend describes it as an incarnation of Uma, who came forth out of a hole created by Shiva's trident after Sage Kashyap's request to release her in the form of a river.[67] Due to this belief, Verinag was also called

Sulaghata (*sula* means 'a shaft pointed like a trident').

Situated on a plateau near the village of Khribal, Martand is very close to Mattan, another large village that took its name from the sun temple. Of the many sun temples in India, three are particularly large: namely, the Khatarmal Sun Temple in Uttarakhand, Martand in Kashmir, and Konark in Odisha. Among them, Martand is the oldest. It is not the largest though, contrary to what the guides there will tell you. Konark is the largest, despite the demolition of its primary shikhara, and Martand holds the second position.

Kalhan, Jonaraja and Sukha have also written about the temple. The grandeur of this structure does not fail to inspire awe in the minds of onlookers, even in its dilapidated state. The locals there call this temple the Pandu Ladan and attribute its construction, as usual, to the Pandavas. And, rather strangely, this temple dedicated to the worship of the sun is not built facing the east but the west.

Kalhan informs us that the Martand Sun Temple was built by Lalitaditya Muktapida in the eighth century CE and states that alongside the temple, Lalitaditya also built 'a township which rejoiced in grape vines'.[68] The second reference to this sun temple comes to us during the reign of King Kalasha of Kashmir in the eleventh century CE. Kalhan laments that due to some unexplained reason, Kalasha removed the copper idol of the sun from the Tamaraswamin Temple and carried away the brass Buddhas from the Viharas.[69] Soon after, he fell sick, bleeding from the nostrils, and that is when he presented a golden statue to the Martand Sun temple, seeking forgiveness for his transgression. In 1089 CE, Kalasha died at Martand,[70] and his six queens followed him to the funeral pyre, becoming sati.

Going by the size of the ruins of Martand and the remains of its pillars, this structure, before its destruction, must have been at least ten storeys high. Between 1389 and 1413 CE, Sikandar Shah destroyed the temple.[71] In 1532 CE, Mirza Haidar Muhammad Dughlat attacked Kashmir for the second time and subdued the valley. A pitched battle was fought near the ruins of the Martand Temple in which the defenders were routed.[72]

Dughlat, in his description of the ruins of the temple, starts with this sentence: 'Kashmir is among the most famous countries of the world, and is celebrated both for its attractions and its wonders.'[73]

His narration manages to transport the reader to his times, and brings them under the shade of a mulberry tree when he writes, 'Among the wonders of Kashmir are the quantities of mulberry trees, cultivated for their leaves, from which silk is obtained.' Next, he describes another wonder, its Hindu temples:

> First and foremost among the wonders of Kashmir stand her idol temples. In and around Kashmir, there are more than one hundred and fifty temples which are built of blocks of hewn stone, fitted so accurately one upon the other, that there is absolutely no cement used. These stones have been so carefully placed in position, without plaster or mortar, that a sheet of paper could not be passed between the joints.

He also notes that the blocks are from three to twenty *gaz* (yard) in length, one gaz in depth, and one to five gaz in breadth. According to him, 'The marvel is how these stones were transported and erected. The temples are nearly all built on the same plan.'[74]

In describing the layout of these structures, he comes to the part that should be quoted:

> The capitals, the ornamentation in relief, the cornices, the 'dog tooth' work [intricate design], the inside covering and the outside, are all crowded with pictures and paintings, which I am incapable of describing. Some represent laughing and weeping figures, which astound the beholder. In the middle is a lofty throne of hewn stone [...] which I cannot describe. In the rest of the world there is not to be seen, or heard of, one building like this. How wonderful that there should here be a hundred and fifty of them![75]

His description of this temple matches that of the Martand Sun Temple.

Sukha, the author of the fourth *Rajatarangini*, mentions that Akbar visited Martand during his first trip to the valley (in 1580 CE) after the Mughal conquest of Kashmir. According to Sukha, Akbar gave gifts of gold to Brahmin boys and also went see the Martand Temple and donated cows adorned with jewels.[76]

Abul Fazal, however, does not confirm Sukha's claim, but mentions the ruins of Martand in his *Ain-i-Akbari*. He says, '*Matan* stands upon a hill and once possessed a large temple. There is a small pool on the summit, the water of which never decreases. Some suppose this to be the *Well of Babylon*, but at the present day there is no trace of anything but an ordinary pit.'[77]

Dughlat's great grandnephew, the Mughal emperor Jahangir, also mentions, 'The idol temples that were built before the appearance of Islam are still standing. They are all of stone, with huge dressed blocks weighing to forty maunds placed one on top of another from the foundation to the roof.'[78]

Godfrey Vigne, who visited Kashmir between 1835 and 1838 CE, has also mentioned the presence of about seventy to eighty temples in Kashmir albeit in a ruined state.[79] Taking note of the wondrous ruins of the Martand, Vigne compared it with the sun temple of Palmyra in Syria,[80] stating that between the two, Martand was far superior in every aspect, including its location.

Well, I have not been to Palmyra, for my wife and I had a bad experience in Syria and were literally escorted out of the country and 'returned' to Jordan; thus I cannot say much about Vigne's comparison. I, however, can compare the Martand Sun Temple with another ruin that I visited at Tala in Chhattisgarh. The reason behind this comparison is that I found certain similarities between these two sites. By the looks of the ruins of the Devrani Jathani temple complex of Tala, I found that structurally it was either inspired by Martand or vice versa. It would be an incredible coincidence if these two ruins separated by a distance of 1,929 km were built by the same guild, or if the two were connected somehow.

The striking similarities that I noticed between the temple of Tala and Martand are the rounded pillars, the high, straight walls, large sculptural embellishments, and sloping roofed niches. This type of structure can be said to contain elements from Greek architecture.

The architectural style of the Martand Sun Temple is an amalgamation of the Indian and Greek styles of temple-building, with high walls, tall pillars and a sloping roof.

Another structure that can be compared to Martand is the Avantiswami temple complex, which is located about 36 km from the former. The two temples are like mirror images of each other in their ruinous state. Both these structures were built in the Indo-Greek style, which is typical of Kashmiri temples. They are embellished with sculptures that appear to have been carved by the same set of artisans, even though Avantiswami was built a century after Martand. However, in terms of scale and grandeur, Martand takes the cake.

During an archaeological excavation done on the site in the years 1932–33 CE, a considerable number of earthen jars were found buried in the courtyard of the temple. There, archaeologists also came across the remains of an earlier temple of a smaller dimension, whose base was utilized to build the larger structure of Martand. This earlier structure, according to historian Ram Chandra Kak, was built by King Ranaditya.[81] Ranaditya, also known as Tunjina, according to Kalhan, built a temple for Martand in the village of Simharotsika.[82] We, however, don't know for sure whether Simharotsika was a former name of the place where the Martand Sun Temple is situated.

Like most temples of that era (the Gurjara-Pratiharas were building great edifices in the plains of North and Central India), Martand too was embellished with countless relief sculptures. Their remains can still be seen, albeit with unmistakable signs of the work of an iconoclast's hammer on them. Most of the sculptures carved in the distinctive Kashmiri style are so badly damaged that identifying the deity becomes an impossibility. However, the few that I could identify are of Shiva holding a skull mace, a Mahisasuramardini, a large Ganga Devi image on the left-hand wall of the temple's porch, a Yama, and a flute player, amongst some others.

The remains of eighty-four small shrines and their arches can be counted surrounding the main temple in a rectangular layout. The primary structure of the sun temple still has three gigantic arches, which somehow refused to cave in after the horrendous deed perpetrated by Sikandar Shah.

Looking at the size of these arches, constructed in a threefold manner, one can estimate the size of the temple, which during its heyday must have stood at about 100 feet in height. Another aspect of this ruin is a part of the 'retaining' wall that exists on three sides of the structure. This wall was once a part of the temple's extension and served as a circumambulation corridor, where the worshipper would go around the *garbhagriha* (sanctum sanctorum) in reverence to the Sun God. Below the raised platform above which the temple is built are to be found several damaged idols. The artistry of these carvings is nonpareil, and they exude grace even in their pitiable state. All around are scattered the remains of the temple's parts and a few damaged sculptural pieces.

When the temple existed in all its glory, it was made to stand as an island amidst flowing water that was channelled from a system of canals that can still be seen on the plateau above the complex. This canal still carries water from the upper reaches of the mountains behind the temple and is now being used for irrigation purposes.

The attractions of Martand are captivating to say the least. At the complex I came across several tourists from different parts of the country and a group of young Kashmiri men and women making sketches of the temple. Seeing one of them sketching the central arches of the temple, a surprising realization dawned on me; strangely, it hadn't occurred to me while I was walking about within the ruins that the presence of the arches in Martand refutes the old concept that ancient Indians did not build arches, and that the knowledge of that came with the Muslim conquest.

2
Haridwar: The Spiritual Gateway

A Personal Anecdote Leading to Haridwar and Kaliyar

In the year 2001, I was staying in Delhi for two reasons: studying for my UPSC exams and also trying to sell my paintings through various art galleries. Initially I had enrolled in a coaching centre, where I made a friend named Rose Singh. We are still friends and keep in touch despite our busy lives. Rose, as his name implies, is a handsome Sikh, the pink tinge of whose cheeks shows from underneath his carefully manicured beard. Being attractive and knowing the power of this natural trait, he employed it in the most envious way possible, by becoming a heartthrob for several Delhi *kuddi*s.

The rosy-cheeked lasses with their constant chatter about 'discs' (that's how these girls pronounced 'discos') and dances took turns to make themselves available to him for weekly trips to CJ's, then a happening dance club at Le Meridian Hotel. Five pretty ladies were the last count, after which I gave up keeping track of his liaisons with the fair sex. Apart from being naturally endowed in terms of his looks, he also had as his *vahan* (vehicle), a handsome car that always had a bottle of whiskey in it.

On day one at the coaching centre by Hailey Road, we became friends and he offered to drop me at my lodge in Karol Bagh. En route, he stopped by at Connaught Place and asked me if I wanted a drink. The coaching classes got over by 8.00 p.m., and it being winter, it was not a bad idea to warm one's innards over a plate of tandoori chicken. Since he was dropping me off, I thought of buying a small bottle to return the favour, to which he laughed and said that a Sardar's car, more than the fuel in it, always had one of the two most important things in life, whiskey and women. Pointing at the soft-drink dispenser before the parked car, he asked me to get two tall cups of Pepsi with straws in them. I complied and he poured a strong peg for me... That was the beginning of our friendship. The reason why I brought up the memory of my friend Rose Singh is that it is because of him that I went to Haridwar for the first time.

Rose happened to be a devotee of the Sufi saint Qutbuddin Bakhtiyar Kaki, whose dargah is in Mehrauli. The chief *pir* of the dargah—named Fahimuddin, a direct descendant of Kaki—and Rose were very close friends. Three days after our acquaintance, he asked me whether I wanted to experience something crazy. Crazy, like *crazy*, he said, and added that it did not involve girls. Seeing the disappointed look on my face, he said that it was beyond the mere pleasures of the flesh and so stimulating that I would never forget it.

After the class, instead of heading towards Karol Bagh, he drove to Mehrauli, past the illuminated Qutub Minar, to the dargah of Qutbuddin Bakhtiyar Kaki. He then introduced me to Pir Fahimuddin, who was sitting surrounded by his *chelas* in a dingy domed room adjacent to the dargah complex.

Rose was a much-loved figure among his chelas and was heartily welcomed by them. He then produced a bottle of whiskey, which delighted the pir and the rest. Ironically, the pir liked his alcohol, which was something of a shock for me; then one of his chelas named Panna brought out the first *chillum* (clay pipe) of the evening.

Panna, from Howrah in West Bengal, was a dwarfish person with an oversized head, and was a husband to three wives and father to eight children, or so I was told. He had taken a special liking to me due to our Bengali link. His story was strangely exciting; he was abandoned as a child in Kaki's dargah, where he grew up begging, and now he was the right hand of the 'badshah of Mehrauli', which was how he often addressed the pir.

The pot went around the room with everyone taking a single puff and reverentially passing it on. When it came to me, I refused to partake of it at first, out of some stupid sense of god-knows-what. The kohl-eyed pir, father to as many sons as would make up an entire football team, quipped that I was the first Bengali he had met who turned down the best smoke available in the universe. The dismal domed room built several centuries ago, with no ventilation and filled with unknown faces, had brought about a sense of scepticism in me. Also, I barely knew Rose and there I was, in a situation that triggered an instinctive sense of caution...but then I had been in situations far more 'dangerous' than this during my college days, so, seeing the waiting faces, including Rose's, I pacified my wandering mind and pulled so hard at the pipe that the embers on top lit up in a flame.

Seeing a dying chillum light up like a beacon brought about shouts of joy amongst the gathered, especially the pir. He began praising my 'inner strength', and his chelas doubled up on his praises and began stating that it was destiny that had brought me to the dargah. Well, I wouldn't credit Destiny or her sisters, but my friend Rose for taking me there.

For the next year, on every Thursday of the week I accompanied Rose to Mehrauli. After about six months, on a certain Thursday evening we stayed behind because the pir had planned to visit Haridwar and a dargah near it.

Early next morning, we drove towards Haridwar in the pir's car. Panna kept up the supply of the holy smoke by filling cigarette after cigarette whenever his master desired, which was punctually at an interval of every half an hour. As if in a trance, we travelled the distance and reached Kaliyar by late afternoon. Kaliyar is about 200 km from Mehrauli, and Haridwar is a further 25 km from there.

Kaliyar

Straightaway, we went to the *khanqah* (residence) of an extremely aged pir named Baba Garib Shah. This elderly pir was the chief of the dargah at Kaliyar, locally called Piran Kaliyar. The khanqah, situated beside a smaller dargah named Imam Sahib, was built on the rampart of a fort-like structure, from where the panorama of the surrounding mustard fields in bloom was a pleasant sight to behold. Between the Imam's grave and a grand gateway that was being constructed by the aged pir, was a water body.

Just like the domed room of Pir Fahimuddin, the entire atmosphere of the place transported one back to the times of the Delhi Sultanate. After a cool refreshing bath from a tube well, the aged pir welcomed us with a sumptuous lunch of khichdi and saag, and thereafter we took a nap in order to get ready for the evening's 'spiritual' merriment.

The large village of Kaliyar is divided by the Ganga Canal, on whose east bank is the khanqah. The main Piran Kaliyar Dargah, also known as Kaliyar Sharif, is on the west bank of the canal. The primary object of veneration at Kaliyar is the grave of Alauddin Ali Ahmed Sabir, a Sufi who was born in Multan towards the end of the twelfth century CE. He was the nephew of another well-known Sufi saint named Baba Farid Ganjashakar, and was brought up by him in Pakpattan in present-day Pakistan. An information booklet on the shrine that I purchased outside the entry gate mentioned that Alauddin Ali Ahmed came to Kaliyar in 1252 CE, and died in 1290 CE, corresponding to the year of Sultan Jalaluddin Khilji's enthronement. Local tradition claims that the last Delhi sultan, Ibrahim Lodhi, had most of the tombs constructed over the graves of those buried there. However, nothing of the Lodhis remains except one tomb.

Back then, my interest in monumental architecture was still in the sack; thus, I obviously failed to take note of any of the ancient structures, except the rampart below the khanqah.

The Unbottled Djinn and the Spiritual Merriment

After a sound sleep of several hours extending well into the night, we went to the Piran Kaliyar Dargah around midnight. When we entered the compound, *nakkara* drumbeats announced our entry, as was done for sultans. Several black-clad pirs rushed ahead to embrace Pir Fahimuddin and Rose. Seeing a new face, they extended the warmth of their bosom to me too, which I gladly accepted.

The first task for our group was to visit the grave of Alauddin Ali Ahmed Sabir.

When I approached his tomb at the heart of the compound, I was shocked to see about a dozen or so teenage girls, some tethered by chains and ropes to the marble lattice windows of other structures. They were acting funny, as if straight out of some B-grade Hindi horror movie. I nudged Rose for an explanation, to which he replied that they were possessed.

'By what?' I retorted.

'Djinn,' he replied, and added that Hazrat Sabir was believed to be their nemesis, thus this place also served as a mass detoxifying centre.

What the hell! For indeed, the trancey head-banging being done by these girls could put any death-metal fan to shame. Some of them were taking it a little too far by throwing themselves against the marble floor of the courtyard and making deep, throaty sounds, each trying to outdo the other in their verbal exposition of displaying the type of djinns that dwelt within them.

While some just let their hair loose—literally speaking—the others allowed the ghosts in them to swing in concord with the shrill screams of the qawwals. When these singers' dry distinctive claps accentuated the rhythm of their harmonium and kept abreast with the fast-paced drumming, those possessed girls increased their rocking as well. If not for the occult angle, these girls could have been mistaken for a crowd jiving crazily in a qawwali concert.

Well, it was a strangely amusing sight to see, and for a while I had this naughty inclination of getting these girls to sniff a sweaty sock and shake the djinn out of the bottle. Seeing these women inside the main compound, albeit acting crazy, was a better sight than Kaki's dargah in Mehrauli, where ladies are prohibited from visiting his grave. They have to make do with paying their respects from afar through a latticed marble separation.

Ignoring these howling girls, we then sat in the pir's enclosure near the entry gate. Here, a central yagna-like firepit had smouldering logs in it and around it were seated several Muslim holy men. They, like their Hindu counterparts, were bedecked with loads of garlands of *rudraksha* and other beads. It was now time for the *mahaprasad*.

Pir Fahimuddin was presented with a foot-long chillum which he lit with the fire supplied from the pit in one drag, to the cheers of '*mashallah*' from everyone. It looked as if he was smoking the Olympic torch. As is customary, the chillum was passed around... After a while the langar of the dargah provided biryani for us, post which we returned to the khanqah.

Before I conclude my experience of Kaliyar, let me tell the readers that in the morning I was rudely woken by a deep growling noise coming from the courtyard of the arched hall. I went out to find the cause of the cacophony, only to see a girl who alone was swooning to music of her own making; another possessed soul out there in the morning trying to get the attention of the aged Baba Garib Shah, who was sitting nearby, surrounded by middle-aged ladies clamouring for some pieces of paper that he was throwing at whomever he fancied.

I went near the girl, making signs of 'shhhhh!' with my finger to my lips. Seeing me disapprove of her antics, the djinn in her complied and she quietly left the courtyard. After two more hours of rest, we visited Haridwar, for Pir Fahimuddin wanted to bathe in the Ganga before we returned to Delhi.

Well, it's good that he did not take a dip in the Ganga Canal that flowed through Kaliyar, or I wouldn't have visited Haridwar in 2001. During my 2014 art exhibition in Delhi, I met the pir for the last time in Mehrauli. He had become quite old and had a tough time recognizing me. Before I began writing this chapter about Kaliyar, I called Rose, who informed me that Pir Fahimuddin had passed away a few years ago.

The First Train in the Subcontinent

While trying to find out about the history of Kaliyar, on which not much information is available, I came across an interesting piece of information that I feel compelled to add here: according to an article in *The Hindu* dated 10 August 2002, a librarian at IIT Roorkee chanced upon some information about the first train in the country, hauling clay between Roorkee and Kaliyar on 22 December 1851. This was groundbreaking, because it is generally believed that the first steam train in India made its journey in 1853 CE, between Mumbai and Thane.

This clay was removed from mounds in Kaliyar in order to excavate the Ganga Canal. The news article claimed that the librarian found this information in a book titled *Report on the Ganges Canal Works* by Col. P.T. Cautley, published in 1860 CE. I combed through both the volumes of Cautley's book in vain for a reference to such a train. I also searched for information in Cautley's second book, titled *Ganges Canal*, published in 1864 CE, without any result. The second volume of his first book, however, does contain two references to steam engines being imported from England to work the machines installed in a workshop built in Roorkee for the purpose of excavating the canal.

In 1851, the first steam machine was imported to India. It was a 10-horsepower condensing steam engine with boilers; along with drilling, punching, planning, sawing and grinding, it could work three lathes, which also arrived from England.[1] Perhaps I have overlooked and missed the part that the librarian found which mentioned the laying of a temporary train line to aid in the canal work... Anyway, let us go to the Kaliyar of today.

Today's Kaliyar

Fourteen years after my first visit, I returned to Kaliyar. This was during one of my rides to see the ancient remains of the Garhwal region. I had taken a detour to Kaliyar to relive the nostalgic experience of my first visit. The grand gateway was completed and done up with kitschy green and pink. The old pir Baba Garib Shah was long gone, sleeping peacefully beside his khanqah.

Several hotels have come up in Kaliyar, which now looks like a typical North Indian town; and as for the main dargah of Alauddin

Ali, everything about it looked overcrowded and did not match the memory I had of it in my mind. This deterred me from entering its premises, and I then rode through the 'town' trying to explore its dirty streets for any signs of the ancient vestiges left uncovered by bathroom tiles.[2] Near the square pool called Sabri Hauz, I saw an old, dilapidated tomb that looked like a Lodhi-era structure.

A possible reason behind the disappearance of old tombs from Kaliyar was the Ganga Canal, whose construction began in 1842 and was completed in 1854. The first 32 km of the canal were paved with locally sourced bricks, and the next 32 km were covered with materials scavenged from '...an ample supply of native bricks [procured] from different ruins in the vicinity...'[3]

Haridwar and Its Ancient History

Like Banaras, Haridwar, being one of the holiest places in the geography of the Hindu mind, is always full of pilgrims. The town, set on both the banks of the Ganga, has many temples, none of which is old. The ancient vestiges of its past have been eradicated on several occasions: the reason being wanton iconoclasm by intolerant Muslim monarchs.

When I say both the banks of the Ganga, I am slightly incorrect. The main focus of the pilgrims' attention is the several ghats on the Ganga Canal at Kankhal. Here, the canal flows west towards Dhanouri and takes a sharp southwest turn to flow past Kaliyar and on to Roorkee. From Roorkee, the canal flows parallel to the Ganga, and terminates as the Lower Ganga Canal at Panki in Kanpur in Uttar Pradesh. Every time I visit my wife's school at Panki, I cross this canal, which, from its source, is a good 600 km in length.

Haridwar ('Hari' refers to Vishnu and *dwar* means 'gate'), as the name implies, means 'the gateway to God' or Devbhoomi, i.e. 'the land of gods'. For the devotees of Shiva, Haridwar is pronounced 'Hardwar', as 'Har' stands for Shiva. At Haridwar, the Ganga, flowing down the Garhwal Himalayas, also called Devbhoomi, joins the plains. It is at Haridwar that the last of the Shivalik Himalayas vanish into the great North Indian plains. And also, it is from here that the ancients began their arduous journey upstream into the mountains following the course of the Ganga. Due to this, Haridwar is also called Gangadwar, or 'the gateway to the Ganga'. Al Biruni has also used the term Gangadarara/Gangadwar[4] for the place where the Ganga emerges from the mountains. Basically, the place was important to its erstwhile kingdoms not only for its religious sanctity but also for its strategic location as the entry point into the Himalayas.

Legendary Accounts

The history of this place is as old as time, being recognized as a tirtha in the post-Vedic period. The Mahabharata, whose story is from that era, has on several occasions mentioned the sanctity that Haridwar embodies as a place of pilgrimage. However, Haridwar was not always known by that name, for it had several; Kapila being one of them. Tradition asserts that Haridwar came to be called Kapila after Sage Kapila's ashram there. Kapila is also believed to have had an ashram at the confluence of the Ganga with the Bay of Bengal at Gangasagar in present-day West Bengal. Timur, in his autobiography titled *Malfuzat-i-Timuri*, has called Haridwar 'Kutila',[5] which is an obvious mispronunciation of Kapila.

The upper reaches of the Ganga, particularly the region from Haridwar to the Gangotri glacier, were called Bharadwaja during the third and fourth centuries BCE.[6] The ancient Brahmin *gotra* Bharadwaja originated from the Garhwal region.

In the small museum of the Bharat Mandir of Rishikesh (about 31 km north of Haridwar), I came across a life-sized two-armed ithyphallic sculpture of Lakulisha and a life-sized sculpture of a Yakshi carved in spotted Mathura red sandstone. The style of these two is unmistakably from the Mathura region, and they were dated to the second century CE, corresponding to the reign of Kanishka and his successor Huvishka. These sculptures, along with other damaged carvings from temples, were unearthed during the excavations done around the Bharat Mandir. The Kanishka era sculptures from Mathura, which also happened to be the eastern capital of the Kushan monarch, are clear proof of the connection between Mathura and Haridwar. It would not be premature to state that the northern Ganga area was a part of the far-flung Kushan Empire.

During the fourth century CE, Haridwar was known as Kankhal. Kalidasa, a Sanskrit playwright from this era, used the name Kankhal in his *Meghaduta* while referring to the region.[7] The eighth century CE *Skanda Purana* mentions Kankhal as the place of Daksha's sacrifice.[8]

Hieun Tsang's Account of Haridwar

Another name for Haridwar is Mayapur. This name is still in use but not for the entire town, only a portion to its north. In the seventh century CE, the Chinese pilgrim Hieun Tsang visited Mayapur and left behind a detailed description of the place. From Sugh in present-day Yamunanagar in Haryana, he went to Haridwar. The pilgrim calls Haridwar 'Moyulo',[9] identified by Cunningham as Mayapur, named after the temple of Mayadevi[10] that exists on the hill to the north of the town. The temple of Mayadevi is a Shakti Peeth and the goddess is the titular deity of Haridwar.

Hieun Tsang mentions that this country was ruled by a king from the lower castes who was not a Buddhist. He also records that there existed twenty Buddhist monasteries of the Hinayana sect in the region with 800 monks living in them. Since it was not a Buddhist kingdom, it had fifty Deva temples. He also states that the Buddhist master Gunaprabha composed a treatise in a small monastery situated a little distance south of Mayapur. Lama Taranath, the sixteenth century CE Tibetan monk, who wrote the book *History of Buddhism in India*, mentions that Gunaprabha was born in a Brahmin family in Mathura and raised in a monastery in Agrapuri in Mathura.[11]

Hieun Tsang describes Haridwar as being situated on the eastern bank of the Ganga (presently it is concentrated on the western bank); to its north was a great Deva temple. Near the temple, the Ganga was diverted by a clever means into a man-made canal, which the people of the Five Indias called the gate of the Ganga, where people bathed to wash away their sins.[12] Even today the bathing takes place primarily in the canal, which was constructed by the British. British engineers basically developed and re-excavated the ancient paved ghats that were built to facilitate ritual dips in the rapid currents of the river.

In fact, the first record of Kumbh at Haridwar is by the Chinese pilgrim, who tells us how hundreds and thousands of people gathered there from all the corners of the country to wash away their sins. He also notes that the kings of different kingdoms established *dharamshalas* at Mayapur to take care of the needs of the pilgrims.[13] From Haridwar, this pilgrim travelled north to Brahmapura, which Cunningham identified as the kingdom of the Kumaon and Garhwal mountains.[14]

We don't know the definite name of the king that ruled the region in the seventh century CE. It is, however, certain that whoever the monarch was, he was under the vassalage of Harshavardhan. However, Lama Taranath mentions that during the lifetime of Dharmakirti, a revered Buddhist monk and teacher at Nalanda University during the seventh or eighth century CE, the ruler of Haridwar was Sakya Mahabala.[15] The Lama also mentions that Mahabala's rule extended up to Kashmir, which contradicts Kalhan's history of the state. During the eighth century CE, Shankaracharya passed through Haridwar and Rishikesh on his way to Kedarnath and Badrinath.

The Sequence of Haridwar's Desecration

The first invasion of Haridwar happened at the hands of Mahmud of Ghazni in 1019 CE. Mahmud was in pursuit of Trilochanpal from the Hindu Shahi Dynasty of eastern Afghanistan. Trilochanpal had fled east and, after crossing Haridwar, camped on the banks of the Ramganga (flowing through the Jim Corbett Forest). After crossing Haridwar, Mahmud met the Hindu Shahi king at Ramganga and defeated him in battle.[16]

In the year 1192 CE, Qutbuddin Aibak conquered Meerut. Hasam Nizami, in his *Taj-ul-Masir*, informs us that all the Hindu temples in the city were destroyed and converted to mosques.[17] We do not know whether Aibak went a further 140 km from Meerut to Haridwar.

The Sufi dargah at Kaliyar maintains that in 1252 CE, Alauddin Ali Ahmed Sabir arrived at Kaliyar, setting up his base near the 'nest of infidels' and began the overt and covert work of proselytizing, as was the agenda of all Sufi mystics of that time. For such an important Sufi site—which was once patronized by the Lodhis, with Sikandar being one of the greatest iconoclastic Delhi sultans—to be so close, does tell us why no ancient temples exist in Haridwar.

Ironically, in the twenty-first century, a large section of North Indian Muslims, influenced by the Sunni–Wahhabi school of thought espoused by Deoband, consider those early mystics as the epitome of *shirk*. Bowing to their grave is akin to idolatry, which is haram. I have observed that such puritanical ideas have crept into the minds of many Indian Muslims, particularly the 'educated' lot. One example of such 'change' is the greeting 'Allahhafiz' that is meant to replace the Persian 'Khudahafiz'.

In 1254 CE, the Delhi sultan Nasiruddin Mahmud crossed the Ganga at Miyapur/Mayapur and marched along the base of the hills to the banks of the Rahab.[18] The Rahab is the Ramganga River. Nasiruddin Mahmud had also destroyed all the temples that existed in the foothills of the Himalayas in Pinjore.[19] It becomes apparent that when he passed through Haridwar, his soldiers must have obliterated those that still remained.

It is only through inference that we know why no ancient temples exist in Haridwar at present. Except one specific record of the destruction of the temples in Haridwar, evidenced in the form of broken bits of sculptural parts seen by Cunningham and those in the Bharat Mandir Museum in Rishikesh, there are no others that I have come across as yet.

Timur's Massacre at Haridwar

In the year 1399 CE, Timur, after plundering and destroying Delhi, marched north following the course of the Ganga. He arrived at Meerut and captured its fort under the command of Ilyas Afghan and his son Maula Ahmed Thanesari. After his conquest of Meerut, he ordered the left wing of his army, which was under the command of Amir Jahan Shah, to proceed west towards the [Yamuna] and '...take every fort and town and village he came to, and to put all the infidels of the country to the sword.'[20] He took the northern route and proceeded upstream.

During his march towards Tughlaqpur, he heard that a large number of Hindus had collected on the bank of the Ganga. He immediately sent his commanders Mubashar Bahadur and Ali Sultan Tawachi, commanding 5,000 horsemen, to massacre them. It was here that he received intelligence about Hindus in forty-eight boats sailing down the river 'with the intention of fighting'.[21]

His horsemen waded along the shallow Ganga and soon dispatched the defenders; their dead bodies were thrown in the river, writes Timur. After this incident, he reached Tughlaqpur and camped there. In Tughlaqpur, he once again received intelligence about some thousands of Hindus congregating on the banks of the Ganga. The psychopath from Samarkand says that this group of Hindus was led by Mubarak Khan, who, being informed of Timur's approach, had arranged 10,000 men to oppose him. At that time, Timur only had a thousand horsemen, for the rest of his army was busy plundering the tract. Timur had lost hope and was praying for victory, which he says was answered by the coincidental return of his army from the Yamuna expedition: 'If it had not been so I might here have said farewell, for I could hardly have escaped,' he notes. Mubarak Khan's army was routed, and the non-combatants that staggered around the main force were killed, their wives and children made prisoners, and their goods and cattle taken in the form of booty.[22] Timur's conquest of the region had coincided with what was most likely the ongoing Kumbh Mela in Haridwar; that is the reason why so many families were by the river hoping to travel upstream, perhaps unmindful of the calamity that had befallen Delhi a month ago.

After this victory, he received intelligence about a '...large number of Hindus assembled in the valley of Kutila [Kapila/Haridwar], on the side of the Ganges, having made that valley a place of refuge.'[23] He immediately mounted his horse, leaving the rest of his army to collect the plunder, and charged ahead with only 500 horsemen. The rest of his troops soon caught up with him. Near Haridwar, he came across thousands of pilgrims and charged through them. Here, he was opposed by one Malik Shaikha (possibly Shekhar), who he says was in charge of the infidels.[24]

Shaikha was soon overpowered and killed. He then once more received intelligence that in Haridwar, which was only four kilometres away from the place of the last encounter, there was a large number of Hindus along with their families and properties awaiting plunder.[25] Timur fell upon the pilgrims and slaughtered thousands of people. He writes that they put up a slight resistance but that it was negligible: 'All the wives and children of the infidels were made prisoners, and their property and goods, gold, money and grains, horses, camels [...], cows and buffaloes in countless numbers, fell as spoils into the hands of my soldiers.' Well, I shudder even to imagine the scale at which the massacre of all those countless individuals must have happened, whose existence would be forgotten if not for Timur, which is ironic to say the least.

The genocidal maniac writes:

> The Hindu infidels worship the Ganges, and once every year they come on pilgrimage to this place, which they consider the source of the river, to bathe and to have their heads and beards shaved. They believe these acts to be the means of obtaining salvation and securing future reward. They dispense large sums of money in charity among those who wear the Brahminical thread, and they throw money into the river. When infidels die in distant parts, their bodies are burned, and the ashes are brought to this river and thrown into it. This they look upon as a means of sanctification. When I learnt these facts, I resolved to war against the infidels of this place, so that I might obtain the merit of overthrowing them.'[26]

In Haridwar he was once more informed that about 25 km upstream, there were thousands of Hindus. On 13 January 1399 CE, at dawn, he set out to plunder Rishikesh. The geographical distance from the valley of Kapila to the place upriver given by him matches Rishikesh. This religious centre was now being defended by the scattered pilgrims. Then the battle commenced with the beating of drums and sounds of fury. After the first charge, the pilgrims' defences were overwhelmed. Once again, thousands were slaughtered, and their '...blood ran down the mountains and plains, and thus (nearly) all were sent to hell'. He continues:

> The few who escaped, wounded, weary, and half dead, sought refuge in the defiles of the hills. Their properties and goods, which extended all computation, and their countless cows and buffalos, fell as spoils into the hands of my victorious soldiers. When I was satisfied with the destruction I had dealt out to the infidels, and the land was cleansed from the pollution of their existence, I turned back victorious and triumphant, laden with spoil.[27]

Timur then notes that on the same day, he crossed the Ganga, which implies that Haridwar and Rishikesh were on the eastern bank of the river, unlike today. After that, he began his westward march towards what is now Dehradun. While marching in the western direction through the valley between the Shivalik and the Dhaulkhand ranges, he was challenged by the king of the Shivalik Mountains, whom Timur names Bahruz and calls the most powerful mountain chief of Hindustan.[28] Once again, Timur inflicted a crushing defeat on the defenders and captured a large amount of booty. This event took place in the 'country of Miyapur', which is, of course, Mayapur/Haridwar.

The identity of the hill king Bahruz is difficult to ascertain. An article titled 'History of Uttarakhand (Garhwal, Kumaon, Haridwar): Part 139' by Bhishma Kukreti, published in the e-magazine of the Government of Uttarakhand, dated 10 September 2013, discusses Timur's invasion of Haridwar and mentions that Bahruz was Baccharaj, a local king from Salan (near Dehradun). While travelling through the valley, Timur plundered a few more places and reached the Yamuna. After crossing it he was challenged by Ratan Sen, the king of Sirmour...[29]

Haridwar under the Mughals

During the reign of Mughal Emperor Akbar, Haridwar was also called Mayapur. The *Ain-i-Akbari* by Abul Fazal mentions that Maya/Mayapur on the banks of the Ganga was one of the seven holy sites of the Hindus.[30] Abul Fazal further informs us that Akbar only drank the water of the Ganga. When the emperor was in Agra or in Fatehpur Sikri, the water was supplied from Soron in the present-day Eta district of Uttar Pradesh. When the court moved to the Punjab, the water arrived from Haridwar.[31]

On 18 December 1621 CE, Jahangir visited Haridwar. He calls it Hardwar and not Mayapur. He describes the place as '...one of the major temple sites of the Hindus, and many Brahmins and hermits lead a life of seclusion here, worshipping God according to their religion.' In Haridwar, he '...gave alms of cash and goods to each and every one according to their merits. Since [he] didn't like the climate of these foothills, and no place suitable for residence had been seen, [he] set out for the foothills of Jammu and Kangra.'[32]

The First Europeans in Haridwar

During Jahangir's reign, the first European to visit Haridwar was the Jesuit priest Anderada, and his companion Manuel Marquez, in 1624 CE.[33] They were on their way to Tsaparang in Guge via Srinagar, the capital of Garhwal.

The first Englishman to visit Haridwar and leave behind a description of it was Thomas Coryat, also during the reign of Jahangir. We don't know exactly when he visited the place but it was before 1617 CE, when he died in Surat and was buried there.[34] In a letter Coryat wrote in October 1616 CE to Edward Terry,[35] he had expressed his desire to travel to Haridwar and then to the Jawalamukhi Temple near Kangra. From Edward Terry we know that Coryat carried out his intention and visited both the places.[36] Cunningham gives us a quote from Coryat's letter to Terry: '[At] Haridwara, the capital of Siba [Shiva], the Ganges flowed amongst large rocks with a pretty full current.'[37]

Haridwar after Jahangir

During the reign of Shah Jahan, the son of Jahangir, the chief of Haridwar was Nagar Das, who was given the charge of the thana of Chandi by Shah Jahan after the conquest of the Dun (the valley between Dehradun and Rishikesh) area by his general, Khalilulla Khan.[38]

During the struggle for the Mughal throne after the illness of Shah Jahan, Aurangzeb set upon his elder brother Dara after having overthrown his father. Sulaiman Shikoh, Dara's son, fled to Haridwar and from there he reached the court of Raja Prithi Shah in Srinagar.[39]

After the fall of the Mughal Empire and the subsequent rise of the Marathas, Haridwar came under their sway. In 1786 CE, the notorious Rohilla Afghan warlord Gulam Kadir invaded Dehradun via Haridwar.[40]

The next Englishman to visit Haridwar and leave behind a record of it was Captain Hardwicke in 1796 CE, who witnessed a massacre during a Kumbh Mela at Haridwar.[41]

After the capture of Garhwal by the Gurkhas in 1804, Har Ki Pauri in Haridwar was turned into a slave market by them. During his survey of the Ganga, Capt. F.V. Raper visited Haridwar in 1808 CE and witnessed the sale of captured Kumaonis and Garhwalis by the Gurkhas. He writes that the price of individuals of both sexes aged between three and thirty varied from ten rupees to 150 rupees each.[42] Raper notes, 'Those slaves are brought down from all parts of the interior of the hills, and sold at *Haridwar*, from ten to one hundred and fifty rupees.'[43]

Cunningham's Haridwar

Cunningham, during his visit to Haridwar in 1863–64 CE and after the completion of the Ganga Canal, had mapped the town. In his map published in his book, *Four Reports Made During the Years 1862-63-64-65*, Vol. II, he gives us the visuals of some ancient sites that once existed there.[44] He informs us that the old city of Mayapur was pointed out to him by the people there. This city corresponds to the area immediately north of the Narayan Shila Temple in the map drawn by him. South of the Narayan Shila Temple, beside the Ganga Canal, was a large fort, which he calls the fort of Raja Ben. Ben is the anglicized version of Vena, a legendary Puranic king from whose arms had emerged Prithu, associated with the Earth Goddess Prithvi.

It would be puerile to believe that the fort seen by Cunningham belonged to Raja Vena, who, if he existed at all, did so during the Jurassic age, if not before that. The fort could have been built after Jahangir's reign, for when he visited Haridwar there was no place suitable for his residence there, as mentioned by him in his memoir.[45] Presently, the Rishikul State Ayurvedic College occupies the spot of the fort.

Kankhal on Cunningham's map is shown to be south of the fort on the other side of the canal. At the Narayan Shila Temple, he reports seeing several broken sculptures that belonged to an older temple existing at the site. Here he also came across a small image of the Buddha surrounded by attendants.[46]

The Mayadevi Temple, he reports, was made entirely of stone. Seeing the remains of an inscription at the entrance, he concludes that the temple was constructed in the tenth or eleventh century CE. At present, the Mayadevi Temple is covered with cement plaster and surrounded by ugly buildings.

At Har Ki Pauri Ghat, Cunningham reports that the original footprints of Vishnu on stone were lost to the river, and had been replaced by different ones, which he saw fixed to the upper wall of the ghat. This ghat had been constructed by Akbar's commander-in-chief, Raja Man Singh of Amer, but due to the torrent had turned ruinous. In 1819 CE, during the Kumbh Mela, 430 pilgrims lost their lives at the ghat owing to the pressure of the crowd. Most drowned in the river while some succumbed to a stampede. In 1820 CE, the British Government reconstructed the ghat in order to prevent any such catastrophe.[47]

The Kumbh Mela at Haridwar

The main river flows past the hustle and bustle of the teeming masses at Kankhal, towards the southeast of Haridwar. The eastern part of Kankhal is the site for the Kumbh Mela that takes place every twelve years, determined by calculations based on the Hindu calendar. The Kumbh at Haridwar is called the Mesh Kumbh and takes place when Jupiter enters Aquarius and the Sun is in Aries. During this gathering, the Niranjani Akhada has the right to take the first dip in the Ganga, accompanied by the Juna, Abahan and Ananda *akhada*s (arenas). After them, the sadhus from the Nirvani and the Atal akhadas take the dip.[48]

These akhadas are clans of Shaivite sadhus that were formed after Shankaracharya reorganized the Brahminical religion, better known as Hinduism. Ten clans of sadhus, collectively called the Dasnamis ('ten-names'), were grouped into symbolic arenas with the motto of upholding *shastra* (scriptures) and *astra* (weapons). The members of these clans, also called the Naga Sanyasis (naked sages), subsequently militarized themselves and continue to uphold that tradition even today.

The order of precedence for the ritual bathing was put in place by the British in order to prevent large-scale sword fights that would erupt between the sadhus of the different akhadas. On several occasions, thousands of lives were lost because of the scramble to bathe first at the holiest moment during the Kumbh Mela, which falls on the Makar Sankranti.[49] The earliest recorded battle between the sadhus during the Kumbh Mela took place in 1253 CE, between the Nirvani Akhada and the Bairagi Sadhus in Haridwar.[50] The Vishnu-worshipping Bairagis were massacred.

In 1749 CE, the Nirvani Akhada had another showdown in Haridwar with the Ramdal and destroyed this group of Rama worshippers. Immediately after this, they came into conflict with the Marathas, who defeated the armed sadhus and planted their saffron flag in the latter's camp in Haridwar.[51] The Marathas were in possession of Haridwar and did not tolerate their authority being challenged, thus the conflict.

Once again in 1760, on the last day of the ritual bath during a Kumbh Mela, another great battle took place between the Dasnamis and the Bairagis at Kankhal, in which 18,000 Bairagis lost their lives.[52]

In 1796 CE, the first British account of the Kumbh at Haridwar was written by Capt. Thomas Hardwicke, who visited the gathering with Dr Hunter. Hardwicke gives us the details of what transpired between the Naga Sadhus and the Sikh Nihangs (armed Sikh sadhus clad in blue), who also take a dip in the Ganga during the Kumbh. On the morning of 10 April 1796 CE, on the last day of the Kumbh, about 12,000 to 14,000 armed Sikhs assembled on the banks of the Ganga and indiscriminately attacked every sadhu who happened to be nearby. A total of 5,000 sadhus were killed on that fateful day in Haridwar.[53] The Sikhs revere Haridwar because of Guru Nanak's visit to the holy place and his dip in the Ganga in 1504 CE. The Nanakwara Gurudwara marks the place where the first Sikh guru bathed in the river.

Today's Haridwar

One interesting aspect of Haridwar is its many Brahmins, who keep genealogical records of pilgrims and have with them registers of names of families that go back even twenty generations. This traditional method of record-keeping is also practised in Banaras and Gaya, but at Haridwar it is categorical and is an integral part of funeral rites. Once the funeral sacraments are completed with the assistance of a Brahmin, he notes down the particulars of the family. This ensures that when another member from the same family dies, the sacramental rites are done by the same Brahmin or a member of his family; thus, a link is established that is maintained over generations.

Today, the pilgrim town of Haridwar is a bustling city of swanky hotels and humble dharamshalas. The ghats are all safely concretized, which light up in the evening, making the place glitter like in a carnival. The town, rather city, seen from the compound of the Mansa Devi Temple situated on the hill immediately to the west makes for a grand sight. At night, the Ganga glitters with the lights that illuminate its banks. Sometimes the river itself lights up with thousands of floating diyas offered to it by devotees. I was told by an attendant of the Mansa Devi Temple that from where I stood, the sight of Haridwar during Diwali was heavenly. I could well imagine the galaxy of stars that would descend to this ancient place and light up every corner of it. This thought evoked in me a yearning to go back to primordial times, to the memory of its past as the place where the great river ended her angry flow and began a placid journey, rendering Indic civilization synonymous with the Gift of the Ganga.

3

In Krishna's Cradle

Mathura, alongside Banaras and Ayodhya, holds a position of immense sanctity in the minds of Hindus as a hallowed place that has been continuously occupied for the past 3,000 years. The geography of India is replete with places, rivers and mountains that have been named after the Ganga, Yamuna, Saraswati, Kailash, Kashi, Ayodhya and Mathura. To maintain a link with these venerated geographic locations, the residents of various places adopted their names and reused them. In this regard, the name Mathura too can be found to have been given to villages strewn across the length and breadth of the country; I know of one near my mother's ancestral place in West Bengal. I also know of another called Sar Mathura in the Dholpur district of Rajasthan. It is also believed that the name of the famous temple town Madurai in Tamil Nadu is derived from Mathura.

Mathura in Myths and Legends

The Mathura or the Vraja/Braj region of hoary antiquity exists as post-Vedic era mounds within the present city and without. These mounds have yielded ancient artefacts and evidence of settlement that attest to the city's earliest mentions in the Ramayana and the Mahabharata. The earliest Purana, the *Harivamsa*,[1] a supplement of the great epic dealing specifically with the life of Krishna and Balarama, is set primarily in Mathura. Due to this, the *Harivamsa* is also called the *Mathura Harivamsa*, amongst its other names.[2]

Mathura is synonymous with the Yadava clan, and is known as the place where this cattle-herding caste originated. The name

Yadava is derived from Yadu, the son of Devyani and Yayati. Legend says that King Yayati had requested Yadu to exchange his youth for his father's old age, which he refused. The king then cursed him saying that his progeny would be deprived of their kingdom. From the line of Yadu was born a descendant named Haihaya, and from his descendant, the mighty Kartavirya Arjuna, a warrior with a thousand arms, who had vanquished Ravana. Kartavirya Arjuna was ultimately killed by Parasurama, the sixth incarnation of Vishnu. Ironically, the eighth incarnation of Vishnu, i.e. Krishna, was born into the dynasty of Kartavirya Arjuna.

One of the descendants of Kartavirya Arjuna was Vrisha, whose son was Madhu, who had a vast brood of sons, the eldest of whom was named Vrishni. Krishna was born into this Vrishni clan, one of whose branches was called the Surasena.[3] Madhu was a contemporary of Dashrath of Ayodhya, the father of Rama. Madhu established his stronghold on the banks of the Yamuna, which came to be known after him as Madhuvan ('the forest of Madhu').[4] The site of the first settlement of Madhuvan/Madhura/Madhupura/Mathura has been identified by Cunningham as the Maholi locality of Mathura.[5]

Madhu's son Lavanya was defeated by Shatrughana, the youngest stepbrother of Rama. It is believed that after defeating Lavanya, Shatrughana cut down the forest of Madhuvana and established another settlement, believed to be the site of Katara, where the present-day Shahi Masjid and the Sri Krishna Janmabhoomi Temple stand. The Yamuna had once flowed past Katara, but changed its course a few years before Tavernier visited Mathura in the seventeenth century CE.[6]

After the son of Shatrughana was ousted, the region around Madhuvan once again came under the control of the Yadavas, led by Bhima Satvata, the grandson of Lavanya. While Bhima Satvata was reigning in Mathura, the ancient Battle of Dasrajan ('battle of the ten kings') took place. This great event of antiquity, predating the composition of the Mahabharata, is spoken about in Mandala 7, Hymn 18 of the Rig Veda, composed by Rishi Vasishtha.[7] A confederation of ten tribes, which also included the Vrishnis, was defeated by the Bharata king Sudas on the banks of the river Ravi.[8]

Mathura from the Harivamsa

Ancient Mathura, and the region of Vraja on both banks of the Yamuna, has been described piecemeal in the *Harivamsa*. The city proper on the west bank of the Yamuna was the capital of the Surasena people, whose king was Kansa.[9] The story of his evil deeds that led to the birth of Krishna in his dungeon in Mathura and the baby Krishna's immediate removal to Gokul is well known.

The narrative that proceeds from the birth of Krishna in the *Harivamsa*, including his heroic feats, has snippets of information about the socio-political life of the people of the region.

We know that the Mathura of Kansa was a fortified city with several gates. Within the palace compound was an arena for gladiatorial fights where Kansa was killed by Krishna.[10] Surprisingly, the description of Mathura's rural tracts, like Gobardhan, as given in the *Harivamsa* is true to form even today. The *Harivamsa* notes:

> That charming village [Gobardhan] was filled with milk-maids. The roads, for carriage, were spacious there. It was covered with thorns and its outside was filled with fallen huge trees.
>
> All through the circumference there were stakes fixed on the ground and ropes for the calves; and it was filled with cow-dungs. The temples and cottages there were covered with grass. [...] The ground there was saturated with the leavings of curd and the drains were covered with moss and it was filled with the sound of the churning bangles of milk-women. The cow-sheds were all properly protected by well-shut doors; inside them were the houses for cows. It was filled with the playgrounds of milk-men and abounded in boys wearing feathers of crows. The youthful damsels of milk-men, clad in blue raiments, prepare clarified butter and accordingly there blows sweet-scented air. Having their heads adorned with garlands of wildflowers and their breasts covered with jackets, the milk-maids, with jars of milk on

their heads, always walk about there. The road, on the bank
of Yamuna, was also filled with milk-maids, carrying water.[11]

Today we can disregard the part about carrying drinking water from the Yamuna due to unchecked pollution, which is toxic for all life in it. Even that long ago, the *Harivamsa* narrates an instance of the river's pollution, then attributed to the gigantic serpent named Kaliya, who had, for a while, made the Yamuna his home.[12] Young Krishna ultimately vanquishes him and sends him out to the ocean, cleansing the Yamuna in the process.

From the *Harivamsa* we also get some idea of the river's geography as it flowed past Mathura and Vrindavan and a few clues to its changing course. In one instance, the *Harivamsa* narrates the acts of mischief by the powerful but inebriated Balarama, who, in his drunken state, becomes enamoured with Yamuna and wishes to marry her. He asks her to approach him in her human form, which she ignores. This throws the already hot-tempered Balarama into a rage, and he, using his celestial plough, drags the river up to Vrindavan, which forms the northern suburb of Mathura.[13] The part about Balarama dragging the river can be interpreted as a sudden change in the river's flow, recorded in a myth as the doings of a god.

After the death of Kansa, his father, the old Ugrasena, was reinstated to the throne by Krishna. Thereafter, the city suffered a total of eighteen sieges by the forces of Magadha, led by Jarasandha, who was the father-in-law of the slain Kansa. The fortification of the city withstood all these assaults, and each time, Jarasandha was defeated by Krishna and Balarama. The frustrated Jarasandha then had his powerful ally, a Greek named Kalayavana, assist him in the siege of Mathura.

An Interpretation of a Greek Invasion of Mathura as Narrated in the Harivamsa

In the story of Kalayavana, the Black Greek, we find the earliest recorded memory of Mathura being sieged by forces from outside the subcontinent. Kalayavana has been mythicized as an invincible demon who was fed on iron dust, or as being born from the union of the Yadava priest Gargaya and a milkmaid with the blessing of Shiva, in order to explain his dark complexion. The myth explaining the second part of his name, 'yavana', states that the child born to these two was reared in the family of a Yavana king, and since he had a dark complexion unlike a Greek, he was named 'the Black Greek'.[14]

His approach forced Krishna and the Vrishni clan of the Yadavas of Mathura to migrate out of the city and head for sanctuary to a faraway place. There, they established a city called Dwarka on the shores of the sea.[15]

The Possible Historicity of Kalayavana

The historical reference to the conquest of Mathura all the way to Ayodhya and Pataliputra by the Indo-Greek ruler Demetrius is found in the *Yuga Purana* by Vriddha Garga, composed before the advent of the Kushans in India.[16] The Hathigumpha Inscription of Kharvela, dated to the first half of the second century BCE, mentions the name of this king as a vanquished monarch who was ousted from Pataliputra and compelled to return to Mathura.[17]

Bana, the seventh century CE author of *Harshacharita*, tells us that there was once a king of Mathura named Brihadrath, who was defeated and killed by Vidurath. This Brihadrath is different from the Mauryan king who was slain by Pushyamitra Sunga, about whom also Bana writes.[18] We don't know the identity of Brihadrath of Mathura, but we know that Jarasandha's father was named Brihadrath. The possible mention of Jarasandha's family in conjunction with Greek invaders does tell us that the legend of Kalayavana's attack on Mathura holds water.

Al Biruni, the eleventh century CE scholar, refers to a calendar called Kalayavana that was once used by Indians. He confesses that apart from the name, he knows nothing about that era due to its antiquity. He states that this era was an epoch at the end of the last Dwapar Yuga when a fierce Yavana had subjugated India and their religion.[19] He also notes that Mathura, being crowded with Brahmins, was famous due to its association with Krishna, who was born and brought up there in the neighbourhood called Nandgola (Gokul).[20]

Today, the memory of the Kalayavana era is long forgotten. Had it not been for Al Biruni, we wouldn't have known about the existence of such a calendar that kept alive the memory of Mathura's first conquest by foreign forces—the first among several.

Mathura in Foreign Sources

The earliest mention of Mathura in foreign sources is by Megasthenes, when he states that the river Jomanes (Yamuna) flows through Methora (Mathura) and Carisobora before joining the Ganges.[21] Cunningham has identified Carisobora as Vrindavan. He states that Vrindavan's original name was Kalikavartta, or 'the whirlpool of Kalia'.[22] He also uses the name Klisoboras, taken from Arrian, who quotes Megasthenes.

Arrian writes that Hercules (mistaken for Balarama and Krishna) was held in high esteem by the tribe of Sourasenoi (Surasena). These Sourasenois lived in two cities, namely Methora and Cleisobora, beside which flowed a navigable river called Iobares (Yamuna).[23]

Pliny mentions the river Jomanes flowing between the cities of Methora and Calisobora. Regarding the identity of Carisobora/Klisoboras, I think it is not Vrindavan but the ancient metropolis of Kausambi, situated far downstream on the banks of the Yamuna before it merges with the Ganga at Prayagraj. Ptolemy has also mentioned Mathura as 'Modoura', calling it 'the city of the gods'.[24]

Mathura in Buddhist and Jain Literature

The mention of Mathura as a holy place is not limited to Hindu sources alone but is found in Buddhist as well as in Jain literature. The *Ashokavadana* tells us that the Buddha had visited Mathura in the company of Ananda and foretold the birth of Upagupta.[25] The city was then the capital of the Surasena Mahajanapada, one of the sixteen principal republics of North India, which was the westernmost part of Madhyadesha.[26]

Upagupta, a famous Buddhist monk, was from Mathura and is believed by the northern school of Buddhism to be the spiritual master of Emperor Ashoka. From the story of Upagupta in the *Ashokavadana*, we get a sense of Mathura as a great city with many guilds, whose chiefs, such as Nata and Bhata, would go on to construct monasteries.[27]

Upagupta's father, named Gupta, was a perfumer, and like him, the yet-to-be-venerable elder Upagupta stepped into the family business of manufacturing essence. He earned a pretty penny because of the malodour that prevailed in the city of Mathura on account of the evil Mara. Soon, the fame of Upagupta spread throughout the city and caught the attention of the courtesan Vasavadatta, who amorously longed for him. Upagupta the Virtuous turned a blind eye to the courtship of Vasavadatta, until finally he found her abandoned in the crematorium bereft of her ears, nose and all the extensions of her body. She had brought this plight upon herself because she happened to have had a rich merchant robbed of his gold and thrown into a dung heap when he had come to her for satisfying his sexual urges. As a punishment for her crime, the king of Mathura had had her mutilated.[28] The story then goes that before she died, he saved her soul by revealing to her the tenets of Buddhism.[29] Rabindranath Tagore's poem 'Abhisara' is about Upagupta and Vasavadatta, in which he depicts her as an abandoned creature suffering from the pox and then being cared for by Upagupta.

The *Ashokavadana* was composed in Mathura before the third century CE,[30] which could only mean that the composition was done during the heyday of Kushan rule over North India, corresponding to either Kanishka's time or after him. Other Buddhist works that give importance to Mathura as a great urban centre are the *Lalitavistara Sutra* and the *Mahavamsa* of Sri Lanka.

The Pali grammarian Mahakaccana was a resident of Mathura.[31]

Jain texts like *Vividha Tirtha Kalpa* associate Mathura with Suparshvanatha, the seventh Tirthankara. Neminatha (Aristanemi), the twenty-second Tirthankara, was from Mathura. He is also believed to be the cousin of Krishna and Balarama. The last Tirthankara, Mahavira, is also believed to have visited Mathura, as is Jambuswami, the last Kevalin, who performed his penance in the city.[32]

The importance of Mathura as a centre where Jainism thrived alongside Buddhism can be ascertained from the numerous archaeological finds from Kankali Tila, which will be discussed separately.

The Historic Period of Mathura Attested to by Its Earliest Sculptural, Numismatic and Epigraphical Finds

The Surasenas were ousted from Mathura by the powerful Nandas in the fourth century BCE.[33] Alexander's arrival in the subcontinent created a new upheaval that changed the socio-polity of North India. And after Alexander died, the realm that he had conquered was divided between his generals. The Indian portion came under the lordship of Seleucus Nicator, and was soon wrested from him by the rising star Chandragupta Maurya.[34]

Megasthenes, who we know was sent to the court of Chandragupta in Pataliputra as an ambassador by Seleucus Nicator,[35] informs us that across the Hemodos mountains (Caucasus) lived the Skythians (Scythians), also called the Sakais (Saka).[36] Two centuries after Megasthenes, these Sakas would overwhelm North India and, in turn, be defeated by another nomadic tribe from Central Asia called the Yuezhi, who would play a major role in the history of Mathura.

With the advent of Chandragupta Maurya, the Nandas were obliterated, and their vast empire was now a Mauryan realm. It is rather strange that so far very few Mauryan era sculptures have been unearthed in Mathura, even though Mathura was a great centre of Buddhism, as attested to in the *Ashokavadana* and later by Fa Hien and Hieun Tsang, who had noticed three stupas there built by Ashoka.[37]

In the Mathura Museum, a few small terracotta figurines of toy elephants with riders from the Mauryan period can be seen. However, a spotted red sandstone bas-relief excavated from Kankali Tila of Mathura, presently displayed in the Allahabad Museum, depicts an Ashokan pillar surmounted with a lion. Below it is the image of a man and a woman circumambulating it. The man is facing the viewer while his partner's back and long braided hair are turned at them. We don't know whether the pillar depicted was an Ashokan monument erected in Mathura or the lion capital pillar of Kolhua from Vaishali in Bihar.

After the murder of the last Mauryan king, Brihadrath, by Pushyamitra Sunga, a new dynasty was established in North and East India. The plastic arts propagated by the Mauryan emperors took a great leap during the Sunga period, particularly in Mathura. This was the birth of the genre called the Mathura School of Art. It is a distinctive category of sculptures that uses the characteristic spotted red sandstone quarried from areas to the west and south of Mathura such as Gobardhan, Barsana, Bharatpur and Sikri.

A gigantic sculpture of Yaksha Manibhadra from Parkham village near Mathura (equidistant from both Agra and Mathura, discovered by Cunningham in 1882–83 CE) and one of Yakshi Layava, currently placed in the Mathura Museum, are, in fact, two of the earliest such artworks that have been found in the Mathura region. The free-standing statue of Yaksha Manibhadra[38] is 2.59 m tall and on its pedestal is inscribed the name of the sculptor Gomitaka, the pupil of Kunika.[39] The sculpture of Yakshi Layava mentions the name of Naka, pupil of Kunika from Najala Jhinga. Both these sculptures have been dated to the second century BCE. Seemingly, Kunika was a master craftsman whose two disciples were the carvers of Yaksha Manibhadra and Yakshi Layava, respectively, and belonged to the guild of Nibhada, which flourished in Mathura.

While the Sungas were progressing as empire builders, their patronage of the sculptural arts was flourishing far and wide. The large gamut of sculptures unearthed in and around Mathura depicts a strong Sunga influence, particularly the small, exquisite terracotta figurines displayed in the Mathura Museum. It is perhaps from such influences flowing in from the east and the west that Mathura came to be one of the chief centres of the sculptural arts, reaching its pinnacle during the Yuezhi/Kushan rule of the first and second centuries CE.

It is also possible that the Indo-Greek king Menander I, reigning from Sagala (present-day Sialkot),[40] had conquered Mathura in the third century BCE. Several coins of his and of his son, Sotar, have been found in Mathura.[41]

We are not certain whether the Brahminical Sungas ever overwhelmed Mathura, but our conjecture suggests that they did. A large cache of coins bearing the image of Lakshmi and suffixes like 'mitra' has been unearthed in Mathura. From this horde, we get the names Gomitra, Brahmamitra, Dridhamitra, Indramitra, Sumitra, Suryamitra and Vishnumitra.[42] The suffix of their names makes one assume that they either belonged to the clan of Pushyamitra Sunga or were their allies.

Another line of local kings is known to have ruled Mathura. Their suffix is 'datta', with names like Bhavadatta, Kamadatta, Purushadatta, Ramadatta, Shashachandradatta, Seshadatta and Uttamadatta. These kings were followed by rulers named Ajadeva, Aparanta, Balabhuti, Tijyavega and Upatikya.[43] During the reign of the mitra and the datta kings, the Bhagavata cult of Krishna and Balarama gained prominence in Mathura as the predominant religion of the place.[44]

During the second century BCE, Mathura had become a major metropolis. The *Mahabhasya* of Patanjali written around that time refers to Mathura as a city that equalled Pataliputra, Sankissa, Saketa, Banaras (now Varanasi), Kausambi, Hastinapur, Gavidhumata (modern-day Kudarkot), Ahikshetra and Kannauj in prosperity.[45]

The Sakas, who had overwhelmed the Indo-Greeks, set their eyes on Mathura in the first century BCE and overwhelmed the city. An inscription called the Yavanarajya Inscription from Maghera near Mathura indicates the region conquered by them. The engraving, dating back to 69 BCE, states that the name of the kingdom is 'Yavanarajya' and mentions the excavation of a well and a tank by Ahogani, the mother of a merchant named Virabala. This engraving is on a red sandstone slab that was found in a field.[46] This long slab, broken in two, is in the Mathura Museum at present.

Epigraphic evidence tells us further about the Sakas who ruled Mathura. An inscription on the twin lion capital of Mathura mentions the names of several Saka kings. These two outward-facing badly sculpted lions, with a square slab on their back on which the Buddhist Triratna diagrammatic design is engraved, mention the name of King Maki (Maues), Mahasatrapa Rajavula, his wife Queen Abuhola, their daughter Hana and their four sons, one of whom was titled Satrap Sudasa.[47] Furthermore, the inscription mentions five other Saka satraps from Sakastana (present-day Sistan).[48] This capital was erected by Rajavula on the death of Maki, who had established Saka rule over North India. In 1869 CE, the capital was discovered by Dr Bhagvanlal Indraji on the steps of a temple dedicated to Goddess Sitala, situated on Saptarshi Tila in Mathura.[49] It is now in the British Museum.

Another inscription from an ancient well in the Mora village of Mathura mentions the name of Rajavula. The inscription is in Sanskrit (one of the earliest) and it talks about the building of a magnificent stone temple dedicated to the five Vrishni heroes (Krishna, Balarama,[50] Pradyumna, Aniruddha and Samba) by a lady named Tosha.[51] From an *ayagapata* (votive tablet) belonging to a Jain temple on the famous Kankali Tila, we also get the name of Mahasatrapa Sodasa, the son of Rajavula, as the ruler of Mathura.[52] This inscription is dated to 24 BCE.[53] We know of two other Saka kings who ruled Mathura after Sodasa from their coins. These Sakas had become Indianized by then, which reflected in their names, such as 'Shivadatta' and 'Shivaghosha'.[54]

The Kushan Period

The greatest historical epoch of Mathura is the reign of the Kushans over the entire tract stretching from the Aral Sea to as far as Kausambi and Patna, as evidenced by the Rabatak Inscription in Afghanistan.[55] The first Kushan king to have included Mathura within his realm was Vima Takto, the grandfather of Kanishka. An inscription on the pedestal of a headless monarch sitting on a lion throne notes the name of the king as Maharaja Rajatiraja Devaputra Kushanputra Shahi Vima. It further says that an official of his named Humaspala, the *bakanapati* of Taksuma, had a *devkula* (temple), a garden, a tank, a wall and a gateway built.[56] He also had the statue carved and placed in that temple. Vima Takto had wrested Mathura from the descendants of either Rajavula or another king named Gondophares, the Indo-Parthian ruler of Taxila.[57]

Shahi Vima, also known as Vima Kadphises, was the son of Vima Takto and Kanishka's father. His statue is in the Mathura Museum and shares space with that of his son, which, like his, is also headless.

The headless statue of Kanishka is so iconic that most children in Indian schools have tried to add a head to it in their history books. I remember doing so in mine and in the books of my classmates. That particular life-sized sculpture is of Emperor Kanishka, standing straight with his Charlie Chaplin legs clad in soft leather boots, wearing a starched long skirt above which his slightly rotund belly can be seen. His left hand is shown gripping the sheath of his straight sword, while his right hand is resting on the grip of a mace. And right below the knees is an inscription that notes his name as Maharaja Rajatiraja Devaputra Kanishka.[58]

These two important statues and two other extremely damaged sculptures, one of which is a standing figure of some Kushan prince (the statue is missing with only his legs remaining), were excavated from the Tokri mound in Mant by Pandit Radha Krishna in 1912. The village of Mant is 23 km north of Mathura on the east bank of the Yamuna. On the pedestal of the statue of the 'missing prince' is an inscription that records the repair of a temple undertaken during the reign of Huvishka, the son and successor of Kanishka.[59]

The headless statue of Vima Kadphises is broken into two, exactly at the waist. The upper half, prior to being united with its lower portion, was worshipped by the locals of Mant as Varuna. These statues were once worshipped as Yaksha figures in the once-existing Kushan temple at Mant. By the look of the seemingly deliberate damage done to their heads and the pulverization of the rest of the parts, it appears to be the work of iconoclasts who ravaged Mathura, destroying its places of worship. There are two contenders for the identities of these barbarians. The earliest of note were the ravaging hordes of Hunas, who fell upon the subcontinent during the fourth century CE and continued to do so till the seventh century CE. And the second is Mahmud of Ghazni, who most definitely sacked Mathura in the tenth or eleventh century CE.

Under Kanishka, Mathura became the second capital of his vast empire and established itself as the centre of various enterprises, particularly the guilds that were involved in the business of sculpting. Kanishka was a great patron of Buddhism and was held in great reverence by Buddhist elders; he occupies a pedestal slightly lower than Ashoka. So far, about thirty inscriptions mentioning the name of Kanishka have been discovered, and twenty of them are from Mathura.

A Kushan era sculpture discovered in the Chaubara mound of Mathura has an important inscription on its pedestal. This sculpture (rather, a small part of it, which includes a seated Buddha's feet in the lotus posture and the pedestal below), presently in Lucknow Museum, notes the name of a lady who was the disciple of Monk Bala as its donor.[60] This inscription also states the name of Mathura as Madhura-vanaka. The monk Bala was a renowned mendicant who lived in Mathura during the reign of Huvishka and Kanishka, as attested by two inscriptions bearing his name found on two gigantic Bodhisattva sculptures crafted out of spotted red sandstone from Mathura and taken to Shravasti and Sarnath.[61]

Hieun Tsang tells us that Kanishka had convened a Buddhist council in Kashmir and had built a stupa on the spot.[62] Kalhan, in his *Rajatarangini*, has also named Kanishka as one of the kings of Kashmir. He writes that although he belonged to the 'Turushka' race, he was a Buddhist and built many Buddhist structures, including chaityas in Kashmir,[63] like the one that I came across in Harwan near Srinagar. Kalhan also mentions that during the reign of Kanishka, the great Buddhist preacher Nagarjuna came to Kashmir and lived in a monastery called Sadarhadvana,[64] which has been identified by Aurel Stein as Harwan.[65]

The Tibetan Buddhist monk and historian Lama Taranatha, in his *History of Buddhism in India* written in 1608, mentions that Kanishka, who was then the monarch of Jalandhar, held the Third Buddhist Council at the Karnikavana Monastery in Kashmir. The Lama also mentions that many believe that this council took place at the Kuvana Monastery in Jalandhar.[66]

The evidence of Kanishka's patronage of Buddhism provided by the above authors corroborates the numerous Buddhist sculptures belonging to the Kushan epoch unearthed from various sites in Mathura. Apart from these are several masterpieces of Hindu and Jain images that were crafted during the Kushan rule. These masterfully done images displayed in the Mathura Museum and in other renowned museums all over the world are the sole witnesses of the once thriving industry of temple-building in Mathura that began during the Kushan period, and ended after the Islamic conquest of North India by Muhammad Ghori in the first decade of the thirteenth century CE.

Kanishka died sometime in 150 CE, and was succeeded by Vasishka, as evidenced by the Isapur and Jamalpur inscriptions from Mathura.[67] Epigraphs from Sanchi also mention his name as a ruler. Kalhan also mentions the names of Huska and Juska as the Kushan kings of Kashmir.[68] Juska is believed to be Vasishka, and Huska, Huvishka. Vasishka and Huvishka jointly ruled over Mathura for a while, as evidenced by an inscription found from the Jamalpur mound in Mathura.[69] The inscription states that Huvishka had a monastery constructed there.

Towards the latter part of Vasishka's reign, the Kushan empire got divided between him and Huvishka.[70] Huvishka was succeeded by Kanishka II, who was succeeded by Vasudeva I. He was the last great Kushan. Inscriptions unearthed at Mathura mention his name as the ruler.[71] The later Kushan kings were Kanishka III and Vasudeva II, dated to 201 CE from their coins.

The Cult of the Toddy-Drinking Balarama and the Worship of Nagas in Mathura

One interesting aspect of Mathura was the prevalence of the worship of Balarama and the Nagas during the Kushan period and after. The worship of Balarama is denoted by the presence of palm capitals, which I have come across in the Gujari Mahal Museum in Gwalior,[72] the Rani Durgavati Museum in Jabalpur, and inside the compound of the Heliodorus pillar in Vidisha.

Balarama is believed to be fond of drinking; thus the palm tree from which toddy is produced is associated with him as his emblem. But strangely enough, the climate of the Vraja region is not conducive to the growth of the toddy palm, which is found aplenty in Bihar, Bengal and the South. I have not come across any toddy palm in the rural environs of Mathura, or Agra for that matter.

Revering Nagas was a common form of worship in Mathura and the adjoining region, as attested to by the discovery of several Naga images. An inscription on a stone slab dated to the Kushan period reads that a votive tablet was erected during the rainy season at a spot sacred to the Naga god Dadhikaran in Mathura by a group of boys who were the sons of the actor brothers Chandaka.[73] This inscription, now in the Lucknow Museum, was unearthed at the Jamalpur mound (the present District Magistrate's office complex), which had a Buddhist temple built by Huvishka.[74]

The Naga Dadhikaran finds mention in the *Harivamsa* as a serpent king, who, among other Nagas and celestials, is invoked in the mantra recited by Balarama for the protection of his nephew Pradyumna.[75]

In 1908, a colossal sculpture of a Naga deity was discovered by Pandit Radha Krishna at the Chharhgaon village, situated 18 km south of Mathura towards Agra. The image, which has the hood of a seven-headed snake above its head, is 7 feet 8 inches in height. This idol was crafted during the Kushan times, as implied by an inscription behind it that notes the name of King Huvishka, during whose reign two friends named Senahastin and Viravriddhi had the image carved.[76]

Another similar Naga image, but smaller in size, was found by F.S. Growse in Kumargram in Shahbad. Yet another similar Naga statue was discovered in the village of Khamni between Mathura and Govardhan. Apart from these, several more images with prominent snake hoods and some holding wine cups were found in and around Mathura. All these have been ascribed to the Kushan period and are believed to be images of Balarama, who is believed to be the human embodiment of Vishnu's celestial serpent, Shesh Naga.

It is evident that the cult of Balarama, a deity associated with agriculture and iconographically represented with a plough and a multi-hooded snake, encompassed ancient snake worship within its ambit, merging as one in this part of India. In the east, the worship of the Nagas is independent of Balarama and is carried out in the person of a goddess named Manasa.

Mathura under the Naga Dynasty

The vacuum created by the weakened Kushan kings was filled by the Naga Dynasty, who wrested control of Mathura from the last Kushans. The *Vayu* and the *Brahminda* Puranas state that before the advent of the Guptas, North India was ruled by two Naga dynasties—one family ruling over Padmavati (present-day Pawaya in Madhya Pradesh) for nine generations and the other over Mathura for seven generations.[77] Many coins of a powerful Naga ruler named Virasena have been found in Mathura and elsewhere.

From the Allahabad Prasasti of Samudragupta (fourth century CE), engraved on an Ashokan pillar inside the Allahabad Fort, we find the mention of a few Naga kings killed by him, namely Ganapatinaga, Nagasena and Nagadatta.[78] We know that Ganapatinaga's coins have been found in Padmavati as well as Mathura. Based on this, one can ascertain that Ganapatinaga was the last Naga ruler to have held sway over Mathura before the city and the entire tract on both the banks of the Yamuna became a part of the Gupta Empire.

The Gupta Epoch over Mathura

In 1853 CE, Cunningham discovered a red sandstone fragment of a pillar on which there is an inscription belonging to Chandragupta II, from the Katara Gate in Mathura. The inscription, being fragmentary, is dated to 380 CE and mentions the lineage of Chandragupta II, the son of Samudragupta.[79] Nothing else can be garnered from this inscription except a confirmation of the conquest of Samudragupta, which made Mathura a major centre of the *Antarvedi Vaishya* (central province).

The poet and playwright Kalidasa, who lived during the Gupta period, states Mathura's importance in his *Raghuvamsa*, where we find ample praise showered on Mathura, the Surasenas, the Yamuna, Govardhan and Vrindavan.

During the Gupta rule of the Vraja/Braj region, Mathura flourished as a major centre for culture and Hinduism. A large cache of terracotta and stone sculptures attributed to the Gupta epoch has been found there. These artworks, now displayed in the Mathura Museum and elsewhere, attest to the resurgence of Hinduism in the region, which coincided with the eclipse of Buddhism. Of special mention are lingas with Shiva's face on them. Some lingas are shown to have multiple faces with a horizontal third eye.

Since the Guptas were primarily Vishnu worshippers, several excellently sculpted Gupta era images of Vishnu and his various avatars have been found in Mathura and the adjoining region. These images are masterfully crafted, which can only speak of the great heights the city had reached. To add a cherry to the cultural cake that was Mathura, there was the nonpareil life-size standing image of the Buddha, draped in a pinstriped raiment that clung to his body. Even though the great master's right hand is broken and his nose damaged, the aura this masterpiece exudes can only attest to the perfection attained by the artists of Mathura. The rather large halo behind the head of the Buddha is another work of art that accentuates the overwhelming presence of the Buddha in the Mathura Museum. Apart from Hindu and Buddhist works, several

Jain images and inscriptions from the Gupta period have also been unearthed. These inscriptions have mentions of the names of a few of Chandragupta's successors, like Kumaragupta I.

Fa Hien's Account of the City

Being on the banks of the Yamuna, which was navigable at that time (till the nineteenth century), and also strategically situated on the land route connecting the west to the east and the north to the south, Mathura's importance as a trade hub gained prominence during the Gupta era. This can be seen in the work of Fa Hien, a Chinese pilgrim who visited India during the first decade of the fifth century CE, corresponding to the reign of Chandragupta II. Fa Hien notes that on both the banks of the Yamuna in Mathura were to be found a total of twenty Buddhist monasteries, with approximately 3,000 monks residing in those establishments.[80] He also states that to the south of Mathura, India was called the Middle Kingdom (*Antravedi Vaishya*).

Fa Hien mentions that Mathura had a ruler who '...governs without decapitation or (other) corporal punishments.'[81] Regarding the civil society of Mathura he writes:

> Criminals are simply fined, lightly or heavily, according to the circumstances (of each case). Even in cases of repeated attempts at wicked rebellion, they only have their right hands cut off. The king's body-guards and attendants all have salaries. Throughout the whole country the people do not kill any living creature, nor drink intoxicating liquor, nor eat onions or garlic. The only exception is that of the Chandalas. That is the name for those who are (held to be) wicked men and live apart from others. When they enter the gate of a city or a market-place, they strike a piece of wood to make themselves known, so that men know and avoid them, and do not come into contact with them. In that country they do not keep pigs and fowls, and do not

IN KRISHNA'S CRADLE ✦ 59

sell live cattle; in the markets there are no butchers' shops and no dealers in intoxicating drink. In buying and selling commodities they use cowries. Only the Chandalas are fishermen and hunters and sell flesh meat.[82]

The First Recorded Destruction of Mathura by the Invading Hunas

The decline of the Imperial Guptas coincided with Huna incursions into India. These marauding barbarians from Central Asia overwhelmed West India and reached as far as Eran in Madhya Pradesh. Led by Toramana, these Huna hordes overwhelmed Mathura and laid everything to waste wherever they went. The catastrophe faced by the people of North India is best described by Hieun Tsang and Kalhan. The Chinese pilgrim who visited India 200 years after Fa Hien informs us about Toramana's son and successor Mihirkula the Hun's occupation of North India. He states that Mihirkula captured the throne of Kashmir after being ousted from the Punjab by Baladitya of Magadha.[83] Baladitya has been identified as Gupta Emperor Narshima Gupta (495–530 CE).

Kalhan corroborates Hieun Tsang's account and mentions a 'Mihirkula of violent deeds', who overran the land with his 'Mleccha hordes'. The scale of destruction brought about by the Huns is best described in the phrases that Kalhan uses for Mihirkula: 'another god of death' and 'royal Vetala', whose 'approach became known by the sight of vultures, crows and the like, eager to feed on those being massacred by his encircling army, to the population fleeing before him.'[84]

Kalhan also mentions his destructive raids in the mainland into Lata (modern-day Gujarat), Chola (Dravida country) and Karnata (Karnataka). After his raids, he turned back to Kashmir and indulged in further atrocities. It is largely believed that Toramana and Mihirkula, particularly the latter, were Shiva worshippers,[85] and thus destroyed the Buddhist establishments of Mathura.

Mathura under Harshavardhan in the Seventh Century CE as Recorded by Hieun Tsang

After the decline of the Gupta Empire, Mathura went back to being ruled by the erstwhile Surasena feudatories, who ruled as independent kings until they either were subjugated by the Maukharis of Kannauj[86] or willingly submitted to Harshavardhan of Thaneshwar, who replaced the Maukharis in Kannauj. In 1889 CE, during the course of laying a railway line over the lower terraces of the Katara mound connecting Mathura to Vrindavan, several Buddhist sculptures were unearthed, including an inscription belonging to the Maukhari king of Kannauj, Mahaditya.[87]

Hieun Tsang arrived in India during the reign of Harsha. He throws an illuminating light over Mathura, which had fallen from its elevated status and become a provincial town between two power centres, namely Thaneshwar and Kannauj.

Hieun Tsang arrived in Mathura after visiting Paryata (Bairat). About Mathura he writes that the place produced fine cotton and gold, and confirms Fa Hien's mention of the twenty Buddhist monasteries existing in Mathura. He also states that the city has five deva temples, which is rather few considering it is one of the chief centres of Hinduism. In Mathura, he came across three stupas built by Ashoka and several other stupas that held the bodily relics of Sariputra, Maudgalyana, Purnamaitrayaniputra, Upali, Ananda, Rahula and Manjushri.[88] The *Ashokavadana* has stated that a hillock named Urumunda in Mathura had a small cave that was used by Upagupta to meditate.[89]

Hieun Tsang has mentioned this cave as existing in the east of the city, which by the seventh century CE had many caves for monks to meditate in. These cells and a stupa on the hillock, which contained the nail clippings of the Buddha, were constructed by the Buddhist monk Upagupta. Hieun Tsang also mentions the location of the stone-built residence of Upagupta that was to the north of the said hillock.[90]

At present, there is no such hill to the east of Mathura that corresponds to the description given by the pilgrim. It is not surprising, as over the years small hillocks are known to vanish due to quarrying; I have seen several being flattened in the Mahoba district of Uttar Pradesh. Cunningham, however, states that the old fort of Mathura, constructed on a low hillock and locally known as 'Kans Ka Quila', was the site of Upagupta's cave.[91]

The Polity around Mathura after Harsha

After the death of Harsha, which probably happened in 647 CE, his vast realm got fragmented. At that time, Mathura was being ruled by the Surasena kings, namely Ajitha, Durghabhatta and Durgadama.[92] Around the seventh century CE, a Surasena prince from Mathura named Jinadatta migrated south to Karnataka from Mathura and established the Kalasa Karkala kingdom. His descendants were called the Santara Dynasty.

After the rise of Yasovarman of Kannauj in the eighth century CE, Mathura was overwhelmed by him. The Surasena rulers of Mathura, named Devraja and Vatsadaman, continued being feudatories of Kannauj like their predecessors. From an inscription found on a Hindu pillar reused to construct the mosque in Kaman in Rajasthan, we find the name of Vatsadaman. The inscription traces Vatsadaman's genealogy to seven generations, beginning with a certain Pakkha. The purpose of the inscription was to record the building of a Vishnu temple by Queen Vachchhika, the mother of Vatsadaman.[93] The name of Pakkha is also found in the Bayana Inscription of Queen Chitralekha of the Surasena Dynasty.[94]

With the conquest of North and Central India by Lalitaditya Muktapida of Kashmir about eighty years after the death of Harshavardhan, Mathura came under his sway. Lalitaditya's first major success was against Yasovarman of Kannauj.[95]

After the fall of Yasovarman, Mathura came under the rule of the Bhandi Dynasty, a family founded by Harshavardhan's powerful general named Bhandi, often mentioned by Bana in his *Harshacharita*.[96] The Gurjara-Pratihara ruler Vatsaraja wrested control of eastern

Rajasthan from this clan based out of Mathura sometime in the last quarter of the eighth century CE. Vatsaraja was, in turn, defeated by the Rashtrakutas from Karnataka, who forced him to escape to western Rajasthan.[97] An inscription discovered on the Katara mound attests to the Rashtrakuta conquest of Mathura.[98]

For about a century, three powerful empires, namely the Gurjara-Pratiharas from the west, the Rashtrakutas from the south, and the Palas from the east, fought for supremacy over North India, particularly for the imperial city of Kannauj. This Maukhari capital held the same status that was accorded to Delhi at that time. The entire tract east and west of Kannauj was known as Aryadesh/Aryavarta at that time and had three principal cities, two of which were Mathura and Banaras. These three places, including the imperial capital, were tossed from one hand to the other, until the Gurjara-Pratiharas emerged victorious in the tug of war known as the Tripartite Struggle in Indian history.

By the ninth century CE, Mathura came to be ruled by the Surasenas/Yadavas once again. They had established their centre at Mahaban on the east bank of the Yamuna.[99] A branch of this family later shifted to Bayana and established their rule over the entire tract, which included Mathura in its eastern extremity. The Yadavas of Bayana claimed to have descended from Krishna, whose seventy-seventh descendant, Dharmapal, had established the lineage, and whose present members are the erstwhile rulers of Karauli.

In Mahaban in Mathura, Cunningham discovered an inscription dated to 1150 CE, mentioning the name of the Yadava king Ajaypal Deva, who was a descendant of Dharmapal.[100] We know the name of the king ruling over the tract in 1032 CE: Lakshinivasa. Lakshinivasa can be identified with the Surasena ruler Lakshmana, whose name we get from the Bayana Inscription from 956 CE.[101]

The First Muslim Conquest of Mathura

In 1018 CE, a scourge fell upon Mathura. The city was devastated by Mahmud of Ghazni. After devastating Baran,[102] which is now called

Bulandsahar, Mahmud marched towards Mathura, his destination being Kannauj. Al Utbi, the author of *Tarikh-i-Yamini/Kitab-i-Yamini*, relates the manner in which Mathura and its temples were destroyed.[103]

Mahaban on the east bank was the centre of Mathura at that time. Mahmud besieged the fort of Mahaban, whose ruler, according to Utbi, was Kaljand/Kaljam. He resisted the invaders tooth and nail: '...five thousand perished and went to hell, and Kaljam drew his dagger, killed his wife, and then, ripping himself up, became a partner of his forces on their road to hell. Of their wealth 185 head of elephants, with other kinds of profit and plunder, came to the Sultan.'[104] Another translation of Al Utbi's narrative gives us the number 50,000 for those who perished during the siege of Mathura.[105]

Al Utbi continues with the sordid tale of Mahmud's religious war and the destruction of Mathura:

In that place, in the city, there was a place of worship of the Indian people; and when he came to that place he saw a city, of wonderful fabric and conception, so that one might say, this is a building of Paradise, but its accidents or qualities could only come by the aid of the infernals, and an intelligent man would hardly receive favourably the account of it. They had brought immense stones and had laid a level foundation upon high stairs (or steps). Around it and at its sides they had placed one thousand castles, built of stone, which they had made idol temples, and had (cemented) fastened them well. And in the midst of the city, they had built a temple higher than all, to delineate the beauty and decoration of which the pens of all writers and the pencils of all painters would be powerless and would not be able to attain to the power of fixing their minds upon it and considering it. In the memoir which the Sultan wrote of this journey he thus declares, that if anyone should undertake to build a fabric like that, he would expend thereon one hundred thousand packets of a thousand dinars, and would not complete it in two hundred years, with the assistance of the most ingenious masters (architects). And amongst the mass of idols there were five idols made of pure gold, of the height of five cubits in the air; and of this collection of idols there were (specially) two, on one of which a jacinth was arranged, such a one that if the Sultan had seen it exposed in the Bazar, he would have considered as under-priced at fifty thousand dinars, and would have bought it with great eagerness. And upon the other idol there was a sapphire (hyacinth) of one solid piece of azure water, of the value of four hundredweights of fine *miskals (five weights of a dram and a-half)* each, and from the two feet of an idol they obtained the weight of 400,400 miskals of gold. And the idols of silver were a hundred times more, so that it occupied those who estimated their standard weight a long time in weighing them. They devastated (all that city) and passed therefrom towards Kanuj...[106]

The identity of Kaljand/Kaljam has been narrowed down to Kulachandra.[107] The plunder of Mathura, which was called 'Maharatu Al Hind' by Al Utbi,[108] went on for twenty days.[109] Al Utbi concludes the narrative with the following statement: 'The Sultan gave orders that all the temples should be burnt with naphtha and fire, and levelled with the ground.'[110]

After the scourge had passed, the holy city tried to rebuild itself. The surviving descendants of Kulachandra, or members of his dynasty from Bayana, continued ruling from Mahaban. Their names are known to us from inscriptions on the pillars of the Chaurashi Khamba temple in Mahaban.[111] This temple, situated in the fort of Mahaban, was converted into a mosque and then reclaimed by the Hindus after the decline of the Mughal Empire. Another inscription dated to 1170 CE from the same temple mentions Ajaypaldeva's successor Haripaldeva.[112]

An inscription dated to 1149–51 CE, named the Mathura Prasasti, was discovered by railway contractors on 10 February 1889 CE while laying the Mathura–Vrindavan tracks. This engraving was recovered from the mound above which once stood the temple of Keshav Rai, built by Bir Singh Bundela during Jahangir's reign. The site is occupied by the Shahi Idgah Masjid of Aurangzeb at present. This Sanskrit inscription gives us the family lineage of Asika, whose father Jajja had built a grand temple dedicated to Vishnu.[113] Jajja had an ancestor named Shimaraja. This family was the vassal of Ajaypaldeva, whose name is mentioned in the *prasasti* (eulogy) as either Vijaypala or Ajaypala, as most of the inscription on the slab is worn out due to the fact that people had ground spices on it.

The lofty temple constructed by Jajja and left under the charge of several trustees, whose names are engraved on the slab, had once stood where now stands the Shahi Idgah Masjid. Jajja's was a reconstructed structure after an older temple on the same mound that was destroyed by Mahmud of Ghazni.

The Repeated Destruction of Holy Places in Mathura by the Delhi Sultanate

Within decades of Haripaldeva's rule, Delhi was captured by Muhammad Ghori from Prithviraj Chauhan III in 1192 CE. Within months, Mathura fell to the invaders and was annexed to the realm of Bayana, which was captured by Bahauddin Tughril, a slave general of Muhammad Ghori.[114] From his base in Bayana, Tughril began launching military raids to nearby territories, reducing the places to rubble and destroying the ancient temples found therein.

After the death of Tughril, the local Yadava rulers of Mathura asserted their independence in 1210 CE. Iltutmish had to march over Mathura subduing the local kings as far as Banaras.[115]

During the reign of Sultan Balban of the Delhi Sultanate, Mathura was being ruled by a local Yadava chief named Gopal.[116] It is for certain that the local Yadava chiefs were not independent but enjoyed a tributary status.

With the ascension of the powerful Delhi sultan Alauddin Khilji, Mathura was completely wrested from the control of the Yadava chiefs and placed under the administration of Sayid Yahyah from

Mashad (in Iran). He was made the *faujdar* of Mahaban by Alauddin Khilji, who destroyed all the temples in the place and constructed the Chaurasi Khamba Mosque in Mahaban.[117] In 1298 CE, Ulugh Khan, the commander-in-chief and brother of Alauddin Khilji, built a mosque at Sami Ghat in Mathura.

The sanctity of Mathura as a holy city persisted in the minds of the Hindus, even though it came under the occupation of Muslim governors who left no stone unturned to obliterate the remains of its ancient temples. For two centuries, the people of the city continued to live a peaceful life, worshipping at the reconstructed temples on the banks of the Yamuna, till the time that Mathura came to the attention of Sikandar Lodhi in 1501 CE.

Chronicler Abdullah, the author of *Tarikh-i-Daudi*, informs us that Sikandar Lodhi completely destroyed the temples of Mathura and turned the places of worship into caravanserais and madrasas. He had the destroyed stone idols used as weights to weigh meat and prohibited all Hindus of Mathura from shaving their heads and beards and performing their ablutions in the Yamuna. This strict policy of his put an end 'to the idolatrous rites of the infidels there; no Hindu, if he wished to have his head or beard shaved, could get a barber to do it.'[118]

Mathura during Akbar's Reign

Despite such oppressive measures, the city continued to live and for a brief while regained its past glory, albeit in a diminished manner, in the sixteenth century CE. In 1515 CE, Chaitanya Mahaprabhu, the famous Bhakti saint from Bengal, visited Mathura and Vrindavan. Along with him came his disciples Sanatan Goswami and Rupa Goswami, who settled down in Vrindavan and established *matha*s. It is also during this century that the Telegu saint Vallabhacharya, the founder of Pushtimarg, visited Mathura, and after his death his youngest son, Vitthal Nath, established a math in 1565 CE in Gokul, on the east bank of the Yamuna.

During the reign of Akbar and Jahangir, the jungles around

Mathura were Mughal hunting grounds. Abul Fazal mentions that in 1563 CE, Akbar, in the company of a select few of his courtiers, hunted seven tigers, of which five were shot by matchlocks and arrows and two were caught alive. During this hunt, the pilgrim tax levied at Mathura was brought to his notice, which he abolished.[119]

It was during the reign of Akbar that temples began being built in Mathura and Vrindavan by the emperor's prominent Rajput vassals. In 1570 CE, the widow of Raja Bharmal, the mother of Akbar's wife Marium Zamani, committed sati on the banks of the Yamuna. Commemorating her self-sacrifice on the demise of her husband, her son Bhagwant Das, the father of the celebrated Man Singh, constructed a four-storey-high red sandstone tower replete with reliefs of elephants and tigers. This monument near the Vishram Ghat—called the Sati Burj—though displaying a protected status board, is now on the verge of being destroyed. About a kilometre upstream from the Sati Burj is Kans Ka Qila, which was rebuilt by Raja Man Singh as his residence in Mathura. This fort had an observatory built by Raja Jai Singh II.[120]

Despite the protective status accorded to the holy city by Akbar, there were instances of religious persecution of the Hindus there. An incident shared by Badauni regarding the death of a Brahmin from Mathura goes like this: the *qazi* (main mufti) of Mathura, Abdur Rahim, had brought to the notice of the *sadarussudur* (the chief enforcer of Sharia law) of Mathura, Sheikh Abdu-n-Nabi, that a rich Brahmin had appropriated building materials for a mosque that were collected by the qazi and used them to build a temple. On top of that, he had indulged in blasphemous abuses of Muhammad and Islam. Sheikh Abdu-n-Nabi summoned the Brahmin, but he disobeyed and was then taken into custody. The *ulema* (shariat judges) arbitrating the matter were divided between capital punishment and disgrace imposed with a heavy fine. The matter was then brought before Akbar, who sent Birbal and Abul Fazal to investigate. Sheikh Nabi wanted the emperor's sanction on capital punishment, which was publicly denied, but Badauni states that privately Akbar is reported to have said to the sheikh that in regard to religious law, the ulema had the authority to act on offences against Islam. After the sheikh returned to his residence, he ordered the death of the Brahmin, which was promptly carried out. This supposedly infuriated Akbar, who withdrew his favour upon the sheikh and relegated him to the status of a commoner when he attended court. It was also during a heated debate about the death of this Brahmin at the Anup Talav in Fatehpur Sikri that the narrator of this information, Badauni, was publicly censured by Akbar for supporting capital punishment being meted out to the Brahmin from Mathura.[121]

Mathura from the Account of a Jesuit

In 1581 CE, the Jesuit Padre Monserrate visited Mathura with the Mughal army led by Akbar to supress the rebellion of Mirza Hakim in the Punjab. He and his fellow priests left Fatehpur Sikri in February 1581 CE, and after travelling for four days, reached Mathura.[122] About Mathura, the Jesuit writes in the condescending manner of a bigot:

> The city is believed to have been founded by Crustnu [Krishna] who is also called Viznu [Vishnu]; at any rate there is no doubt that he was born in a small town near Maturanum [Mathura]. Temples [ruins] dedicated to Viznu are to be found in many places in the neighbourhood, built in spots where the silly old-wives-fables (of the Hindus) declare that he performed some action. These fanes (or rather 'profanes') are elegantly built in the pyramidical style of India. Their doors face east, and the rising sun bathes the face of the idol with his light.[123]

He further notes:

> Since Viznu is the most famous of the Indian false gods, it follows that Maturanum has for long been the fountain-head of superstitions in India, just as Rome was in Europe. It used to be a great and well populated city, with splendid buildings and a great circuit of walls. The ruins plainly indicate how

imposing its buildings were. For out of these forgotten ruins are dug up columns and very ancient statues, of skilful and cunning workmanship. Only one Hindu temple is left out of many; for the Musalmans have completely destroyed all except the pyramids. Huge crowds of pilgrims come from all over India to this temple, which is situated on the high bank of the Jomanis.[124]

Padre Monserrate was talking about the Krishna Janmabhoomi Mandir, also called the Keshav Rai temple.

Mathura during Jahangir's Reign

Jahangir, like his father, accorded religious protection to Mathura and banned the hunting of big game outside the city. One Saturday, on 23 October 1619 CE, during his visit to meet the sadhu Jadrup who had come to Mathura from Ujjain, Jahangir was informed of a lion in the vicinity of Mathura. He went to hunt it mounted on his elephant. With him was Nur Jahan. She was handed the matchlock, with which she fired a single shot, killing the unfortunate creature. Appreciating her skill as a crack shot, Jahangir tells us that shooting to kill from the shaking howdah—because the elephant, sensing the predator, could not keep still—was a great feat.[125] In 1624 CE, on his fifty-seventh birthday, he was out hunting wild boars in the vicinity of Mathura. There he shot and killed a lioness and had her three cubs captured.[126]

Jahangir's favourite courtier, Bir Singh Bundela, the ruler of Bundelkhand, who had assisted Jahangir's rebellion against his father and was personally responsible for the murder of Abul Fazal, had the imposing temple of Krishna built in Mathura. This structure was called Keshav Rai Mandir and was imposingly tall, which is attested to by Tavernier and Bernier.[127] Manucci too confirms the existence of the imposingly tall temple dedicated to Keshav Rai.[128]

Mathura Witnesses the Destruction of Temples Once Again

During the sixth regnal year of Jahangir's son Shah Jahan, the destruction of Hindu temples restarted, and Jahangir and his father's policy was turned on its head. In 1637 CE, corresponding to his sixth regnal year, an order was promulgated by him that all the temples that were being built in his dominion should be brought down.[129] The governor of Mathura and Mahaban, Murshid Quli Khan, applied the decree and prevented the construction of any new temples there and brought down those that were being built.[130]

In 1639 CE, Aurangzeb's eldest son, Muhammad Sultan, was born in Mathura. In 1658 CE, after the defeat of Dara Shikoh in the Battle of Samugarh near Agra, Aurangzeb and his brother Murad Baksh marched at the heads of their respective armies from Agra and headed for Delhi, in pursuit of Dara. Niccolao Manucci, from whose account this part of history is being retold, had disguised himself as a Hindu mendicant and joined the thousands of followers of the Mughal camp who sold daily items to the soldiers. The two armies arrived at Mathura, where they camped.[131] On 15 June 1658 CE, Aurangzeb sent his eldest son, Muhammad Sultan, to escort his brother to visit his camp, which was at Koli Ki Ghat. This place is the present-day Aurangabad, south of Mathura and on the opposite bank from Gokul.

All through their alliance against their eldest brother Dara, Murad Baksh was under the impression that he would be crowned the emperor. Suspecting foul play, he deferred his visit to Aurangzeb's camp that day, citing illness as an excuse. However, he ultimately threw caution to the wind and, being accompanied by his eunuch Shahbaz, reached Koli Ki Ghat the next day. Manucci narrates that en route, he was given a warning by an ex-officer of Dara about the impending treachery, which went unheeded. Murad Baksh then entered Aurangzeb's tent where he was entertained with wine and a grand feast that went on for two hours. At the end of it, he was asked to rest while the throne was being made ready for him. While Murad Baksh was in repose, the eunuch Shahbaz was seized and strangled to death and his master was rudely awoken with the sound of chains being fettered around his feet and hands.[132] From Mathura, Murad Baksh was sent to Salimgarh Fort in Delhi and later transferred to Gwalior Fort where he was executed in 1661 CE.

Mathura, Aurangzeb and the Building of the Idgah Mosque over Krishna Janmabhoomi

In 1661 CE, the three-domed four-minaret Jama Masjid of Mathura was constructed by the city's governor, Abdurnabi Khan, over the ruins of a temple.[133]

On 19 August 1666 CE, Shivaji and his son Sambhaji escaped from Agra.[134] He rode the entire length of the night for about 50 km and reached Mathura in the morning. There, he disguised himself as a sanyasi and left his son under the protection of a Brahmin.[135] In 1668 CE, Abdurnabi was killed at the hands of the Jats during their rebellion headed by Gokla, the zamindar of Tilpat. That same year, Raja Bishan Singh of Amer, the father of Raja Jai Singh II, was made the governor of Mathura and entrusted with the suppression of the Jat rebellion.

On 18 April 1669 CE, Aurangzeb promulgated the order prohibiting idol worship and the preaching of Hinduism, which resulted in the wide destruction of temples. In December 1669 CE, the Keshav Rai Mandir of Bir Singh Bundela, also called Dehra Kesu Rai, was destroyed on the orders of the bigot.[136]

Saqi Mustad Khan, the author of *Maasir-i-Alamgiri*, writes that the temple of Bir Singh Deo Bundela had cost 33 lakh rupees to build after obtaining permission from Jahangir. Over the demolished structure, Aurangzeb laid the foundation of a mosque and changed the name of Mathura to Islamabad.[137]

This mosque is the controversial Shahi Idgah mosque of Mathura, built over the spot that is believed by the Hindus to have been Kansa's jail where Krishna was born. The idols from the temple of Keshav Rai were brought to Agra, which Saqi Mustad Khan states were buried under the steps of the Jama Masjid near the Agra Fort, '...in order that they might be pressed under foot by the true believers.'[138] The name of Vrindavan was also changed to Muminabad.[139] Manucci also notes that Aurangzeb ordered the destruction of the temples of Mathura and other chief pilgrimage centres of the Hindus like Banaras, Ayodhya and Haridwar.[140]

Adjoining the Shahi Idgah mosque is the modern Sri Krishna Janmabhoomi temple. This entire area is heavily guarded by the police due to the raging issue of Hindus demanding that the mosque be demolished, and they be allowed to rebuild a temple over its remains. Just like the Ram Janmabhoomi–Babri Masjid issue of Ayodhya that has been resolved, and the unresolved Kashi Vishwanath–Gyanvapi Mosque issue in Banaras, the Krishna Janmabhoomi issue in Mathura is a burning controversy. For a history buff, it is very difficult to get inside the mosque as police personnel deputed to guard the premise prevent anyone from approaching the steps. One can only see a portion of the structure from the dirty railway line below.

Aurangzeb not only destroyed the temples of Mathura but also extended his benevolence to memorials erected in the memory of the dead. He also had the top portion of the Sati Burj demolished as an exposition of his pious nature that did not deviate from the Quranic injunctions against ostentatious grave markers.[141]

The story of his mindless acts of intolerance and conversion of Hindu places of worship into mosques had far-reaching consequences, which can be felt even today. The ire that his acts drew from the descendants of the dwellers of the Vraja region resulted in the desecration of the grave of his great grandfather Akbar. Under the leadership of Suraj Mal of Bharatpur, the Jats conquered Agra on 12 June 1761.[142] He stripped the silver doors of the Taj and looted the Agra Fort of its treasures. He even dismantled marble structures from the Agra Fort, like the famous marble swing of Nur Jahan, and had them reassembled at the Deeg Palace in Rajasthan. Local lore states that some soldiers from his army exhumed Akbar's corpse from his mausoleum at Sikandra and cremated it.

Mathura under Jat Rule and the Conquest of the City by Ahmad Shah Abdali

After the death of Aurangzeb in 1707 CE and the subsequent disintegration of the Mughal empire, Mathura came under the rule of Churaman Jat of Sinsini. Churaman was succeeded by Badan Singh with the help of Raja Jai Singh II. It was during the reign of Badan Singh that the Jats of the Braj region gained prominence and established a kingdom, which came to be called Bharatpur. Jat ascendency gained prominence under the leadership of Badan Singh's son, the powerful Suraj Mal, who became the undisputed leader of the Jat nation and extended his conquest to Agra. In 1739 CE, the Persian ruler Nadir Shah invaded Delhi, which caused its residents to seek shelter in Mathura.

Despite Mathura now being directly in the hands of Hindu rulers, it did not gain any respite from iconoclastic activities. Just like the previous catastrophe that befell it, another devastating calamity was yet to arrive in the ancient metropolis of Krishna.

On 4 February 1757 CE, the defeated Maratha commander-in-charge of Delhi, Antaji Manekshaw, reached Mathura. There, Suraj Mal came to meet him and refused to join hands in a combined march against the Afghan scourge headed by Ahmad Shah Abdali. Suraj Mal left Mathura for his stronghold in Kumbher, leaving his son Jawahir to defend Mathura.[143]

On 26 February 1757 CE, Ahmad Shah Abdali ordered his commander Jahan Khan and the Rohilla warlord Najib-ud-Daulah to invade and sack every Jat town and village. They were specially ordered to demolish every temple in Mathura and put everyone to the sword.[144] The Afghan army, infused with the slogan of Jihad and equipped for plunder, reached Mathura. Preceding the Afghans, the residents of Delhi had already fled to Mathura and Agra with their riches and sought shelter under the protection of Suraj Mal.[145] Unlike earlier times, during Nadir Shah's invasion, the refugees leaving Delhi for Mathura were stopped by the Jats at every checkpost beginning from Badarpur, and extorted for money.[146]

The Maratha garrison of Antaji had, in the meantime, fled from the city, leaving it undefended. The only defence that was put up was carried out by 10,000 Jat peasants who were led by Jawahir at the village of Chaumuhan, some 18 km north of Mathura.[147] On 28 February, a desperate battle was fought there for nine long hours, at the end of which about 10,000–12,000 soldiers lay dead from both sides. The Jats had done their part; the survivors melted away to their villages, leaving the road to Mathura open for the invaders to fall upon the city.

Bloodbath and Genocide

On 1 March 1757 CE, the Afghan troops under Jahan Khan fell upon the city and began the indiscriminate slaughter of its inhabitants. This carried on for four hours, at the end of which several thousand innocents lay dead and their temples demolished. Jahan Khan then moved south, headed for Agra, and left the city at the mercy of the Rohillas, who, like vultures, fell upon the dead and started devouring and demolishing everyone and everything, and this went on for three days.[148]

According to the eyewitness account of a certain Samin, the streets of Mathura were strewn with headless bodies and the water of the Yamuna flowed red, which after seven days turned yellow. The reason for so many decapitations was that a bounty of five rupees had been offered per Hindu head. At Vrindavan, Samin notes that he found the headless bodies of two hundred children in a heap.[149]

Ahmad Shah Abdali, whose nose was allegedly affected by leprosy, followed his vanguard and after crossing the Yamuna, reached Mahaban. From there, he prepared to sack Gokul and plundered its temples.[150] Four thousand naked Dasnami Sanyasis were defending Gokul.[151] In the terrible battle that ensued, about 2,000 monks died. The battle ended after an envoy of the Bengal subedar named Jugal Kishor convinced Abdali that hermitages like those in Gokul contained no wealth.[152]

While his commander Jahan Khan was plundering Agra, Abdali had remained in his camp on the banks of the Yamuna. Due to the innumerable putrefying bodies choking the shallow river, a cholera epidemic broke out in his camp.[153] This prompted him to send word to his contingent in Agra to wind up the campaign and return to Delhi in the north.

The slaughter that was carried out from Delhi all the way to Agra, a stretch of a good 200 km, was unprecedented. The eyewitness, Samin, notes that at midnight soldiers on horseback would leave their camps, leading some twenty horses like a camel caravan, and they would come back laden with plunder. Between the looted goods would be young girls and slaves whom they had captured, on whose heads were loaded the bundled heads of those they had decapitated. These heads would fetch a price of five rupees each and they would be displayed as pillars. And this went on for days. The camp, being filled with such sights, would also be filled with the shrieks of those young girls who would be gang-raped. They and the other slaves would then be made to grind corn, after which their heads would be cut off and added to the pillars. Suraj Mal, in the meantime, stayed hidden in his stronghold as Mathura was being ravaged, only to venture out after Abdali reached Delhi.[154] Abdali's primary objective was to exact tributes from Suraj Mal, because of which he had campaigned into the Jat country. Instead, he ended up destroying the entire stretch and killing about one lakh people, without getting a penny out of the king of Bharatpur.[155] That same year, in 1757 CE, the English won a resounding victory at Plassey and established themselves as a prominent political power in the subcontinent.

In 1761 CE, the Marathas were decimated by the forces of Abdali and his Rohilla allies in the Third Battle of Panipat. The situation in Mathura had not yet recovered from its earlier devastation at the hands of the Muslims. Many fleeing Marathas sought shelter in Mathura and in the Jat stronghold of Deeg. Suraj Mal, repeating his previous response, remained neutral, but helped the defeated Marathas by giving them asylum. That same year, a peace conference was arranged at Mathura between Abdali, the Marathas, the Rohillas, the Jats, the Bangash Afghans and Shuja-ud-Daula of Awadh. On 19 April 1761 CE, the conference commenced and was disbanded after two months due to the machinations of Suraj Mal and the agents of the Peshwa.[156] On 12 June 1761 CE, Suraj Mal captured the Agra Fort and became the master of all its hoarded treasures.

In 1763 CE, Suraj Mal was killed in a Rohilla ambush by a small tributary of the Hindon near Ghaziabad.[157] This was during a battle against Najib-ud-Daulah. In his memory, a splendid cenotaph was built by his son Jawahir Singh on the side of a small lake named Kusum Sarovar in Gobardhan, near Mathura. This cenotaph is a delight to the eye and is a must-visit for any tourist visiting Mathura and its surrounding areas.

Jawahir Singh became the next Jat king and died five years later at the hands of a soldier whom he had patronized and then disgraced.[158] He was succeeded by his brother Ratan Singh, who was also murdered. This incident happened in Vrindavan, when a mendicant named Rupanand stabbed him to death. The next Jat king was Nawal Singh, another son of Suraj Mal, who was defeated by his youngest brother Ranjit Singh at Gobardhan on 5 April 1770 CE. In the struggle for the Jat throne, Ranjit Singh was aided by the Marathas.[159]

Mathura under the Marathas

The Jat fratricidal struggle was an opportunity waiting to be siezed by the Maratha leader Scindia, who, by now, had become the regent of the inept Mughal Emperor Shah Alam II. Mathura came into Maratha hands and was soon taken away by Ismail Beg, the nephew of Muhammad Hamdani, the governor of Agra in 1783 CE. The powerful Mahadji Scindia was away on a campaign in Malwa at that time. Ismail Beg was quickly ousted from Mathura by a Maratha commander named Devji Gauli, who made Vrindavan his base. The Rohillas had occupied the Mahaban fort, from where they were ousted in 1788 CE.[160]

On 10 August 1788 CE, the Rohilla chief Gulam Qadir blinded Shah Alam II at the Red Fort. Mahadji Scindia was then residing in Mathura. Gulam Qadir was soon apprehended and handed over to Scindia in Mathura, where he was mutilated.¹⁶¹ Khairuddin Muhammad, author of the *Ibratnama*, gives us graphic details about the way Scindia avenged the blinding of Shah Alam II. After Gulam Qadir was brought to Mathura in chains, his ears were sliced off and hung about his neck. His face was blackened and he was paraded around the city. The next day, his nose and lips were cut off and he was paraded around once again. The third day, he was blinded and paraded around another time. The day after that, his hands and feet and, finally, head were taken and the badly damaged corpse was hung neck-down from a tree. Scindia then sent his eyes and ears to Shah Alam…¹⁶²

The English in Mathura

After the death of Mahadji Scindia, his nephew Daulat Rao became the Maratha chief. He soon came into conflict with the English, led by Lord Lake. The defeat of Daulat Rao's forces in Delhi came at the hands of the English in 1803 CE, when the English forces advanced from Delhi to Mathura and occupied the city. On 30 December 1803 CE, the Treaty of Surji–Arjungaon ended the Second Anglo-Maratha War. The treaty stipulated, among other terms, the handing over of the Scindias' northern territories to the English. This resulted in Mathura and Agra, among other places, coming under the direct control of the English East India Company.

On 15 September 1804 CE, the Maratha leader and king of Indore Yashwant Rao Holkar captured Mathura from the English during the Third Anglo-Maratha War. After a month of occupying Mathura, Holkar then advanced towards Delhi. After the end of the Third Anglo-Maratha War, Mathura saw peace till the beginning of the Great Mutiny of 1857 CE. In 1832 CE, the city of Mathura was made the headquarters of a district named after it.¹⁶³

On 14 May 1857 CE, Mathura was abuzz with the news of the mutiny. The district collector, Mark Thornhill, and his deputy,

Gulam Hussain, sent for reinforcements from Bharatpur. Within the English army in Mathura a rebellion was brewing, which was affected when a sum of 5.5 lakh rupees was being loaded onto carts from the district treasury for transfer to the Agra Fort. One of the subedars assigned to the task gave a signal and the sepoys broke rank, shooting their commanding officer Lt Burlton dead. He was in charge of transporting the money train.[164] After plundering the chests, the sepoys marched on to the court house, which they set on fire. They then proceeded to Delhi hoping to join the main body of the mutinous troops.

On 6 July 1857 CE, the rebel troops from the contingent in Agra entered Mathura. Meanwhile, Collector Thornhill, disguised as an Indian, fled to Agra. These sepoys stayed at Mathura for two days, from where they marched off to Delhi. On 26 September 1857 CE, the retreating rebel soldiers from Delhi reached Mathura, from where they crossed the Yamuna and went on to Hathras.

The Romance of Vrindavan

The axis around which the worship of Radha and Krishna revolves is the ancient place of Vrindavan, about 10 km north of Mathura. This suburb of Mathura is intrinsically linked with Radha, who epitomizes the essence of *bhakti* (devotion) for the divine soul represented by Krishna.

The *Harivamsa* says that when Krishna and his elder brother Balarama were still children, they decided to shift from their village of Vraja/Mathura to Vrindavan. The reason given in the supplement to the Mahabharata is that Vraja had become unliveable, being devoid of beauty because of increasing urbanization.

The *Harivamsa* states:

> [Vraja] has been divested of grass and twigs and the milk-men have up-rooted the trees. This beautiful forest has been destroyed by us. All the forests and woods, that were thick (with trees), are now all looking blank like the

sky. All these eternally beautiful trees, that were in the cow-sheds well-protected by walls and wooden bolts, have been destroyed by the fire of cow-sheds. The trees and grass, that were near us, have been all thrown away on the ground at a great distance. The trees have been destroyed by the people of this extensive village. The birds have fled away from the useless trees. This forest, divested of birds, has become disgusting like rice without curry and other vegetable dishes. Even the delightful winds do not blow here. Woods and vegetables, grown in the forest, are now being sold. The grass is all destroyed, and this village has taken the appearance of a city. Let the wealthy inhabitants of Vraja repair to another forest filled with new trees and grass [...]. When excrement and urine fall on grass its juice becomes poisonous. The cows do not like to graze on it and it is unwholesome for milk. We wish to range, with our kine, in the charming new woods which are almost like dry ground. Let this station of milk-men be also transferred there. I have heard that there is a charming forest on the bank of Yamuna abounding in profuse grass, endued with all the virtues and freed of thorns and insects. It is named Vrindavana.[165]

To make the residents of Vraja comply with his wishes, Krishna produced packs of wolves from the hair on his body and let them loose on the unwilling villagers. Out of the fear of being eaten by these bloodthirsty carnivores, the people of Vraja packed up their cattle and their kettles and shifted to Vrindavan.[166]

Reading between the lines of the mythological account shared above, we get to know about the pastoralist lifestyle of the Yadavas, who were basically cattle-rearing nomads. As Vrindavan on the Yamuna was settled, the *Harivamsa* included it in the Vraja tract as a single geographic location, with a new set of adventures that make up the story of Krishna and Balarama.

The legend of how the Yamuna came to flow past Vrindavan is interesting. This story is associated with Balarama. While Balarama and Krishna were growing up at Vrindavan, away from the clutches of Krishna's maternal uncle Kansa, the boys indulged in various heroic activities that form a corpus of divine acts centred around Vrindavan. One fine morning, Balarama was sporting with the local lasses in one of the many groves of Vrindavan, when Varuni, the daughter of the water god Varuna, enchanted him with her essence. Due to her presence the woods became aromatic, and she transformed herself into nectar and intoxicated Balarama, who later came to be known as the Indian equivalent of Bacchus. In his inebriated state, he desired to bathe in the Yamuna, which was then flowing near Mathura. He summoned her, but Yamuna, the twin of Yama, paid no heed to the slurred command of a tippler. This slight infuriated him. He flashed his weapon, the divine plough, and hooked the river with it, dragging her to Vrindavan.[167] Thereafter he threatened to unbraid her into many streams and destroy her flow. Yamuna begged for mercy, and he forgave the river goddess. It is believed that since then the Yamuna began flowing beside Vrindavan.

Krishna's story also flowed like the dark Yamuna's cascading hair, which, one day, happened to become clogged by an unearthly being. A gigantic lake had formed beside the river, which a deadly five-hooded serpent named Kaliya had created as his abode. His poisonous breath was harming the aquatic life in the river and the avian life above it. Kaliya was basically a refugee who had sought shelter inland, swimming upstream from the sea. He was afraid that Vishnu's mount, the powerful Garuda, would devour him.[168]

So, the young Krishna, climbing atop a kadamba tree that overhung the abode of Kaliya, jumped into the lake and began wrestling the gigantic serpent. The tumult resulting from this great struggle caused the water to turn like a wheel, forming a whirlpool. Soon enough, Krishna got the upper hand and stood on its central hood and began dancing on it. Unable to bear the weight of his vanquisher, Kaliya yielded and made a request to the young hero to let him live, which was granted. Krishna ordered him to leave the Yamuna and get back to the ocean without fearing Garuda. The act of dancing on his hood had engraved Krishna's footprint on it; Garuda would recognize it as his master Vishnu's (Krishna is the eighth avatar of Vishnu) and accord clemency to the serpent. Tradition ascribes the duel to have taken place at Kaliya Ghat on the Yamuna.[169]

Now, with the Yamuna flowing by the forests of Vrindavan, where the young Krishna sported with his many *gopi*s (village girls tending to cattle), a few complications arose in the love life of Radha and Krishna, which, at this juncture, involved the river goddess Yamuna.

Seeing the dark and handsome Krishna, the dusky Yamuna (thus the name Kalindi) fell in love with him but could not profess it for fear of Radha, who ultimately cursed her. Much later in life, when Krishna came back as a mature man to the place of his childhood accompanied by the Pandavas, Yamuna met him once more. This time Krishna took her to Indraprastha and from there to Dwarka, where he married her. Radha was not that lucky. Yamuna is also known as one of the twelve principal consorts of Krishna, who were Yamuna/Kalindi, Rukmini, Mitravinda, Sudatta, Subhima, Saivya, Jambavati, Satyabhama, Lakshmana, Pauravi, Madri and Nagnajiti.[170]

The legend of Krishna and his association with Vrindavan is a story that has forever been told and retold over aeons. Vrindavan gets its name from 'vrinda', which is the shrub called 'tulsi' (basil). This plant is sacred to Hinduism and most rural households have one in their courtyard.

The legend describing how the place came to be called Vrindavan is as follows: One of the many gopis that Krishna sported with was called Vrinda. She is believed to be an aspect of Lakshmi, just like Radha. In order to be all around Krishna, the lovelorn Vrinda took the form of the basil shrub and grew everywhere in the area. Krishna reciprocated her love by indulging in sporting with her through his *leela* (divine game). He further honoured her by being partial towards any offering made to him that contained a basil leaf. Unfortunately, the love of the gopi Vrinda for Krishna got eclipsed by Radha's longing for the dark god. As a result, Vrindavan came to be associated more with Radha than the personification of the aromatic basil.

The Historicity of Radha

Mythology aside, we don't know for sure whether Radha was a historical personality or the creation of some bard's romantic mind. But if one goes by folklore and oral history, which, of course, should not be shelved as mere cultural concoctions, we can say that this tragic personality did exist, just as Laila and Majnun existed in the fifth century CE at the Al Aflaj oasis, 290 km south of Riyadh in Saudi Arabia. Here I must state that in 2007, I visited the small town of Layla at Al Aflaj, believed to be the home of these tragic lovers.

The historical Radha is believed to have grown up in Barsana, a village in the shadow of four narrow ridges, about 40 km from Vrindavan. She was the daughter of Vrishabhanu, a Yadava chief, who found her inside a lotus. The name Barsana is the corrupted version of Brahma-Sanu, which means 'the hill of Brahma', where each ridge denotes the creator god's four faces.[171]

Gradually, as it happens with every story that gets embellished by every bard who enriches it down the millennia, Radha's tale too became more elaborate. Having survived in people's memory as a celebrated recital, it got immortalized as a story of eternal love, giving rise to the essence of Bhakti, a philosophical path to the realization of the divine. This, on a temporal scale, would be defined by me as the indescribable pain of longing on the altar of separation.

Bhakti is the embodiment of the Radha Syndrome, which post the sixteenth century, for generations and across cultures and languages, has inspired poetry, songs, dance, paintings and sculptures. In addition to that, it has inspired schools of philosophy that have the tragic story of Radha as their embryonic ethos.

However, the iconographic image of Radha is conspicuously absent from sculptural representations in temples that are 700–800 years old or older than that. A huge cache of pre-fifteenth-century sculptures depict all aspects of Krishna and his heroic deeds, sans two vital features that have now become synonymous with him, the flute and Radha. Surprisingly, the Mahabharata and the *Harivamsa* do not mention Radha at all. However, the word *radha* in Sanskrit has been used as a noun denoting prosperity, synonymous with Lakshmi, the consort of Vishnu.

One of the earliest written references to Radha as a name attached to a personality that we get is from the Sanskrit poem *Gita Govinda*, written in the twelfth century CE by the Bengali/Odiya poet Jayadeva in faraway Bengal/Odisha. Radha, the principal character of the poem, is mentioned as greater than her object of devotion and love, i.e. Krishna. Perhaps Jayadeva must have heard a bard sing about a cowgirl named Radha when he was a student of Sanskrit in Puri in Odisha, for we have no knowledge of him travelling to Vrindavan or Mathura where he could have heard her story, to be so inspired. The revered persona of Radha as the consort of Krishna, however, finds mention in several other literary canons like the Puranas, Bhakti literature, and Chandi Das's *Shri Krishna Kirtan*, among several others, but these are later compositions.

The Rediscovery of Vrindavan

One must credit the sixteenth century Bengali reformer and Vaishnav saint Chaitanya Mahaprabhu and his disciples Sanatan and Rup Goswami with the rediscovery of Vrindavan. This proponent of Bhakti visited Vrindavan in 1515 CE and located the places associated with the legends of the luckless Vrinda and Radha. The first site that the reformer identified was the mound of Seva Kunj, on which he established a small temple dedicated to Vrinda.[172]

While Chaitanya Mahaprabhu entered the domain of legends, being deified as an incarnation of Krishna, Radha of Vrindavan emerged from her legendary identity to become an idea that is as tangible as the Yamuna that flows past it. And Vrinda, just like the temple dedicated to her, vanished from public memory, living on only as a noun, Vrindavan, a jumbled, crowded settlement by the Yamuna, whose narrow gullies metaphorize the complicated relationship young Vrinda had with Krishna.

Post the sixteenth century CE, many temples were built in Vrindavan in her honour that rivalled those present at Mathura. With the change in the religio-politics of northern India after the death of Aurangzeb, in the wee years of the eighteenth century, Mathura and Vrindavan re-emerged as the twin centres of the Vaishnavite universe. This was despite the cultural and genocidal trauma suffered by the Hindus of Mathura and Vrindavan due to the iconoclastic zeal of intolerant Islamic rulers over the centuries. The memory of the massacres and the destruction lingers on in the edifice of the Shahi Idgah Masjid that towers over Mathura. It is still festering after so many centuries, without any hope of reconciliation as long as the issue of Aurangzeb's mosque remains unresolved.

Vrindavan too experienced this trauma, particularly at the hands of Abdali's general Jahan Khan and the bloodthirsty Rohilla Afghan hordes of Najib-ud-Daulah. However, the resilience of the survivors of Mathura and Vrindavan in keeping alive the memory of those destroyed places of worship is commendable. Many temples were built anew, and are intact to this day.

In 1570 CE, Emperor Akbar visited Vrindavan and permitted the construction of four temples there. His heir Jahangir, along with his favourite queen Nur Jahan, visited Vrindavan during his fourteenth regnal year. On his way to Kashmir, Jahangir stopped outside Mathura and went to Vrindavan to see the 'idol temples' built by the 'Rajput Amirs' during his father's time.

At Vrindavan he also met Jadrup, the famous ascetic from Ujjain, whom he had once gone to see and discuss spiritual affairs with while going to Mandu and Ahmedabad.[173] On his way back from Ahmedabad via Ujjain on 13 November 1618 CE, he visited Jadrup's cave for the second time. The sage was then, according to Jahangir, more than sixty years old.[174] His meeting with Jadrup in Vrindavan was his third, which happened on 22 October 1619 CE. Jahangir writes that Jadrup had come to Mathura in order to worship the 'true deity on the banks of the Jumna River'. Once again, Jahangir went to the hut of Jadrup in Vrindavan and met him on Monday, 25 October 1619 CE. On 27 October 1619, he met Jadrup again and bid him goodbye. Jahangir writes, 'Without exaggeration, it was hard for me to part from him.'[175]

The History of the Madan Mohan Mandir of Vrindavan

The Madan Mohan temple, sitting on the Dwadashaditya Tila near Kaliya Ghat, was built in the sixteenth century by Ram Das Kapur, a rich merchant of Multan.[176] The mound on which the temple is constructed has yielded artefacts dated to the Gupta period. This uniquely designed temple, not corresponding to any architectural style employed in Indian temple-craft, is the oldest intact structure of Vrindavan. Its design has, in turn, inspired other smaller structures built in Vrindavan, mirroring the style of its shikhara.

Built using red sandstone sourced from the Fatehpur Sikri area, the temple is without an *amalaka*[177] atop it, as it was destroyed on Aurangzeb's orders. A more ornate temple, replete with panel carvings, was built later on. This taller structure, adjacent to the south side of the Madan Mohan temple, was commissioned most probably by the grandson of Ram Das Kapur, named Gunanda.[178]

The chief *purohit* of the Madan Mohan temple informed me that it was Chaitanya Mahaprabhu who laid the foundation for it. Another piece of information that I garnered from him was that the original idol of Madan Gopal belonging to the temple is no longer there. Anticipating the destruction of the structure at the hands of Aurangzeb, it was smuggled out to Karauli in Rajasthan. What is worshipped here is a replica of the original idol.

Upon reading the history of the structure, I got to know that Ram Das Kapur patronized its construction after an incident where his cargo-laden boat got stuck near the Kaliya Ghat. He climbed up the mound and found the hut of Sanatan Goswami, an acolyte of Chaitanya Mahaprabhu, which had the idol of Madan Gopal. Sanatan Goswami had received that idol from a person in Mathura and established it atop the ancient mound in a makeshift temple. At the request of Sanatan Goswami, the merchant Kapur addressed his prayer to the idol of Madan Mohan, which immediately had an effect. His boat was released from the sand bank. After he had sold all the goods in Agra, Kapur decided to build a temple there on his return.[179]

The present structures within the complex have been reconstructed after their destruction at the hands of Aurangzeb's minions. Below the mound but within the compound of the protected place is the *samadhi* (burial site) of Sanatan Goswami, who is buried under a Bengali-style *charchala* structure (four sloping thatched roofs of a hut, a style incorporated by the Mughals and Rajputs to build domed roofs over their palaces). In 1875 CE, the temple complex of Madan Mohan was renovated under the guidance of F.S. Growse.

The History of the Govind Dev Ji Mandir of Vrindavan

In 1570 CE, Emperor Akbar visited Vrindavan and permitted the construction of four temples there. Built on the Goma Tila is the gigantic red sandstone temple of Govind Dev Ji, one of those constructed following Akbar's orders. This splendid structure, albeit damaged, is about 2 km from the Madan Mohan temple and was constructed by Raja Man Singh under the direction of Sanatan and Rup Goswami in 1590 CE.[180] It is believed that Sanatan and Rup Goswami had dug out a small idol of Krishna from a cow shed at Nand Gaon and installed it in a makeshift temple atop the Goma Tila, near the Brahma Kund stepwell.[181]

An inscription found outside the northwest part of the temple declares that in the thirty-fourth regnal year of Akbar (corresponding to 1590 CE), Maharaja Man Singh, the son of Bhagwant Das, founded this temple in Vrindavan. The construction was supervised by Kalyan Das, assisted by Manik Chand Chopar. Its architect was Govind Das from Delhi, and the mason was Gorakh Das.[182]

On 21 October 1619 CE, Jahangir went to visit the temple of Govind Dev Ji. He notes that though the Rajput kings built temples in their '...own style, i.e., extremely ornate outside, inside so many bats and owls had nested that it was impossible to take a breath on account of the stench. "From without, as corrupt as an infidel's grave, from within, the wrath of God."'[183]

In anticipation of Aurangzeb's temple demolition spree, the

primary idol of Govindji was shifted out to Jaipur.[184] This temple, like all others, suffered the strokes of an iconoclast's hammer. Its sanctum was demolished, and what the devotee now sees is a reconstructed temple, built in 1854 CE.[185]

This humongous temple, presently four storeys in height, is replete with ornate window struts. The superstructure of the temple makes the shape of a Greek cross when seen from above. It was supposed to have five imposing shikharas with a gigantic central dome. The shikharas were never completed; the dome was damaged and on it a tall wall was built by Aurangzeb to deter the reconstruction of the temple if ever the Hindus tried to do so. An old photo of the temple clearly shows that wall, which was demolished in 1873 CE, during the restoration of the temple initiated by F.S. Growse and financed by the Maharaja of Jaipur.[186]

The Govind Dev Ji temple is an architectural masterpiece. The architect, Govind Das, incorporated the best of Rajput and Mughal elements and magnified them to conceive the structure, which, if it had been complete or not been demolished, would have been a wonder of its age.

The poet, novelist and amateur sketch artist Emily Eden, on her way back from the Punjab and Shimla, visited Vrindavan, Mathura and Govardhan in December 1839 CE. Her account of the religious place is very brief, except for the description of an old Jain temple that was destroyed and its statues beheaded on the orders of Aurangzeb.[187] Another part of her visit was an account of their breakfast in the midst of menacing monkeys in one of the temples.[188] And while she was sketching what appears to be the Govind Dev Ji temple, a monkey carried off her Indian rubber, which was vital for the correction of the wrong strokes.

Mathura and Vrindavan Today

I have, on several occasions, ridden to Mathura and Vrindavan, particularly to see the masterpieces in the Mathura Museum, the Madan Mohan temple, the Govind Dev Ji temple and the post-Vedic archaeological mound of the Gosna Tila, just outside Mathura city on the way to Hathras.

It is at this mound that I came across the famed Northern Black Polished Ware (NBPW) pottery pieces for the first time. The black lustre on the thin pot shards that litter the mound has still been retained despite their age. This, I feel, metaphorizes the continuation of ancient Mathura and Vrindavan into the modern world. Just like the million fragments of the NBPW wares at Gosna, the history of Mathura and Vrindavan has been shaped, destroyed, rebuilt and destroyed and rebuilt, the cycle continuing since the hoary days of yore. Yet, the fragmented story of the place is as tangible as the pot shards of Gosna, if one only cares to notice.

The present-day city of Mathura is like any other modern Hindu holy place, filled with thousands of temples built after the demise of the Mughal Empire. These temples share cramped spaces with houses along the riverbank and extend beyond it. Replete with dharamshalas and hotels, Mathura and Vrindavan, like Banaras and Haridwar, are primarily pilgrim towns dominated by the minarets of the Shahi Idgah mosque and the shikhara of the modern Krishna Janmabhoomi temple adjacent to it.

During Holi and Diwali, particularly in the evenings, the area around the Madan Mohan temple seems to drag its past into the modern times. Amazingly, it appears as if the caravan of time has paused there on those days, forcing the last camel to catch up with the first. This seamless overlapping of time that is witnessed in Mathura and Vrindavan can be equated with the tangibility of collective memory that never actually dies, but lives on as long as civilization continues to flow like a river.

Suffice to say, Mathura and Vrindavan are where the eternal lovers Radha, Vrinda and Yamuna still dwell. Their presence is palpable in the air, in the silent flow of the river, on the shiny backs of the many turtles that call the Yamuna home, and in the smell of burning incense that invisibly rends the air. One also feels the presence of these lovers in the devotion visible on the faces of devotees sporting necklaces made up of bits of basil twigs (the twigs from the branches of the tulsi/vrinda shrub), in the harrowing stare of the beggar outside a crowded temple, and in the haste of the pilgrims who come from every part of India, wishing to visit as many temples as possible before the scheduled arrival of their trains (due to such haste, a good friend of mine from Barasat came under a bus at Vrindavan and never returned home). One hears the voices of these lovers in the *kirtans* that waft out of the temples and dharamshalas, flowing over the placid Yamuna, filling every cranny of this timeless place.

Being jealous of Yamuna's desire to touch Krishna, taking on his hue as *Krishnasoma* ('black as Krishna'), Radha cursed her to be polluted and ravaged for her transgression. Can that be the justification for the pollution the Yamuna braves, slowly dying as a river? Well, while I ride across her black waters away from Vrindavan, I sense the sorrowful tale of these three lovers, whose longing for the eternal soul will forever inspire devotion in the minds of millions.

4
The Ruins of Kannauj

My visit to Kannauj commenced on a fine winter morning of January in 2019, when I rode out of Kanpur and was on my way to Shimla. After crossing Bilhaur I decided to head straight for the Kannauj Archaeological Museum, which is situated outside the town, beside the Grand Trunk Road. Mr Deepak Kumar, the curator of the museum, gave me an erudite tour of the exhibits, and we discussed the lack of Buddhist artefacts in the museum. We also talked about the genesis of the Gypsies, known as the Roma, from Kannauj.[1]

In December 2018, an international Roma conference was held in New Delhi. Participating delegates had also visited the museum where a talk was held. Mr Kumar informed me that some of the delegates went to visit a Kali Mandir in Kannauj as their chief deity was Kali. This information puzzled me because the deity Kali in its present iconic form is not older than the sixteenth century CE, and was largely conceived by a tantric named Krishnananda Agamvagisha, a resident of Navadwip in Bengal. What I later learnt was that the Roma people consider Kali Sara ('the black Sarah') as their patron deity, whose origins are believed to have come from Shakti worship in India. A memory of this deity has survived, albeit in a syncretic form, as an amalgamation of Roman Catholic saints and Hindu elements from the Roma's past.

Many sculptures have been unearthed from different locations in and around Kannauj and displayed in the museum. Surprisingly, Buddhist remains are conspicuous in their absence, except a solitary head, carved out of spotted red sandstone that came from Mathura. That partial image from an idol of the Buddha had not yet been placed amongst the exhibits. Mr Kumar credited that extremely rare find to the guard of the museum, who got it from a villager residing close by. He also lamented the general apathy of the government's archaeology department towards putting together a task force and collecting the thousands of sculpture parts strewn about in makeshift shrines and kept in heaps near ancient mounds around Kannauj town.

Kannauj, situated at the confluence of the Kali and the Ganga in Uttar Pradesh, is an ancient place, and for close to 500 years, it was considered the capital of the then North India, known as Panchala,[2] Aryavarta, Madhyadesha and Mahodaya.[3] At present, this district town is an unkempt conurbation known primarily for its perfume manufacturing units, attributed to the Islamic capture and settlement by Persians, Afghans and Turkic peoples in the thirteenth century CE.

This erstwhile megapolis from the bygone world was once a thriving city, whose skyline against the Ganga was studded with the spires of innumerable temples and stupas. The city during the ninth century CE was the centre of the Tripartite Struggle. Three prominent empires, namely the Gurjara-Pratiharas of the west, the Rashtrakutas of middle India, and the Palas of east India fought devastating battles for its conquest. Eventually, the Gurjara-Pratiharas, led by Nagabhatta, gained prominence and held on to the city, till Nagabhatta's descendant Rajyapal was chased out by Mahmud of Ghazni in 1018 CE and later murdered by Arjuna of Dobkund, a vassal of Chandela ruler Vidyadhara.[4]

Its Hoary Past in Ancient Literature

The story of Kannauj, however, goes back to times beyond recorded history and is etched in the cultural memory of India from mythical times under the name 'Kanyakubja'. In the Bala Kanda of the Ramayana, we come across the story of Sage Vishwamitra's ancestors, which he narrates to Rama and Lakshmana. In the story, the venerable sage and author of the famous Gayatri Mantra from the Rig Veda states that one of his ancestors, named Kushnabha, founded the city named Mahodaya.[5] From his marriage to a celestial entity named Ghritachi,

100 beautiful daughters were born. Vayu, the wind god, fell in love with them and proposed marriage, but was turned down by the girls, citing their need to seek approval from their father. This insult angered Vayu, who entered their bodies and distorted them, giving each one a hump. Since then, the city of Mahodaya came to be called Kanyakubja (or 'the hunched maidens'), whose colloquial pronunciation is 'Kannauj'.

King Kushnabha then had the girls married to a king of Kampila called Brahmadatta. He was the child of the pious sage Chuli and a celestial entity named Somada, the daughter of the *apsara* Urmila. Immediately after the wedding, their deformity was cured. King Kushnabha then set out to perform a sacrifice to beget a son, who was named Gadhi. This Gadhi was the father of Vishwamitra. It is interesting to note that Kannauj was also called Gadhipura in the ancient times.[6]

The *Harivamsa*, on the other hand, informs us that King Kushnabha, the son of Kush, belonged to the dynasty of Amavasu, and that Gadhi was not his son but that of his brother, Kushika.[7] Kannauj also finds mention, in the Mahabharata, in the works of Patanjali, and a host of other ancient works. Anyway, let us keep myths in their realm and not allow them to confuse us with their jumbled-up narration, and get back to the story of the city of the hunchbacked damsels.

The story of the hunchbacked damsels is repeated by the Chinese pilgrim Hieun Tsang in his *Si-Yu-Ki*, though fascinatingly altered. He writes that ancient Kannauj was called Kusumapura and was ruled by Brahmadatta, who had 100 beautiful daughters. A sage who was meditating on the banks of the Ganga had gone into a deep state of trance and become emaciated like a twisted log. Unmindful of the birds, who thought him to be a tree, he remained oblivious to their droppings on his head and shoulders, from which sprang a nayagrodha (banyan) tree. After the sage woke up, he tried to get rid of the tree growing from his shoulders but decided to let it go as many birds had nested on its branches. In such a condition, he went to the banks of the Ganga and saw the girls of the king playing. Their gambols stirred the desire for love and sex in his heart. He then went to the king and asked for the hand of one of his daughters in marriage. The king, in turn, asked his daughters whether they wanted to wed such a strange-looking person. Their answer was an obvious no, except for the youngest's, who consented, fearing a calamity befalling her father from the curse of the sage. The king then took his daughter to the sage, who was angered by her gawky looks. In his rage he cursed the other ninety-nine girls with an ungainly hump on each of their backs. And since then, writes the pilgrim, the city has been called Kanyakubja.[8]

The Historical Kannauj

The antiquity of the city is undoubted. Claudius Ptolemy, the second century CE geographer, mentions a town named Kanagora on the banks of the Kali/Kalindi.[9] This name is a corrupted form of Kanyakubja/Kannauj.

Archaeologists have found remains of settlements yielding Painted Grey Ware (PGW) and NBPW pottery pieces that date back to post-Vedic times. Excavations carried out by the ASI on a mound in Kannauj revealed 40-foot thick deposits, the earliest of which were dated to 1000 BCE. Period one yielded PGW and period two of the dig, NBPW. Period three, being subdivided, yielded Kushan era artefacts, and period four belonged to the later medieval times.[10]

Fa Hien's Kannauj

The Kannauj of the Gupta era has been briefly documented by Fa Hien, the elderly Chinese monk who visited India during the suzerainty of the Imperial Guptas (fouth–sixth century CE). The city that he documented was situated beside the Ganga, where he found two monasteries belonging to the Hinayana doctrine. Some distance west of the city he came across a stupa and another one on the other side of the river, built to commemorate the spot where the Buddha had preached his doctrine.[11] These two stupas were those built by the Mauryan emperor Ashoka, and Hieun Tsang also mentions seeing them when he visited Kannauj about 230 years after Fa Hien.

The Maukharis of Kannauj

Once a part of the Gupta Empire, Kannauj emerged as the capital of the Maukharis. This dynasty started out as vassals to the Imperial Guptas and after their decline, they asserted their independence, effectively controlling a vast tract of land stretching from Kannauj to Barabar in Jahanabad, Bihar.

Maukhari is an ancient clan name that dates back to the Mauryan times; a version of this name, 'Mokhalinam', has been found stamped on a Mauryan era clay seal discovered in Gaya by Alexander Cunningham.[12] According to the seventh–eighth century CE Sanskrit grammarian Vamana from Kashmir, the word 'Maukhari' denotes one who descended from a progenitor named Mukhara.[13]

The existence of this clan was scattered far and wide throughout upper India. Three inscriptions on three stone *yupa*s (sacrificial post) dated to 239 CE, from a village named Barwa near Anta in the Baran district of Rajasthan, mention a Vedic sacrifice conducted by a powerful Maukhari commander named Bala and his sons Balavardhan, Somadeva and Balasimha.[14] We don't know whether the Maukhari chiefs of eastern Rajasthan were related to the Maukharis of Kannauj.

During the fifth–sixth century CE, a Maukhari family was ruling in the area around Gaya. The inscriptions, particularly belonging to Maukhari king Anantavarman, are found inscribed on the walls of the Lomas Rishi, the Gopika and the Vedatika caves of Barabar in the Jahanabad district of Bihar.[15]

At the time of the resurgence of the Later Guptas,[16] the Maukharis, led by Isanagupta, battled the forces of Kumaragupta. The Apasad Stone Inscription of the Later Gupta King Adatiyasena from which we get the above information also mentions that his great grandfather Damodargupta (560 CE), the son of Kumaragupta, lost his life fighting against the Maukharis, whose war elephants had effectively trampled over the armies of the invading Hunas.[17]

The Haraha Inscription found in the village of Haraha in the Barabanki district of Uttar Pradesh was engraved during the reign of the first powerful Maukhari monarch named Isanavarman, dated to 553 CE. This inscription gives us a list of the names of Maukhari monarchs starting from Harivarman, Adityavarman, Iswaravarman,[18] and Isanavarman.[19] The inscription states that the dynasty descended from the mythical Asvapati ('lord of horses'), who according to the Ramayana was the king of Kayakaya, from where Rama's stepmother Kaikeyi hailed.

Furthermore, we get to know that Isanavarman, like his father, had defeated the Andhras (also known as Vishnukundins), the Sulikas of Odisha, and an unnamed king of Gauda (present-day Bengal).[20] The inscription also states that Suryavarman, who was the son of Isanavarman, while on a hunt, came across an old and dilapidated temple of Shiva and over that edifice had a grand structure built in the year 553 CE. After Suryavarman followed Avantivarman, and after him came Saravarman.[21] The Asirgadh Copper Seal Inscription of the Maukhari king Saravarman confirms his ancestry as mentioned above.[22]

Bana's Kannauj in the Seventh Century CE

While the Later Guptas and the Maukharis were involved in a tussle for hegemony over the Ganga–Yamuna tract east of Kannauj, there arose a powerful dynasty in North India at Thaneshwar/Kurukshetra in Haryana. This was the Pushpabhuti/Pushyabhuti Dynasty, whose greatest monarch was Emperor Harshavardhan, better known as Harsha.

King Prabhakarvardhan, the father of Harsha, seeking a groom for his daughter, Rajyasri, found a match in the heir to the Maukhari throne, Prince Grahavarman of Kannauj. Grahavarman was the son of the Maukhari king Avantivarman, about whose lineage Banabhatta, the biographer of Harsha, writes: '...now at the head of all royal houses stand the Mukharas, worshipped, like Civa's foot-print, by all the world.'[23]

Despite the strategic alliance that the wedding brought about, the region was troubled by two menaces. The Huna scourge coming from the west and the constant strife with the newly established kingdom of Shasanka at Karnasubarna in Gauda had the Ganga–Yamuna Doab in turmoil. It was possibly due to these two factors that the Pushyabhutis and the Maukharis sought out this nuptial match, which got mired in tragedy.

Bana writes that the wedding '…at length united the two brilliant lines of Puspabhuti and Mukhara, whose worth, like that of the Sun and Moon houses, is sung by all the world to the gratification of wise men's ears.'[24] This happiness lasted only for some years, for soon, Prabhakarvardhan died of natural causes and Harsha's mother Yasomati committed sati on the banks of the dwindling Saraswati that flowed by Thaneshwar.[25]

On the throne would now sit Harsha's eldest brother Rajyavardhan, who, when the king and the queen were being cremated, was busy in a campaign against the Hunas.[26] However, this was not to be, as Bana tells us that when the heir arrived after the funeral, a messenger too arrived from Rajyasri, conveying bad news. He reported that on the day King Prabhakarvardhan was consumed by the flames, the king of Malwa (Devagupta, an ally of Shashank) had conquered Kannauj and killed their brother-in-law Grahavarman and incarcerated their sister. Furthermore, he was planning to march upon Thaneshwar, preparing to that effect. This emergency was tackled by Rajyavardhan who, postponing his coronation, marched at the head of 10,000 horses led by his general Bhandi[27] to challenge the invasion and free his sister. The teen Harsha, according to Bana, was ordered to remain in Thaneshwar by Rajyavardhan. Bana has been criticized for overtly dramatizing an event in history to the extent that some historians consider his chronicle of Harsha's life a work of fiction.

It is true that the *Harshacharita*, replete with exaggerated narrative, does read like fiction, but the same can be said about the *Akbarnama* of Abul Fazal, with its excessive panegyrics. Here, one must understand that for a court chronicler, it made no sense to falsify a sequence of events as grave as these; after all, he had written the biography during the lifetime of Harsha, and it was meant for the monarch to read and reflect on. Having said that, the campaign against the king of Malwa was successful, but despite that, Rajyavardhan fell victim to treachery and was murdered by Shashank.[28]

Soon, the news arrived at Thaneshwar that '…though he [Rajyavardhan] had routed the Malwa army with ridiculous ease, [he] had been allured to confidence by false civilities on the part of the King of Gauda [Shashank], and then weaponless, confiding, and alone, despatched in his own quarters.'[29]

Both Bana and Hieun Tsang write that Harsha became king with great reluctance. He then marched at the head of his army towards Kannauj, hoping to expel the forces of Bengal and find his sister, who had, in the meantime, fled to the Vindhyas.

The *Harshacharita* then talks about the alliance between Harsha and the prince of Kamrupa, Bhaskarvarman, who made common cause against Shashank. The biography ends with Harsha saving his sister from consigning herself to the flames on the banks of Sone River somewhere in the Vindhyas in the nick of time, after which he sets out on 'the conquest of all the seven Dvipas'.[30]

Harsha's Occupation of Kannauj

After his enthronement at the tender age of sixteen, Harsha marched from his paternal kingdom of Thaneshwar to Kannauj, occupying the now empty throne and making this city the seat of his power. It is possible that he relegated the surviving family of the Maukharis to the background. We have seen a similar example with the Wadiyars of Mysore, who were left as a royal house by Hyder Ali within the city of Mysore while he ruled their domain. The same can be said of the Maratha Empire that was ruled by the Peshwas, while the descendants of Shivaji lived as titular monarchs elsewhere in Satara, Kolhapur and Tanjore.[31]

However, the story of the occupation of the Maukhari throne by a Pushyabhuti is a bit more complicated than Bana's narration. There is more to it than meets the eye. After the fall of the Imperial Guptas, due to constant attacks by the Hunas and internal weakening, several small vassal states became independent. Thaneshwar, ruled by the Pushyabhuti Dynasty, was one such vassal state. The Huna invasions of North India did not stop even after their first defeat at the hands of Bhanugupta, a lesser-known Gupta Monarch at Eran near Vidisha, and their second at the hands of Yasodhavarman, the king of Malwa, in 654 CE.[32] These marauding hordes from Central Asia were also resisted by the father of Harsha, Prabhakarvardhan.

A vacant throne in Kannauj and another vacant throne in Thaneshwar, coupled with the constant harassment by 'barbarian' forces, prompted Harsha to shift towards the centre of North India, which was the best option for him. At Kannauj, the Ganga and Kali rivers provided protection from attacks; from this strategic situation he could now tackle the constant provocation from Shashank and avenge his brother's death. Also, Kannauj was then a richer city than his parental property, Thaneshwar, which, in a way, had become a provincial state with little prestige by then. One can also say that he rose to the challenge at such a tender age to stand as a bulwark against the forces of Shashank, a religious bigot, (dis)credited with having cut down the Bodhi Tree at Bodh Gaya.

Harsha gradually became a powerful emperor and extended his rule as far as Kamrupa (in present-day Assam) in the east and across the Sutlej in the west. He also subjugated the kingdoms of Central India. While marching across the Narmada, he met with reverses at the hands of the Chalukyan emperor, Pulakeshin II.[33]

Well, Harsha is much revered in Buddhist sources, especially by Hieun Tsang, as Buddhism's great patron, second only to Ashoka. In my opinion, Harsha could have, in a personal capacity, embraced Buddhism, but Kannauj as a city did not do so, as described by the Chinese pilgrim. Several excavations at Kannauj have yielded scanty Buddhist artefacts, yielding, instead, plenty of Jain and Hindu sculptural remains, evidenced by their presence in the museum.

These factual findings, or rather the lack thereof, make one doubt Kannauj's, rather Harsha's, religious leanings. His seals, however, attest to the fact that he was a Shaivite. If we filter information based on the analysis of these stories, he comes across as a secular, tolerant person who was the epitome of benevolence, under whom Kannauj emerged as the principal city of North India and remained so till the advent of Muhammad Ghori and his conquest of it.

Hieun Tsang's Account of Kannauj Corroborated by Inscriptions

The Chinese pilgrim had reached Kannauj when Harsha was its ruling monarch and had been so for thirty-three years.[34] There is a remarkable similarity between Bana's and the pilgrim's chronicle of Harsha. Like the former, the pilgrim gives us the lineage of Harsha and also mentions his ally from Kamrupa. He also states the name of General Bhandi.[35]

The names of Harsha's brother and father, as mentioned by the pilgrim and Bana, are corroborated by the following inscriptions:

1. The Sonipat seal of Harsha dated to 606 CE was found in the possession of a merchant named Moharsingh Ram Ratan Mahajan from Sonipat, about 120 km south of Kurukshetra and 40 km north of Delhi. This oval seal has in it the mention of Harshavardhan, to whom the royal stamp belonged. Apart from this, we also get other names from his genealogy, starting with Rajyavardhan I and his wife Mahadevi, their son Adityavardhan and his wife Mahasenagupta Devi, their son Prabhakarvardhan and his wife Yasovati, and their sons Rajyavardhan II and Harsha.[36] The *Harshacharita* is silent about the first four names.

2. The Banskhera plate of Harsha, dated to 628–9 CE, was found in the village of Banskhera about 40 km from Shahjahanpur in Uttar Pradesh in the year 1894 CE. This copper plate grant is presently in the Lucknow Museum. From it, we get the following information about the genealogy of Harsha: Naravardhan and his wife Vajrini Devi had a son named Rajyavardhan I. He and his wife Apsara Devi had a son, Adityavardhan, who married Mahasenagupta Devi. Their

son Prabhakarvardhan and his wife Yasovati Devi had two sons, Rajyavardhan II and Harsha.[37]
3. The Madhuban copper plate dated to 632 CE, found by a farmer while ploughing his field in the Madhuban village near Azamgarh in Uttar Pradesh in 1888 CE, gives us the same genealogical information as the Banskhera grant.[38] The Madhuban plate mentions the defeat of Devagupta at the hands or Rajyavardhan, who, in turn, died in 'the mansion of his foe'.[39] This grant corroborates Bana's account of Rajyavardhan's treacherous murder after his victory over Devagupta of Malwa.
4. The clay seal of Harsha found in Nalanda matches Bana's description. This seal also mentions the names of Naravardhan and his wife Vajrini Devi, their son Rajyavardhan I and his wife Apsara Devi, their son Adityavardhan and his wife Mahasenagupta Devi, their son Prabhakarvardhan and his wife Yasovati, and their sons Rajyavardhan II and Harsha.[40] Bana's description of the seal of Harsha states that it was made out of gold and had a bull for its emblem. The seal was used on clay to stamp his decree, which once inauspiciously fell from his hand.[41] This small incident has been noted by Bana.

Hieun Tsang's Description of the City

Kannauj's many structures, however, were built during the Maukhari reign, about which Hieun Tsang remains silent. He had reached Kannauj after visiting Sankissa (whose ancient name was Kapitha) on the banks of the Kali River, which is situated about 85 km northwest of Kannauj.

Hieun Tsang's physical description of Kannauj is rather vivid.[42] Situated on the western bank of the Ganga, the city had a dry ditch around it and was watched over from tall towers at regular intervals. This fortification beside the dry ditch must have been towards the western portion of the metropolis, as its north and east were defended by the Kali and the Ganga. It was a bustling place of commerce with several lakes and gardens, and the people were prosperous and learned. The Buddhist and the non-Buddhist (Hindu and Jain) citizens were equal in number. A hundred Buddhist monasteries and 200 non-Buddhist temples existed in Kannauj. At the south of the city, beside the Ganga, there existed three Buddhist monasteries that had in them 'highly ornamented statues' of the Buddha and his tooth. This tooth, the pilgrim states, was acquired by Harsha from the king of Kashmir by force and enshrined in his capital.[43]

In front of these monasteries, there were two stupas, about 100 feet in height, whose foundations were of stone but their walls were made of bricks. These stupas had two decorated statues of the Buddha, one made of gold and silver and the other, copper. To the southeast of this stood a great temple/stupa about 200 feet tall, embellished with numerous sculptures depicting the life of the Buddha. Above this structure was placed a gem-studded copper statue of the Buddha, measuring 30 feet in height. And near this stupa were two equally large temples dedicated to the Sun and another to Shiva. These two structures were made of lustrous bluish stones (green schist) and embellished with many sculptures. On the east bank of the Ganga there was another great stupa, which the pilgrim states was built by Ashoka. And some distance from there, about 100 li (around 50 km), was the town of Navadevakula (identified by Cunningham as Newal/Nanamau).

Hieun Tsang also shares with us the mythological history of Kannauj that I have already narrated. Unlike Bana, the pilgrim mentions that Harsha belonged to the Vaishya caste (Baniya) and on assuming the throne, had assumed the name 'Shiladitya', as well as 'Kumar Raja', which can be understood, because he remained unmarried throughout and died without an heir.

Harsha, according to Hieun Tsang, was a devout Buddhist who, like Ashoka, forbade the unnecessary slaughter of living beings and:

> ...built on the banks of the river Ganges several thousand *stupa*s, each about 100 feet high; in all the highways of the towns and villages throughout India he erected hospices,

provided with food and drink, and stationed there physicians, with medicines for travellers and poor persons round about, to be given without any stint. On all spots where there were holy traces (*of Buddha*) he raised *sangharamas* [monasteries].[44]

Every five years he held a large assembly called Moksha, where he emptied his treasuries for charity. *Moksha* means 'liberation', and this assembly is most likely the Kumbh Mela. The pilgrim was witness to two such melas. The first was held in Kannauj and the second at Prayag.

The pilgrim met Harsha due to a summons he received from the monarch when he was in Kamrupa, where he had gone from Nalanda on the invitation of Bhaskarvarman, the ruler of Kamrupa. He writes that he and Bhaskarvarman went to the camp of Harsha, which was at Kajughira. Cunningham has identified Kajughira as Kankjol,[45] a town in present-day Jharkhand about 18 km from Farakka in West Bengal. Interestingly, the pilgrim notes that the royal camp of Harsha was a 'travelling palace'.[46]

Bana has described the royal camp of Harsha in vivid detail. Just like the pilgrim, he too was summoned by the monarch, who was camped at Manitara on the banks of the Achiravati.[47] He too mentions the royal building inside the camp, which he visited for an audience with the king.

The pilgrim states that Bhaskarvarman, who was also known as Kumar Raja, travelled with Harsha on his way back to Kannauj. While Harsha, at the head of a vast army, marched back on the southern bank of the Ganga, Bhaskarvarman and his troops took the northern bank and reached the city after travelling for three months.

Description of a Religious Gathering at Kannauj

At Kannauj a great religious conference was convened in the month of January/February. On the west bank of the Ganga, a great building was constructed with a tall tower beside it. Between these two structures was a pavilion that held a life-sized golden image of the Buddha. The pilgrim then describes a golden image of the Buddha, about three feet in height, placed on an elephant and paraded with Harsha, who was dressed as Indra, holding an umbrella above the statue. Bhaskarvarman, dressed as Brahma, walked on the other side of the beast.

This ensemble was led by an escort of 500 war elephants clad in armour, while another 100 elephants followed behind carrying musicians. While this procession was in progress, coins and other valuables were being scattered for the people to pick up and keep for themselves. The pilgrim also narrates that at the end of this ceremony that went on for several days, there was an attempt on Harsha's life by conspiring Brahmins.

Shaman Hwui Li, the biographer of Hieun Tsang, informs us that the pilgrim was accorded the honour of presiding over the religious gathering and managed to defeat everyone in debate.[48] Also according to Hwui Li, Harsha had arranged another religious gathering at Prayag, which, in fact, was the Kumbh Mela. Here, too, the pilgrim was given the great honour of presiding over a conference as its president.[49] After the completion of the conference in Prayag, Hieun Tsang sought Harsha's permission to return to China, to which the monarch reluctantly consented, making arrangements for it to happen.[50]

Harsha from Lama Taranatha's Fanciful Account

There is an interesting story about Harsha shared by Lama Taranatha in his *History of Buddhism in India* written in 1608 CE. He writes:

> Sriharsa was incomparable as a king. He wanted to wreck the religion of the *mleccha-s* [Muslims]. In a small place near Maultan, he built a *masita* [masjid], that is a big monastery of the *mleccha-s*. The whole of it was made only of wood. He invited all the *mleccha* teachers there, lavishly offered gifts to them for several months and made them collect all their scriptural works there. Then he set fire to it, and, as a result, twelve thousand experts of the doctrine of the *mleccha-s* perished.
>
> At that time, there lived in Khorasan only a weaver well-versed in the *mleccha* religion. From him the *mleccha-s*

of the later period gradually grew in number. As a result of this wreck (of the *mleccha* religion) by this king, there remained for about one hundred years only a few to follow the religion of the Persians and Turuskas.[51]

Even though Muhammad, the founder of Islam, was a contemporary of Harsha, I doubt whether Islam had reached so far from Arabia to Multan to present itself as a threat. We know that even during the lifetime of Muhammad, Arab Muslim traders had begun to arrive in India, to Kerala and Gujarat, but they were peaceful merchants braving the peril of the sea and land to make a living. Political Islam as we know it did not take root in the subcontinent during the seventh century CE, but about seventy-nine years later, after the death of Muhammad in 632 CE. Well, all I can state is that the above information given by the venerable Lama is a cooked-up story, made to soothe the throbbing pain of wanton iconoclasm by the then Muslim rulers of India.

Kannauj after Harsha

Harsha died in 647 CE, aged about fifty-seven, possibly in Kannauj. He had left behind a vast realm without an heir, and three Sanskrit plays (so far discovered): namely *Nagananda*, *Ratnavali* and *Priyadarshika*.[52] As expected, squabbles broke out among his vassals to fill that vacuum, and the kingdom was sieged by a minister of his named Arjuna, who occupied the throne.

One forgotten chapter of India's history is the Tibetan conquest of Nepal, North Bihar, North Bengal and Assam. This adventure on the part of the powerful Tibetan king Songtsen Gampo in 646–7 CE, after the death of Harsha, followed a military incursion by a Chinese envoy, Wang Hiuen Tse, into the court of Kannauj. Wang's misadventure in North India was repulsed with the aid of small tribal kingdoms in Nepal.

The Tibetan king Songtsen Gampo,[53] who was then the suzerain of Nepal by virtue of his queen, the Licchavi princess Bhrikuti Devi, threw his hat in the ring and was successful in capturing a large swathe of land in the subcontinent.[54] His motivation to attack Kannauj was the misbehaviour of Arjuna, a minister of Harsha, who had usurped the throne of Aryavarta. By 702 CE, the occupying Tibetans were defeated, and India fell back into its internecine strife for lack of a strong controlling authority.

Kannauj as Mentioned in the Chachnama

The *Chachnama*, which has the oldest chronicle of the Islamic conquest of the subcontinent in the eighth century CE, gives us some interesting information about Kannauj and its ruler named Sayar/Satbar, the son of Rasal Rai.[55] The chronicle states that when Raja Chach, the ruler of Sindh, had besieged Brahamanabad (modern-day Lahore), the capital of Agham Luhana, the latter had asked Sayar for assistance against the siege. After the death of Agham Luhana, Chach once again marched against Brahamanabad, and captured it.

We hear of Kannauj once more in the *Chachnama*. Chach was succeeded by his brother Chandra, who was not warlike. Mattah, the king of Siwistan, went to Kannauj and sought assistance from Sayar. Sayar, in turn, involved the king of Kashmir in the conquest, and together they marched against Chandra. This venture ended in a stalemate and the siege was lifted.

It is extremely difficult to ascertain the identity of the ruler of Kannauj from the Chachnama. However, we know that Chandra was succeeded by his nephew Raja Dahir, the son of Chach.[56] Raja Dahir was a contemporary of the Umayyad governor of Baghdad named Hajjaj (661–714 CE), whose commander, Muhammad Bin Qasim, defeated and killed Dahir in 711 CE and conquered Sindh, establishing Islamic rule in the subcontinent for the first time.

Yasovarman of Kannauj from Vakpatiraja's Gaudavaho

We know that in the eighth century CE, Kannauj was the capital of Yasovarman, a powerful ruler eulogized in Vakpatiraja's Prakrit composition *Gaudavaho*.⁵⁷ This monarch, like Harsha, also had a brief rule, in the course of which he conquered a vast realm, including Gauda. Vakpati, the author of *Gaudavaho*,⁵⁸ a eulogistic poem extolling the virtues of his patron Yasovarman, gives us a brief account of the conquests of his lord and the slaying of the king of Gauda/Magadha. The historical aspect of the poem narrates the conquest of Yasovarman after he reached the valley of the Sone River and then visited the ancient cave shrine of Goddess Vindhyavasini in the Vindhya mountains, south of present-day Mirzapur.⁵⁹ From there he embarked on the conquest of Gauda and Vanga and vanquished his enemies, emerging victorious. After that, he subdued parts of Central and West India and reached Srikanta/Thaneshwar, bathing in the Brahma Lake of Kurukshetra. From there, he reached Ayodhya, and after subduing some kingdoms in the Himalayas, he returned to Kannauj.⁶⁰

An inscription found in the debris of the southern veranda of Monastery 1 at Nalanda mentions Yasovarman as the sovereign of the tract who '...placed his foot on the heads of all kings.' The engraving records the donation a certain Malada, a minister of King Yasovarman, had made to the temple erected by the feudatory king Baladitya.⁶¹

It is strange that we know nothing about the genealogy of such a powerful king. My hypothesis is that he could have belonged to the subdued line of the Maukharis, who, after the expulsion of the Tibetans, asserted their right over what rightfully belonged to them, i.e. Kannauj, and lost it once again to the Kashmiris. Before Yasovarman lost his sovereignty to Lalitaditya, he had embarked on a grand campaign of conquest. Kalhan's *Rajatarangini* corroborates Vakpatiraja's panegyrics about this ruler.

Yasovarman of Kannauj from the Rajatarangini

The next phase of the history of Kannauj comes to us from the *Rajatarangini* of Kalhan. The powerful Lalitaditya Muktapida of Kashmir (724–60 CE) ascended the throne of Kashmir seventy-seven years after the death of Harsha. He, like Harshavardhan, established an empire which was short-lived. Lalitaditya's first major success was against Yasovarman of Kannauj, whose capital, according to Kalhan, was Gadhipura (another name for Kannauj). Yasovarman capitulated and sought a peace treaty.

Kalhan writes that in the document prepared by Yasovarman, Lalitaditya's minister for war and peace, Mitrasarman, noticed that Yasovarman's name preceded Lalitaditya's, making it state: 'This is the treaty of peace concluded between Yasovarman and Lalitaditya.' Considering this to be an insult towards the victorious monarch, Yasovarman was reduced to 'the position of a ministerial'. Kalhan, with a lot of sympathy for the vanquished king and the irony that life had imposed upon him, mentions that once upon a time his court was illuminated by great poets like Vakpati, the author of *Gaudavaho*, and Bhavabhuti, the author of the *Malatimadhava*, *Mahaviracharira* and *Uttararamachatita*.[62]

Kannauj after Yasovarman

Jain sources like the *Prabhakacharita* inform us that Yasovarman was succeeded by his son Ama, whose capital was Kannauj, and his territory extended till Gwalior. He, like the previous rulers of Kannauj, was involved in constant strife with the kingdom of Lakshmanavati (Gauda), then ruled by a king named Dharma.[63] Ama was succeeded by his son Dunduka. His son Bhoja succeeded to the throne of Kannauj after committing patricide.[64] It has to be said that the historicity of Ama and his progeny is unverifiable...

From Rajshekar's Prakrit language play *Karpuramanjari*, written in the ninth century CE, we know that a certain ruler named Vajrayudha, belonging to the Ayudha Dynasty, had his capital at Kannauj. The Jain *Harivamsa* also states that a ruler named Indrayudha ruled Kannauj in 784 CE.[65] He was defeated by Dharmapala, the son of Gopala and the founder of the Pala Dynasty of Bengal.[66]

Indrayudha was followed by Chakrayudha, who was put on the throne by Dharmapala. The Khalimpur Copper Plate Grant of Dharmapala, dated to the earlier half of the ninth century CE, confirms the reinstatement of the ruler of Kannauj by him, and this appointment was accepted by a host of kingdoms like Bhoja, Matsya, Madra, Kuru, Yadu, Yavana, Avanti, Gandhara and Kira.[67]

The Beginning of the Mad Scramble for Kannauj and Its Conquest by the Gurjara-Pratiharas

The above inscriptions make it obvious that Kannauj had ceased to be a sovereign realm and a mad scramble for it had begun, making the city the epicentre of the Tripartite Struggle that carried on for nearly a century.

I remember that as a school student, the most boring part of Indian history was the study of this 'struggle', wherein several large kingdoms, namely the Pala Empire of Bengal, the Gurjara-Pratiharas from Gujarat and Rajasthan, and the Rashtrakutas from Maharashtra and Karnataka, fought incessantly for a century to 'own' Kannauj.

The ultimate 'victory' was of the Gurjara-Pratihara ruler Nagabhatta II, the son of Vatsaraja, who after defeating Chakrayudha and Dharmapala occupied Kannauj.[68] He was, in turn, defeated by the Rashtrakuta ruler Govinda III. The Rashtrakuta conquest of Kannauj did not last long, as the city was reconquered by Nagabhatta II, who in 815 CE made it his capital.[69] In 833 CE he was succeeded by his son Ramabhadra, who died within three years. The baton was then passed on to Ramabhadra's son Mihir Bhoja. The Barah Copper Plate Grant of Mihir Bhoja, dated to 18 October 836 CE, discovered in the village of Bara situated 35 km from Kanpur on the Kalpi Jhansi road, informs us that he was the lord of Mahodaya (another name for Kannauj) and the son of Nagabhatta, who was the son of Ramabhadra.[70]

Mihir Bhoja was the greatest ruler of Kannauj. Epigraphical, numismatic and historical information about Mihir Bhoja is found aplenty in public libraries. The metropolis of Kannauj reached a new pinnacle under Mihir Bhoja. The stability that he brought to Aryavarta was unprecedented and echoed the rule of Harsha. Kannauj began to increase in size with new structures being added to it once again.

Bhoja's empire, centred at Kannauj, stretched from parts of Bengal in the east to the Narmada in the south. The realm engulfed the entire western tract of Rajasthan and went beyond the Thar to northern Haryana and the mountainous kingdom of the Himalayas in Himachal and Uttarakhand. It was during his reign that a new impetus was given to temple architecture in India, the examples of which can be found strewn across northern India and even in the Himalayan states of Himachal and Uttarakhand.

An inscription from the temple of Garibnath at Pehowa[71] in the Kurukshetra district of Haryana mentions the names of three horse dealers, amongst others, who had built temples in Kannauj. These rich traders were named Guhaditya, who built a temple of Vishnu in Kannauj, Kadambaditya, who built a temple in Gotirtha at Kannauj, and Brahmin Bhuvaka, who built two temples dedicated to Vishnu in Pehowa and Bhojpura near Kannauj. The inscription is dated to 882 CE, corresponding to the reign of Mihir Bhoja.[72]

Bhoja was succeeded by his son Mahendrapala I, who, like his father, was a powerful monarch and patronized art, architecture and eminent authors like Rajshekar, who was also the tutor of the emperor.[73] Another horse dealer's inscription from Pehowa mentions that during the reign of Mahendrapala, a *triratna* temple dedicated to Vishnu was built in Pehowa. The inscription, dated to 882 CE, states that the local ruler was a Tomar chieftain named Jajjuka, the son of Jaula, a vassal of Mahendrapala.[74] This inscription, which is in the Lucknow Museum, is the last known record of the ruler, who possibly died around that time.[75]

After the death of Mahendrapala, possibly in 882 CE, a civil war broke out between his sons, which marked the first stage of the decline of the Gurjara-Pratiharas. The immediate successor of Mahendrapala was Bhoja II,[76] who was overthrown by his stepbrother, Mahipala. Rajshekhar was also patronized by Mahipala, as mentioned by the poet in his *Karpuramanjari*.[77]

Mahipala's rule lasted till 910 CE,[78] after which there were different kings ruling from Kannauj, till one named Vijayapal was defeated and killed by his vassal, Dhanga, the Chandela ruler of Jejakabhukti (present-day Bundelkhand).[79] This event occurred around 990 CE. By then, the Gurjara-Pratihara Empire had broken up into different independent kingdoms established by the Chandelas, the Chauhans, the Solankis, the Parmars, the Kachchhapaghatas, and a host of other principalities. It was at this juncture that there appeared in the subcontinent the murdering hordes of Mahmud of Ghazni. Before I can get back to Kannauj and what befell the city at the hands of Mahmud, let me conclude the brief narrative of the last two Gurjara-Pratihara rulers of Kannauj.

From an inscription found inside the ruins of the temple site of Dobkund in the Palpur Kuno forest near Gwalior, we get to know that a certain Kachchhapaghata general named Arjuna defeated and killed another ruler of Kannauj named Rajyapal in 1027 CE.[80] He was fighting on behalf of his lord, the Chandela monarch Vidyadhara, the grandson of Dhanga.

Rajyapal was succeeded by his son Trilochanpal, whose reign barely lasted, and he was succeeded by the last known Gurjara-Pratihara ruler Yashpal in 1036 CE; after this, we do not hear of the dynasty of Nagabhatta I founded in the first half of the eighth century CE, and established firmly with Kannauj as the capital by his grandnephew Nagabhatta II.

Kannauj's Destruction by Mahmud of Ghazni

Needless to state that Kannauj remained in prominence for nearly 371 years after Harsha, till it was first destroyed by Mahmud of Ghazni in 1018 CE. Even during the time when Mahmud was making his plundering raids in India, Kannauj, albeit diminished in stature, had the aura of an imperial city that was accorded to Delhi during the Islamic phase of India's history.

Al Biruni, who arrived with the army from Ghazni, lived for some time in Kannauj and Banaras. His book, the *Kitab al-Hind*, has an entire chapter dedicated to the geographic location of every known urban centre in India measured from Kannauj, which he reiterates was the capital of Madhyadesha.⁸¹

His description of the city is rather sad to read. He writes that Kannauj '...lies to the west of the Ganges, a very large town, but most of it is now in ruins and desolate since the capital has been transferred thence to the city of Bari, east of the Ganges.'⁸²

The cause for the transfer of the capital was the weak Gurjara-Pratihara ruler Rajyapal. Unable to defend his capital from the attacks of Mahmud of Ghazni, he had left Kannauj to its fate and fled across the Ganga. For his cowardice, he was severely rebuked by the Chandela monarch Vidyadhara, and a punitive force was sent under the Kachchhapaghata general Arjuna, who killed him in battle.⁸³

Al Utbi's Description of the Conquest of Kannauj

Al Utbi, the biographer of Mahmud of Ghazni, has narrated in his *Kitab-i-Yamini* the fall of Kannauj in a detailed manner. After destroying Mathura and all the towns between it and Kannauj, which was then being ruled by Haipal/Jaipal/Vijaypal,⁸⁴ Mahmud of Ghazni arrived at the gates of the city.

I quote Al Utbi:

> The Sultan then opposed the fortresses of Kanuj; and he beheld seven castles, placed upon the margin of the water of the Ganges. Nearly ten thousand temples were built in these forts, and these dotard and lying idolaters declared that the date of the commencement of those fabrics was two or three hundred thousand years, and from this confident belief derived pride and pretension. Their trust in them was continually recurring, under all circumstances, for they were desirous to deposit money therein, and in time of need made processions around them, humbly imploring aid. The greater number of the people had deserted their homes, from terror [of] the Sultan, but some remained. The Sultan in one day took all those fortresses and plundered them, and thence turned to the fortress of Manaj, called the *Brahmins' Castle*.⁸⁵

From there he proceeded further and reached Manaj/Manaich (the old name for Jaunpur) and besieged it; after that he captured the fort of Asni, and then marched on to Banaras, plundering, killing and taking captives. After the completion of his raids, he returned loaded to Ghazna and commenced building the Jama Masjid there, which was the grandest mosque of the Muslim world.

Al Utbi also informs us that the number of slaves he took along with him to Ghazna was mindboggling. He writes:

> When the Sultan returned from Hind in victory and light, with abundant wealth and no scanty amount of gems, and so many slaves that the drinking-places and streets of Ghazna were too narrow for them, and the eatables and victuals of the country sufficed not for them, and from the most distant parts tribes of merchants betook themselves to Ghazna, bringing so many slaves from Khurasan, and Mawarannahr, and Irak, that their number exceeded the free, and a white freeman was lost among them [...][86]

Khondamir's Account of the Fall of Kannauj

Khondamir, in his *Habib-us-Siyar*, informs us that after the conquest of Mathura, Ghazni marched on to capture Kannauj. He notes that the then king of Kannauj was Jaipal, who had fled his capital, abandoning it to its fate. The Kannauj described in Khondamir's narrative consisted of seven forts on the banks of the Ganga, and in one day Ghazni captured the undefended city. He then set about the destruction of all its temples, of which Khondamir gives the exaggerated number of 10,000. The number of slaves he took back in this expedition was so high that each one's price did not exceed 10 dirhams.[87]

Far-Flung Repercussions

One sad aspect of Kannauj's destruction was the exodus of skilled craftsmen from the central part of India, who migrated east. While speaking to a few sculptors in their studio homes at the historic site of Lalitgiri near Jajpur in Odisha, I got to know that these artists, who practised their craft over generations, were migrants from Kannauj. They could not for certain recall the exact tales of their ancestry but knew for sure that they were settlers from North India.

The Dewal Prasasti of Lalla, a Chhinda chief of a small principality near Pilibhit in Uttar Pradesh, was engraved by the artist Somnatha from Kannauj.[88] This prasasti was engraved in 992 CE, before the sack of Kannauj by Mahmud of Ghazni. What I am trying to imply here is that artisans from Kannauj did continue sculpting in far-flung places. And when the chisel finally split the rock twenty-six years later, there was no stopping their escape from the wrath of the iconoclasts.

Another point to be noted is that the slaves taken to Ghazna had exceeded demand and were being sold dirt cheap, which compelled the city authorities to free them as they were expensive to maintain. This was the genesis of the Roma people of Europe and the Americas. After the slaughter of the Brahmins and Kshatriyas, particularly the male gentry, whoever remained of the working population, especially the Shudras, was mercilessly marched to Ghazna, which has prompted historians to conclude that the name Roma is derived from the Shudra sub-caste of the Dom people.[89]

The Gahadavalas of Kannauj

After this first catastrophe, the kingdom of Kannauj somewhat established itself under the Gahadavalas, whose rise began immediately post the departure of Mahmud. Intermittently, several other Ghaznavid incursions happened in this part of India. Mahmud's son Sultan Masud and nephew Salar Masud followed him and ravaged those places that remained.

The *Diwani-i-Salman* of Said Bin Salman informs us that during his conquest of Agra, Sultan Masud (998–1040 CE) defeated its ruler Jaipal, and the war elephants captured in this campaign were handed over to a local Hindu named Chand Rai, who took them to Kannauj.[90] It is believed by some historians that this Chand Rai was the founder of the Gahadavala Dynasty of Kannauj, whose last great king was Jayachandra/Jaichand.[91]

The dynasty originated from a person named Yasovigraha.[92] It is possibly a branch of the Rashtrakutas that had once captured Kannauj under Govinda III, during the Tripartite Struggle. An inscription excavated from Shravasti, dated to 1119 CE, mentions that a person named Vidyadhara had built a Buddhist monastery in Shravasti. He was the son of Janaka, a minister of the king of Gadhipura named Gopala, who belonged to the Rashtrakuta (also known as Rathore) dynasty.[93]

The idea of the Rashtrakuta origin of the Gahadavalas is further strengthened by the Budaun Inscription of Lakhanpal, found in the ruins of a temple that is now the Jama Masjid of Budaun. The undated inscription, which was most likely engraved towards the end of the twelfth century CE, mentions the building of a Shiva temple and gives us the lineage of Prince Lakhanpal, who was the chief of the town of Vodamayuta (Budaun). This prince traced his ancestor to one Chandra, who belonged to the Rashtrakuta clan. The inscription also informs us that one of his grand uncles, named Madanpal, effectively checked Islamic incursions by defeating the armies of the 'Hambiras', a generic name used for Amirs/Muslims.[94] It is highly likely that Chand Rai is the Chandra of the Budaun inscription.

For ease of understanding, I have presented a simplified list of the Gahadavala kings who ruled the Gangetic tract from Budaun to Banaras, based out of Kannauj. The information regarding their lineage has been taken from *Epigraphia Indica*, Vol. 4, which lists a total of twenty-one copper plate inscriptions issued by Vijayachandra and his son Jayachandra.[95]

1. Chandradeva, the son of Mahichandra (first half of the eleventh century CE)[96]
2. Madanpala (1104–13 CE) or Gopala of the Shravasti Inscription

3. Govindachandra (1114–54 CE).[97] He defeated an Islamic army sent possibly by Masud III, the ruler of Ghazni, and saved Banaras from being ravaged by them.[98]
4. Vijayapala/Vijayachandra (1155–69 CE)[99]
5. Jayachandra/Jaichand (1170–94 CE)
6. Harishchandra (1194–7 CE)[100]

The second-last ruler, Jayachandra, was defeated and killed in the Battle of Chandawar between Agra and Firozabad in 1194 CE by Muhammad Ghori.

Epigraphic information about Jayachandra is found aplenty,[101] and testifies to the extent of his realm that incorporated almost the entire state of Uttar Pradesh. The Kamuli Copper Plate Inscription of Vijayachandra and Yuvaraj Jayachandra dated to 21 June 1170 CE informs us about the consecration of Jayachandra as the heir apparent of the throne of Kannauj. The ceremony took place in a ghat at Banaras, after the completion of which Jayachandra granted a village named Haripura to the Brahmin who presided over it.[102]

Suffice to say, history has not been kind to Jayachandra, whose name as Jaichand is synonymous in North India with betrayal, similar to the example of Mir Jafar in Bengal. The reason for such an unkind epithet is the imaginary story about his daughter Sanyukta and his arch-rival Prithviraj Chauhan III, the powerful monarch of Ajmer who sought to subdue the entire northern part of India.

While extolling the virtues of Prithviraj III, Chand Bardai, the author of *Prithviraj Raso*, a eulogistic poem composed in Brajbhasa (an earlier form of Hindi spoken in North India), has mentioned a romantic connection between him and Jayachandra's daughter. As a child, I had read that quaint part of the romance in a kitschy illustrated comic book, wherein Prithviraj bravely carries Sanyukta off from her *swayamvara* the moment she garlands the effigy of Prithviraj kept at the door of the wedding hall as an insult.

The poem eulogizes Prithviraj III to the extent that the people reading it are made to believe that Muhammad Ghori died at his hands. Bardai writes that after his defeat, Prithviraj III was blinded and taken to the capital of Ghori, where he, assisted by Bardai, shot an arrow at the sultan and killed him. And after that, the duo died honourably by stabbing themselves to death.

Here, one must excuse the bard Bardai for his poetic license. As with every other historical narrative, fictionalized or not, one man's hero is the other's villain. Take for instance the *Parmal Raso* by Yagnik, the court poet of Parmardideva, the Chandela ruler of Jejabhukti. The Alha Khand of that encomium portrays Prithviraj as the bad guy, keeping in mind his sacking of Mahoba during Parmardideva's reign. Alha Khand extols the bravery of the Banaphar brothers Alha and Udal, who fought to defend Mahoba from Prithviraj Chauhan III.

If one reads between the lines, the rivalry between them is much more than what is implied by the panegyrist pen of Bardai or Yagnik. Prithviraj III, the Chauhan monarch of Ajmer, was continuing with the subjugation of the kingdoms of North India begun by his grand-uncle Vigraharaja IV, also called Visaldeva. The Tomars of Delhi had been defeated by the latter, extending the Chauhan realm all the way to the Punjab in the north and the borders of Jayachandra's kingdom in the east. Prithviraj III, following in the footsteps of his predecessors, had continued with the conquest against the Solankis of Gujarat, the Parmars of Malwa, and the Chandelas. He had effectively sacked the Chandela capital Mahoba and forced its king Parmardideva to sue for peace. Jayachandra was next on his list, who, according to Bardai, had sought aid from Muhammad Ghori. This, I think, is utter balderdash.

After the defeat and the death of Prithviraj III at Taraori (also known as Tarain), 15 km north of Karnal in Haryana, in 1192 CE, the entire tract lay open to Ghori, who, along with his generals, began the conquest of North India. After the conquest of Meerut and Delhi, Qutbuddin Aibak, the slave general of Ghori, marched on Kol (present-day Aligarh) and invaded it in the year 1201 CE.[103] The following year, Muhammad Ghori returned to India and began his march east, towards Kannauj and Banaras.

The Last Stand for Kannauj

At Chandawar, on the banks of the Yamuna, about 7 km south of Firozabad, Jayachandra met Ghori in battle, in which he was defeated and killed.[104] A lucky arrow downed Jaichand, who was on his elephant. This changed the course of the engagement.[105] It is a strange coincidence of history that the Second Battle of Panipat, fought 262 years later between Akbar and Hemu's forces, should mimic the end of Jayachandra. The entirety of the elephant corps of Jayachandra, numbering 300, fell into the hands of Ghori. After that, his general, Aibak, continued with his conquest and invaded Kannauj, Banaras, Budaun, Ayodhya, Kalinjar, Gwalior, and several other urban centres.[106]

Once again, Kannauj saw the gory days when Mahmud of Ghazni had utterly destroyed the metropolis. And this time, it never recovered its past glory, getting buried in its own rubble, over which stand the Islamic structures that we see today.

The Gahadavala Dynasty of Kannauj did not come to an end after the death of Jayachandra. Whichever family members of Jayachandra managed to survive must have fled east. Local tradition around Banaras states that a son of Jayachandra named Laxman carried on the fight after his father's death.

Cunningham has come across a pillar lying in a field at Belkhara, about 25 km from Chunar in the Mirzapur district of Uttar Pradesh, which names a certain king of Kannauj as the overlord of the region. The engraving on the 11.7-foot long pillar was dated to 1196 CE, i.e. three years after the death of Jayachandra. The name of the king in the inscription is given as 'Sweta', which Cunningham conjectures is an alias of Laxman. The engraving informs us that during the reign of this king in Kannauj (by then, Kannauj had been destroyed) the pillar was raised by a mason named Jalauna who resided at Belkhara, and whose chief was Vijayakarna.[107]

We also know of Jayachandra's son named Harishchandra from the Kamuli inscriptions that record the prince's *jatakarma* ceremony (post-natal ceremony) on 10 August 1175 CE in Banaras.[108]

The Machhlishahr Copper Plate Inscription of Harishchandra, dated Sunday, 6 January 1197 CE, informs us that he as the king had made a grant of a village named Pamahar to one Rahihiyaka.[109] We don't know more than that regarding the young Harishchandra, who was only twenty-two years of age when the Machhlishahr grant was made.

Did the Gahadavalas who ruled Aryavarta from Kannauj for nearly 170 years get completely wiped out? It appears not to be so from the lore of the Rathore Rajputs of Jodhpur, who claim descent from Jayachandra.[110] Also, the name 'Gahadavala' still exists in the form of Gaharwar, a Rajput surname.

Kannauj under the Delhi Sultanate and the Mughals

A few years after Ghori's conquest of Kannauj, the city was once again assaulted. This time, it was Iltutmish, the third sultan of the newly established Delhi Sultanate, who took 'Kinnauj-i-Shergarh'.[111]

The Moroccan traveller Ibn Battuta visited Kannauj during the reign of Muhammad Bin Tughlaq (1325–51 CE). He writes that the city was surrounded by a great wall and exported sugar to Delhi, on account of it being cheap there.[112]

In 1392 CE, Kannauj once again suffered devastation at the hands of the Delhi Sultanate. Sultan Muhammad Shah Tughlaq, after subduing the rebellion of Sarvadharan, the Rathore Rajput *jagirdar* of Etawah, marched to Kannauj and '...punished the infidels of Kannauj and Dalamau'.[113] Whatever stood of Kannauj's destroyed temples was all levelled to the ground and its Hindu populace massacred, as a punishment for the rebellion of the Rajputs of the Doab.

One rather strange episode that concerned Kannauj during the Sultanate period was the shifting of the last Tughlaq sultan Nasiruddin Muhammad Shah to Kannauj, who settled there, never to return to Delhi. In 1401 CE, Mallu Iqbal Khan, the powerful minister of the Tughlaqs and the de facto ruler of the Sultanate, began his march against Jaunpur and reached Kannauj. Nasiruddin Muhammad Shah, resenting the status of a prisoner accorded to him by Mallu Khan, was compelled to accompany him.

Ibrahim Shah Sharqi, the sultan of Jaunpur, had also reached Kannauj and camped on the opposite side of the Ganga. While they were getting ready for battle, Sultan Nasiruddin Muhammad, under the pretext of going for a hunt, crossed the Ganga and reached the camp of Ibrahim Shah, who received the sultan with scant regard and refused to help him against Mallu Khan. In disgust, the last scion of the Tughlaq dynasty returned to Kannauj, and with the aid of the residents, drove out the city's governor and made it his *iqta* (landholding).[114] Some years later, Kannauj was annexed to the Jaunpur Sultanate, until its dissolution at the hands of Bahlol Lodhi and his son Sikandar Lodhi in 1493 CE.

The Account of the Battle of Kannauj Fought in 1540

Skipping forty-seven years, we come to 1540 CE, when the last great battle was fought in Kannauj on the plains across the river. In this rather strange encounter, Sher Shah Suri defeated Humayun, the second Mughal emperor, on 17 May 1540 CE. Mirza Muhammad Haidar Dughlat, a cousin of Babur and later the ruler of Kashmir, was an eyewitness to this rout.

He gives a vivid description of the Battle of Kannauj in his *Tarikh-i-Rashidi* and says that Sher Shah defeated the Mughal army, comprising 40,000 soldiers, with a mere 10,000 men: '...they fled before 10000 men, and Sher Khan gained a victory [...], where not a man, either friend or foe, was wounded. Not a gun was fired, and the chariots [cannon carriage] were useless.'[115]

Abbas Khan Sherwani, the author of *Tarikh-i-Sher Shahi*, gives a slightly different version in which he notes that a wing of Sher Shah's army was defeated by Humayun's troops. During the battle that took place on the east bank of the river, Humayun ordered a retreat, fearing 'supernatural beings fighting against him'.[116] He managed to successfully cross the bridge of boats that he had constructed, but not so the thousands of his armour-clad troops, who drowned when the bridge broke in the middle. Sher Shah Suri then occupied the city and after '...having speedily settled the country around Kannauj, he betook himself in the direction of Agra',[117] effectively chasing out Humayun from Hindustan.

The buildings of Kannauj had by then changed form, with no traces of its Hindu, Jain and Buddhist past left above ground. To add to that, Sher Shah Suri demolished whatever remained of the ancient metropolis and tried to rebuild a fort, naming it after himself.

Now, the city's non-Islamic past is coming back to life with findings of sculptural remains displayed in the Kannauj Museum. As stated at the beginning of the chapter, there are many mounds, locally known as 'tilas', adjoining Kannauj that are yet to be excavated. Hopefully, the government will wake up from its apathy and go about doing the needful.

From an Imperial Capital to a Provincial Town Famous for Its Perfumes

Kannauj was made a *sarkar* (administrative town) within the *subah* (province) of Agra by Akbar. Akbar's successor Jahangir awarded Kannauj to the poet Abdur Rahim, the Khan-e-Khana.[118]

William Finch, whose eyewitness account of Jahangir's reign throws a great deal of light on the temperamental monarch, had visited Kannauj from Agra. About the city he writes that it '...is great and unwalled, seated on an ascent, and the castle on the height well fortified; at the foot whereof anciently Ganges [took] his course, but hath now broken a passage [through] the valley some 4 kos distant, notwithstanding as yet a small branch [remains] there. Ganges is within his bounds three quarters of a mile broad, but with great [rains swells] over his [banks], covering the whole valley [near] 10 kos.'[119]

Today, Kannauj is famous for its *attar* perfumes. There is no definitive record about how the town came to be the capital of the attar industry, but one can assume that the manufacture of a variety of attars in its many units must have begun during the reign of Jahangir, because the *Ain-i-Akbari* gazetteer from Akbar's reign, which has a long chapter on perfumes and their manufacture, is silent about Kannauj being the place where such fragrances were made.[120]

In the middle of Jahangir's eighth regnal year, corresponding to 1613 CE, Nur Jahan's mother, Asmat Begum, accidentally invented a rose fragrance while preparing rose water. About this, Jahangir writes:

> While she was making rose water, grease formed on the utensils she was using to get the hot rose water out of the pot. Little by little she collected the grease, and when a lot of rose water had been made, there was a palpable amount of grease.
>
> In fragrance it is of such a degree that if one drop is rubbed on the palm it will perfume a whole room and make it seem more subtly fragrant than if many rosebuds had opened at once. It cheers one up and restores the soul.
>
> As a reward for this invention I gave the inventor a pearl necklace. Salima-Sultan Begam[121]—God rest her soul—was present and named the oil Jahangiri attar.[122]

Being wishful, it is highly likely that Kannauj, with its fertile soil, became conducive for the production of roses from which the attar, then known as 'Jahangiri', began to be manufactured.

The Archaeological Rediscovery of Kannauj

Alexander Cunningham was the first archaeologist to investigate Kannauj for its antiquities, in 1838 CE and in 1862 CE.[123] His 1862–63 report mapped the Kannauj of the day, beginning with the high triangular mound west of the present town called the Quila, which was the ancient fort of the Maukharis, Harsha, the Gurjara-Pratiharas and the Gahadavalas.

Below the Quila once flowed the Ganga, which has now shifted about 2 km away. The northern extremity of the Quila is marked by the dargah of Khwaja Haji Zindani. Cunningham reports that on its southwest was the temple of Ajaypal, which I think is the present-day Phoolmati Mandir.[124] On its southeast, above a large bastion, the dargah of Makhdoom Jahaniya is situated.

The dargah of Sayid Jalal Makhdoom Jahaniya is the most

important Islamic era monument to be found in Kannauj. This complex is situated atop the topmost mound of the ancient fort on its southeastern end, in the Sekhana Mohalla. It overlooks the wide plains, at the eastern end of which flows the Ganga. The complex consists of three domed tombs with several graves in them and a mosque. The grave of Makhdoom Jahaniya was constructed by his son Raju in 1476 CE. The pillared mosque beside the tomb complex was also constructed at around the same time by Hussain Shah Sharqi of Jaunpur. In fact, the entire complex occupies the spot over which an ancient temple had once stood.[125]

In the dargah of Makhdoom Jahaniya, Cunningham came across a broken idol of the goddess Shashti which was 'built into the entrance steps' leading to the complex. There, he also came across a pedestal on which he discerned an inscription that had the date 1136 inscribed on it.[126] He also mentions seeing three damaged idols outside the doorway of the dargah and a large statue under a tree close by. During his second visit to Kannauj, these statues and the inscription were gone.

Getting to know that the tahsildar of Kannauj had caused all the images to be chiselled off and removed, Cunningham sent for him, and recovered the inscription, behind which there used to be a sculpture.[127] The man had removed the inscription to chisel off the image, damaging the entire thing in the process.

Trying to identify the places in the Quila where the temples mentioned by Hieun Tsang once stood, Cunningham conjectures that the temple of the sun and Shiva stood on the spot where the dargah complex stands now.[128] He also tried to identify the places on the mound where once stood tall stupas and viharas of the seventh century CE; here a large-scale excavation, if carried out, might yield results.

Cunningham's search for antiquities took him to some suburban villages around the town where he found sculptural remains of idols and temple parts. He writes that in the village of Singh Bhawani beside the Kutalupur locality, now a part of the town, a six feet tall stele of Vishnu surrounded by his avatars was discovered about a hundred years before his second visit. Apart from that, he came across images of Buddhist goddess Vajra Varahi with her seven hogs below her, an image of Mahisasuramardini, and a stele of Shiva-Parvati seated atop Nandi. At Kutalupur he found a door lintel with an image of Vishnu carved in the centre, indicating that the piece belonged to the *garbhagriha* of a Vishnu temple.[129]

In Makrand Nagar, the locality behind the Kannauj Museum, he came across a dried lake bed called the Surajkund ('the lake of the Sun'), being planted with the newly introduced potato crop. On the banks of this lake bed, an annual fair was held in the months of August–September. Close to the lake bed was a 'modern' Shiva temple built over an ancient one. To the southwest of Makrand Nagar, he came across three mounds '…covered with broken bricks and pottery, and under a tree on the south mound are collected a number of fragments of sculpture at a spot dedicated to Morari Devi.'[130]

He ended his report on Kannauj with this: 'I think it probable that excavation on this mound would be attended with success, as the two temples are said to have been built of stone, which no doubt furnished the whole of the materials for the masjid and the tomb of Makhdoom Jahaniya.'[131]

Antiquities in Kannauj Today

Since I visited Kannauj from Kanpur, the first monument that I came across was a crumbling tomb of an unnamed person, locally called Mir Baba Ka Maqbara. The tomb of Mir Baba is situated in the middle of the Saraimira locality beside the Grand Trunk Road. This large domed structure built on a raised platform is crumbling and utterly uncared for at present. From the architectural aspects of this building, it appears to have been constructed in the seventeenth–eighteenth centuries and exhibits elements associated with that era. The identity of Mir Baba is unclear, but considering that the locality is named the Sarai of Mir after him, he must have been an important personality of his time. Asking the locals about the identity of the person interred within, I came across a blank wall. Except for the name 'Mir Baba', I could gather no other information about this person.

Situated about 1.5 km north of the dargah of Makhdoom Jahaniya is the tomb of Bala Pir. This complex consists of two identical single-domed tombs, whose corners are surmounted with domed cupolas. These two buildings are constructed out of red sandstone and overlook the town. Cunningham notes that several old coins were found from the tomb complex. In 1834 CE, twenty-nine gold ingots weighing about a kilo each were unearthed below the buttress of the remains of the Rang Mahal palace, which was close by. Only nine were handed over to Wemyss, the collector of the Kanpur district, while the rest remain untraced.[132] I tried to search for the remains of the Rang Mahal palace but in vain. It appears that the ruins have completely vanished; prompted by the discovery of the treasure, they must have been uprooted from their foundation.

A stone's throw from the tomb of Bala Pir is the open expanse of a mound called the Fort of Jaichand. This rather tall and gigantic mound, about 60 feet in height, occupies the central part of the ancient Quila, and from its eastern edge begin cultivated plains on the receded Ganga. If not for a rusty signboard beside the road that I was taking to visit the riverbank, I wouldn't have come to know of the mound.

Climbing up the steep incline of this mound, one comes across innumerable brickbats, indicative of the existence of a once thriving settlement, and the remains of a fort. The narrow gullies formed on it due to the rains had revealed even more brickbats. There is nothing intact on this mound except the remains of a foundational wall embedded into it, and the sky above, the only witness to what happened below that is now buried underneath the ground. If only the mound could speak, I wonder how sad its tale would be...

At a walking distance from the tomb of Bala Pir through the crowded locality, one comes to the Jama Masjid of Kannauj, which occupies the top of a lofty mound. This Friday Mosque is also called Madina Masjid and was constructed by Ibrahim Shah Sharqi of Jaunpur in 1406 CE, most likely over the remains of a Jain temple. James Fergusson in his *History of Indian and Eastern Architecture* has noted that the mosque was locally known as Sita ki Rasoi ('Sita's kitchen').[133]

Cunningham's report on the mosque adds the following points: the inscription that mentioned when the structure was built was damaged, but a copy of the engraving was shown to him by one Rajab Ali, the teacher of the madrassa within the mosque compound, and it mentioned the name of the builder and the date given above. Between his first and second visits, the pillar arrangements of the mosque were changed by the tahsildar of Kannauj before 1857 CE. This person had removed all the images of idols from the pillars of the mosque and the walls of the building, just as he had done for the dargah of Makhdoom Jahaniya.[134] At present, the pillars of the Jama Masjid are whitewashed like the rest of the structure and nothing ancient or medieval can be discerned inside the building.

A Buried City

Unlike Banaras, whose name is greater than the city itself, there seems to be more to Kannauj underground than there is above. The city, which for close to 700 years was the capital of North India, was larger than what the old chroniclers have recorded. Due to the continuous occupation of the ancient metropolis despite the unfortunate catastrophes it had to endure, the remains of Kannauj lie underneath its modern avatar. The memory of its ancient past only comes alive when one happens to read the *Harshacharita* or the *Si-Yu-Ki*.

Speaking of the *Si-Yu-Ki*, I was pleasantly surprised to learn about a certain individual named Deepak Anand from Bodh Gaya. This gentleman, an ardent history enthusiast and Buddhist scholar, retraces the steps of Hieun Tsang in India. Like the pilgrim, he too walks to the places mentioned in the *Si-Yu-Ki*. In doing so, he visited Kannauj to investigate the existence of the Ashokan stupas mentioned in the *Si-Yu-Ki*.[135]

Mr Anand has effectively photo-documented several sculptural remains of ancient artefacts, Buddhist and Hindu alike, near mounds that are found outside the town.[136] One particular mound that he documented, called Gadhi, is situated to the north of Kannauj, about 4 km away in the Dahelpur village. He believes that this was one of the Ashokan stupas mentioned by Hieun Tsang, which according to the pilgrim was situated on the northwest of the ancient metropolis. Interestingly, the lofty Gadhi mound on the banks of the Kali River has yielded several ancient bricks and broken sculptures, whose photos Mr Anand has shared on his blog. Another interesting aspect of the mound is its name, Gadhi; it echoes the town's ancient name, Gadhipura.

While visiting the Kannauj Museum, I rode through Makrand Nagar from the Quila, past Surajkund and the shrine of Morari Devi. The utterly unkempt nature of Kannauj, with plentiful filth clogging its roads, reminded me of Bihar's Sasaram and, frankly, put me off. The only consolation was that unlike Sasaram, which stinks of an unholy mixture of faecal matter and the stench of the dead, Kannauj smelt somewhat of roses and the sweat of tanners.

5
Lord Rama's Janmabhoomi

For long, I had been planning a ride to Ayodhya, which, due to circumstances not in my hand, kept getting postponed. I had planned to take the northern route via Ayodhya and Kushinagar and reach Siliguri for my ride to the northeastern states. That had to be put on the back burner, firstly because of the anti-NRC and CAA agitations of 2019–20, and secondly due to the blight of Covid-19 that had us all stay in a lockdown situation. The year 2020 passed by, leaving thousands dead in its wake, and 2021 was no better, even though a vaccine against the virus had been developed and the process of administering it had begun on a war footing.

Ironically, the summer of 2021 was the worst. The death toll of the devastating second wave of the virus began climbing upwards, mimicking the mercury in thermometers. It shattered families and brought down small businesses already struggling under the impact of the first wave. The death toll all over the world, including India, crossed five million and kept mounting. I lost a young riding friend. My extended family suffered immense losses; Richa, my wife, lost an aunt and her husband, who died within days of her passing. And after three months of this tragedy, my father-in-law passed away due to the virus.

The inevitability of life is that it goes on for those left behind. With the ebb in the second wave, travel sanctions and the lockdown situation eased a bit. Flights, trains, hotels, and other necessary industries resumed their operations. I made use of this window and decided to finally ride to Arunachal Pradesh, Nagaland, Manipur, Mizoram, Tripura and Meghalaya. These states were the only provinces of India I had not been to on my motorcycle. Visiting them would help me fulfil my self-made goal of riding solo to all the states and union territories of mainland India.

After visiting Ayodhya, I comfortably rode to all these states and visited most of their historical sites. In Mizoram, I had planned to go to the village of Vangchhia in the border district of Champhai and document a newly discovered archaeological site containing numerous sculptured monoliths. This did not happen due to the extreme location of Vangchhia, right on the Indo-Myanmar border. Also, that morning I suffered a minor accident near Saitual after crossing Aizawl. These two factors made me change my mind and decide against riding further through the jungle roads of Mizoram.

Coming back to the topic of Ayodhya: I finally reached the place on day one of my Northeast ride, having started my journey from Kanpur. After crossing Lucknow, I reached Ayodhya at noon.

What was it that I was expecting to see in Ayodhya—the debris of the Babri Masjid or the ghats of Ram Ki Paidi on the palaeochannel of the Sarayu? For nothing from ancient Ayodhya remains above ground, except the age-old belief that the seventh avatar of Vishnu was born in that ancient place. Well, such intangible beliefs do not stir me enough to risk a solo ride over roads filled with more rash drivers than potholes. And yet, Ayodhya had to be seen to fulfil that old craving of bearing witness to the continued history of a place that is as ancient as the myths allow it to be.

Of the places I visited in Ayodhya (adjacent to the town of Faizabad) were the eighteenth century mausoleums of Bahu Begum and Nawab Shuja-ud-Daula called the Gulab Bari Imambara. In Ayodhya proper, I went to the Hanumangarhi temple and the Ram Ki Paidi ghats. The plan to go see the demolished site of the Babri Masjid and the ongoing construction of Rama's temple over it was shelved because of the security cordon around the place. And yet I had to visit Ayodhya…the place etched in my memory since my teenage years.

Ayodhya from Historical and Modern Sources

While doing my research on the history of Ayodhya, I came across an interesting introductory line in a book published in 1870, *Historical Sketch of Tahsil Fyzabad, Zillah Fyzabad* by P. Carnegy, the officiating commissioner and settlement officer of the district. Carnegy begins by writing, 'He who essays to write the History of Ajudhia [Ayodhya], in detail, must first of all master all that has been written of three distinct ages, and that is not little.'[1]

The writings covering the first age of Ayodhya must customarily include the Ramayana, followed by the *Raghuvamsa* of Kalidasa and the *Ayodhya Mahatmya*, which is a later text extolling the 'special virtues of the different shrines in and around Ajudhia.'[2]

The second age is described in historical records found in the works of Fa Hien, Hieun Tsang, and the Muslim chroniclers of the Sultanate and Mughal periods.

To understand the third age of this ancient place, which is the modern period, Carnegy suggests studying about '...Oudh, under its Nawabs and Kings, which would entail familiarity with a host of recent writers from Macaulay downwards.'[3]

Here, I will add another age to this age-old place, which begins from 6 December 1992. I vividly remember that day for two things; I was in eighth grade and, with bated breath, awaiting the result of the promotion exam, in which I had messed up, particularly in the agonizing maths paper. On that particular day, my cousin's wife had asked my mother about my results, and in her sarcastic tone, had added that English-medium schools awarded inflated marks to their pupils, unlike the government school where her son was studying, who, despite the apparent constraint, had still managed to score above 60 per cent in all subjects.

This had a great impact on my mother, who, time and again, adjusted her disciplinary actions on the basis of the inputs shared by the ladies of the extended family. So, I was pulled up for my poor performance earlier, given an ineffectual whack, and threatened with withdrawal from my school if I failed to get promoted to Class IX.

The whacks of the past years had ceased to matter, as I had grown taller and towered over my mom, but the prospect of having to seek admission in a village school, after having spent the entire length of my primary years in a hostel in the hills of Kurseong, was a tad unpalatable. Brooding over the potential consequences if I failed, I spent the afternoon imagining a bleak future, till my friend Rintu came by to inform me about a 'picnic' that had been arranged in another friend's house in Kazipara, a Muslim locality a bit far from our house in Barasat in West Bengal.

While we were enjoying the spicy beef curry and rice, the news of the demolition of the Babri Masjid in Ayodhya by the *karsevak*s (volunteers) was shared by my friend's brother. The news of the destruction of a little-known mosque in a faraway place mattered little to us teenagers, but this started a chain reaction of events filled with misery, which engulfed the nation and spilled over its borders. Old wounds were reopened, riots began, and a series of devastating bombings was carried out by the underworld kingpin Dawood Ibrahim in Mumbai. Hindus and their temples in Bangladesh and Pakistan began to be attacked anew. The CPI(M)-affiliated babus began targeting all those that supported the karsevaks and, contrary to logic, made common cause with the regressive *maulvi*s (Islamic scholars), who for long had been known to address them as the spawn of the devil for their atheistic beliefs.

And then there was some clamour that the next to fall would be the Shahi Idgah Masjid of Aurangzeb, constructed over the temple of Keshav Rai/Krishna Janmabhoomi Mandir of Mathura, and the Gyanvapi Masjid, also built by Aurangzeb, over the demolished Kashi Vishwanath Mandir in Banaras.

The socio-political situation in Bengal, and perhaps in the rest of India, was so skewed then that every intellectual worth their salt began to beat around the bush, without touching a leaf of the plant under whose shadow was hidden the question, 'What are mosques doing on the most hallowed spots of Hindus?'

Another question that demanded an answer was, 'Were those

mosques built over the holiest places of Hindus made to celebrate the holiness of the Hindu deities?'

If the answer to the above was yes, it would be blasphemy as per the tenets of Islam; so the obvious answer was no. And that naturally meant that these mosques were built with the might of arms to insult the people of the predominant religion, which even a dunce knows.

What I find the most surprising is that despite the knowledge that these mosques were forcefully built over demolished Hindu temples, the Muslim community is adamantly against the demand for these holy spots to be returned to the Hindus. If a power decided to demolish the Kaaba and build a church/synagogue/temple over it, would they remain silent?

Ironically, that question occurred in my mind much later in life, when I began to understand the meaninglessness of religious beliefs. Anyway, let me leave it to the logical mind and the courts to decide whether these historical wrongs should be made right, and get on with the brief history of Ayodhya, starting from the Ramayana.

A Disclaimer, Since the Subject Is Very Sensitive in India

A word of caution: I must warn the readers to not make the mistake of putting me in the bracket of a left- or right-leaning person while reading this chapter. For too long, my generation has suffered the fear of being put under the umbrella of two distinctive groups, the Left and the Right, based upon one's acceptance or rejection of the prevailing historical narrative.

To be candid, I grew up reading the rosy version of the history of the Sultanate and Mughal periods spoon-fed to school children. When these children grow up and happen to read the sources that supplied the historical matter, a strange loathing wells up inside for the historians responsible for craftily hiding the horrors of history, and framing the portraits of tyrants in such a manner that their demeanour mimics an ice cream seller's jollity.

To cite an example: I remember an elaborate section in my school history book about the pious nature of Babur when he exchanged his life for his ailing son Humayun. This story, originally narrated in the *Humayun-Nama* by Princess Gulbadan Banu Begum, is filled with pathos and makes for a great read.[4] In the same chapter on Babur, the school book cleverly omitted mentioning his mindless order to destroy the immensely tall standing sculptures of more than fifty Jain Tirthankaras carved on the rock faces below the Gwalior Fort.[5] This collection of gigantic Jain sculptures is the only one of its kind in the world, and each sculpture had its face and genitals chiselled out on the order of Babur.

Suffice to say, I am not a fan of the polished historiography by 'leftist' historians, whose Oxford accents mellow the genocides of Mahmud of Ghazni and Timur. I also do not take seriously the historical perspectives narrated by WhatsApp intellectuals of the right wing, strictly abhorring the idea espoused by some of them that the Taj Mahal was once a Shiva temple, and that everything about ancient India was hunky-dory.[6]

I have my own understanding of historical events and am clear-headed enough to avoid the binary narration of India's past thrown at children from the politically fortified bastions of these two groups. Basically, what I understand from their historiography is that they artfully avoid calling a spade a spade. Come to think of it, sometimes I feel as if the author of my old school history book saw us as Native Americans celebrating Columbus Day with aplomb. Imagine!

Thus, I urge everyone reading this chapter to exercise their faculty of comprehension with logic and independently grasp my rendering of Ayodhya's history.

The Earliest Literary Sources

The earliest mentions of Ayodhya and Saket (another name of the city often used interchangeably during the Gupta Era) come to us from several literary works like the Ramayana and the Mahabharata in its Vana Parva section, and other places in the epic. The Jain holy canon, Buddhist literature, Brahminical literatures like the Puranas,[7] and a host of other Sanskrit works also mention this holy place as an ancient metropolis.

A comprehensive list of canonical literature that mentions Ayodhya is given in the book *Ayodhya Revisited* by Kishore Kunal, IPS (retd). Here, I am mentioning a few names from this book: the *Yuga Purana* of the *Gargi Samhita*, the *Buddhacharita* of Ashvaghosha (a native of Ayodhya), Buddhaghosha's commentary on *Phenapindupama Sutta, Satyopakhyana, Samyutta Nikaya, Ghata Jataka, Saketa Jataka*, Bhasa's *Pratima Natakam* and *Abhisheka*, Kalidasa's *Raghuvamsa*, the *Mahabhasya* of Patanjali, the *Kathasaritsagara*, and the *Adi Purana* of Jinasena, among others.

The *Aitareya Brahmina* and the *Sankhayana Srauta Sutra* describe Ayodhya as a rural settlement.[8] The *Nilamata Purana* of Kashmir describes Ayodhya as a great city. The *Mahaparinirvana Sutra* too states that Ayodhya was a great city. This reference to Ayodhya in the sutra comes up when Ananda asks the Buddha why he chose Kushinagar as his place of death instead of great centres like Campa, Rajgriha, Sravasti, Kausambi, Banaras and Saketa (Ayodhya).[9]

The *Ayodhya Mahatmya*, a book on the holy places of Ayodhya and part of the *Skanda* and *Padma* puranas, gives us a detailed description of the places within the city and the religious sanctity attached to them. This book is in the form of a conversation between Shiva and Parvati and was first translated into English and published in the *Journal of the Asiatic Society of Bengal* for 1875 CE.[10]

I have come across a rather dense viewpoint shared by a few 'artists/thinkers' I know that the real Ayodhya is a metaphorical allusion to a perfect place akin to Utopia and that no such city existed in history. It would be not only insensitive but also foolish to even think that Ayodhya is just a figment of collective imagination, and that no such place existed in India that could be identified with the Ayodhya of the Faizabad district as the hallowed place of antiquity.

Quite often, overtly rational personalities dismiss oral and literary history as mere myths due to all the fantastical and unbelievable embellishments these works are decorated with. They metaphorically throw the baby out with the bathwater. In contrast to these 'thinkers', bigots swallow all the mumbo jumbo found in mythological stories hook, line and sinker, and refuse to exercise logic, which is sacrificed on the altar of faith.

Speaking of faith, the epic Ramayana narrates the story of Rama, his life and adventures, and mentions that Rama was born in the capital city of Kosala, Ayodhya, to the family of Dasharatha of the Ikshvaku lineage. The Bala Kanda of the Ramayana gives us a vivid description of the city on the banks of the Sarayu.[11] We also get another description of Ayodhya on the day of his return from Lanka.[12]

The physical rendering of the city as described in the Ramayana can be seen in a gigantic model of Ayodhya in the Nasiyan Jain Temple of Ajmer in Rajasthan. According to Hindus, the tradition of celebrating Diwali, the festival of lights, began when the residents of Ayodhya lit lamps to welcome their beloved Prince Rama (he had not been crowned king yet).

Jain sources also mention that Ayodhya was the birthplace of Rishabh Deva, the first Tirthankara, who was born thousands of years before Rama. The Jain literary canon also tells us that the second Tirthankara Ajitnath, the fourth Tirthankara Abhinandananath, the fifth Tirthankara Sumatinath, and the fourteenth Tirthankara Anantanath were all born in Ayodhya.

We know that Ayodhya was also called Vinita, Ikshvaku Bhumi, Ramapuri and Kosala. The *Bhagavata Purana* calls Ayodhya a city and the *Skanda Purana* gives its overall shape as that of a fish.[13] Ptolemy calls Ayodhya 'Sagoda the metropolis',[14] which is the Greek version of Saket, and mentions the name of the river Sarayu as Sarabos.[15]

During the second century BCE, the mighty Mauryan Empire was ended by the machinations of Senapati Pushyamitra Sunga.[16] This Brahmin general of the last Mauryan monarch Brihadrath established the Sunga Empire after the murder of his overlord.[17] This empire had stretched across a vast tract of the subcontinent, which had also included Ayodhya as one of its provinces. The *Yuga*

Purana, composed in the first century BCE, tells us that a Yavana (Greek) invasion had taken place that conquered Saket, Panchala, Mathura and Pataliputra.[18]

The powerful Jain monarch Kharvela of Kalinga, who flourished in the second century BCE, defeated an Indo-Greek king named Demetrius, who had occupied Pataliputra, and forced him to return to Mathura.[19] Undoubtedly, Ayodhya was an important part of the once powerful Mauryan Empire that had become so weak that it could not defend its capital from being ravaged by the Indo-Greeks.

It is simplistically understood that this event resulted in the overthrow of the last Mauryan king, and over his corpse a new dynasty called the Sungas was established by Pushyamitra Sunga in a coup d'état in faraway Pataliputra. Ayodhya, as an important part of the Mauryan empire, remained a province of the newly established Sunga realm.

An inscription on a flat stone slab found at the eastern entrance of the samadhi of Baba Sangat Baksh testifies to this. This samadhi was constructed during the reign of Nawab Shuja-ud-Daula in the eighteenth century CE, in Ranopali near the Rishikund Park between Ayodhya and Faizabad. The inscription, dated to the first century CE, is important not only for establishing the Sunga domain over Kosala (Ayodhya) but also because it is the only one of its kind to corroborate the existence of Pushyamitra, who, so far, had only existed in literary sources like the *Vishnu* and *Bhagavata* Puranas, the *Divyavadana*, the *Mahabhasya* of Patanjali, and Kalidasa's Sanskrit play *Malavikagnimitram*.[20]

The two-line inscription records the building of a shrine in honour of Phalgudeva, the father of Dharmaraja, who was the then king of Kosala. The inscription mentions Kaushiki as Dharmaraja's mother and says that he was the sixth descendant of Pushyamitra, the *senapati* who had performed the Aswamedha Yagna twice.[21]

The *Yuga Purana* states that after the Indo-Greeks left Madhyadesha (region corresponding to the Ganga–Yamuna Doab) due to wars that were raging in their own country, seven kings ruled Ayodhya, who with the force of their arms conquered several kingdoms and devastated the land they ravaged.[22] The Purana, however, does not tell us the names of these kings. Based on evidence from inscriptions and coins, we know the names of the three dynasties that ruled over Ayodhya post the Sunga period. First came the Deva Dynasty of Phalgudeva, followed by the Datta Dynasty and then the Mitra Dynasty.[23]

Foreign Traditions about Ayodhya

A Korean legend narrates the story of a princess named Suriratna/Heo Hwang Ko from Ayodhya. This princess had left her home in Ayodhya in 48 CE and reached Korea. Here, she was married to King Kim Suro. The couple had many children, and the descendants of these children still trace their ancestry to this royal couple. Koreans have no doubt that Suriratna was from Ayodhya of India and no other place with the same name.

Different places in Southeast Asia are verily named after Ayodhya in honour of the sanctity attached to this ancient city. The most famous Ayodhyas outside of India are Ayutthaya, the old capital of Thailand, and Yogyakarta in Indonesia. If Princess Suriratna did indeed belong to Ayodhya, then she could have been from the family of Phalgudeva. It is important to note that the Sakya clan of the Buddha also traced its descent from the legendary Ikshvaku Dynasty of Rama. Thus, royalty from Ayodhya, even if unrelated to the Ikshvakus, would have an elevated position in the minds of people who were ardent followers of Buddhism in areas far from mainland India.

The Revival of Hinduism in Ayodhya during the Gupta Epoch

During the fifth century CE, Ayodhya was a part of the Gupta Empire, as attested to by an inscription engraved during the reign of Kumaragupta I (415–55 CE). This inscription, dated to 436 CE, engraved on a Shivling from the village of Karm Danda in the Faizabad district, mentions the name of the Gupta monarch Kumaragupta I as the overlord of Prithivisena, a minister of Kumaragupta I. The inscription further mentions that the donors to the temple of Saileswara, where the linga was installed, were Brahmins from Ayodhya, living within the vicinity of said temple.[24]

The Gaya copper plate inscription of Gupta monarch Samudragupta, dated to 328–9 CE, was issued from his victory camp in the city of Ayodhya. Due to the suspicious nature of the way in which the main body of the engraving is attached to the seal of Samudragupta, it was concluded that this grant was not genuine. The seal, however, is genuine and appears to have belonged to some other grant from where it was removed and attached with this copper plate. The inscription was obtained by Cunningham from Gaya.[25]

During the decline of Buddhism and the subsequent reestablishment of the Brahminical religion by the Imperial Guptas, Ayodhya became an important Hindu centre once again. Powerful local tradition tells us this story: it is believed that after the death of Rama because of his *jalsamadhi* (suicide by drowning) in the Sarayu, the city, and the kingdom of Kosala, became dilapidated. His descendant King Sumitra's sons migrated to different parts of India and founded independent kingdoms, and Ayodhya became engulfed by forests. Due to Ujjain's King Vikramaditya's efforts, the jungles were cut and Ayodhya once again regained its sanctity as a holy city, where Vikramaditya is believed to have built 360 temples.[26]

Let us pause here and examine the above sentence; the historicity of King Vikramaditya is often questioned, but we know that he is the founder of the Vikram Samvat calendar that starts from 57 BCE, commencing after he defeated the Sakas. Fa Hien and Hieun Tsang clearly mention that Ayodhya was an important Buddhist centre in the Gupta and the post-Gupta periods, albeit in decline during the latter's visit. Over the ages, Vikramaditya became a symbol for a strong and righteous monarch. We know that the Brahminical doctrines began flourishing after the advent of the Gupta Empire in the fourth century CE. We also know that several Gupta rulers adopted Vikramaditya as a suffix to their name, particularly Skandagupta, who had also defeated the Central Asian tribe of the Hunas.[27]

From coins and inscriptions, we know that Skandagupta's regnal years corresponded to 455–67 CE, and that he had taken up two titles, Kramaditya and Vikramaditya.[28] He had restored the glory of his kingdom, which had eroded due to devastating wars with the Pushyamitra kingdom on the banks of the Narmada. He also defeated the Hunas around 458 CE or immediately after,[29] just like the legendary Vikramaditya of Ujjain vanquished an invading horde from Central Asia. It is possible that the memory of these victories got confused over the ages as one event and became associated with the memory of Vikramaditya of Ujjain. This could explain why local tradition attributes the construction of many temples in Ayodhya to Vikramaditya of Ujjain and not the Gupta Emperor Skandagupta.

Fa Hien's Account

Fa Hien had visited Ayodhya during the Gupta Era, corresponding to the period when Kumaragupta I was the emperor between 415 and 455 CE. He has left behind a small account of Ayodhya as a place where the Buddha had planted his tooth-cleaning twig that sprouted roots and became a small plant. The Chinese pilgrim had reached Ayodhya via Kannauj. He mentions that Buddhism was practised there, and that he paid homage to the four stupas built on spots where earlier Buddhas had sat (these are mythological Buddhas believed to have appeared on earth before the coming of the historical Buddha).[30] He calls Ayodhya 'Sha-che', which is Chinese for Saket.

The Post-Gupta Ayodhya

In the sixth and seventh centuries CE, Ayodhya was ruled by the Varman Dynasty. Many coins belonging to different monarchs from this dynasty have been unearthed at Bhitaura near Ayodhya.[31] Approximately 139 years after Skandagupta, the celebrated Chinese pilgrim Hieun Tsang visited India during the reign of Harshavardhan in the seventh century CE. Banabhatta, the biographer of Harshavardhan and a contemporary of Hieun Tsang,[32] has mentioned Ayodhya in the *Harshacharita*[33] while referencing the incident of the murder of King Jarutha of Ayodhya by a lady named Ratnavati. Bana also makes a reference to Mandhatri and the righteous king Harishchandra, both from the Ikshvaku Dynasty of Ayodhya, in the *Harshacharita*.[34]

Ayodhya during Hieun Tsang's Visit

Hieun Tsang's account of Ayodhya gives us an elaborate description of the place. Like Fa Hien, he started his journey to Ayodhya from Kannauj but took a different route via Navadevakula. This place has been identified by Cunningham as Nanamau on the banks of the Ganga, about 33 km from the present-day Kannauj town. From Nanamau, Hieun Tsang crossed the Ganga and proceeded to Ayodhya. Hieun Tsang stated that to the north of the city, 40 li (20 km) away, flowed the Ganga, on whose bank was an old monastery, beside which was a 200-foot tall stupa built by Ashoka. The 'Ganga' he mentions is a definite mistake for it should be Ghagra, which is another name for the Sarayu that flows past the holy city.

Unlike Fa Hien, he calls the place O-Yu-To (Ayodhya). He states that there were one hundred Buddhist monasteries in the kingdom and ten deva temples. In the capital of this country, i.e. the city of Ayodhya, he visited the old Buddhist monastery, in which the famous fourth century CE Buddhist preacher from Gandhara named Vasubandhu resided and composed many works.[35]

Besides this monastery, he also mentions the existence of the four stupas of the previous Buddhas. A little distance to the west of the then urban centre of Ayodhya was a stupa that contained the relics of the Buddha. To the north of the Buddha's relic stupa, he came to the ruins of another monastery where Silabhadra composed the *Vibhasha Shastra*. Silabhadra was more than 100 years old when Hieun Tsang studied under him at Nalanda. To the southwest of the city, he came to an extensive grove of amra trees. In this grove was an old monastery where Vasubandhu's brother, Asanga, had lived and formulated the *Yogacharya Shastras*[36] and other doctrines. To the northwest of this amra grove was another stupa that also contained the relics of the Buddha.

Cunningham's Identification of the Places Mentioned by Hieun Tsang

During his visit to Ayodhya in 1862, Alexander Cunningham tried to identify some stupas mentioned by Hieun Tsang. He writes:

> There are several very holy Brahminical temples about [Ayodhya], but they are all of modern date, and without any architectural pretensions whatever. But there can be no doubt that most of them occupy the sites of more ancient temples that were destroyed by the Musalmans. Thus *Ramkot* [Fort of Rama], or *Hanuman Garhi*, on the east side of the city, is a small walled fort surrounding a modern temple on the top of an ancient mound.[37] The name Ramkot is certainly old, as it is connected with the traditions of the *Mani Parbat*, which will he hereafter mentioned; but the temple of Hanuman is not older than the time of Aurangzeb [...] The only remains at [Ayodhya] that appear to be of any antiquity, are three earthen mounds to the south of the city, and about a quarter of a mile distant. These are called *Mani-Parbat*, *Kuber-Parbat*, and *Sugrib-Parbat*. The first, which is nearest to the city, is an artificial mound, 65 feet in height, covered with broken bricks and blocks of *kankar* [...] Five hundred feet due south from the large mound [Mani-Parbat] stands the second mound called *Kuber-Parbat*, which is only 28 feet in height. The surface is an irregular heap of brick rubbish, with numerous holes made by the people digging for bricks, which are of large size, 11 inches by 7¼ by 2. It is crowned by two old tamarind trees and is covered with *jangal*. Close by on the south-west there is a

small tank, called *Ganesh-Kund* by the Hindus, and *Husen Kund* or *Imam Talao* by the Musalmans, because their *Tazias* are annually deposited in it. Still nearer on the south-east there is a large oblong mound called *Sugrib-Parbat*, which is not more than 8 or 10 feet above the ground level. It is divided into two distinct portions; that to the north being upwards of 300 feet square at top, and the other to the south upwards of 200 feet.[38]

These mounds, according to Cunningham, were ancient stupas and Buddhist monasteries that once dotted the city.[39]

Ayodhya from the Eighth–Tenth Centuries CE

During Hieun Tsang's visit to India in the seventh century CE, Kannauj was the capital of the empire of Harshavardhan. The extensive region immediately attached to the core of Harsha's kingdom was called Aryavarta. Even now, the tract around Kannauj is remembered as Aryavarta. After the death of Harsha, Kannauj retained its paramount position as the greatest city of northern India and was the capital of the powerful Yasovarman of the Varman Dynasty. This king is the hero of Vakpatiraja's poem *Gaudavaho* and is responsible for reestablishing the power of the Varmans over the region. Vakpatiraja mentions that Yasovarman had built a temple in the city of Harishchandra (Ayodhya). Kalhan mentions that Lalitaditya Muktapida (724–60 CE), the greatest Kashmiri king from the eighth century CE, had defeated Yasovarman and captured a large tract of land extending up to Bengal.[40] If Kalhan's account of Lalitaditya is to be believed, then Ayodhya too was overwhelmed by Kashmiri forces.

During the ninth and tenth centuries CE, the Kalachuris were masters of Ayodhya, as attested to by an inscription found in Kushinagar.[41] This dynasty is credited with building many temples whose remains can be primarily found in Chhattisgarh, and the Amarkantak and Jabalpur areas of Madhya Pradesh, among other places. The famous Rama temple called the Rajeev Lochan Mandir of Rajim, in Chhattisgarh, was built in 1145 CE by a general of the Kalachuri king Prithvideva II, named Jagapala.[42] We get this information from an inscription found in the temple. Interestingly, the composer of this inscription, a scribe named Jasananda, belonged to Ayodhya.[43]

Ayodhya during Mahmud of Ghazni's Plundering Raids in the Eleventh Century CE

The eleventh century CE Iranian polymath Al Biruni had come to India in the retinue of Mahmud of Ghazni during one of his plundering raids of the various cities and temples of India. This was during the waning period of the once powerful Gurjara-Pratihara Empire, which was on its last legs, with its king Rajyapal ruling from Kannauj in a diminished state.

After reading Al Biruni's exhaustive work on the religion, sciences and geography of the subcontinent, whose English translation is titled *Al Biruni's India*, one can easily understand that he lived for a few years in India, particularly in Kannauj and Banaras. His discussion on the different kingdoms and cities in the country begins with Kannauj as the centre point. The distance to every place in India at that time is measured from there. He does not specify whether he had visited Ayodhya but gives us the distance to and direction of the place via road from Kannauj passing through Bari.[44] This Bari is possibly Bangarmau on the eastern bank of the Ganga, and is very close to Kannauj, which is on the western bank (there is another Bari near Dholpur in Rajasthan).

Around 1018 CE, Kannauj, the greatest city of India at that time, was plundered by Mahmud of Ghazni. He also captured and destroyed several other places around Kannauj.[45] Al Utbi, Mahmud's biographer, is silent about the army from Ghazni marching further east from Kannauj towards Ayodhya, which, being an important religious centre, held an immense amount of riches.

However, we know of an Islamic zealot named Salar Masud, reportedly the nephew of Mahmud, who, in 1030 CE, invaded the region and captured Barabanki, from where he began plundering Ayodhya.[46] Abul Fazal notes that this *ghazi* was a blood kin of Mahmud of Ghazni and died in battle fighting Suhar Deo/Sahal Deva and Har Deo.[47] He is buried in Bahraich, 115 km northwest of Ayodhya, where his grave is a major place of pilgrimage for local Muslims.

In the eleventh century CE, under the kingship of Chandradeva, a new Rajput power rose in the region with Kannauj as its capital. Chandradeva, the founder of the Gahadavala Dynasty, established his realm in the wake of Mahmud's departure from Kannauj around the last decade of the eleventh century CE. His domain extended up to Banaras in the east and Ayodhya in the southeast.

The Chandravati copper plates of Chandradeva,[48] dated to 1192–93 CE and 1198–99 CE, inform us that Maharaja Chandraditya Deva had bathed at the confluence of the Sarayu and the Ghagra in Ayodhya during a solar eclipse on 23 October 1093 CE.[49] The name of the ghat where he bathed is mentioned as Swargadwara ('the gate of heaven'). This is interesting because the present Ram Ghat on the confluence of the Sarayu with the Ghagra, near the Ram Ki Paidi ghats on the palaeochannel of the Sarayu, is also called Swargadwara.

Jain sources also mention that a Chalukya monarch named Kumarpala (twelfth century CE) installed a Jain image in a temple at Ayodhya.[50]

The Complete Destruction of the Holy City by Bakhtiyar Khilji, and Later by the Sultanate of Delhi

Jaichand Gahadavala, the last Hindu king of Kannauj, was defeated and killed by Muhammad Ghori after the Battle of Chandawar, fought in 1193 CE.[51] Minhaj-us-Siraj, the author of *Tabakat-i-Nasiri*, gives us the names of the places conquered by Ghori. In this list, we find the mention of the territories of Awadh (Ayodhya).[52]

It is safe to assume that after the Battle of Chandawar, the realm of the Gahadavalas automatically became Ghori's, after whose death Qutbuddin Aibak, his slave general, established himself as the first

Muslim sultan of northern India. The history of Ayodhya in the years immediately after the establishment of Muslim rule, which happened 163 years after the death of Mahmud of Ghazni, is sketchy and has been compiled from the inscriptions that I have already discussed in the chapter.

It was during the hegemony of the Delhi Sultanate that Ayodhya and the province around it came to be known as Awadh. The period after the death of Jaichand Gahadavala saw Ayodhya being attacked by a large Muslim army led by Jurjan Ghori in 1193 CE. The defender of Ayodhya was a general named Bartuh (Prithu), who defeated the invaders and killed Jurjan Ghori.[53]

After the establishment of the Delhi Sultanate under Qutbuddin Aibak, the mercenary marauder Muhammad Bin Bakhtiyar Khilji began plundering places in and around Ayodhya.[54] Going by the usual 'tradition' established by Islamic rulers, it is no secret that they indulged in the wholesale destruction of Hindu and Jain temples. Here, I will not waste words in citing source materials from Muslim authors, who wrote about the sultans and their effort to gain religious merit by indulging in iconoclasm.

Yet, in defence of my statement, I must mention the presence of the infamous iconoclast Bakhtiyar Khilji in Ayodhya. According to his biographer Minhaj-us-Siraj, he:

> ...proceeded into Awadh to the presence of Malik Husamuddin and Aghul Bak. As he had shown activity and gallantry, Bhagwat or Bhugwat and Bhiuli were conferred upon him in fife: and being a man of valour and intrepidity, he was in the habit of making incursions into the territory of Muner and Bihar and used to obtain booty from it, until he acquired ample resources in the shape of horses arms and men.

From his base in Ayodhya, he then invaded '...Bihar and ravaged that territory'.[55] Basically, what he did after destroying Ayodhya was to move on to destroy the Odantapuri and Nalanda universities in present-day Bihar Sharif.

Whatever was left behind in Ayodhya, which, if pictured, would verily resemble a ruined field of crops after a locust attack, was taken care of by Nasiruddin Mahmud Shah, the eldest son of Iltutmish, to whom the province of Awadh was entrusted in 1226 CE. Nasiruddin defeated and killed Bartuh of Awadh. Minhaj-us-Siraj tells us that Bartuh was responsible for the total destruction of an army of 'a hundred and twenty thousand Musalmans',[56] indirectly referring to rout faced by Jurjan Ghori.

It is understood that after the complete annihilation of the forces of Bartuh, the once sprawling metropolis of Ayodhya and its numerous temples were obliterated. After completely subduing the province of Ayodhya, Nasiruddin then marched on to Bengal.[57] A strange aspect of India's history is that Barthu/Prithu is completely forgotten, except as a one-liner mentioned by Minhaj-us-Siraj in his *Tabakat-i-Nasiri*. The gazetteer of Faizabad district tells us that he could have been a chief of the Bhar tribe that dominated the tract.[58] In between the centuries, the city did exist as a holy site, but completely under the mercy and the whims of the Muslim governors posted there. Eventually, the Mughals finally gave the city the last iconoclastic blow.

Babur's Visit to Ayodhya

Here I am brushing past 225 years of Ayodhya's history after Nasiruddin Mahmud Shah and going straight to Bahlol Lodhi, the founder of the Lodhi Dynasty in 1551 CE.

Bahlol Lodhi had appointed Muhammad Farmuli (also known as Kala Pahad)[59] as the governor of Awadh after the conquest of the Jaunpur Sultanate,[60] under whose jurisdiction Ayodhya happened to remain since the times of the Tughlaqs. Farmuli's son-in-law, Mustafa, succeeded him as the governor after his death. After Mustafa's death, his younger brother Bayzid was appointed governor by Ibrahim Lodhi, the last sultan of Delhi.

It is because of Bayzid's rebellion against the newly established Mughal rule that Babur visited Awadh during a campaign against this rebellious Afghan, immediately after the completion of his campaign against Medini Rai of Chanderi in 1528. Babur, who founded the Mughal Empire after defeating Ibrahim Lodhi in the First Battle of Panipat in 1526 CE, had to fight several other battles in the subcontinent for consolidation and new gains, the most frustrating one being the pursuit of Bayzid and Biban.

The *Baburnama* lists out the names of the provinces from where Babur collected revenue. The province of Awadh and Bahraich yielded a total annual revenue of 11,701,369 rupees.[61] This conclusively proves that Ayodhya was within the domain of the first Mughal. Ironically, he had confirmed Bayzid's post as the governor of Ayodhya before the latter's rebellion.

The Babri Controversy

In the minds of Hindus, the importance of Ayodhya is primarily due to the belief that this city was the birthplace of Rama, and secondarily because of the Babri Masjid, which was built after demolishing a temple that marked the birthplace of Rama. Popular tradition attributes the destruction of the main temple of Rama inside Ramkot and the building of a mosque over its ruins to one Mir Baqi, a general of Babur. For several centuries, this mosque was known as the Janmsthan Masjid (the mosque of the birthplace)[62] and was infamous as the Babri Masjid. This disputed structure was demolished by a frenzied Hindu mob on 6 December 1992.

Here, the controversy begins with one segment of India's historians claiming that no temple ever existed on the spot of the Babri Masjid and another maintaining that a temple was indeed destroyed by Mir Baqi to build the mosque over it. Interestingly, Kishore Kunal, in his book *Ayodhya Revisited*, has given a slight twist to this controversy by stating that the Babri Masjid was not built by Mir Baqi but by Faidai Khan Koka, the foster brother of Aurangzeb, during his governorship of Ayodhya.[63] This well-researched book tries to give evidence to prove that Babur had nothing to do with the destruction of Rama's temple or the building of a mosque there, which I do not agree with.

If one looks at the old image of the Babri Masjid of Ayodhya and compares it with an image of the Kabuli Masjid of Panipat, which was constructed by Babur, the similarity in the architectural aspects between them becomes apparent. Both mosques exhibit the early Mughal style with simple and bulbous domes fronted with another simple façade below which is the arched entry into the building. This design is unlike the style employed to construct the Shahi Idgah Masjid of Mathura and the Gyanvapi Masjid of Banaras, both of which were constructed by Aurangzeb.

In case of the three-domed Babri Masjid, we strangely do not have any 'literary' evidence of Mir Baqi's destruction of a temple or the construction of a mosque. Babur's autobiography, which is otherwise meticulous in its documentation of events, conquests and iconoclasm, is silent about it. The portion that was supposed to detail his stay near Ayodhya to 'settle the affairs of Aud [Awadh]' is missing from the manuscript.

The missing portion from 2 April to 18 September 1528 is presumed to be lost.[64] The *Baburnama* does not mention the name of Mir Baqi as a general in his army but mentions two Baqis.

The first was Baqi Shaghawal (chief scribe), who was given charge of Dipalpur,[65] in the Okara district of Pakistan. After making Baqi the governor of Dipalpur, Babur sent him to Balkh on a military expedition. The mention of this personality happens in the *Baburnama* during the siege of Chanderi in 1528 CE. By then, Baqi Shaghawal had been promoted and was the commander of 1,000 troops. In his autobiography, Babur also calls him Baqi *ming-bashi* (head of a thousand),[66] deputed to peruse Bayzid.

When Babur was camping outside Awadh near the confluence of the Ghagra and another river named Sird (Sarda/Kali River), about 160 km from Ayodhya town, Baqi and a few others managed to capture some Afghans and bring them to him as prisoners.[67]

The other Baqi was his general named Baqi Tashkindi, who was put in charge of his troops that were occupying Ayodhya. Babur writes that on 13 June 1529 CE, while he was camped at Dalmau,

'Baqi Tashkindi came in with the army of Aud and waited on me.'[68] It was during this time that the Babri Masjid was constructed.[69]

After the unsuccessful conclusion of the campaign against Biban and Bayzid, Babur once again mentions the name of Baqi Tashkindi, who, on 20 June 1529 CE, was permitted to get back to Ayodhya with the Mughal army under his command.[70] At this point, it is difficult to say whether Baqi Tashkindi from Tashkent is the same as Baqi Shaghawal the scribe to whom the construction of the Babri Masjid is attributed.

Ayodhya during the Mughal Hegemony

The *Ain-i-Akbari* mentions that Ayodhya, one of the largest cities in India, was the capital of the subah of Awadh. It was also one of the holiest places of antiquity on account of Rama.[71] Abul Fazal writes that around the environs of the city, people obtained gold by digging the earth (possibly from the sand from the wide Ghagra). Akbar had established a mint in Ayodhya. The coins produced in Ayodhya during the reign of the lesser Mughal Muhammad Shah bore the inscription 'Akhtarnagar Awadh'.[72] It is believed that Tulsidas composed the *Ramcharitmanas* in Ayodhya in 1575 CE, when Akbar was the Mughal Emperor.

Between 1608 and 1611 CE, William Finch visited India during Jahangir's reign. He went to Ayodhya, which was then the seat of a 'Potan' (Pathan/Afghan) king, and reported seeing Ranichand's (Ramchandra's) castle and house, which was in a ruined state (Ramkot). These ruins he mentions were built 400 years ago, which corresponds to the Gahadavala rule over Ayodhya. He noted that the Brahmins living nearby write down the names of all the pilgrims who, after bathing in the river, come to visit the place where they claim Rama was born.[73]

Some 3 km to the further side of the river, he reports the existence of a deep cave whose entrance was narrow. He tells us that people believed that the ashes of Rama were buried inside the cave. Pilgrims from different parts of India would visit this cave.

Like Abul Fazal, he also reports the mining of gold in Ayodhya. Finch, being a merchant (indigo dealer), mentions that Ayodhya was famous for its trade in the sale and craft of rhino horns made into buckles and drinking cups.[74]

While writing about Ayodhya in his compilation titled *The Empire of the Great Mogol*, Joannes De Laet has also mentioned the existence of the fort of Rama. He writes that Ayodhya, an ancient city, once the seat of Pathan kings but now almost deserted, is 50 *cos* from Lucknow, and:

> Not far from this city may be seen the ruins of the fort and palace of Ramchand, whom the Indians regard as God Most High: they say that he took on him human flesh that he might see the great *tamasha* of the world. Amongst these ruins live certain [Brahmins] who carefully note down the name of all such pilgrims as duly perform their ceremonial ablutions in the neighbouring river. They say that this custom has been kept up for many centuries. About two miles from these rivers is a cave with a narrow mouth but so spacious within and with so many ramifications that it is difficult to find one's way out again. They believe that the ashes of the god are hidden here. Pilgrims come to this place from all parts of India and after worshipping the idol take away with them some grains of charred rice as proof of their visit. This rice they believe to have been kept here for many centuries.[75]

His observation of Ayodhya appears to be directly influenced by Finch's...

In 1632 CE, Shah Jahan promulgated a general order that decreed the destruction of temples throughout his domain. Abdul Hamid Lahori, in his *Badshah Nama*, writes that seventy-six temples in the district of Banaras were demolished.[76] He, however, does not mention whether temples in Ayodhya were demolished. Aurangzeb, Shah Jahan's son, caused the destruction of many renowned temples within the Mughal empire, which included Ayodhya.

Niccolao Manucci, in his encyclopaedic account of the last days of Shah Jahan and the subsequent reign of Aurangzeb, compiled in the book *Storia Do Mogor*, mentions that on the order of Aurangzeb, the temples in Hajudia (Ayodhya), Caxis (Kashi/Banaras), Matura (Mathura) and Maisa (Mayapur/Haridwar) were demolished.[77]

In 1767 CE, the Jesuit priest Joseph Tieffenthaler visited Ayodhya. This was during the reign of Shah Alam II. In his book titled *Description Historique et Geographique de l'Inde*, he mentions that Aurangzeb had demolished the fortress called Ramkot and erected on the same place a mosque with three cupolas. He also says, 'Others believe that it was constructed by Babor.'[78] Several more Europeans like Buchanan, Mantell, Malte Brun, William Ward and M'Culloch, amongst others, mention the iconoclastic deeds of Aurangzeb at Ayodhya. The mention of Aurangzeb by these authors has led many like Kishore Kunal to conclude that it was Aurangzeb who had destroyed the primary temple of Ayodhya.

The Founding of Faizabad outside Ayodhya by the Early Nawabs of Awadh

Throughout the Mughal period, Ayodhya remained the capital of the province of Awadh. The era of the independent nawabs of Awadh began in 1732 CE, after the appointment of Sadat Ali Khan I as its governor. Prior to Sadat Ali Khan's appointment, Chabile Ram was made the governor by the lesser Mughal Emperor Farrukhsiyar. And after Chabile Ram, his nephew Girdhar Bahadur Naga became the representative of the Mughal court in Awadh. In 1732 CE, Girdhar was transferred to the Deccan and Sadat Ali Khan was sent to Ayodhya from Agra.

Sadat Ali Khan I is credited with the founding of the town of Faizabad, which is adjacent to Ayodhya. Earlier, this newly established township was called Bangla, and the name was frequently used. The story behind this name is interesting. After his posting to Ayodhya, Sadat Ali Khan I had a mud fort built on the banks of the Ghagra near the Lakshman Ghat, and named it Qila Mubarak. This was his residence. Faizabad was a thickly wooded tract at that time, where he would often go hunting. In this jungle, on an elevated part of the land, he had a shooting box built out of wood.[79] This structure, called Bangla, gave the place its name.

Khan started the construction of the Dilkhush Palace, and in 1739 CE, consumed poison and despatched himself to the nether world. Abdul Mansur Ali Khan, better known as Safdar Jung, his son-in-law, became the governor of Awadh in 1759 CE, and thereafter this post became hereditary.

Safdar Jang's son Shuja-ud-Daula succeeded him in 1754 CE as the Nawab of Awadh. In 1754 CE, he died in mysterious circumstances and was buried in the beautiful Gulab Bari Mausoleum in the heart of Faizabad. While riding to Ayodhya, I first visited this monument. Shuja-ud-Daula is credited with building most of the old Islamic structures seen in Faizabad. He was succeeded by his son, Asaf-ud-Daula, who transferred the capital of Awadh from Faizabad to Lucknow. Once again, decay set in around this age-old place, and, with the exception of the Gulab Bari tomb and garden, one can see this decay on the façade of every other Nawab era structure in the town.

The Reclamation of Ayodhya by the Hindus

In July 1855 CE, during the reign of the last Nawab of Awadh, Wajid Ali Shah, there was a battle fought between the Bairagi Sadhus and Maulvi Shah Ghulam Hussain in Ayodhya. The cause of this bloodbath was the Hanumangarhi temple. During the reign of Aurangzeb, this temple had been vandalized and a mosque was constructed beside it.

Nawab Shuja-ud-Daula, while on his way to Buxar to assist Mir Qasim in his fight against the British, had a temple built at the site. This is the present structure of the Hanumangarhi temple, whose single spire towers over the crowded locality. The mosque of Aurangzeb fell to ruins, and the temple was later fortified with a strong wall by Raja Darshan Singh over the ruins of Aurangzeb's mosque. [80]

The local Muslims of Ayodhya, led by the Sunni cleric Maulvi Ghulam Hussain and his disciple Maulvi Muhammad Shah, began a vigorous campaign to reclaim the mosque. On 28 July 1855 CE, Shah Ghulam Hussain led a group of 400–600 people who had come to wrest the Hanumangarhi temple from the Hindus. The temple compound was defended by 8,000 people, overwhelming the raving fanatics led by the maulvi.[81] In this skirmish, seventy members from Shah Ghulam Hussain's mob lost their lives.[82]

In February 1856 CE, Awadh was annexed to the British domain. Faizabad was made into a separate district and a division. The first commissioner posted there was Col. P. Goldney, assisted by W.A. Forbes. Captain Reid and O.E. Bradford were also posted to assist the commissioner and his deputy Forbes in administering the district.[83] The Great Mutiny of 1857 that engulfed the entire region was effectively suppressed in Ayodhya and its neighbouring regions at the cost of several thousand lives.

The First Puja inside the Babri Masjid

In November 1858 CE, a certain Nihang Singh from the Punjab, along with twenty-five other Sikhs, entered the Babri Masjid and, after placing an idol of Rama inside it, performed puja and a yagna. This act of theirs was to commemorate Guru Nanak's visit to Ayodhya in the sixteenth century. Another important reason for them to do this was the belief that Guru Nanak's clan, the Bedis, trace their descent from Rama's elder twin son Lava, while Guru Gobind Singh's clan, the Sodhis, trace theirs from Kush.[84]

After these incidents, the simmering tension between Hindus and Muslims over the ownership of the Babri Masjid lingered on for a century, with a lengthy litigation and intermittent riots until 1949. On 23 December 1949, members of the Akhil Bharatiya Ramayana Mahasabha placed an idol of Rama inside the mosque, forcing the government to lock up the premises and declare it a disputed site.[85]

Now the question here is, was the Babri Masjid built over a temple or on vacant land? Let us see what material evidence tells us in the paragraphs below.

Epigraphic and Archaeological Evidence

Where literary evidence is lacking, epigraphy and archaeology have filled in the gap. There is ample proof to state that below the foundation of the Babri mosque there once existed a temple.

In the archaeological report titled *The Sharqi Architecture of Jaunpur: With Notes on Zafarabad, Sahet-Mahet and Other Places in the Northern-Western Provinces and Oudh*, A. Fuhrer mentions that 'Babar's Masjid' was built by Mir Khan in 1523 on the 'very spot where the old temple of Janmasthanam of Ramchandra was standing'.[86]

The first inscription found in the masjid, numbered in Roman numerals in the book as XL, is a Shahada ('there is no God but Allah and Muhammad is His Prophet'). The second inscription, XLI, mentions that the mosque was built by Mir Khan on the orders of Babur. The third inscription, XLII, mentions that in the presence of Babur and one of the grandees 'who is another king of Turkey and China', Babur's minister laid the foundation of this building in Hijri 930, corresponding to 1523 CE. This inscription calls the mosque a 'fort masjid' and names the composer of the engraving as Fatahullah Ghori.[87]

Right after giving the translations of the inscriptions, Fuhrer adds these lines:

> The old temple of Ramachandra at Janmasthanam must have been a very fine one, for many of its columns have been used by the Musalmans in the construction of Babar's masjid. These are of strong, close-grained, dark-coloured or black stone, called by the natives *kasauti*, 'touch-stone slate', and carved with different devices. They are from seven to eight feet long, square at the base, centre and capital, and round or octagonal intermediately.[88]

Fuhrer also notes another inscription numbered XLII that he came across at Ayodhya. This engraving on a red sandstone fragment belonged to a mosque built by Aurangzeb over a temple called Svargadvara Mandira.[89] Inscription number XLIV, dated to 1184 CE, corresponding to the reign of Jayachandra, mentions the name of the last Gahadavala king of Kannauj as the builder of a temple dedicated to Vishnu. The stone slab originally belonged to said temple, whose destroyed remains were used by Aurangzeb to construct the masjid over the temple named Treta Ki Thakur.[90]

Fuhrer's translations of the inscriptions were reviewed by two other epigraphists, viz. Annette Susannah Beveridge and Maulavi M. Ashraf Hussain, who corrected the mistakes made by Fuhrer. The translator of the *Baburnama*, Annette Susannah Beveridge, had procured the Persian text of the second and third inscription (nos. XLI and XLII) from the deputy commissioner of Faizabad and found some faults with Fuhrer's translation. Her corrected version of the second inscription reads:

> (1) By the command of the Emperor Babur whose justice is an edifice reaching up to the very height of the heavens.
> (2) The good-hearted Mir Baqi built this alighting place of angels.
> (3) It will remain an everlasting bounty, and (hence) the date of its erection became manifest from my words: It will remain an everlasting bounty.[91]

In the chapter titled 'Inscriptions of Emperor Babur' by Maulvi M. Ashraf Hussain in *Epigraphia Indica: Arabic and Persian Supplement (In continuation of Epigraphia Indo-Moslemica) 1964 and 1965*, we get a fresh translation of all the three inscriptions. Maulvi Hussain's translations of the second and third inscriptions are not very different from Beveridge's but differ vastly from Fuhrer's. In the introduction to his translation, he briefly talks about Ayodhya's importance as the birthplace of Rama. He also goes on to state that '...at the Muslim conquest three important temples are reported to have existed here,' viz. the Janmasthan, the Treta Ki Thakur, and Svargadvara Mandir. On the site of the first, the Babri Masjid is believed to have been built, and the second and the third were destroyed by Aurangzeb.

The Flemish researcher and Indologist Koenraad Elst has provided the following information regarding Aurangzeb's activities in Ayodhya:

'The best-known and clearest testimony is certainly the one by the Austrian Jesuit Tieffenthaler, who wrote in 1768: Emperor Aurangzeb got demolished the fortress called Ramcot and erected on the same place a Mahometan temple with three cupolas. Others believe that it was constructed by Babor.'[92]

Coming back to Maulvi Hussain, he writes:

> The Baburi-Masjid, which commands a picturesque view from the riverside, was constructed according to A. Fuhrer in A.H. 930 (1523-24 A.D.), but his chronology, based upon incorrect readings of inscriptions supplied to him, is erroneous. Babur defeated Ibrahim Lodi only in A.H. 933 (1526 A.D.), and moreover, the year of construction, recorded in two of the three inscriptions studied below, is clearly A.H. 935 (1528-29 A.D.). Again, it was not built by Mir Khan as stated by him. The order for building the mosque seems to have been issued during Babur's stay at Ajodhya in A.H. 934 (1527-28 A.D.), but no mention of its completion is made in the *Babur Nama*. However, it may be remembered that his diary for the year A.H. 934 (1527-28 A.D.) breaks off abruptly, and throws the reader into the dark in regard to the account of Oudh.[93]

The salient points of Maulvi Ashraf's translation of the third inscription are: '...in his court [Babur's], there was a magnificent noble, named Mir Baqi the second Asaf, councillor of his government and administrator of his kingdom, who is the founder of this mosque and fort-wall [...] The time of the building is this auspicious date, of which the indication is nine hundred (and) thirtyfive (A.H. 935=1528-29 A.D.).'[94]

The Vishnu Hari inscription of Ayodhya, claimed to have been found in the debris of the demolished Babri Masjid by one Ashok Chandra Chatterjee, a resident of Faizabad, though riddled with holes, is important from the point of view of Ayodhya's history. It is interesting to note that the Vishnu Hari inscription in chaste Sanskrit, dated to the middle of the twelfth century CE on palaeographic ground, mentions the name of King Govindachandra. This king was from the Gahadavala dynasty and '...ruled over a fairly vast empire from 1114 to 1155 A.D'.[95] Furthermore, it mentions the name of his son, Alhana, and nephew, Meghasuta, who had been made the governor of Saketa-mandela (Ayodhya province). Meghasuta had a grand stone temple dedicated to Vishnu Hari built at Ayodhya.

The inscription goes on to tell us that his younger brother Ayusychandra succeeded him as the governor of Ayodhya and set up his residence in the city. He also built many palaces and temples and excavated many water bodies throughout Saketa-mandela. Lastly, the inscription tells us that Ayusychandra warded off an invasion from the west.

On the orders of the Lucknow High Court, the ASI carried out a series of digs that started on 12 March 2003 and carried on until 7 August 2003. Archaeologists dug ninety trenches, from where they unearthed the following:

1. NBPW Pottery dated between 1000 and 300 BCE.
2. Terracotta mother goddess and other figures belonging to the Sunga period corresponding to the first and second centuries BCE.
3. Terracotta figurines of humans and animals belonging to the Kushan epoch (first–third centuries CE).
4. Terracotta figurines and a copper coin with Sri Chandra (Chandragupta) written on it, attributed to the Gupta Epoch (fourth–fifth centuries CE).
5. A circular brick shrine with a *pranala* chute dated to the seventh century CE.
6. Huge structural remains of a temple dated to the eleventh–twelfth centuries CE, with fifty pillar bases. This structure was not a residential complex but a temple over which the Babri Masjid was built in the sixteenth century.
7. Also unearthed were mutilated sculptures of divine couples, carved door jambs, *amalaka* (fluted circular disc found atop temples in North India), lotus motifs, and broken octagonal shafts of black schist pillars, among other things.

The conclusion arrived at was that the Babri Masjid structure was constructed directly above the remains of a once massive temple.[96]

The Battle for Ayodhya in the Supreme Court

The Supreme Court's verdict on the Babri Masjid dispute, which is available in the public domain, also has detailed archaeological evidence in it.[97] The verdict was given on 9 November 2019 in the favour of the Hindus. From the perspective of history, this judgement is very important and put to rest a long-standing dispute between India's Hindu and Muslim communities. Here I will discuss certain parts of the 929-page-long verdict that details empirical evidence used by the judges to come to a logical conclusion.

The first paragraph of the verdict's introduction mentions the importance of the site to both the Hindus and Muslims, the former claiming it to be the birthplace of Rama and the latter as a mosque built by Babur. The third paragraph of the introduction informs us that the disputed land is a part of Ramkot in Ayodhya and is believed by Hindus to be the spot where Rama was born, while the Muslims claim that the Babri Masjid was constructed on a vacant piece of land.[98] Part G of the verdict, given on pages 85–104, mentions three inscriptions from Fuhrer's report as evidence and discusses their merits in the case.

The above-mentioned epigraphic evidence does not say anything about the destruction of any temple by Mir Baqi to construct a mosque in 1528–29 CE, just a year before Babur's death. The evidence for the existence of a temple below the said mosque comes to us from archaeological digs, whose findings are cited in the Supreme Court's judgement in Part N of the court document titled 'N 9. Archaeological Report' (pp. 507–99). After going through several reports prepared by the ASI, the honourable court conclusively states:

> The ASI report does find the existence of a pre-existing structure. The report deduces 17 rows of pillar bases (a total of 85 of which 50 were exposed in sections, in parts

or whole). The report concludes based on the architectural fragments found at the site and the nature of the structure that it was of a Hindu religious origin. The report rejects the possibility (urged by the Sunni Central Waqf Board) of the underlying structure being of Islamic origin. But the ASI report has left unanswered a critical part of the remit which was made to it, namely, a determination of whether a Hindu temple had been demolished to pave way for the construction of the mosque.[99]

The judgement document also posits the following:

(i) The Babri mosque was not constructed on vacant land;
(ii) The excavation indicates the presence of an underlying structure below the disputed structure;
(iii) The underlying structure was at least of equal, if not larger dimensions than the disputed structure;
(iv) The excavation of the walls of the underlying structure coupled with the presence of pillar bases supports the conclusion of the ASI of the presence of a structure underlying the disputed structure;
(v) The underlying structure was not of Islamic origin;
(vi) The foundation of the disputed structure rests on the walls of the underlying structure; and
(vii) Artefacts, including architectural fragments, which have been recovered during excavation have a distinct non-Islamic origin. Though individually, some of the artefacts could also have been utilised in a structure of Buddhist or Jain origins, there is no evidence of the underlying structure being of an Islamic religious nature.

The conclusion which has been drawn by the ASI that the nature of the underlying structure and the recoveries which have been made would on stylistic grounds suggest the existence of temple structure dating back to the twelfth century A.D. would on a balance of probabilities be a conclusion which is supported by evidence. The conclusion cannot be rejected as unsupported by evidence or lying beyond the test of a preponderance of probabilities, which must govern a civil trial.[100]

On 22 January 2024, a grand temple dedicated to Rama was inaugurated in Ayodhya. This structure has been built on the original site of the Ram Mandir above which the Babri Masjid used to exist. The temple, built in the Nagara style of temple architecture, was designed by temple architect Chandrakant Sompura and his sons.[101] Contrary to popular belief that the BJP would win great electoral dividends after the construction of the Ram Mandir, they fared rather poorly in the 2024 general elections. Also, the strange irony that a democratic India witnessed was the defeat of the BJP candidate of the Faizabad Lok Sabha seat, Lallu Singh, by Awadesh Prasad of the Samajwadi Party.[102]

6
Prayagraj: The Immortal Tree and the Invisible Saraswati of the Sangam

In Indic religions, an ideal place of pilgrimage is almost always beside a water body. The Sanskrit word for such a place is *tirtha-sthal*, meaning 'a ford that has to be crossed in order to reach the place of pilgrimage'. Metaphorically, it can mean a variety of things related to one's spiritual journey and the subsequent upliftment. Geographically, it denotes a place that is difficult to reach, sanctified as holy due to its remoteness and the purity associated with it. Distant mountains and confluences of rivers are the most sought-after sites. Over the aeons, remote places in the subcontinent have been associated with holiness, making them important religious sites. It is precisely because of the sanctity associated with these far-flung places that the idea of Bharat as a nation made cohesive sense even before its political unification could be conceived.

Of the various tirthas, be it a differently shaped boulder, the pinnacle of a hill or a mountain, a cave inside a desert or a jungle, a sacred forest with a spring at its centre, a riverside mound, or any conceivable geographic anomaly, the most common is the confluence of two or three water bodies. Over the ages, these locations saw people congregate around them, because of which shrines came about; these were enlarged into temples and around these temples were established urban localities.

This phenomenon is not unique to India. It is historically certain, and logically so, that civilization begins beside water bodies. After the decline of the Indus–Saraswati urban centres, the next phase of urbanization in the Ganga–Yamuna valley most probably also began in a similar manner: beside water bodies, but with the additional impetus of holiness attached to some of those places. Several ancient urban centres have continued to be occupied throughout, like Ropar, the Indus–Saraswati sites of Rakhigarhi and its surrounding villages, and Kalibangan, but, ironically, never re-developed as the ancient cities they once were.

Many modern cities in the subcontinent whose antecedents go back to the Later Vedic Age are built around some place of religious significance: Pushkar, Haridwar, Banaras, Prayagraj, Thaneshwar, Mathura, Ayodhya, Gaya, Madurai, Dwarka, Ujjain, Kanchipuram, Rameswaram, Tirupati and Trivandrum, to name a few. Of these cities, Banaras and Prayagraj came up on the confluences of rivers, which in Sanskrit is called 'sangam'. The word 'prayag' too denotes the same.

Sangam at Prayagraj

In India, most confluences of rivers have a temple or two near them, and the most important of these sangams are the ones on the Ganga. A series of confluences on India's holiest river begins from the Uttarakhand Himalayas at Ganesh Prayag on the Bhagirathi.[1] On the Alaknanda part of the Ganga, the first important sangam is Vishnuprayag, then Nandaprayag, Karnaprayag, Rudraprayag, and Devprayag. The last sangam is between Bhagirathi and the Alaknanda, after which the river flows through the mountains as the Ganga. These confluences are important to Hindus from a religious point of view.

After the Ganga reaches the plains past Haridwar, the river is joined by several tributary streams from the north as well as the south. The river, overall, travels a distance of about 900 km from Devprayag, till it comes to its chief feeder, the Yamuna, at Prayagraj. The confluence of the Yamuna and the 'Saraswati' with the Ganga here is the holiest of all the sangams, thus the name 'Prayagraj'.[2]

The justification for its sanctity comes from the mythological event of the churning of the ocean by the gods and the demons. The elixir of immortality was acquired in a *kumbha* (pot), a few drops of which spilled in four spots, namely Ujjain, Nasik, Haridwar and Prayagraj. Indic belief states that bathing at these spots not only washes away sins but also grants the bather a place in heaven, particularly in the month of January, when the sun in its transition enters the zodiac of Capricorn. The sangam at Prayag is so important precisely due to this belief, and the Kumbh Mela that takes place there is called Makar Kumbh. Apart from this, Prayagraj is also associated with several beliefs adhered to by practising Hindus, one of them being the story of Brahma's first sacrifice on the spot and another of Rama and Sita's visit to the ashram of Rishi Bhardwaj and the Akshay Vat banyan tree.[3]

For as long as civilizational memory can recall, Prayag holds a preeminent position as the tirtha-sthal to beat all such places with religious sanctity that humanity has ever conceived of. It is here that during the Maha Kumbh Mela, which takes place every twelve years, people gather in such large numbers. The Maha Kumbh of 2001 saw a record number of about 7 crore people congregate in one place over a period of six weeks.[4] This gathering at Prayagraj was the largest recorded assembly of humans over a single area measuring about 10 sq. km. The second largest gathering of humanity takes place during the month-long Hajj at Mecca, the largest number recorded there being 2.5 million pilgrims in 2019.[5]

Prayagraj in Myths, Legends and Archaeology

Of the umpteen mentions of the sangam at Prayag in different Indic religious and literary works, the earliest come to us from the Ramayana, the Mahabharata, the *Rig Veda Parisista* (a supplementary),[6] and the *Harivamsa*. The Ramayana informs us that the exiled Rama, Sita and Lakshmana had reached the ashram of Rishi Bhardwaj on the sangam, and spent the night there before proceeding to Chitrakoot.[7] While walking away from the ashram, they were asked by Rishi Bhardwaj to cross the Yamuna and pay their respects to an ancient banyan tree there,[8] which, according to the Ramayana, was on the other bank of the Yamuna corresponding to Arail.

Since ancient times, Prayagraj and the nearby areas along the banks of the Ganga and the Yamuna have been home to several ashrams of sages. An ancient mound on the Ganga at Sringaverapura, about 40 km from Prayag, is believed to be the ashram of Rishi Sringa from the Ramayana. Excavations done there have unearthed remains of building complexes, which, according to tradition, was the palace of the king of the fisherfolk, who received Rama, Sita and Lakshmana on their way to exile. The earliest layer of the excavated site has been dated to 1000 BCE.[9]

Local tradition posits that an ancient mound within the perimeter of the University of Allahabad—near the Anand Bhavan mansion owned by Motilal Nehru—used to be an ashram of Rishi Bhardwaj. Archaeologist B.B. Lal, excavating the site in two series of digs, first in 1978-79 and then in 1982-83, unearthed the earliest layer, belonging to 1000 BCE.[10] From this period, an early form of NBPW pottery shards was found. Following this, PGW, Red Ware, and Black Slipped Ware were recovered. The dig showed a break in the occupation of the site, which regenerated in the fifth century CE. Apart from the usual pottery pieces, eight terracotta figurines, several parts of terracotta animals, and seals were unearthed from the last layer. Also recovered were copper and iron implements of daily use, beads, shell bangles, and miscellaneous objects.

Prof. Lal's Conclusion

The archaeologist concluded that the site of the Bharadwaj Ashram was associated with the epic Ramayana, writing that the earlier excavations at Ayodhya, Sringaverapura, etc., show a similar type of cultural traits in their lower levels that flourished in the beginning of the first millennium BCE. In this regard, the excavation at the Bharadwaj Ashram is significant in corroborating the historicity of the Ramayana.

Prof. Lal tells us to assume for the sake of debate that the events of the Ramayana are the imaginative creation of Valmiki, informing us that scholars have accepted that the Ramayana of Valmiki was codified between the third century BCE and the third century CE in several stages. The assumption made is belied by the fact that in this period the places associated with the Ramayana were all occupied, as excavations have shown. However, the Bharadwaj Ashram was the only one that was not under occupation in the period mentioned.

The professor now asks a pertinent question: How was it that the name of the Bharadwaj Ashram was used by Valmiki when its trace had been lost? To this question, he responds that the only means by which the name of the ashram could have survived was in the memory of the people, kept alive in the ballad of Rama, which was put to writing in the centuries mentioned above.

Adding information to prove his hypothesis, the professor cites three significant pieces of evidence from the excavated site of the Bharadwaj Ashram. The first is the topography—it is a flat piece of land, sans any mound on top like at Ayodhya or Sringaverapura. But adjacent to the flat land, the ground slopes towards the Ganges and drops by 5–6 m. According to the locals, the river water would often reach the site of the ashram during floods, which has now been prevented after an embankment was constructed. This sloping aspect of the land proves beyond any doubt that once upon a time the river had flowed right past the ashram.

The second piece of evidence cited by him states that the lower levels of the excavated ashram did not yield any brick structures like the upper levels. However, NBPW shards were found sporadically in the sandy loam that was at the lowest level. It is in this sandy loam that lumps of clay deposits bearing impressions of reed were discovered, indicating the existence of wattle-and-daub huts. The professor writes:

> This scenario fits well into the picture of an asrama (hermitage) by the side of the Ganga. Surely, archaeology cannot tell us that it was the asrama of sage Bharadvaja, since we have not come across any inscription from the site certifying the same. For all we know, writing was not in vogue at that time. The earliest inscriptions that we have

as of now are datable to the fourth-third century BCE. The third point of interest is that, the site was re-occupied only during the Gupta times. It is well known that it was during the Gupta period that there took place a great revival of the Brahminical religion. Since oral tradition, perhaps through ballads, must have carried down the centuries the memory of the association of this site with the Rama story, it was but natural for the people to revive its glory by re-occupying it.[11]

Prayagraj in Early Historical Sources

The *Indica* of Megasthenes also mentions the confluence. Even though the *Indica* is lost, other Greek historians quoting from the *Indica* inform us that Megasthenes, while going to Pataliputra, had crossed the confluence of the Ganga and the Yamuna.[12] The Buddhist work *Majjhima Nikaya* also mentions Prayag as a holy place in the chapter titled 'Vetthupama Sutta' ('the Simile of the Cloth').[13]

A part of the larger *Sutta Pitaka*, the *Majjhima Nikaya*, composed between the second century BCE and the second century CE, notes that while giving a discourse on inner cleanliness in the Jetavana Vihara in Sravasti, the Buddha was asked by a Brahmin named Sundarika Bhardwaj why he went to the Bahuka River (Rapti River) to bathe. The Buddha in turn asked, 'what can the Bahuka River do?' The Brahmin's reply was that the river, according to many, liberated one's soul and washed away one's sins. The Buddha, in reply, recited a poem that went like this:

> Bahuka and Adhikakka
> Gaya and Sundarika too,
> [Prayag] and [Saraswati],
> And the stream Bahumati—
> A fool may there forever bathe
> Yet will not purify dark deeds.
>
> What can the Sundarika bring to pass?
> What the [Prayag]? What the Bahuka?

They cannot purify an evil-doer,
A man who has done cruel and brutal deeds.[14]

The poem recited by the Buddha was primarily talking about holy rivers, in which he used Prayag as a synecdoche for the Ganga. Needless to state that the Ganga finds several mentions in the Buddhist canon, and Prayag, for the first time, in the *Majjhima Nikaya*. The reverence the place commanded during the lifetime of the Buddha is undoubted, but at what point of time the grand melas began to be held on the confluence cannot be said for certain.

The Sanctity of the Sangam since Ancient Times as Attested to by the Ashokan Pillar

Over the centuries, being continuously inhabited, Prayagraj has lost the vestiges of its past. The presence of an Ashokan pillar inside the Allahabad Fort at the confluence testifies to the importance that even Ashoka attributed to the spot. It should be noted that there already exists another Ashokan pillar at Kausambi, without any edict, but with some undeciphered inscriptions in the shell script of the Gupta times.

However, the presence of the Ashokan pillar inside Akbar's fort on the sangam testifies to the ancient nature of the gathering there, which the Mauryan emperor utilized to spread certain messages relating to dharma. The erection of the pillar there was in fact a very sensible act, as this confluence attracted pilgrims from all religions and had quite a gathering throughout the year. Compare this to today's advertising hoardings and their placement above crowded squares. For Ashoka, who was passionate about having scribes scribbling 'dharmic' instructions on pillars and boulders, Prayagraj was the best choice for a site for one of his pillars and the edicts on it, as this would have been the most visible one among all his inscriptions.

Historians argue that the pillar originally belonged to Kausambi and was brought to Prayagraj by some monarch, most probably Samudragupta or Firuz Shah Tughlaq, as suggested by Cunningham.[15]

Due to this hypothesis, the pillar is also called the Allahabad Kausambi Pillar. Because of a mention of Kausambi on one of Ashoka's edicts on the polished Chunar sandstone shaft, some historians attribute the pillar's original place of erection to Kausambi. The 35-foot (the total length of the pillar is 42 feet 7 inches) tall column has on it a schism edict that warns the monks of Kausambi not to attempt to split the *sangha*, on the threat of expulsion.[16]

The attempted schism in the Buddhist order that took place at Kausambi is also mentioned in the *Majjhima Nikaya*, occurring first during the lifetime of the Buddha, when he was residing in the Ghositarama Monastery of Kausambi.[17] We are not certain whether another schism took place during the reign of Ashoka, but an engraving on a pillar 50 km away from Kausambi, warning against the possibility of such an event occurring, tells us that it most probably did happen. Apart from this, Ashoka had seven other edicts engraved there, including an engraving from his second queen Kaluvaki, the mother of his son Tivala.[18] The number of Ashokan edicts on the pillar at the sangam that saw a considerable gathering of pilgrims on certain days of the year tells us that the pillar was originally erected there and not transported from anywhere else.

Through the detailed study of history, Cunningham's hypotheses about the pillar being moved by Firuz Shah Tughlaq were proved wrong. There are several other factors proving that the original location of the pillar was Prayagraj. The first is logistical; transporting such a heavy stone monolith from Chunar via the riverine route would have been extremely difficult. Prayag comes before Kausambi on the route from Chunar, which is where the monolith originated. The approximate distance between the two places is 170 km by boat. Kausambi is a further 60 km from there if one took the riverine route. We have detailed logistical information of the relocation of two Ashokan pillars from Topra and Meerut to Delhi, done by Firuz Shah Tughlaq in 1356 CE.[19] Such an endeavour during the fourteenth century CE was Herculean enough to merit mention in the *Tarikh-i-Firoz Shahi* of Shams Siraj Afif. If at all Firoz Shah had attempted another such endeavour, it would have been written about by his chroniclers. The very absence of such a mention negates any hand the Delhi sultan might have had in the column's transfer.

Apart from the Ashokan inscription, the pillar also has numerous other engravings from later ages, studying which gives us clues about the pillar's original location. The second important engraving on it was posthumously dedicated to Samudragupta, the powerful Gupta monarch who ruled a vast tract of the subcontinent between 335 and 375 CE. The engraving was commissioned during the reign of Samudragupta's heir Chandragupta by a minister of justice named Harisena.[20] The inscription begins by stating that the column was erected like an arm of the earth. This is indicative of the state of the monolith, which clearly notes that the pillar was made to stand there, possibly from a lying position. Had it been transported from Kausambi, some indication of it would be in the inscription.

Another clue to the pillar's fallen state is the scribbles left by pilgrims in early Gupta script, done in a vertical manner.[21] These engravings predate Harisena's prasasti for Emperor Samudragupta. Had the pillar been standing, it would have been impossible to carve such vertical scribbles on it.

The third important inscription on the pillar belongs to Akbar's minister Birbal, the son of Gangadas, who noted that in the month of Magh (November–December) in 1575 CE he had visited Prayagraj, the chief of holy places, and successfully completed his religious obligations.[22] He was there to participate in the Kumbh Mela, which was then called the Magh Mela. This inscription proves that the pillar stood in situ before Akbar built the fort on the sangam or Jahangir carved his inscription on it, which is the fourth important inscription. Well, so much for the inscriptions, which I was deprived of seeing as I was not allowed entry by the military sentry to the area where this lofty column stands.

The Account of Hieun Tsang

Having discussed the Ashokan pillar at the chief of all sangams at length, let us now see if the place had any temples. The absence of ancient temples in such an important holy site is rather glaring. This confluence of the Yamuna with the Ganga over millennia was and is still used as a sacred place for bathing rituals. According to popular belief, the river Saraswati also joined the confluence as an invisible entity. The legend behind this present non-existent Saraswati is not utterly concocted but has an element of truth to it, which I will come to later in the chapter.

Since ancient times, Prayagraj had existed as a kingdom by itself, sometimes independently but mostly under the subjugation of more powerful rulers. Well before Ashokan and Gupta times, Prayagraj was a part of the ancient kingdom of Prathistana, ruled by the legendary Pururava.[23] The *Harivamsa* informs us that King Pururava, who was the son of King Buddha, '...ruled over the sacred province of Prayag, so highly spoken of by the great Rishis.'[24] The *Harivamsa*, being one of the earliest Puranas, composed in the second or first century BCE, also mentions that the capital of Prayag was Pratisthana.[25]

An urban sprawl called Jhusi on the left bank of the Ganga opposite the sangam was ancient Pratisthana. Archaeological excavations on the mound called the Ulta Quila (Opposite Fort) or the fort of Haribong Raja at Jhusi have revealed a city that dates back to the sixth century BCE. This archaeological site has an ancient well believed to have been excavated by Emperor Samudragupta. At present, Jhusi is a confusing maze of lanes and by-lanes that run between houses. In earlier times, though, this was an important urban centre due to its strategic location and was somewhat the go-to destination for the people of ancient Bhita and Kausambi on the Yamuna.

One of the last phases of its grandeur was during the Gurjara-Pratihara rule, when it was being controlled from the then capital of Aryavarta at Kannauj. The Jhusi copper plate inscription of the Gurjara-Pratihara ruler Trilochanpal, dated to 1027 CE, was unearthed in Jhusi. The inscription states that Trilochanpal, being in residence on the banks of the Ganga near Prayagraj and after having bathed in the river and worshipped Shiva, informed the officers, mahatmas, and other inhabitants of the Lebhundaka village in Asurbhaka district about the donation of said village to 6,000 Brahmins, who were residents of Pratisthana (Jhusi).[26]

It is difficult to visualize a place from mentions in grants given by monarchs. However, travelogues of ancient pilgrims do help us piece together the story of any place, particularly one as important as Prayag, and for that, let us go back in history to the seventh century CE and read the memoirs of Hieun Tsang. Strangely, Fa Hien, who visited Kausambi from Sarnath 200 years earlier, has not written anything about Prayag, despite the fact that such an important place as this fell en route.

Hieun Tsang's Description of Prayagraj, the Akshay Vat, and the Kumbh Mela

Hieun Tsang gives a rather detailed account of the sangam in his *Si-Yu-Ki*, writing that the capital of the country of Prayagraj lies between two branches of the river. The people there '... love learning, and are very much given to heresy. There are two *sangharamas* [monasteries] with a few followers, who belong to the Little Vehicle. There are several Deva temples; the number of heretics is very great.'[27] To the southwest of Prayag was a champak grove, inside which was a stupa built by Ashoka. The pilgrim reports that this structure had sunk into the ground, yet it was still about 100 feet in height. Beside it were several stupas, one of which enshrined the hair and nails of the Buddha. Close by was an old monastery in which a South Indian monk named Deva had written a shastra.

The pilgrim also informs us about the presence of a tall temple with beautiful ornamentation. The sanctity of the place was such that if a man donated a coin there, he would accrue religious merit to the power of a thousand.

The presence of temples in Prayag as attested to by the Chinese pilgrim is further confirmed by the Tibetan Lama Taranatha's *History of Buddhism in India*. He writes that during the reign of the Palas in Bengal, particularly Mahipala, a Buddhist monk named Acharya

Bhago had built a big temple dedicated to the Buddha at Prayagraj and another in Karnataka.[28]

Another interesting aspect of the place noted by Hieun Tsang was that people found it meritorious to die at Prayagraj, a practice that was carried out even during British times. Before the hall of the ornamented temple was 'a great tree with spreading boughs and branches'.[29] This was the ancient Akshay Vat banyan tree of Prayagraj, from whose branches pilgrims often plunged to death. The pilgrim writes that the grisly practice of ritualistic suicide took place because of a demon who resided on the tree; the bones of his victims could be seen to the right and the left of it, and from 'very early days till now this false custom [had] been practised'.[30] He also notes the practice of ritualistic suicide that pilgrims committed at Prayagraj by drowning in the Ganga, hoping to be reborn in heaven.

The ancient tree of Prayagraj has the story of the first Tirthankara of the Jains, Adinatha, meditating under it. The twelfth century CE Kashmiri historian Kalhan in his *Rajatarangini* also mentions this banyan tree in association with the birth of King Ranaditya of Kashmir.[31]

Hieun Tsang's description of the Kumbh Mela at Prayag is invaluable. Harsha's camp was pitched on the north bank of the Ganga, corresponding to the highland on which the fort now stands. The camp of his ally from Kamrupa, Bhaskarvarman, was where Jhusi is, and the king of Malwa Dhruvabhatta's camp was where Arail is situated. He writes:

> To the east of the capital, between the two confluences of the river, for the space of 10 li or so, the ground is pleasant and upland. The whole is covered with a fine sand. From old time till now, the kings and noble families, whenever they had occasion to distribute their gifts in charity, ever came to this place, and here give away their goods; hence it is called *the great charity enclosure*. At the present time Siladitya-raja [Harshavardhan], after the example of his

ancestors, distributes here in one day the accumulated wealth of five years. Having collected in this space of the *charity enclosure* immense piles of wealth and jewels, on the first day he adorns in a very sumptuous way a statue of Buddha, and then offers to it the most costly jewels. Afterwards he offers his charity to the residentiary priests; afterwards to the priests (*from a distance*) who are present; afterwards to the men of distinguished talent; afterwards to the heretics who live in the place, following the ways of the world; and lastly, to the widows and bereaved, orphans and desolate, poor and mendicants.[32]

He furthermore writes that the benevolence of Harsha was to such a degree that the king, after having exhausted his wealth, gave away his personal adornments like his diadem and necklaces. Immediately after this, his vassals made their tributes to him, replenishing the depleted treasury. The sequence of events given by Hieun Tsang is repeated by his disciple Hwui Li but with embellishments, adding that after having given away everything, Harsha begged his sister for a garment, wearing which he offered prayers to the Buddha.[33] From Hwui Li's biography of Hieun Tsang, we know that he had presided over a Buddhist conference in Prayagraj, where a humongous mass of people, close to 5 lakh, had gathered.[34]

Oddly, Hieun Tsang has omitted mentioning the Ashokan pillar. This is rather strange, because the pilgrim has not failed to tell us about monoliths wherever he found one. However, he does mention a pillar at Prayag that he saw in the middle of the river. Pilgrims had raised a high column there, atop which some ascetics practised the rite of bidding goodbye to the sun by balancing on it with one hand and a leg.[35]

A question that arises is that the biography of Harsha by Bana mentions nothing of the sort described by the pilgrim, except a stray reference to Prayagraj as the place where the Ganga and the Yamuna meet.[36] Well, the *Harshacharita* is a eulogistic history of Harsha before he became an emperor. The narrative had to be limited to the span of the first eighteen years of Harsha's life, from the time of the emperor's birth till the rescue of his sister after the deaths of her husband and their elder brother, in that order.

The Corroboration of Hieun Tsang's Mention of Ritualistic Suicide in the Sangam

Several inscriptions and latter-day chroniclers have noted the ritualistic suicides at Prayagraj. From those engravings it appears that it was not an unusual practice to give up one's life voluntarily when one felt that one had nothing to contribute to society at large.[37]

The first epigraphic mention of ritualistic suicide at the sangam comes from the Aphsad stone inscription of Adityasena, dated on palaeographic as well as historic grounds to the seventh century CE. King Adityasena belonged to the line of lesser Guptas, who ruled parts of Bihar under the hegemony of the Maukharis and Harshavardhan. The inscription informs us that Adityasena's great-great-grandfather Kumaragupta, after his defeat at the hands of the Maukhari king Isanavarman, committed suicide at Prayagraj by immolating himself in a pyre on the banks of the Ganga.[38] The stone inscription of Chandela ruler Dhanga dated to 1001–02 CE, discovered in the Vishwanath Temple of Khajuraho, informs us that after a long and eventful reign, King Dhanga immersed himself in the sangam at Prayagraj, committing ritualistic suicide.[39] The Khairha Plates of Kalachuri ruler Yashahkarna (1070–1123) state that his grandfather Gangeyadeva, the father of the famous Kalachuri Karnadeva, had committed ritualistic suicide alongside his hundred wives below the Akshay Vat tree.[40]

Al Biruni, who arrived in the subcontinent with the army from Ghazni in the eleventh century CE, notes in his *Kitab-Al-Hind* that between Kannauj and the ancient Akshay Vat banyan, on the confluence of the Ganga and the Yamuna, there were several urban centres like Jajamau (Kanpur), Abhapuri, Kuraha (Kara/Kade) and Barhamshil. He further adds that Prayagraj was '…where the Hindus torment[ed] themselves with various kinds of tortures, which are described in the books about religious sects.'[41]

The cantankerous Badauni also notes the suicides, writing, 'The infidels consider this a holy place, and with a desire to obtain the rewards which are promised in their creed, of which transmigration is one of the most prominent features, they submit themselves to all kinds of tortures. Some place their brainless heads under saws, others split their deceitful tongues in two, others enter Hell by casting themselves down into the deep river from the top of a high tree...'[42]

Upheavals in the Province of Prayagraj

Between the seventh and ninth centuries CE, the kingdom of Prayag was tossed between different monarchs, starting with Yasovarman of Kannauj, Lalitaditya Muktapida of Kashmir, the Palas of Bengal, and the Gurjara-Pratiharas, who eventually held the province for the longest duration, till it was conquered from its last nominal monarch Yashpal by the powerful Chandela monarch Dhanga.[43]

After his plunder of Kannauj in 1018 CE, Mahmud of Ghazni marched east, destroying and pillaging urban and religious centres as far as Banaras. Prayag, being en route to Banaras, fell like other cities, its temples bearing the brunt of the iconoclast's hammer strokes. In the wake of Ghazni's destruction rose the Gahadavala Dynasty, who, within fifty years, managed to make themselves the masters of the Ganga–Yamuna Doab. However, the reign of the Gahadavalas was soon eclipsed by the arrival of Muhammad Ghori in 1192 CE, after which the history of the subcontinent took a destructive turn, mimicking the torrent of a long-suppressed river that bursts out of its banks to inundate everything in its path. The destruction of ancient temples resplendent with sculptures commenced like falling hail over a field of ripe paddy. Prayagraj, being at the heart of the route that connected the west to the east of India, was levelled to the ground to such an extent that not a single ancient edifice remains to connect its past to the present, except the Ashokan pillar.

It was primarily due to this that when Babur reached Prayagraj on 8 March 1528 CE, he merely wrote, 'We reached the meeting of the waters of Gang and Jun [Ganga and Yamuna] at the Evening Prayer, had the boat drawn to the flag side, and got to camp at 1 watch, 4 *garis* (10:30p.m.).'[44] He was camped at the confluence for the next two days and then moved on to Bihar. Had there been anything worthy of note like a temple or the ruins of one, his keen eyes would not have missed it.

In 1565 CE, Ali Quli the Uzbeg, also known as Khan Zaman, who had served under Humayun, rebelled, compelling Akbar to send a strong force led by Asaf Khan and besiege the bastion of Kara.[45] Two years later, Khan Zaman rebelled once again. In the battle fought at the village of Mankarwal, a dependency of Jhusi and Prayagraj, Ali Quli was defeated and killed, being crushed under the foot of an elephant named Narsing.[46]

Prayagraj as Allahabad, Its Fort and the Saraswati

The next episode in the history of Prayagraj begins with Akbar laying the foundation of a fort at the confluence in 1574 CE.[47] He then renamed Prayagraj 'Allahabad', or 'the city of God'. The Allahabad Fort at the sangam was built around the ancient Akshay Vat tree. Regarding this event, Badauni informs us that on his journey to conquer Bengal, Akbar had reached Prayagraj, where he camped. There, he writes, did the emperor lay the foundation of a great fort and change the name of the city to Allahabad.[48]

Abul Fazal, unlike Badauni's vituperative criticism of Hindu rituals pertaining to self-mortification and death, simply states in the *Ain-i-Akbari* that Akbar changed the name of the place and constructed a grand fort where the Ganga, Yamuna and the invisible Saraswati meet. He added that the Hindus regard this confluence as the 'king of shrines'.[49] The fort, being the largest built by the great Mughal, took a considerable number of years to construct, during the course of which Akbar would visit the confluence and reside in the yet-to-be-completed bastion.

Badauni notes that in the year 1583 CE, while on a pleasure cruise on the Yamuna, Akbar reached his fort, where he resided for four months. While he was at Allahabad, Birbal and Zain Khan Koka had gone to Chauragarh/Panna to receive the homage of the Baghel king Raja Ramchandra Bhatta. Birbal was earlier in the employment of this king and so was the famed singer Tansen. During his stay in Allahabad, several courtiers began building grand palaces inside the fort.[50]

In conjunction with the building of the fort, I believe that the stones from the destroyed temples at the sangam were used in the bastion's construction. As discussed in the beginning of the chapter, several ancient temples had existed at Prayagraj and the conspicuous absence of any of their remains obviously directs me to this conclusion. How else can one account for the complete absence of any temple remains in Prayagraj, the likes of which were found aplenty in Delhi, Mathura, Agra, Kannauj, Kara, Sarnath, Banaras, and almost every other ancient place?

The Earliest Accounts of Prayagraj by European Travellers

It appears that even during the reign of Jahangir, the construction of the fort was not completed, as reported by English merchant William Finch, who passed through Allahabad in 1610 CE. He reports that the place was formerly known as Prayag and was one of the wonders of the east. Several Muslim kings had failed in their attempts to build a fort on the confluence, except Akbar, whose structure was still being constructed forty years after its foundation. He also notes that when Prince Salim/Jahangir rebelled against his father Akbar, he used the bastion as his stronghold. It was to Allahabad that Bir Singh Bundela had sent the severed head of Abul Fazal on the orders of Jahangir in 1602 CE.[51]

While describing the red sandstone bastion, Finch verily mentions the Ashokan pillar that stood inside it, which he thought was erected by Alexander. He also gave detailed accounts of several multi-storey palaces and the main darbar, close to which were several temples below an arched vault. Near this complex of buildings, now called the Patalpuri Mandir, was the Akshay Vat banyan, which '...the Indians call the tree of life ([being] a wild Indian [fig] tree), for that it could never [be] destroyed by the Potan [Muslim] kings and this man's ancestors (Jahangir's), which have sought to [do] it by all means, stocking it up and sifting the very earth under it to gather forth the sprigs; it still springing [again], insomuch that this king lets it alone, seeking to cherish it.'[52] By the time Finch passed through Allahabad, two more Mughal forts had been built, one at Jhusi and the other at Arail.[53]

Finch was not the first English traveller to cross Prayagraj. Ralf Fitch was there between the years 1583 and 1591 CE. His report of Prayag is brief, concentrating on describing the naked sadhus that he saw there. Of this lot, one particular mendicant caught his attention due to the sheer size of his body, who Fitz writes '...was a monster among the rest'.[54]

The famous English traveller Thomas Coryat, in a letter written from Agra in 1616 CE, stated that he was planning to visit a fair on the banks of the Ganga to see the gathering of people on the confluence. It is uncertain whether he was writing about Haridwar or Prayag when he wrote:

> ...[four] hundred thousand people go thither of purpose to bathe and shave themselves in the river, and to sacrifice a world of gold to the same river, partly in stamped [money], and partly in massy great [lumps] and wedges, throwing it into the river as a sacrifice, and doing other strange ceremonies most worthy the observation. Such a notable spectacle it is, that no part of all Asia, neither this which is called the Great Asia nor the Lesser, which is now called [Anatolia], the like is to be seen. This [show do] they make once every [year], coming thither from places almost a thousand miles off, and honour their river as their God, Creator, and Saviour...[55]

The mention of the multitudes does tell me that he was most likely referring to Prayagraj and not Haridwar. In that letter, he also wrote that after his visit to the Ganga, he would visit Lahore, which would be a journey of twenty days. Coryat had walked all the way to India from Aleppo and preferred the leg over wheeled traffic; so, I guess he was not referring to Haridwar, from which Lahore is a week's journey on foot.

On 7 December 1665 CE, the French gem merchant Tavernier reached Allahabad from Agra. He was on his way to Bengal in the company of the Frenchman Bernier, the royal physician of Aurangzeb, and a merchant named Racheport.[56] Close to Prayaraj, Tavernier reports that the Dutch had a factory on the banks of the Ganga and never drank the water of the river unless it was boiled. On reaching the river, the three musketeers from France drank a glass of wine each mixed with the Ganga water, which caused them to fall ill. He however states that the royal household only drank the water of the Ganga, noting that everyday there was a constant stream of camels, '…which [did] nothing else but fetch the water from the Ganges'.[57] His description of Prayagraj is brief, mentioning that on the confluence existed the fort with a double ditch and a large town outside it.

Manucci's Account of the Saraswati at the Sangam

Of the few accounts of Prayagraj we get from foreigners, Manucci's is the most important. Like the three Frenchmen who were his contemporaries, the Venetian too reached Prayagraj from Agra en route to Bengal. Accompanying him were two fugitive Jesuits. After travelling for 12 days, they reached Allahabad. He begins by describing Akbar's fort on the confluence. He then informs us that during his stay there, a physician named Hakim Mumin, who treated Governor Bahadur Khan, invited him for dinner on the ramparts of the fort. From there he observed a clear stream flowing from the rocks above which the fort wall stood. I quote Manucci:

> …petty stream with blue waters, which is called Tirt (Tirth); it goes by a straight course, like a tongue, between the two rivers until it flows into them. Just as if the said two rivers held those waters in respect, on account of their birthplace,

Kashmir: The once gigantic Avantiswami temple of Awantipora. A dome of a modern mosque can be seen in the background.

The Martand Sun Temple, Khribal, Kashmir. Presently this ruin is a centre for local picnickers who throng the protected site during the Eid celebrations.

The Martand Sun Temple, Khribal, Kashmir. The temple has numerous large sculptures, and each one bears the marks of the ravages it has sustained over the ages. In fact, if these sculptures could speak, then they would narrate a tale so filled with sorrow that no pen of any chronicler could whitewash Kashmir's history.

Kumbh Mela at Haridwar. The photo is of Har Ki Pauri bathing ghat.

Haridwar: The present Kaliyar Dargah.

Ancient potsherds from Mathura's Gosna Tila mound.

Northern Black Polished Ware (NBPW) pottery pieces from Mathura's Gosna Tila mound.

The Madan Mohan temple on the ancient Dwadashaditya Tila of Vrindavan.

A colossal headless image of Vima Kadphises, the father of Emperor Kanishka, now in the Mathura Museum.

The famous life-size headless statue of Emperor Kanishka holding a royal mace and a sword and wearing a fashionable lower dress, while his upper body is left bare bearing his corpulent stomach. The sculpture is in the Mathura Museum.

A Kushan-period Ekmukha Shiva Linga in the Mathura Museum. During the first–second centuries CE, the third eye of Shiva was depicted in the horizontal manner as seen on the image, unlike later-day depictions.

Life-size stone head of a Kushan man discovered in Mathura, on display at the Mathura Museum.

Barsana, the birthplace of Radha Rani. Seen on the hill is the Radha Rani temple.

Parking my bike beside the Yamuna at the Kaliya Ghat of Vrindavan.

A Buddha head found in Kannauj by the guard of the Kannauj Museum. I was shown this small sculpture carved out of spotted red sandstone of Mathura by the curator, who had not yet displayed it as an exhibit as there were some delays due to red tapism.

A Nawabi-period mosque between Ayodhya and Faizabad.

The Ram Ki Paidi Ghat of Ayodhya on the palaeochannel of the Sarayu.

A Nawabi-period gate between Ayodhya and Faizabad.

The Sangam, where the Yamuna meets the Ganga, and where a spring that emerged out of the rocks from below the Allahabad Fort once flowed into. That streamlet was believed to be the Saraswati.

Vendors selling abir and some ayurvedic medicinal stuff near the Sangam at Prayagraj.

Prayagraj: Ramparts of Akbar's fort by the Sangam.

The Ratneshwar Mahadev Temple, also called the leaning temple of Banaras, at the famous Manikarnika Ghat of Banaras.

Feeding seagulls on the Ganga at Banaras. It is rather surprising that these sea-dwelling birds have made the eternal city their home during the winters.

The Kardameshwar Mandir, which I consider the luckiest temple of Banaras to survive destruction at the hands of iconoclasts.

The Kardameshwar Mandir of Banaras.

The Nepali Temple of Banaras.

Exquisite wooden sculptures atop the main door of the Nepali Temple of Banaras.

Buddhist tourists from Southeast Asia at the Dhamek Stupa of Sarnath.

The Chaukhandi Stupa of Sarnath, which has a hexagonal tower built during the Mughal times.

The ancient Deer Park monastery complex of Sarnath. The Dhamek Stupa can be seen in the background.

Kashmir: The once gigantic Avantiswami temple of Awantipora. A dome of a modern mosque can be seen in the background.

The Martand Sun Temple, Khribal, Kashmir. Presently this ruin is a centre for local picnickers who throng the protected site during the Eid celebrations.

The Martand Sun Temple, Khribal, Kashmir. The temple has numerous large sculptures, and each one bears the marks of the ravages it has sustained over the ages. In fact, if these sculptures could speak, then they would narrate a tale so filled with sorrow that no pen of any chronicler could whitewash Kashmir's history.

Kumbh Mela at Haridwar. The photo is of Har Ki Pauri bathing ghat.

Haridwar: The present Kaliyar Dargah.

Ancient potsherds from Mathura's Gosna Tila mound.

Northern Black Polished Ware (NBPW) pottery pieces from Mathura's Gosna Tila mound.

The Madan Mohan temple on the ancient Dwadashaditya Tila of Vrindavan.

A colossal headless image of Vima Kadphises, the father of Emperor Kanishka, now in the Mathura Museum.

The famous life-size headless statue of Emperor Kanishka holding a royal mace and a sword and wearing a fashionable lower dress, while his upper body is left bare bearing his corpulent stomach. The sculpture is in the Mathura Museum.

A Kushan-period Ekmukha Shiva Linga in the Mathura Museum. During the first–second centuries CE, the third eye of Shiva was depicted in the horizontal manner as seen on the image, unlike later-day depictions.

Life-size stone head of a Kushan man discovered in Mathura, on display at the Mathura Museum.

Barsana, the birthplace of Radha Rani. Seen on the hill is the Radha Rani temple.

Parking my bike beside the Yamuna at the Kaliya Ghat of Vrindavan.

A Buddha head found in Kannauj by the guard of the Kannauj Museum. I was shown this small sculpture carved out of spotted red sandstone of Mathura by the curator, who had not yet displayed it as an exhibit as there were some delays due to red tapism.

A Nawabi-period mosque between Ayodhya and Faizabad.

The Ram Ki Paidi Ghat of Ayodhya on the palaeochannel of the Sarayu.

A Nawabi-period gate between Ayodhya and Faizabad.

The Sangam, where the Yamuna meets the Ganga, and where a spring that emerged out of the rocks from below the Allahabad Fort once flowed into. That streamlet was believed to be the Saraswati.

Vendors selling abir and some ayurvedic medicinal stuff near the Sangam at Prayagraj.

Prayagraj: Ramparts of Akbar's fort by the Sangam.

The Ratneshwar Mahadev Temple, also called the leaning temple of Banaras, at the famous Manikarnika Ghat of Banaras.

Feeding seagulls on the Ganga at Banaras. It is rather surprising that these sea-dwelling birds have made the eternal city their home during the winters.

The Kardameshwar Mandir, which I consider the luckiest temple of Banaras to survive destruction at the hands of iconoclasts.

The Kardameshwar Mandir of Banaras.

The Nepali Temple of Banaras.

Exquisite wooden sculptures atop the main door of the Nepali Temple of Banaras.

Buddhist tourists from Southeast Asia at the Dhamek Stupa of Sarnath.

The Chaukhandi Stupa of Sarnath, which has a hexagonal tower built during the Mughal times.

The ancient Deer Park monastery complex of Sarnath. The Dhamek Stupa can be seen in the background.

they allow them to pass down for a long distance without their colour being modified. Thus, you can plainly see the water of this streamlet flowing in the middle of the waters of the two rivers, Ganges and Jamnah.[58]

He also noted that every five years a grand bathing festival happened at the confluence, which the Muslim kings permitted after a personal tax of six and a quarter rupees was levied from the pilgrims. The gathering, he wrote, was so multitudinous that many pilgrims succumbed to stampedes, which was not lamented by their relations but boasted about, as those who passed on went 'in grace and holiness'.[59]

Telltale signs of this stream can still be seen when looking at the sangam via Google Earth imagery. At present, the Ganga has shifted further away from the fort, forming a flat plain over which the Kumbh takes place. Here, a question arises: did Akbar deliberately build the fort over the 'Saraswati' stream? I think not, because if Akbar had intentionally tried to stop the flow of the Saraswati, he would have blocked the channel, or diverted its flow. Also, he could have cut down the Akshay Vat inside the fort, which was done by his son Jahangir. According to historian Jadunath Sarkar, the Akshay Vat was cut down by Jahangir and a red-hot cauldron was hammered to its stump. Within a year of this deed, the tree sprang back to life.[60]

Prayagraj Post the Mughals and the Many Assaults It Suffered

In 1739 CE, Prayagraj was ravaged by Raghoji Bhonsle, when he raided the city and carried off an immense booty. The fort also fell, and its deputy governor Suja Khan was killed in the raid.[61] Around this time, the Jesuit missionary Joseph Tieffenthaler visited Allahabad and documented the fort and its Ashokan pillar, illustrating its capital as a sphere topped with a cone.[62]

Prayagraj, just forty years after the death of Aurangzeb in 1707 CE, had become a part of the territory governed by Nawab

Shuja-ud-Daula of Awadh. The lesser Mughal Ahmad Shah had transferred the region to the nawab in 1748 CE, after appointing him as the prime minister of the crumbling Mughal Empire.

The rise of the Shia Shuja-ud-Daula in that decade was disliked by the Sunni Afghan factions in the Mughal court. Due to Shuja-ud-Daula's high-handed act of seizing Farrukhabad from the Bangash Afghans, its nawab, Ahmad Khan Bangash, led an uprising against Awadh. During the progress of this turmoil, Prayagraj was besieged by the Bangash Afghans in 1751 CE, which compelled the deputy governor of the city, Ali Quli, to barricade his troops inside the Allahabad Fort and await bombardment.

The Bangash Afghans began the bombardment of the fort from the Ulta Quila mound across the Ganga. Intermittently, the besieging Afghans would foray into unprotected Allahabad and raid houses for plunder and carry off their women. This went on for three months, with the total number of women taken adding up to 4,000 souls, who were systematically raped by the ruthless Bangashes. The Afghans had set fire to the city from Khuldabad to the fort, and only spared the house of Sheikh Muhammad Allahabadi and the Afghan quarter of Daryabad.[63]

The Martial Spirit of the Dasnamis Exhibited at Prayagraj

The fort held its ground during the Afghan siege, but sat mute to the suffering of those who had nowhere to escape. At this juncture in the winter of 1751 CE, there descended a mass of Dasnami Sanyasis for the ritual bathing festival on the sangam.[64] It is uncertain how many Naga Sadhus had reached Prayag, but one estimate puts it close to 5,000.[65] The arrival of these fierce ash-smeared sword-wielding mendicants brought about a respite from the bombardment. These Nagas were led by Rajendra Giri, who was compelled by the Maratha governor of Bundelkhand, Naro Shankar, to leave his fort at Moth near Jhansi and go elsewhere.[66] Since the time for the Sankranti festival was at hand, Rajendra Giri had decided to shift east to the sangam, which was 350 km away from Moth. As usual, they set up camp on the sand bank and, after realizing the burning issue at hand and the misery faced by the residents of Prayagraj, readied themselves to aid the besieged. This was a welcome move for the harried forces of Shuja-ud-Daula.

Unbelievable feats of courage were shown by the Naga Sadhus who, refusing to don armour, stood in open ground, whilst cannon balls whizzed overhead. Rajendra Giri and many other monks on horseback began to raid the Afghan camps and harass them to such an extent that Ahmad Khan Bangash decided to intensify the siege by starving the occupants of the fort through an embargo. He deputed his ally Raja Prithvipat and Mahmud Khan to occupy Arail on the southern bank of the Yamuna.

It was from Arail that the fort was being supplied with food. This two-pronged attack was countered by Rajendra Giri, who now drew out in battle formation and lined his monks between the Allahabad fort and the city, while the besieged forces of the Nawab of Awadh prepared to face the onslaught from Arail on the confluence. This defensive measure had its effect, deterring against all odds the main body of the Bangash cavalry from attacking the fort.

While the stalemate continued, Nawab Shuja-ud-Daula, after crushing the Bangash army posted in Koil (Aligarh), began marching for Farrukhabad, the Bangash capital. This news compelled the Bangash Nawab to lift the siege and rush to the defence of his home, effectively turning himself into a fugitive. In the meantime, his rabid army of rapists and mercenaries turned tail and showed a clean pair of heels.

It was due to the selfless sacrifice of the Dasnamis that Prayagraj was saved from total obliteration. Another aspect to be considered is that after the defeat of the Bangash Afghans at Allahabad, Shuja-ud-Daula induced Rajendra Giri and his monks to join his army and fight on his behalf.

Within six years of this incident, the British gained paramountcy in Bengal in 1757 CE, drawing a new equation on the geopolitical board of the subcontinent.

Prayagraj and the English

In 1758 CE, the ambitious Mughal emperor Shah Alam II shifted to the Allahabad Fort under the protection of Nawab Shuja-ud-Daula, and lived at Prayagraj for four years till he was taken to Delhi. On 27 October 1764 CE, the British decimated the combined armies of Bengal's Nawab Mir Qasim, Shuja-ud-Daula and Shah Alam at Buxar. This humiliating defeat of the three largest native forces made the English the undisputed masters of the entire stretch of the Gangetic Plains, starting from the east till Prayagraj in the west.

Fleeing Buxar, Shuja-ud-Daula reached Banaras, and from there, he went to the fort in Prayagraj. He prepared for a long siege and awaited his English pursuers with 150 pieces of artillery manned by close to 2,000 men. After an intense bombardment of the bastion, the Nawab was compelled to leave the city and shift to Jajamau in Kanpur. The fort was then handed over to the British by Deputy Governor Ali Beg Khan.[67]

At Jajamau, Shuja-ud-Daula was defeated once again and finally surrendered. Against a hefty war indemnity, Shuja-ud-Daula was allowed to retain his dominion, except Kara, Kora and Prayagraj, which were handed over to Shah Alam, who, instead of living in the fort, shifted to the Khusro Bagh, while the English troops occupied the bastion.

The treaty of Allahabad, signed between Shah Alam and the British on 12 August 1765, handed the Allahabad Fort over to the East India Company, who maintained a contingent there, being paid for by the Nawab of Awadh under the terms of the Subsidiary Alliance. The English, unwilling to administer the province directly, sold the revenue rights to Shuja-ud-Daula for 50 lakh.

Later English Accounts of the City

In 1783 CE, the artist William Hodges arrived in the city, travelling from Kolkata on a palanquin.[68] He begins his description of the place with his usual fervour, discussing the sanctity of the confluence and the fort on it, which was then in ruins. He then goes on to describe its Agra

Gate, the expanse of the fort as a supersized bastion requiring many defenders, and a small tomb of an English officer, the engraving on whose grave he was unable to read. Every other structure in the fort was a heap of ruins. Outside its walls was the town, if one could call a multitude of thatched huts urban dwellings, 'with scarcely a vestige of any considerable house remaining'.[69] The fort, he remarked, was now in the possession of Nawab Asaf-ud-Daulah of Awadh, which '...was for some time, the residence of the present Great Mogul, the unfortunate Shah Allum'.[70] After his stay in the city for three days, during which he completed several drawings, he moved on to Kanpur.

On 14 November 1801 CE, Awadh's Nawab Sadat Ali Khan ceded Allahabad to the British, who made the city an important military station and the headquarters of a civil district. It was after this that some of the buildings inside the fort were renovated while the rest were demolished, and European structures built to accommodate the army officers.

The Bishop of Kolkata, Rev. Reginald Heber, reached Allahabad in 1824 CE and got stuck there for ten days due to Diwali, when no blacksmith was available to shoe his newly purchased horse. In between the festivities, where he was in the audience of a Ramleela, he managed to administer to the spiritual needs of the new converts and convert only twenty natives.[71] Between his ecclesiastical endeavours, which, by their results, were probably less than half-hearted, he went around the city documenting its various structures and concluded that it never was a grand city.

Despite its fort, the Khushro Bagh tomb complex, and the Jama Masjid, the city was derogatorily called Fakirabad, the city of beggars, by the locals.[72] Heber writes that the Company-built Sadar Mufassil Adalat (court) with a thatched roof, established in line with the Sadar Diwani Adalat of Kolkata, had brought relief to the uneducated populace. Along with this, he adds a comment that, unpalatable as it is for any Bengali, held true at that time:

The necessity for such a special court had become very great. The remoteness of the [Sadar Diwani] had made appeals to it almost impossible, and very great extortion and oppression had been committed by the native agents of the inferior and local courts, sometimes with the connivance, but more often through the ignorance and inexperience of the junior magistrates and judges. They, when these provinces were placed under British governors, having been previously employed in Bengal and Bihar, naturally took their [Bengali] followers with them, a race regarded by the [Hindustanis] as no less foreigners than the English, and even more odious than Franks, from ancient prejudice, and from their national reputation of craft, covetousness, and cowardice. In fact, by one means or other, these [Bengalis] almost all acquired considerable landed property in a short time among them, and it has been the main business of the [Sader Mufassil Adalat], to review the titles to all property acquired since the English Government entered the [Doab]. In many instances they have succeeded in recovering all or part of extensive possessions to their rightful heirs, and the degree of confidence in the justice of their rulers, with which they have inspired the natives, is said to be very great.[73]

Through Heber's narrative, we are informed of the changes that took place inside the fort, beginning with:

...its lofty towers being pruned down into bastions and cavaliers, and its high stone rampart topped with turf parapets, and obscured by a green sloping glacis. It is still, however, a striking place, and its principal gate, surmounted by a dome, with a wide hall beneath surrounded by arcades and galleries, and ornamented with rude but glowing paintings, is the noblest entrance I ever saw to a place of arms. This has been, I think, injudiciously modernized without, after the Grecian or Italian style, but within, the high gothic arches and Saracenic paintings remain. The barracks are very handsome and neat, something like those of Fort William, which the interior disposition of the fort a good deal resembles. On one side, however, is a large range of buildings, still in the oriental style, and containing some noble vaulted rooms, chiefly occupied as officers' quarters, and looking down from a considerable height on the rapid stream and craggy banks of the Jumna.[74]

The Jama Masjid that stood on the banks of the Yamuna between the fort and the town had first been converted into a residence of the general of the Allahabad cantonment, and then converted to a hall, until Courtney Smith persuaded the government in Kolkata to restore it to its earlier status as a religious structure. When Heber was in Prayagraj, he reported this structure as he saw it, which today I am unable to locate in the city.

The Indophile Fanny Perks, staying in Allahabad in 1828 CE, noted in her memoir that the news of the death of Rev. Heber's successor Rev. Thomas James at the Sandheads was conveyed to the English residents of the city via 'telegraphic intelligence'.[75] In a tone dipped in humour, she observed that three more bishops were to be imported as their demand was so great, and that they should make bishops out of the clergy who had spent time in India, '...and not send out old men who [could not] stand the climate'.[76]

The First Steamer Arrives in Prayagraj

That very year, on 1 October 1828, Prayagraj received its first motorized means of transport, a steamer that, after chaffing upstream from Kolkata for twenty-six days, berthed near the fort on the banks of the Yamuna.[77] It was a spectacle for the natives, who gathered to marvel at the wonder of science.

The Great Sepoy Mutiny and the City

Prayagraj had it terrible during the Great Sepoy Mutiny of 1857. Bholanath Chandra, while visiting Allahabad a few years after the turmoil, wrote about the atrocities committed by the 'avenging' English in his book titled *The Travels of a Hindoo*:

One's blood still runs cold to remember the soul-harrowing and blood-freezing scenes that were witnessed in those days. There were those who had special reasons to have been anxious to show their rare qualification in administering dumb-headed justice. Scouring through the town and suburb, they caught all on whom they could lay their hands—porter or pedlar—shopkeeper or artisan, and hurrying them on through a mock-trial, made them dangle on the nearest tree. Near six thousand beings had been thus summarily disposed off and launched into eternity. Their corpses hanging by two and threes from branch and sign-post all over the town, speedily contributed to frighten down the country into submission and tranquillity. For three months eight dead-carts daily go their rounds from sunrise to sunset, to take down the corpses which hung at the cross-roads and marketplaces, poisoning the air of the city, and to throw their loathsome burden into the Ganges.[78]

Cunningham's Documentation of Prayagraj's Antiquities

Thirty-four years after the arrival of the first steamer to Allahabad and four years after the Great Mutiny of 1857, the great Alexander Cunningham undertook an expedition to document the ancient remains of North India. Prayag's antiquities, he noted, were the Akshay Vat inside the fort, the absence of the ancient remains described by Hieun Tsang, and the Ashokan pillar.

Interestingly, he gives us a sequence of events that happened with this ancient monolith that is a mute witness to every event that transpired there. After it was first erected by Ashoka, the pillar was brought down sometime in the third century BCE, as attested to by horizontal scribblings on it from that era, re-erected by Samudragupta or Harisena, the minister of Chandragupta, in the fourth century CE, and thrown down by Mahmud of Ghazni, a conclusion based on the absence of Pala records on it. It was raised again in the fifteenth century, when several dates starting with 1336 CE down to 1660 CE are scribbled on it. Once again, it was laid on the ground by General Kyd during the building of barracks inside the fort, and finally raised in 1838 by Captain Edward Smith,[79] where to this day it remains in situ.

Note that the first English Nobel Prize winner for literature Rudyard Kipling lived in Prayagraj between 1882 and 1889, while working as an assistant editor for the newspaper *The Pioneer*.

Allahabad to Prayagraj

On 16 October 2018, Allahabad reverted to its old name 'Prayag' with the added suffix of Raj. The city, home to several Indian stalwarts, has given India many of its prime ministers, including Pandit Jawaharlal Nehru, his daughter Indira Gandhi, her son Rajiv Gandhi, Chandra Shekhar and V.P. Singh, and a host of eminent personalities like Amitabh Bachchan, to name one.

Of the places beside the sangam and the fort, which can be accessed from near the confluence to visit the Akshay Vat and the Patalpuri Mandir, I visited the Allahabad Museum inside the Chandra Shekhar Azad Park, adjacent to the wonderfully constructed Vijaynagaram Hall building of the University of Allahabad.

On my first visit to the museum, I was accompanied by a self-taught scholar of Indian iconography named Ajay Singh, whose knowledge on the subject is praiseworthy. On my way to Agra from Kolkata, prior to crossing the Ganga bridge connecting Jhusi with Prayagraj, I had stopped by to see the Ulta Quila on the east bank of the Ganga near the bridge. That visit was a disappointment, particularly because of certain expectations I had from such an ancient place.

That morning, while riding out of Banaras, I had revisited the sculpture-embellished Kardameshwar Mandir outside the hustle and bustle of Banaras city. Perhaps due to the lingering image of the lone Surya sculpture opposite the Kardameshwar Mandir, I expected to come across a few such pieces in the Ulta Quila, but it was not so.

Perhaps they are buried within the mound below the overgrowth and are yet to be exhumed. Perhaps the excavation conducted by the ASI there missed out on areas where some remains are still interred... so many perhaps-es had led to my disappointment. Anyway, Ajay Singh was waiting for me outside the museum, where my roving mind was set at ease when I beheld fantastic ancient works of art, made by hands we know very little about.

The Allahabad Museum

The museum has a great collection of sculptural masterpieces but sadly, the display is pathetic, especially the ramshackle shade in the annexe under which many priceless sculptures are kept. I don't know when we are going to really start caring for our tangible past instead of taking pride in the pseudoscience peddled by superstitious louts and misogynistic nutcases.

Of the various exhibits, the few that caught my attention were:

1. A Sunga era terracotta head of a man with a samurai-styled haircut.
2. A Sunga/Kushan era tiny terracotta torso depicting the small intestines inside the gut; this piece was found in the excavated ruins of Kausambi and was possibly a model used to teach anatomy to students in some *gurukul* there.
3. Three Sunga era moulded terracottas of toy chariots, one drawn by four horses, and several Chandraketugarh-type moulded images of female divinity with weapons sticking out of the hair, all from Kausambi.
4. A Kushan era sculpture, part of a stupa railing, depicting a young man trying to reach out to something while standing on a three-layered human pyramid, like the annual *dahihandi* celebration on Janmashtami day in Maharashtra.
5. A superb sculpture of a Gupta era Ekmukha Linga.
6. A splendidly sculpted Pala era stele of the Buddhist deity Tara.

7
Eternal Banaras

I have been to a few continuously inhabited cities spread around the older parts of Asia, North Africa and peninsular India, and I have been to Banaras. Bagdad, Cairo, Damascus, Constantinople and Jerusalem, even though conquered, were never so mercilessly destroyed. Banaras, being as old as these cities, saw more onslaughts than living memory can recall for certain.

Indian temples, filled with hoards of offerings, attracted the attention of Muslim conquerors. They satiated their greed for gold and bloodlust and 'spiritual merit' by looting temples, demolishing the idols, and obliterating non-believers as the opportunity accorded. The writings from their scriptures were used as a license to justify the genocide perpetrated by them, which, according to the ulema, was not considered a crime, but rather a meritorious act that guaranteed them wine and women in heaven. Banaras, being the centre of the idol-worshipping world, periodically faced devastation to such an extent that except the Kardameshwar Mandir, no other ancient structure there remains standing.

The City of Death and Life

After every round of carnage, the city rebuilt itself over time on the debris scattered by thoughtless barbarians like the Hunas,[1] Ahmed Nialtjin, a general of Ghazni,[2] Salar Masud and his ilk,[3] Muhammed Ghori and his general Qutbuddin Aibak,[4] Iltutmish,[5] Sikandar Lodhi,[6] Shahjahan,[7] and Aurangzeb. The last bigot, through his overzealous acts, not only destroyed the holiest of the holy places of the city, but also constructed mosques over them, which, today, is a bone of contention between Hindus and Muslims.

Aurangzeb demolished the Kashi Vishwanath Mandir, the holiest shrine of the city, and built a mosque over it, making it the cause for another Ayodhya- and Mathura-like situation in modern India. Primarily because of his iconoclastic deeds, a hundred-fold fiercer than his ancestors, this bigoted emperor is the most hated figure in India's history. He thoughtlessly used his unbridled power to demolish all that he considered sacrilegious to Islam. His murderous rule alienated non-Muslims, scattering acrimony as a cultural memory so plagued with injustice that over the past centuries it festered like pus-filled blisters, only to be exploited by radicals of both religious hues.

At present, even after his death in 1707 CE, many Hindus sadly look at their fellow Muslim citizens as his children. On the other hand, I believe this fire of mistrust is fuelled when Indian Muslims, unmindful of Aurangzeb's past wrongdoings, put him on a pedestal and peddle him as an ideal ruler. Apart from this idiocy, any sort of acrimony against any community for the crimes of past sovereigns makes no sense. Not being an apologist for the misdeeds of ancestors or delving into the socio-political side of the bloody past, I will concentrate on the perseverance of Indians as my strength and cite the example of Banaras, which survived despite everything.

Possibly no other city on the face of the earth has seen such misery and untold bloodshed over a span of nearly 700 years. Not for nothing is this place called the city of death—for according to the beliefs of the Hindus, it is spiritually meritorious to die and be cremated there. The pyres at the two crematoriums, namely the Manikarnika and the Harishchandra ghats, never go out.

After each wave of destruction, Banaras rebuilt its places of worship. One must give it to the tenacity of its residents, those who still had their heads on their shoulders, to carry forward the tales of the intended existence of the city to rebuild what was desecrated, again and again. Ultimately, creation prevailed over destruction, and we get the city as it is today. Post the fall of Islamic kingdoms in India, various resurgent Hindu powers like the Marathas, the Rajput kings, zamindars from Bengal, and royals from Nepal and South

India contributed to the work of rebuilding this ancient place that saw constant habitation from about 1000 BCE.

Banaras, as Old as Time

Set between the confluence of the Varuna and the Assi with the Ganga, Banaras is a colloquial pronunciation of an amalgamated name formed by joining Varuna and Assi: Varanasi. Another story emphasizes that the city was named after a king named Banar, who rebuilt it after its destruction by Mahmud of Ghazni. This city is also called Kashi, which comes from the root word *kans* (shining brass), meaning 'the city of eternal light/learning',[8] due to the Brahmins who dwelt there.

It is also called the city of Shiva, as many myths related to the god of destruction are associated with it. The Buddha lived there for many years and preached his first sermon at the north-end of the city at Sarnath. Banaras finds mention in the Mahabharata, the Puranas, Buddhist and Jain texts, and in the works of latter-day travellers. Cunningham is of the opinion that the Kassidia mentioned by Ptolemy is Kashi.[9]

In the pan-Indian psyche and in the sacred geography of the subcontinent, this city is akin to an ideal, which by nature is utopic. Thus, any town or city in India with a considerable number of temples in it is often termed the Banaras of the east, west, north or south. It is also a favourite destination for foreign tourists, who, with their Eurocentric notion of an exotic land lost in time, get a microcosmic experience of India just by walking along the many ghats of this ancient city.

From Myths and Legends

For the sake of context, my effort to reconstruct the history of Banaras would bear fruit by bringing to life the tenacity exhibited by the city during its most perilous hours. I feel as if the city with all its defects is the metaphorical representation of India and its culture, which prevail despite the turmoil they were subjected to. Disruption is nothing new to Banaras and was not instigated by outsiders. If stories from mythological accounts bear even a tiny kernel of truth, then, according to the *Harivamsa*, the first unsettling of Banaras happened at the hands of the powerful Nikumbha, leader of Shiva's *ganas*.[10]

The myth goes that at that point of time, King Divodasa was ruling Banaras, a city he had captured from King Bhadrasena after a lot of bloodshed.[11] Here, one must recall that Divodasa finds mention in the Rig Veda and was the son of King Sudas, the victor of the Battle of the Ten Kings from the Rig Veda. Nikumbha, on the command of Shiva, settled outside the city walls and started granting boons to its citizens. This, alongside him denying the boon of a son to the queen of Divodasa, compelled the latter to destroy the hut of Nikumbha, who then cursed the city and divested it of its population.[12]

After having emptied Banaras, Nikumbha went to Kailasha, the abode of Shiva, who, in turn, moved in and occupied Banaras. Parvati, for some reason, did not like her new abode and decided to move out, to which her husband replied that if she so pleased, she could go back to Kailasha but he would stay put there, and called Banaras 'Avimukta', which is another name for it. The *Harivamsa* relates that for the first three yugas, Shiva lived there, but left it in the Kali Yuga, only to remain there in an invisible form.[13]

While capturing Banaras from Bhadrasena, Divodasa had spared an infant son of the deposed king named Durdama. This child was adopted by Haihaya, the grandson of Yadu, the progenitor of the Yadavas. He returned to Banaras and began ruling it like his father, only to lose it to Pratadana, the son of Divodasa. Alarka, the grandson of Pratadana, conquered an extensive kingdom and laid out the picturesque city of Banaras, and after him ruled kings from his line in succession.

Well, the myth narrated above, for lack of empirical evidence, should not be taken literally. Instead, it should be understood as the story of the conquest of a thriving place, whose immense significance to the psyche of the Indians transcends time and logic.

Banaras in Other Religious Literature

Beyond the *Harivamsa*, almost every Hindu, Jain and Buddhist chronicle has at some point mentioned Banaras as an important religious centre. Brahminical literature like the epics Ramayana and the Mahabharata, and Puranas like *Matsya, Kurma, Linga, Padma, Agni, Skanda* and *Bhavishya* have all acknowledged the importance of Banaras. The *Linga Purana* clearly states that a person who dies in Banaras is freed from the shackles of rebirth.[14]

Buddhist chronicles like the Jatakas, the Pitakas, the *Ashokavadana*, the *Mahavamsa*, and a host of other literary works all mention Banaras and its suburb Sarnath, where the Buddha had preached the law for the first time. The city was also a hub of trade and was well connected via the riverine route and roads to urban centres as far as Taxila.[15]

Several Jain chronicles have mentioned Banaras as a holy city, because four of their Tirthankaras, namely the seventh, Suparshvanatha, the eighth, Chandraprabhu, the eleventh, Shreyansnatha (at Sarnath), and the twenty-third, Parshvanatha, were born there. Due to the immense religious significance that the city holds, it has several names apart from Varanasi/Banaras and Kashi:

1. Avimukha ('not forsaken')
2. Anandavana ('forest of bliss')
3. Rudra Bhasa ('the dwelling of Shiva')
4. Maha Samshana ('the great crematorium'), and those mentioned in the *Skanda Purana*

Historical Banaras as Evidenced by Archaeology

Banaras is divided into three parts. The north is the Omkara Khanda, the centre is the Vishveswar Khanda, and the south is the Kedara Khanda. The historical Banaras, old as it is, can be said to have been established during post-Vedic times in the Omkara Khanda side of the city. Excavations carried out in Rajghat near the confluence of the Varuna with the Ganga, and at Aktha, near Sarnath, reveal the existence of a much older Banaras. It appears that the city began at Aktha and shifted south to the triangular shelter of the two rivers.

Digs in Aktha have revealed the existence of habitation that goes back to 3,300 years,[16] which was anterior to the settlement of Rajghat by a good three centuries. For about five centuries, Aktha and Rajghat co-existed, until the fourth century BCE, when Rajghat emerged as an urban centre. Aktha, on the other hand, remained as the primordial outpost on the periphery of 'civilization' till the sixth century CE, when the village vanished into oblivion.

This is rather strange because of the existence of Sarnath, which during the lifetime of the Buddha in the sixth century BCE was an important place, where learned men who attracted the attention of the affluent in Banaras congregated. The expansion of Banaras from Rajghat to its west and along the river bank is another factor that contributed to the demise of Aktha. It appears that the citizens of the immortal city had demarcated the Varuna as their northern border and refrained from spreading beyond it. To the city's south, the Assi was its delineating margin, and like most ancient metropolises of India, it flourished within the shelter of these natural barriers.

However, it is not that an urban centre can be strictly contained within certain limits, and so the city experienced some peripheral expansion over the eastern banks of the Ganga, at Ramnagar. Excavations carried out near the Ramnagar Fort along the high banks of the Ganga have yielded NBPW, Black Slip Ware pot shards, and other evidence of settled life datable to 700 BCE, down to the Kushan and Gupta period.[17]

Here, one must understand that since Banaras is a continuously inhabited city, most of its ancient past lies interred under the houses that exist in the tightly packed localities on the banks of the Ganga. Seen from the river, its concave edge, exhibiting a medley of exotic structures, unusually stands on artificially elevated ground. It seems as if the river that meandered west and north[18] at Banaras had cut through a hillock on its way east after travelling through a flat stretch, interrupted by the sudden outcropping of the Chunar rock, on which the fort of the same name was built. This 'hillock' on the west bank over which Banaras is, is the evidence of the city's hoary past, which survives as deep-rooted foundations; here, the proverbial phrase 'transcending time' can be used in an elegiac way.

The most important excavation that was carried out in Banaras happened at Rajghat first in 1940 by Krishna Deva. What prompted the dig was a report by a railway contractor. While digging the area around the eighteenth century CE mausoleum of Lal Khan, he had been scavenging for materials to extend the old Kashi railway station.[19]

The 1940 excavation unearthed a seal inscribed in Gupta Brahmi, which had *baranasy-adhishthan-adhikara-nasya* written on it, which means 'the seal of the city administration of Varanasi'.[20] This small object that belonged to the fourth century CE was a momentous find, confirming the city's ancient name through epigraphy.

Krishna Deva's dig revealed five strata, with the topmost part belonging to the era of the Gahadavala rule over Banaras, which ended in 1194 CE. This layer yielded a great cache of destroyed Hindu sculptures from a temple. Two copper plate inscriptions of Govindachandra Gahadavala, the father of Jayachandra/Jaichand, the last ruler of that dynasty, were discovered.

Strata two and three were damaged by the railway diggings. Strata four yielded the largest cache of artefacts and structural foundations, particularly of eight brick-built buildings separated by lanes between them, and several other structures including a temple base. This layer also yielded seals of King Dhanadeva and several others that bore the images of Greek deities. Apart from these, there were several hundred terracotta human and animal figurines that belonged to the Gupta period.

About these sophisticated sculptures, Krishna Deva writes:

> These terracottas share, in some measure, the amazing vitality and expressing qualities of the Gupta sculptural art. Another noteworthy feature is the fine painting of the lines and suitable colours, still preserved on some of the figurines. These show all variety of poses seated, standing, kneeling, and

reclining. Gods and goddesses, men and women, musicians and dancers, boys and children, soldiers and riders, animals, and birds, all varieties of subjects are depicted in multiple pleasing postures. We find on these such diverse themes as amorous couple engaged in love play, mother suckling the baby or hugging it to her bosom, young lady swinging in a cradle, rider galloping on a horse, monkey holding a fruit and so on. The religious figures include representations of Vishnu, Siva, Kartikeya, Ganesha, groups of Kubera and Hariti and Siva and Parvati. Among animal figurines the bull and the horse with their lifelike modelling are particularly remarkable. More interesting than these and decidedly the most artistic are the numerous human heads and busts which deserve special notice. These show exquisitely refined and expressive features with prominent nose, full sensuous lips, large, charming eyes, fine forehead and gliding cheeks; all set in a beautiful oval face. The beauty of these heads is enhanced by the charming style of hairdressing which shows a bewildering variety from the simple unsophisticated parting of hair to the most gorgeous coiffure.[21]

The photos of these figurines can be found in various museums and collectively seen in the book titled *Catalogue of Terracotta Figurines from Rajghat Excavations* by B. Mani and Arundhati Banerji.

The lowest strata of the dig exposed four housing complexes, an ivory seal and two small clay seals bearing the legends Phagunandisa and Balamitasa, datable to the Sunga period. Two test pits below this level revealed seventeen pottery jars, and innumerable pot shards of NBPW ware.[22]

After nearly two decades, Rajghat was once again excavated, this time by A.K. Narain of the Banaras Hindu University (BHU). The digs started on three mounds in 1957 and continued till 1969.[23] Further digs carried out at Rajghat in 2013–14 shed new light on the settlement. The earliest level at Rajghat went down to 800 BCE and continued up to 600 BCE. This phase corresponded with the sixteen mahajanpada political realms that held sway over parts of North India during the lifetime of the Buddha; the Kashi Mahajanpada was one such political entity.

The next stage began after 600 BCE and ended in 400 BCE. This period yielded coarse grey pottery and hand-moulded terracotta figurines. The period after this extended up to the first century CE and yielded evidence of baked brick foundations and stamped Buddhist artefacts.

The next phase, which happened to be the most prolific period, was measured to last till 300 CE. This stratum has revealed numerous artefacts belonging to the Kushan and post-Kushan period with several findings of seals and coins that commonly mention Harisena, who happened to be a monarch. Another important name that was found inscribed on a coin of the Ayodhya category was that of Sivodasa, and another coin called the Kausambi type had Navasa written on it.

The period between 300 CE and 700 CE yielded an apsidal temple and several gold coins, four of which had the names of the Gupta kings Chandragupta and Kumaragupta written on them. Period V, i.e. the phase till 1200 CE, yielded several temple remains and idols lying scattered on the same level, indicative of a sudden destruction that caused these structures to crumble.[24] This timeline corresponds to the murdering raids conducted by Salar Masud and Muhammad Ghori, who, according to their chronicles, destroyed temples of Banaras.[25] The last and the uppermost layer has been dated from 1200 CE to 1700 CE. This stratum has yielded coins from the age of Sher Shah Suri and Akbar, among other items belonging to the Islamic phase of North India's polity.

Banaras during the Gupta Epoch

From the stratified history of Banaras beginning from post-Vedic times, let us arrive at the Gupta Era, particularly during the reign of Kumaragupta I (415–55 CE) and look at the city visited by Fa Hien. This Chinese pilgrim visited Banaras from Pataliputra via the riverine route.[26] After crossing Banaras, he went to Sarnath and stayed there for a while, visiting nearby places like Kausambi. From Banaras, he returned to Pataliputra via the same route. Unfortunately, we learn nothing about the city from him except that it was the capital of the Kashi kingdom.

From the Garuda pillar inscription of Skandagupta in Bhitari (about 50 km east of Banaras), we know that he, the son of Kumaragupta I, had defeated an invading horde of the Hunas on the banks of the Ganga.[27] The pillar, which he erected in honour of Vishnu in the vicinity of a temple complex in Bhitari, was to celebrate his victory. If the battle took place near Bhitari, then it is certain that Banaras would have been overwhelmed by the invading hordes from Central Asia, who were routed during their march into Magadha.

Banaras from the Account of Hieun Tsang in the Seventh Century CE

About 200 years later, in the seventh century CE, the holy city was visited by another Chinese pilgrim. Unlike Fa Hien, Hieun Tsang's account of Banaras is elaborate for a pilgrim concerned with places of Buddhist interest. He writes that the city was 18–19 li in length and 5–6 li in breadth, and was on the western side of the Ganga. If we convert this to kilometres, then the overall size of Banaras during the seventh century CE would be 9 km by 2 km along the Ganga, which is very impressive. Possibly, the pilgrim included Sarnath within the ambit of the city while giving us the measurements of it. And like today, the Banaras of the seventh century CE too was tightly packed, which compelled him to compare the settlement to a small-toothed comb, being densely populated.[28]

About the people he writes:

> The families are very rich, and in the dwellings are objects of rare value. The disposition of the people is soft and humane, and they are earnestly given to study. They are mostly unbelievers, a few reverence the law of Buddha. The climate is soft, the crops abundant, the trees (*fruit*

trees) flourishing, and the underwood thick in every place. There are about thirty *sangharamas* (monasteries) and 3000 priests. They study the Little Vehicle according to the Sammatiya school (Ching-liang-pu). There are a hundred or so Deva temples with about 10,000 sectaries. They honour principally Maheshwara (Ta-tseu-tsai). Some cut their hair off, others tie their hair in a knot, and go naked, without clothes (Nirgranthas); they cover their bodies with ashes (Pasupatas), and by the practice of all sorts of austerities they seek to escape from birth and death.[29]

Regarding the inner portion of Banaras adjacent to the area around the Kashi Vishwanath temple, the pilgrim notes the presence of '...twenty Deva temples, the towers and halls of which are of sculptured stone and carved wood. The foliage of trees combines to shade (*the sites*), whilst pure streams of water encircle them. The statue of the Deva Maheshwara, made of [native copper], is somewhat less than 100 feet high. Its appearance is grave and majestic, and appears as though really living.'[30]

The Ashokan and the Gupta Era Pillar in Banaras

One extremely interesting piece of information the pilgrim shares is the presence of an Ashokan pillar beside a stupa built by Ashoka. I quote him: 'To the north-east of the capital, on the western side of the river Varuna, is a *stupa* built by Ashoka-raja [...]. It is about 100 feet high; in front of it is a stone pillar; it is bright and shining as a mirror; its surface is glistening and smooth as ice, and on it can be constantly seen the figure of Buddha as a shadow.'[31]

The existence of the Ashokan pillar has been attested to by the seventeenth century gem merchant Tavernier. He notes that about 500 paces from the town in the northwest direction there was a mosque beside which there were several well-designed graves. The largest of these graves was a square pedestal about 40 paces in length. In the centre of this platform, there stood a sandstone column about

30–35 feet in height, which three men could embrace with some difficulty. He tried to scratch this column with his knife and failed to do so. He further writes that the column terminated in a pyramid and had a great ball on the point below which large beads encircled. He also states that all sides of the square platform were sculpted with relief sculptures of animals. The antiquity of this platform and the pillar was attested to by the caretaker of the grave complex, who informed him that the platform was the tomb of the king of Bhutan, who was driven out of his kingdom by the descendant of Timur the Lame.[32]

Undoubtedly, Tavernier had seen the Ashokan pillar mentioned by Hieun Tsang. 'The king of Bhutan' is a misinformed epithet for the Buddha or Buddhists, who, according to the guard with no knowledge of history, lay buried beneath the sandstone shaft. But what of the pillar? Sadly, this was destroyed during a Hindu–Muslim riot that took place in October 1809 CE. H.R. Nevill in *Banaras: A District Gazetteer* gives us the circumstance behind the destruction of this ancient shaft that was carved 2,300 years ago in a quarry in Chunar.

During the riots concerning the Kashi Vishwanath Mandir, the Muslims were led by brothers Dost and Fateh Muhammad, while the Hindus were mainly the Rajput inhabitants of the city. What triggered the strife was the construction of a Hanuman temple in the space between Aurangzeb's Gyanvapi Masjid and the rebuilt Kashi Vishwanath Mandir. The Muslims, having collected in large numbers, destroyed the upcoming structure and several other temples. They even attempted to destroy the Kashi Vishwanath, which spurred the Hindus to congregate at Gayaghat and meet a large mob of Muslims on their way to the hallowed grounds of Banaras's holiest temple. A veritable bloodbath followed, in which the Muslims were 'beaten back with the loss of some eighty persons'.[33]

While this battle was going on, another riot broke out near Aurangzeb's mosque, which was quelled by the superintendent of police, Mr Bird. While returning, these enraged Muslims desecrated the Lat Bhairava Mandir in which they slaughtered a cow and toppled the pillar of Ashoka, which was smashed to smithereens.[34]

At some point in time, the Hindus of Banaras had converted the pillar and its surrounding into a Shiva temple, which shared space with the Muslim graveyard seen by Tavernier. This most possibly happened after the fall of the mighty Mughal Empire. Because of its association with Shiva, the pillar came to be known as the shaft of Bhairava Shiva. The aftermath of the destruction of the pillar was gory, as Nevill writes:

> A strong guard was placed at the Lat, but nothing happened during the night, although the Hindus were in a state of great excitement. The next day, however, the storm broke. About noon a vast throng of armed Rajputs, followed by hundreds of maddened Goshains made their way rapidly to the Lat, set the mosque of Aurangzeb on fire, effectually desecrated the spot, and put to death every Muhammadan in the neighbourhood.[35]

Presently a stump of the Ashokan pillar exists in the Lat Bhairava Mandir, which shares space with a mosque. Beside these two places of worship is the Adi Ganga tank, a paved water body that was possibly excavated during the Mauryan times to make the bricks for the Ashokan stupa. The existing stump is covered with a copper sheet and above that an expensive silk cloth. The pillar stands about 8 feet above ground, towering over the worshipper, and has a knob-like projection on it. This, I think, was a strut that once held an Ashokan emblem in place. If my assumption is correct, then the pillar portion that is worshipped as a linga belonged to the topmost part. And what about the Ashokan stupa? The entire area of the Lat Bhairava Mandir exists on raised ground that is undoubtedly the foundational remains of the stupa. The next question pertaining to Tavernier's observation is of the relief sculptures on the platform, which, I believe, were effaced when the *lat* (temple) was pulled down.

I visited the Sampurnananda Sanskrit University in Banaras to see a Gupta era pillar. The pillar is not from Banaras but Parladhpur, 70 km east of Banaras in the Ghazipur district. It was discovered by Capt. Burt in 1838 and brought to Banaras on the orders of

Lt Governor James Thompson in 1853. A year later, it was erected between the university's playground and the observatory by George Franklin Atkinson, to accentuate the Gothic-style architecture of the university building designed by archaeologist and soldier Major Kitteo, in 1853 CE.[36]

The 27-foot tall pillar that looks like an Ashokan shaft is carved out of Chunar sandstone and has two inscriptions on it. The first, in Gupta Brahmi, mentions the name of a certain King Sishupala.[37] The second inscription, in Gupta era shell script, has not been deciphered. While reading about the inscription on the pillar, I got to know that a similar pillar existed in the village of Lathiya about 3 km east of Zamaniya and about 7 km north of Parladhpur.[38] Since that pillar did not have any inscription, it was not brought to Banaras. I don't know if that pillar still exists in Lathiya or not.

The Revival of Hinduism by Shankaracharya at Banaras

In the eighth century CE, there arrived in Banaras a young reformer from Kerala named Shankaracharya. For a brief while, he had lived in Omkareshwar on the Mandhata island on the Narmada. There he was initiated as a sanyasi by his guru Govindapada and asked to go to Banaras, where he studied and postulated his doctrine and commentaries on ancient religious texts. In Banaras, he got his first disciple, an inquisitive young man from eastern Karnataka/Tamil Nadu named Sanandan.[39]

It is from Banaras that Shankaracharya began his extensive travels all over India, preaching the Brahminical doctrine by challenging Buddhist scholars to debates and establishing mathas.

Banaras in Lama Taranatha's Account

The Tibetan Buddhist monk Lama Taranatha mentions one such debate between Shankaracharya and the Buddhist monk Dharmakirti, in which, predictably, Shankaracharya was defeated several times. The

Lama then goes on to inform us that after his defeat he jumped into the Ganga and died.[40] Well, we know that no such thing happened, and that Shankaracharya went on to travel the length of the country and died in Kedarnath.

The Lama also informs us that during the reign of King Ajatshatru of Magadha (a contemporary of the Buddha), the Buddhist sangha had received a hostile response from the inhabitants of the city. They had objected to the giving of alms to the monks due to the crisis of 'surplus'.[41] Furthermore, we learn that at a later date Buddhists from Banaras visited Kashmir en masse for a council that was convened by the reverend monk Madhyantika from Banaras.[42]

The Lama also shares a story about the famous poet Kalidasa, Vasanti, the daughter of King Bhimasukla of Banaras, and a renowned Brahmin named Vararuchi, who was the resident priest of a temple belonging to the king of the city. This story touches upon the legend of Kalidasa's illiteracy and how he became a renowned dramatist after being blessed by Goddess Kali, whose devoted servant he was, changing his name to Kali-dasa ('the slave of Kali'). This story has no historical veracity and may be a concoction of the times when the Lama wrote his book in the seventeenth century CE; Kalidasa, we know, was a poet who flourished in the fourth–fifth century CE in Ujjain.

The Beginning of the Destruction of Banaras by Islamic Forces

At this juncture in the story of Banaras, I am compelled to skip a few centuries, clear past the heyday of the Gurjara-Pratiharas, past the forays upon the city by the Palas of Bengal and by the Kalachuri king Karna, and arrive at the time when India faced the onslaughts of Mahmud of Ghazni, which according to Al Biruni, '...ruined the prosperity of the country.'[43]

The Iranian polymath, who came to India with the ransacking army from Ghazni and lived in Kannauj and Banaras, writes that the severity of his lord's earlier invasion had pushed out learned men to distant parts like Kashmir, Banaras, and other places where 'our hands cannot yet reach'.[44] And that, according to him, was the precise reason why Hindus had 'the most inveterate aversion towards all Muslims'.[45] Well, this dictum might hold true for many Hindus, even after the lapse of a thousand years.

The year 1018 CE is particularly tragic for North India, because it is the year of the fall of Kannauj. After the destruction of the city, Mahmud of Ghazni marched east and sacked Manaj and Astar.[46] From these two places, Banaras was about 65 km away, which then begs the question: Did Mahmud of Ghazni also sack the holy city? The *Kitab-i-Yamini* by Al Utbi is silent about it, and so is the *Habib-us-Siyar* by Khondamir.

Through the narration of Utbi, we know that after the sacking of Astar, Ghazni marched against a king called Chandra, 'who was owner of a very strong fortress'.[47] We are uncertain whether this fortress was at Banaras or Kalinjar, after sacking which Mahmud of Ghazni obtained '...three thousand packets of gold and silver, precious gems, and valuable sapphires, and so great an abundance of slaves that the price of each never exceeded from two to ten dirhems, at the utmost. This victory fixed the embroidered border of the Sultan's prosperity and good fortune, and its renown extended from the East to the West...'[48]

However, Abul Fazal informs us that Mahmud of Ghazni sacked Banaras in 1018 CE, and then, after a gap of six years, invaded the fort of Kalinjar.[49] Within living memory of the first carnage, Ahmad Nialtagin, a general of Mahmud of Ghazni, raided Banaras in 1034 CE, suddenly appearing in the city and plundering 'its markets from morning till midday', and immediately after that, returning to the Punjab with the loot.[50]

Immediately after this incident, Banaras fell victim to another marauder named Salar Masud, who is believed to be the nephew of Mahmud of Ghazni. Masud had sent a force of looters led by Malik Fazal to Banaras and the surrounding areas.[51]

In the intervening centuries between Mahmud's invasions and the establishment of political Islam in India, there arose the Gahadavala Dynasty, which I have discussed at length in the chapter on Kannauj. Banaras fell within the realm of the Gahadavalas and was their eastern capital. We know of several copper plate grants of the Gahadavala monarchs issued from Banaras. Epigraphic records found in Sarnath also testify to the importance accorded by them to the holy city. The Gahadavalas were the last Hindu monarchs of Banaras for the next almost 600 years, after which it became the capital of the Kashinaresh ('king of Kashi') Raja Balwant Singh in the eighteenth century CE.

Ghori's Destruction of the Holy City

After the defeat and death of Jayachandra in 1194 CE, Muhammad Ghori, along with his general Qutbuddin Aibak, reached Banaras. Hasan Nizami, in his *Taj-ul-Masir*, describes the sack of Banaras by Ghori:

> From that place the royal army proceeded towards Benares, 'which is the centre of the country of Hind', and here they destroyed nearly one thousand temples, and raised mosques on their foundations; and the knowledge of the law became promulgated, and the foundations of religion were established; 'and the face of the dinar and the diram was adorned with the name and blessed titles' of the king. The Rais and chiefs of Hind came forward to proffer their allegiance. 'The government of that country was then bestowed on one of the most celebrated and exalted servants of the State,' in order that he might distribute justice and repress idolatry.
>
> When the king had settled all the affairs of the city and its vicinity, and 'the record of his celebrated holy wars had been written in histories and circulated throughout the breadth of the fourth inhabited quarter of the world,' he returned to Ghazna.[52]

Sarnath too is included in the list of destruction by Ghori, as the Muslim chroniclers could not tell them apart because of their proximity.

Banaras during the Early Years of the Delhi Sultanate

Minhaj-us-Siraj in his *Tabakat-i-Nasiri* is very brief about the conquest of Banaras by Ghori and Aibak and includes Banaras as one of the conquests of Iltutmish.[53] Lama Taranatha informs us that during the 'Turushka' conquest of Magadha and Nalanda, the king of Banaras was Buddhapaksha, who fought battles against the invaders.[54] We don't know of any king by that name but know for certain that Jayachandra was the king of these places.

Ferishta mentions that after Ghori's conquest of the Asni fort, the next city to fall was Banaras. At the holy city, Ghori and his slave Aibak destroyed about 1,000 temples and broke all their idols.[55] Some years later, the powerful Delhi sultan Iltutmish raided Banaras and, like his master Aibak, indulged in wanton iconoclasm, destroying the temples there.

The Dhai Kangura Masjid of Mukimganj was constructed after the conquest of Iltutmish, with materials from the destroyed temples. An inscription on a slab dated to 1190 CE, found in the second storey of the mosque, records the construction of several temples. This slab belonged to one of the temples demolished by the early rulers of the Delhi Sultanate.[56] The temples around the Bakaria Kund near the Banaras Railway Station are other such places that were utterly obliterated by the early Sultans of Delhi.

By then, large-scale migrations out of the city were occurring, particularly by Brahmins who went south and north fleeing prosecution. Its temples too were mostly destroyed and survived only as ruined memories of the times when sculptural arts flourished in the act of constructing new places of worship.

Delhi Sultan Firoz Shah Tughlaq notes that he had ordered the destruction of temples within his realm and banned the construction of any new ones.[57] Going by such pronouncements, I assume that orders were probably served to the governor of Banaras to break a few 'surviving' temples. A mosque inside the dargah of Fakhruddin Alwai on the bank of the Bakaria Kund has an inscription that states that the mosque was constructed during the reign of Firoz Shah Tughlaq by one Zia Ahmed.

In 1354 CE, Firoz Shah marched against Bengal from Jaunpur. The route to Bengal falls through Banaras, which leads me to conclude that the invading army, in order to gain religious merit, most probably indulged in large-scale desecration of Banaras; after all, the capital of idolatry was at their mercy and a god-fearing monarch such as Firoz Shah would probably not miss any opportunity to break a few idols.[58]

The City Becomes a Province of the Jaunpur Sultanate

After the complete obliteration of the Tughlaqs, there arose in the region the reign of the Sharqis, who had carved out for themselves a sultanate with Jaunpur as their capital. During the reign of the Jaunpuri sultans, Banaras suffered immensely. Not only were its surviving temples broken, but the stone remains were also carted away to Jaunpur to build mosques.

The Lal Darwaja Masjid of Jaunpur was primarily built by materials sourced from those destroyed temples. An inscription on a pillar inside the masjid, dated 15 May 1296 CE, informs us that a certain Padmasadhu had built a temple dedicated to Vishnu outside the north gate of the Kashi Vishwanath temple of Banaras.[59] The sultanate of Jaunpur was later completely destroyed by Sikandar Lodhi, whose tenure as the sultan of Delhi spelt further doom for the existing non-Muslim structures of North India.

The infamous iconoclast Sikandar Lodhi's campaign against Raja Bhid (Bhiradev) of Panna in 1494 CE was met with reverses, which compelled him to retreat to Jaunpur. The ousted Jaunpuri sultan Hussain Shah Sharqi marched out of Bengal and headed towards Jaunpur. In a hotly contested battle near Banaras, Hussain Shah's troops were defeated.[60]

The *Tarikh-i-Daudi* of Abdullah informs us about the religious zeal of Sikandar Lodhi, which had him decree the destruction of every temple within his realm: '...so zealous a Musalman that he utterly destroyed diverse places of worship of the infidels, and left not a vestige remaining of them.' He further adds: 'Every city thus conformed as he desired to the customs of Islam.'[61]

Under the Mughals

Babur reached Banaras in 1528 CE. The city by the Ganga by then had most likely not a single temple standing, and existed as a small provincial town bereft of its *kash* (sheen). Its fort, the identity of which is uncertain,[62] was the seat of its governor Jalaluddin, appointed by Babur. Due to the amassing of the Afghan powers, which included Biban, Bayzid and Sher Shah Suri, Governor Jalaluddin capitulated his stronghold and fled to the fort of Kara. In this situation, Babur reached Kara and, after having a sumptuous meal of 'cooked meat and other viands',[63] sailed past Banaras and reached the confluence of the Gomti with the Ganga.[64]

We don't know exactly what Babur's appointee Jalaluddin did at Banaras, but all I can state is that if Babur had been involved in the demolition of the city's already destroyed structures, he would have mentioned it in his memoir, like he did with the colossi of Gwalior. The absence of Babur's iconoclastic exploits in his memoir in the heart of the idol-worshipping world can be taken as confirmation of my assumption that there were no known temples standing in Banaras in the sixteenth century CE.

Skipping a few decades past Sher Shah Suri's capture of Banaras from Humayun,[65] we arrive at the time when Akbar was the emperor of Hindustan. This grandson of Babur must be given credit for consolidating Mughal rule over the subcontinent and laying the firm foundations of the Mughal Empire that ruled most of India for the next 170 years. The *Ain-i-Akbari* of Abul Fazal informs us that by the time Akbar consolidated his empire into different provinces, Banaras ceased to be the capital of any province, and instead was relegated to the non-glamorous position of a mere provincial town in the province of Allahabad.[66]

About Banaras, the *Ain-i-Akbari* reports:

> *Baranasi*, universally known as Benares, is a large city situated between the two rivers, the *Barna* [Varuna] and the *Asi*. In ancient books it is styled *Kasi*. It is built in the shape of a bow [the north flow of the Ganga has carved its path westwards] of which the Ganga forms the string. In former days there was here an idol temple [the Kashi Vishwanath Mandir], round which procession was made after the manner of the *kaabah* and similar ceremonials of the pilgrims conducted. From time immemorial, it has been the chief seat of learning in Hindustan. Crowds of people flock to it from the most distant parts for the purpose of instruction to which they apply themselves with the most devoted assiduity.[67]

Under Akbar, Banaras tried to regain a bit of its former glory as a place of Brahminical learning. While the productive socio-politics of Akbar bore fruit in easing out the glaring differences between Hindus and Muslims in statecraft, several prominent Rajput dandies of his court began reconstructing the destroyed temples of Banaras. Particular attention was given to the most hallowed edifice of the city dedicated to Shiva, the Kashi Vishwanath Mandir.

While such activities were in progress, Brahmins from different parts of the country began returning to the city and establishing their *toll*s (Hindu schools that used to exist in the houses of learned Brahmins) there. One such Brahmin was a learned scholar from Bengal named Rudra Bhattacharya, who came from Banaras to Agra and paid homage to Emperor Jahangir in 1621 CE. About him, the son of Akbar writes, 'He was truly learned in the rational and traditional sciences and was perfect in his calling.'[68]

Till about the sixth year of Shah Jahan's reign, Banaras enjoyed an uninterrupted revival, till a decree promulgated by him spelt doom for the ancient city. Due to reports of temples being rebuilt in Banaras, which had commenced during the reigns of his grandfather Akbar and father Jahangir, Shah Jahan, in 1632 CE, decreed that at Banaras, 'the great stronghold of infidelity', and in every other part of his domain, 'all temples that had been begun should be cast down.'[69] Abdul Hamid Lahori in his *Badshah Nama* writes, 'It was now reported from the province of Allahabad that seventy-six temples had been destroyed in the district of Benares.'[70]

The Cauterization of Wounds

The temple-breaking carried on with renewed intensity during the reign of Aurangzeb. Like his father before him, this monarch promulgated a disastrous decree that ordered his governors to begin demolition activities all over the empire. That order was passed on 18 April 1669 CE, corresponding to the twelfth year of his reign. Along with the destruction of non-Muslim places of worship, every school run by Hindus had to be demolished.[71] That same year, the rebuilt Kashi Vishwanath temple was brought down on his orders.[72]

Unlike most other rulers, Aurangzeb used to cauterize the wound by building mosques over the ruined temples, which he did at two places in Banaras. The Gyanvapi Masjid occupies the spot of the Kashi Vishwanath Mandir, and still retains the vestiges of the demolished temple if one looks at this building from the back.

The second mosque is the Alamgir Masjid on the Panchaganga Ghat, which was constructed after demolishing the towering temple of Bindu Madhava (Vishnu). Seen from the river, this mosque is the tallest structure along the riverbank. Further extending his bigotry, Aurangzeb tried to rename Banaras as Muhammadbad, which did not catch on, remaining limited to court papers during his reign.[73]

Four years before the demolition drive at the Kashi Vishwanath Mandir, the Mughal troops were challenged by a large contingent of Naga Sadhus of the Nirvani Akhada. The battle that ensued between them in 1664 CE resulted in the victory of the sadhus, about which Jadunath Sarkar writes: 'From sunrise to sunset the battle raged and the Dasnamis proved themselves heroes; they preserved the honour of Vishwanath's seat. They defeated the Muslims Mirza Ali, [Turang Khan,] and Abdul Ali.'[74]

Rev. M.A. Sherring's observation of the iconoclasm perpetuated by subsequent Muslim rulers is a compelling read. In his book, *The Sacred Cities of the Hindus: An Account of Banaras*, he notes the following:

> It is worthy of notice, as illustrating the nature of Mohammedan rule in India, that nearly all the buildings in Benares, of acknowledged antiquity, have been appropriated by the Musalmans; being used as mosques, mausoleums, dargahs, and so forth; and also that a large portion of the separate pillars, architraves, and various other ancient remains, which, as before remarked, are so plentifully found in one part of the city, now contribute to the support and adornment of their edifices. Not content with destroying temples and mutilating idols, with all the zeal of fanatics, they fixed their greedy eyes on whatever objects was suited to their own purposes, and, without scruple or any of the tenderness shown by the present rulers, siezed upon it for themselves. And thus it has come to pass, that every solid and durable structure, and every ancient stone of value, being esteemed by them as their peculiar property, has, with very few exceptions, passed into their hands. We believe that it was the boast of Alauddin, that he destroyed one thousand temples in Benares alone. How many more were razed to the ground, or transformed into mosques through the iconoclastic fervour of Aurangzeb, there is no means of knowing; but it is not too much to say, that he was unsurpassed, in this feature of religious fanaticism, by any of his predecessors. If there is one circumstance respecting the Mohammedan period which Hindus remember better than any other, it is the insulting pride of the Musalmans, the outrages which they perpetrated upon their religious convictions, and the extensive spoilation of their temples and shrines. [75]

Banaras from the Accounts of European Travellers

Let me pause the tragedy of Banaras and look at it from the perspective of a traveller, starting with Ralph Fitz, who visited Banaras in 1584 CE, during the reign of Akbar. He was perhaps the first Englishman to do so. He had started his journey from Agra in a flotilla of 180 boats laden with salt, opium and *hing*, which were being taken to Bengal for trade.[76] To this English merchant, Banaras came as a shock, compelling him to record his experience at length. His description of the town begins by stating that Banaras:

> ...is a great towne, and great store of cloth is made there of cotton, and shashes for the Moores [Muslims]. In this place they be all Gentiles [Hindus] and be the greatest idolaters ever I [saw]. To this towne come the Gentiles on pilgrimage out of [far countries]. Here alongst the waters side bee very many faire houses, and in all of them, or for the most part, they have their images standing, which be evill favoured, made of stone and wood, some like lions, leopards, and monkeys; some like men and women, and [peacocks]; and some like the devil with [four arms] and four hands. They sit crosse legged, some with one thing in their hands, and some another. And by breake of day and before, there are men and women which come out of the towne and wash themselves in the Ganges.[77]

He furthermore describes the crematoriums on the ghats of the Ganga, and notes that widows immolated themselves in the pyres of their husbands and those who escaped the horrendous practice of Sati had to have their heads shaven and lived in obscurity the rest of their lives.[78] About twenty-seven years after Ralph Fitz, the English merchant William Finch passed through Banaras. He does not give us any details about the place but merely mentions it as a great hub of goods from Bengal.[79]

The first recorded Frenchmen to visit Banaras were Tavernier the gem merchant and Bernier the physician, in 1665 CE. Together they journeyed to Bengal from Agra in the month of November in 1665 CE, parting at Rajmahal.

Tavernier's account of Banaras informs us that the buildings there were of either stone or bricks, and taller than those of other towns in India. The streets between them were narrow, just as they are now, and the city had several caravansaries where silk weavers and other craftsmen sold their goods to merchants.[80] He, however, does not mention the sale of rainbow-hued betel wings, for which Banaras was famous in the nineteenth century CE.[81] These betel wings were sewn into dresses like *kimkhab*s (brocade Banarasi fabric) and gowns of European ladies.

Talking of kimkhabs, the English poet and novelist Emily Eden, who reached the city on 15 November 1837 CE,[82] tells us that while welcoming her and others to his fort at Ramnagar, the raja, who was then the young Ishwari Prasad Narayan, rolled out this expensive cloth on which they had to walk, to her dismay. She informs us that a yard of this cloth cost a pound, and that she had been unsuccessfully bargaining for a week to buy enough of it for a wadded *douillette*, so '...it was a pity to trample on it'.[83] The moment they stepped off it, their servants '...snatched it up and carried it off'.[84] The *Milindpanho* of Buddhaghosha, written in the first–second centuries BCE, also speaks about this expensive cloth from Banaras called *kotumbara* (kimkhab) being sold in Sagala (present-day Sialkot), the capital of the Indo-Greek king Menander.[85]

I find it intriguing that the manufacture of silk in Banaras has been mentioned in the *Ashokavadana*, a hagiographic book on the life of Emperor Ashoka that was composed in the second century CE. Arhat Upagupta of Mathura, while giving a magical tour of places associated with the Buddha's life, shows the monarch the spot outside Kapilavastu where the Buddha '...gave his clothes of Banaras silk to a hunter in exchange for a yellow robe'.[86] If indeed this part of the *Ashokavadana* was composed during the Kushan period, then we have to credit the Kushans with introducing silk into India, to such an extent that this sought-after cloth was being manufactured in India long before the Tibetan conquest of Nepal in the seventh century CE.

Getting back to Tavernier, his description of the Bindu Madhava temple is rather detailed. Reading it, one can form an idea of what the building looked like. He starts by stating that the structure was built in the shape of a cross.[87] The temple was crowned with a large 'dome' that extended upwards like a tower with many sides (shikharas) that terminated at a point. The end of each arm of the 'cross' was topped with towers that could be ascended from the outside. These towers had many balconies and niches. The temple was decorated with 'rudely executed' sculptures of animals.[88]

Near the temple was the palace of Raja Jaisingh of Amer, in which was a school run by Brahmins. There, Tavernier saw, amongst other children, two princes of Amer being educated. He also came across two globes that were gifted by the Dutch, on which he pointed out France to the two inquisitive princes.[89] Apart from these, he also mentions the existence of an Ashokan pillar, which I have discussed at length towards the beginning of the chapter.

Bernier's impression of Banaras, unlike Tavernier's, is more scholarly. Like every traveller that visited India at that time, he also notes the peculiarities and practices of its people and begins by writing:

> The town of *Benares*, seated on the *Ganges*, in a beautiful situation, and in the midst of an extremely fine and rich country, may be considered the general school of the *Gentiles*. It is the Athens of India, whither resort the [Brahmins] and other devotees; who are the only persons who apply their minds to study. The town contains no colleges or regular classes, as in our universities, but resembles rather the schools of the ancients; the masters being dispersed over different parts of the town in private houses, and principally in the gardens of the suburbs, which the rich merchants permit them to occupy.[90]

One very interesting piece of information he shares is about a very large library of Sanskrit manuscripts that included books on philosophy, medicines and other subjects. He then goes on to mention that the Puranas and the Vedas were so scarce that his *agha*, Danishmand Khan, '...notwithstanding all his diligence, ha[d] not succeeded in purchasing a copy. The *Gentiles* indeed conceal[ed] them with much care, lest they should fall into the hands of the *Mahometans*, and be burnt, as frequently ha[d] happened.'[91] After this observation, he dedicates a considerable number of pages to discussing the metaphysics of Indian philosophy and religions.

The Venetian Niccolao Manucci, part soldier, part physician, part author and full-time hustler, was a contemporary of the two Frenchmen and had met them in Agra and Delhi. Travelling to Bengal from Agra, he had reached Banaras from Allahabad by road. He records that the city, though small, was very ancient and venerated by the Hindus due to a temple there that possessed a very ancient idol. He also adds that a few years after he passed through it, that temple was knocked down on the orders of Aurangzeb, who had decreed the demolition of every other temple. The city then produced cloth worked in gold and silver that was exported to every part of the Mughal Empire and other parts of the world.[92] What this Venetian was referring to were the famous Banarasi silks, coveted by every Hindu bride and passed down as heirlooms from one generation to the next.

The Kashi Kingdom

The eclipse that Banaras suffered after 1669 CE took it nearly a hundred years to recover from. Meanwhile, the Mughal Empire crumbled, with a succession of incompetent rulers installed on the throne and just as quickly murdered. Their writ had practically ended outside the walls of the Red Fort. Everywhere new kingdoms were being formed, and the new lord of Banaras was Sadat Ali Khan, the first Nawab of Awadh. He had taken over the administration of Jaunpur, Ghazipur and Banaras from Murtaza Khan in 1722 CE, against an annual payment of 7 lakh.[93]

The Mughal ruler then was Muhammad Shah. Sadat Ali Khan had, in turn, subinfeudated his holding to his subordinate Mir Rustam Ali who, being disposed to pleasure, handed over the administration of Banaras to Mansa Ram, the zamindar of Titharia. He was the father of Raja Balwant Singh, who within years would go on to become the king of Banaras, establishing the Narayan Dynasty, the eldest members of which are still called Kashinaresh.

In 1748 CE, Balwant Singh became somewhat independent from Awadh and established his capital at Gangapur to the west of Banaras. After his capital was sacked by Safdar Jung, the successor of Sadat Ali Khan, he set about constructing the Ramnagar Fort in 1752 CE. This impressive bastion on the east bank of Banaras served as the capital of the Kashi kingdom.

After his death, there arose within his family a struggle for the throne between his legitimate daughter and illegitimate son Chait Singh. The claims of Chait Singh were given prevalence, and he became the ruler with the support of Shuja-ud-Daula in lieu of a massive amount of money. His position was ratified by the involvement of Warren Hastings who, along with Shuja-ud-Daula, conferred on him and his heirs the *sanad* (the right to govern) of Banaras against an annual revenue of 2,248,449 rupees.[94]

The First Rebellion against the British

After the death of Shuja-ud-Daula, his heir, Asaf-ud-Daula, handed over the province to the British. A new agreement was concluded that allowed Chait Singh to remain the king, but he had to appoint an English resident at Banaras. Trouble began brewing in Banaras in 1778 CE, when Chait Singh was ordered to contribute 5 lakh rupees towards the maintenance of English sepoys as part of the subsidiary alliance. The demand increased the next year, and was extracted after British troops appeared outside the walls of the Ramnagar Fort. In 1780, Chait Singh was ordered to provide a cavalry contingent of 2,000 for the impending war against the Marathas and the Nizam of Hyderabad. He refused the demand, which forced Hastings to impose a fine of 50 lakh rupees on him.[95]

In 1781 CE, Hastings marched from Kolkata and was met by Chait Singh at Buxar. The raja was ready for battle and had with him about 2,000 well-equipped soldiers in a large fleet of boats.[96] However, no fighting took place, and Hastings reached Banaras.

Artist William Hodges was present in Banaras when Chait Singh's rebellion broke out in the city. He writes that Markham, the resident, was sent with soldiers to arrest the raja, who was then in his palace in the Shivala Ghat. The raja surrendered, but his forces had gathered at Ramnagar and fell upon the English troops, guarding his residence in Shivala Ghat and killing about 250 soldiers. Chait Singh escaped through a window after climbing down a rope made of tied turbans.[97]

Once again, Banaras witnessed a severe upheaval. The British troops, faring badly in a series of skirmishes, lost about 105 men. This compelled Hastings to flee the city under the cover of darkness and seek shelter in the Chunar Fort. Hodges was in the train of Hastings and managed to escape to Chunar with nothing but a change of clothes and his drawings.[98]

The flames of Chait Singh's insurrection spread to every part of his kingdom, which included west Bihar. The raja, who had managed to evade the English, fought a series of battles in the Mirzapur district from his Latifpur fort in the Kaimur Hills.[99] For a few months the English were at a disadvantage, but after reinforcements arrived, the tables were turned against Chait Singh.

Unable to sustain the struggle due to severe losses, he decided to retreat south. From his fort in Latifpur, he retreated to Bijaigarh.[100] There he left his family and reached Gwalior via Rewa, where he joined the services of Mahadji Scindia.[101] When the Bijaigarh fort was captured, his aged mother and some other female relatives were taken into custody and accorded the kind of respect reserved for royalty.[102] Hearing of his retreat, Banaras was recaptured by the British on 28 September 1781 CE, and they immediately set upon the vacant throne Mahip Narayan Singh, the son of Chait Singh's stepsister.[103] In 1810 CE, Raja Chait Singh died in Gwalior. The present residents of the Ramnagar Fort belong to the line of Mahip Narayan Singh.

The Second Rebellion

Another rebellion that rocked Banaras was the revolt of Wazir Ali Khan, the illegitimate son of Awadh's Nawab Asaf-ud-Daulah. Wazir Ali was deposed from the throne of Lucknow in 1797 CE and accommodated in the garden mansion of Madho Das at Banaras, where he lived a lavish life with a 1.5 lakh annual pension. Getting wind of orders asking for his removal to Calcutta (now Kolkata), on 14 January 1799 CE, he caused the death of Resident George Cherry and three other English officers.[104] The next day, Wazir Ali fled to Azamgarh, and from there to Nepal. This rebellion was supported by Jagat Singh (a person we will read about in the chapter on Sarnath), a relative of Raja Mahip Naryan Singh, and a few others. Within days, the revolt was snuffed out in Banaras, and with the capture of Wazir Ali from Jaipur, the rebellion was forgotten. He was deported to Calcutta and then to Vellore, where he died.[105]

The next momentous incident in Banaras was the bloody riot of 1809 CE, of which I have discussed the part pertaining to the Ashokan pillar at the beginning of the chapter. The aftermath of the riot left a trail of blood and a lot of destruction, including that of fifty mosques.[106] The Great Mutiny of 1857 saw some flare-ups in Banaras for about three hours,[107] which is nothing when compared to the bloodshed witnessed by the city over the course of history.

The Regeneration of Banaras

From the times of Akbar, several palaces of various Rajput kings were built in Banaras. These residences were attached to the temples they constructed. One such palace was that of Raja Mansingh and Raja Jaisingh I of Amer. Even though all the old temples and religious schools were demolished, the residences remained, albeit in diminished glory. It appears that after the death of Aurangzeb in 1707 CE, Rajput rulers renewed building activities in Banaras. And after the advent of the Marathas, Banaras saw a resurgence of religious activities, with new types of temple architecture coming up in all parts of the city. The demolished temples were rebuilt once again with added vigour.

After the English gained ascendency over the subcontinent, the fear of a temperamental Muslim sultan destroying the 'arts' of the infidels at will abated. With the establishment of the Permanent Settlement in Bengal, Bihar, Banaras and Tamil Nadu, the new landed elite that was formed contributed to the growth of the city. Every year a new mansion came up, attached to which were temples. In fact, it is extremely difficult to ascertain the number of temples Banaras has because of this.[108]

The religious significance of this eternal city, which had for ages captivated Indians, magnetized even the non-landed trader from distant parts to set up a dwelling on the banks of the Ganga. Rich Bengalis thronged to Banaras and erected mansions there, particularly in the Bengali Tola near the Kedareshwar Mandir, which became their chief temple. Even those who did not belong to the upper crust of Bengal's landed elite but had considerable agricultural holdings built dwellings in Banaras, which they converted to boarding houses for pilgrims from Bengal. My great-grandfather was one such person, who inherited from his father a house in Banaras and Patna that provided additional income to the family.

For lack of space, the private houses of traders began to climb skywards and reach till the fifth storey, where each floor was occupied by a different family. This observation by Hodges is very interesting, for it denotes that the advent of apartment life in India began at Banaras in the eighteenth century CE. Another observation he makes is of the numerous ruins that surrounded the city. He blames their condition on the 'effects of Muhammadan intolerance'.[109]

Rev. Heber's description of Banaras is a great read that effortlessly tells us the extent to which the city had developed by 1824 CE, when he visited it in the month of September. Wherever he went he was welcomed very warmly, to such an extent that the garlands put around his neck made him '...look like a sacrifice'.[110] He notes that no Europeans lived in the 'town' then, and that some of the houses beside the narrow lanes were as tall as six storeys.[111] Such tall structures had surprised him too. Banaras, he writes, is:

> ...in fact, a very industrious and wealthy as well as a very holy city. It is the great mart where the shawls of the north, the diamonds of the south, and the muslins of Dacca and the eastern provinces, centre, and it has very considerable silk, cotton, and fine woollen manufactories of its own; while English hardware, swords, shields, and spears from Lucknow and Monghyr, and those European luxuries and elegancies which are daily becoming more popular in India, circulate from hence through Bundelcund, Gorruckpoor, Nepaul, and other tracts which are removed from the main artery of the Ganges.[112]

He also gives us the social side to the story of the city, whose occupants had begun incorporating newer ideas of life and bringing about changes within themselves. It was not only Calcutta that stood for modernity in the nineteenth century, Banaras too was going in that direction. Heber's account of a missionary school founded by Kalishankar Gossain is illuminating. This institution taught Persian, Hindustani, English and the Bible. The students in it were mostly Brahmins from middle-class families.[113]

One incident the reverend narrates is so charming that I, as a teacher, feel compelled to share it here. I too have seen such acts by enthusiastic pupils, keen on being complimented by their master. Heber narrates that while he was riding a pony through the busy throughfare of the city, a day after visiting a Sanskrit Vidyalaya near the Alamgir Masjid, a pupil from that school came running up to him:

> ...and with hands joined, said that I 'had not heard him his lesson yesterday, but he could sing it very well to-day if I would let him.' I accordingly stopped my horse, and sate with great patience while he chanted a long stave of Sanscrit. I repeated at proper pauses, 'good, good,' which satisfied him so much, that when he had finished, he called out

'again,' and was beginning a second stave when I dismissed him with a present, on which he fumbled in his mantle for some red flowers, which he gave me, and ran by my side, still talking on till the crowd separated us.[114]

The Ancient Art of Dharna Practised in Banaras

Another observation of Heber's surprised me no end. He states that when the government at Kolkata levied a house tax on the residents of Banaras, the city's inhabitants gathered in large numbers and sat for a dharna, until the unjust legislation was repealed. They were joined by the folks from the nearby villages and numbered to 3 lakh approximately. About this non-violent form of protest, Heber notes:

> To this the natives objected, that they recognized in their British rulers the same rights which had been exercised by the Moguls,—that the land-tax was theirs, and that they could impose duties on commodities going to market, or for exportation: but that their houses were their own,—that they had never been intermeddled with in any but their landed property, and commodities used in traffic,—and that the same power which now imposed a heavy and unheard of tax on their dwellings, might do the same next year on their children and themselves. These considerations, though backed by strong representations from the magistrates, produced no effect in Calcutta; on which the whole population of Benares and its neighbourhood determined to sit 'dhurna' till their grievances were redressed. To sit 'dhurna,' or mourning, is to remain motionless in that posture, without food, and exposed to the weather, till the person against whom it is employed consents to the request offered; and the Hindoos believe that whoever dies under such a process becomes a tormenting spirit to haunt and afflict his inflexible antagonist. This is a practice not unfrequent in the intercourse of individuals, to enforce payment of a debt, or forgiveness of one. And among

Hindoos it is very prevailing, not only from the apprehended dreadful consequences of the death of the petitioner, but because many are of opinion, that while a person sits dhurna at their door, they must, not themselves presume to eat, or undertake any secular business. It is even said that some persons hire brahmins to sit dhurna for them, the thing being to be done by proxy, and the dhurna of a brahmin being naturally more awful in its effects than that of a soodra could be. I do not know whether there is any example under their ancient princes of a considerable portion of the people taking this strange method of remonstrance against oppression, but in this case it was done with great resolution, and surprising concert and unanimity.[115]

To achieve that end, the leading Brahmins of Banaras sent tiny chits to the localities near the Banaras College and some to the nearest village, explaining the reason for the dharna and the need for the people to join the cause. And three days after such chits were issued by the Brahmin leaders, about 300,000 persons, leaving behind their chores, work and other means of sustenance, congregated in Banaras and resolved to fast, sitting 'down with folded arms and drooping heads, like so many sheep, on the plain which surrounds Benares'.[116]

The reverend's question of whether there was any example under India's ancient princes of a considerable portion of the people participating in such remonstrance, is answered in Kalhan and Jonaraja's *Rajatarangini*s, where several mentions of the hunger strikes done by the ancient and medieval Kashmiris for the redressal of their grievances are given.[117] The dharna of Banaras in 1824 CE was successful, and compelled the government in Calcutta to repeal the tax.[118]

The Golden Age of Banaras

The Banaras from the accounts of Heber has not changed: the small shrines by the lane under the eaves of the houses, the carved balconies, the brightly painted walls depicting flowers, animals and gods and goddesses, the gently bellowing bulls that block the passage through the lanes, the monkeys and their antics, 'religious mendicants of every Hindoo sect, offering every conceivable deformity, which chalk, cow-dung, disease, matted locks, distorted limbs, and disgusting and hideous attitudes of penance can show, literally [lining] the principal streets on both sides…men with their legs or arms voluntarily distorted by keeping them in one position, and their hands clenched till the nails [grow] out at the backs.'[119]

In fact, I believe that the golden age of Banaras is not some century in the distant past but the beginning of the nineteenth century, and it continues till date. According to the census of 1828–29 CE, Banaras had a total of 1,000 Hindu temples and 333 mosques.[120] By 1868 CE, the city saw an increase of 454 temples and its mosques decreased in number by 61, making it a total of 1,454 temples and 272 mosques.[121] This clearly tells us about the flurry of activities that were going on in the city.

Reclaiming the City's Holiest Place

The fabled Kashi Vishwanath Mandir, about whose destruction I have written in this chapter, was reconstructed by Rani Ahalya Bai outside its original position, occupied by the Gyanvapi Masjid. Maharaja Ranjit Singh of the Punjab had financed the gilding of the temple's spires, which were first covered with copper and then by gold leaf.[122] To the northwest of the Gyanvapi Masjid is the Adi Vishweswar Mandir (Adi Kashi Vishwanath), which is believed to be the first temple of Shiva that was destroyed by Muhammad Ghori. Nevill writes that this temple is marked by a small mosque built out of the materials from the destruction.[123]

I have not visited the Adi Vishweswar Mandir and the Kashi Vishwanath temple due to the crowd. However, I have seen the back of the Gyanvapi mosque, while buying hawai-mithai from one of those shops behind the northwest corner of the complex. The mosque is so heavily guarded that one is deterred from getting inside it except on Fridays, when people come to offer the Juma Namaz. One also cannot approach the back because of the wire-mesh barricade. The police posted there prohibit tourists from photographing the temple architecture that stands out below the three domes of the mosque.

James Prinsep's sketch of this mosque, done in 1825 CE, vividly details the southwest corner of the structure. At the right-hand corner of the sketch, just near the foot of a seated man, can be seen an unmistakable sculpture of four *bharbahaka*s (load bearers), who are the Indian equivalents of Corinthian load bearers, the topmost portions of pillars that support the lintel of the building. The idols of pot-bellied bharbahakas are characteristic of pillars belonging to Hindu temples that were constructed during the ninth–tenth centuries CE in North India. Immediately next to the foot of the seated man can be seen an idol of a destroyed Nandi, and behind him, three other standing figures and two graves.

In the information portion appertaining to the sketch, Prinsep notes that '…antiquarians will be well pleased that the Musalmans, in their zeal for the triumph of their own religion, discovered a method of converting the original structure into a capacious Masjid, without destroying above one half of its walls; so that not only the ground plan, but the entire architectural elevation, may still be traced out. A specimen of the order has been lithographed in the frontispiece, to shew the proportions of the different mouldings.'[124]

He further adds:

> The Lingam of the original temple of Vishweshwar was looked upon as the genuine type of Mahadeo or Shiva, which fell from heaven upon this spot, and was converted into stone. When the Musalmans set about their work of destruction, it is asserted, the indignant image leaped of its own accord into the Gian Bapee [Gyanvapi/'well of knowledge'] hard by, where it still remains. The well has since been considered to be the centre of the *Untergriha Jatra*, or Holy Circuit, although a modern Shivalaya, erected near the spot, pretends to have reinstated the genuine Lingam, and fashion is rapidly acquiescing in the arrangement.[125]

He also shares a grisly incident that took place in the Kashi Vishwanath Mandir; two persons slit their throats so that their blood might spatter over the linga.

The linga in the well he was talking about is the controversial black linga that has been found inside the Gyanvapi well, whose water was being used for *wudu* (water used for ritual purification by Muslims before prayers). In 2022, a court-ordered videographic survey found what many believe is a Shivling inside the well, whose discovery has flared up the demand for the demolition of the mosque.[126] And the modern Shivalaya from Prinsep's report is the present Kashi Vishwanath temple of Ahalya Bai. Between 1728 and 1783 CE, Maharaja Krishna Chandra of Krishnanagar in West Bengal had a large staircase constructed beside the Gyanvapi well.[127]

Rev. Heber was given a tour of the Kashi Vishwanath temple by Prinsep, who was then one of the magistrates of the city. His description of the temple and the well is worth sharing here. He writes:

> Our first visit was to a celebrated temple, named the Vishvayesa, consisting of a very small but beautiful specimen of carved stone-work, and the place is one of the most holy in Hindustan, though it only approximates to a yet more sacred spot adjoining, which Alamgir defiled, and built a mosque on it, so as to render it inaccessible to the worshippers of Brahma. The temple court, small as it is, is crowded like a farmyard, with very fat and very tame bulls, which thrust their noses into everybody's hand and pocket for gram and sweetmeats, which their fellow votaries give them in great quantities. The cloisters are no less full of naked devotees, as hideous as chalk and dung can make them, and the continued hum of 'Ram! Ram! Ram! Ram!' is enough to make a stranger giddy.[128]

The reverend goes on to write that the temple was very clean and maintained well by the priests. Furthermore, he writes about the Gyanvapi well, which had a small tower over it. Its water came via underground channels from the river, and was considered holier than even the Ganges. The reverend notes the occurrence of a religious riot in Banaras a few years before his visit, which started as the result of a Muslim mob slaughtering a cow beside the well. He writes:

> ...a quarrel having occurred between the Hindoo and Mussulman population of the town, arising from the two religious processions of the Muharam and Junma Osmee [Janmashtami] encountering each other, the Moslem mob killed a cow on this spot, and poured her blood into the sacred water. The Hindoos retaliated by throwing rashers of bacon into the windows of as many mosques as they could reach; but the matter did not end so: both parties took to arms, several lives were lost, and Benares was in a state of uproar for many hours, till the British Government came in with its authority, and quelled the disturbance.[129]

The Alamgir Masjid

Built over the demolished remains of the temple of Bindu Madhava (Vishnu) in 1669 CE on the orders of Aurangzeb, this imposingly tall structure is the tallest of all buildings that line the riverbank. As stated earlier, Tavernier saw Bindu Madhava and visited it.[130]

The Alamgir mosque once had two extremely tall minarets, one of which fell, killing several; the other was brought down by the British government due to concerns of safety. Prinsep's sketch of the mosque shows the left minaret within bamboo scaffolding, possibly being renovated.

Prinsep writes:

> The imperial zealot, not satisfied with triumphing over the religion of the Hindus, chose a method of perpetuating the insult most offensive to their habits and feelings, by carrying his minarets to such a height as to overlook the privacy of their houses, the upper apartments and terraced roofs of which are always tenanted by the females of the family. The Mosque has little architectural beauty to boast of, but the minars have

been deservedly admired for their simplicity and boldness of execution. They are only eight-and-a-half ft in diameter at the base, diminishing to seven ft at the top, while they have an altitude of 147 feet 2 inches, from the *suhun* or terraced door of the masjid to the *kulsa* or pinnacle. The terrace is elevated about 80 feet above the river at low water.[131]

He also tells us:

> In the course of the last ten years, four or five instances have occurred of men throwing themselves from the top of the southern minaret. One of them was a man who had gambled away his money and his wife during the Diwali, another a sailor, who, probably deceived by the height, thought the river within his reach; he fell upon the roof of the house contiguous to the terrace in the sketch, and was killed on the spot; but a remarkable instance is on record of a fakeer having once performed the same feat without suffering material injury; he broke through the tiles and mat work of the roof, which tore the flesh from his sides, but he alighted on the floor beneath, with every bone safe: such an escape was deemed miraculous, and crowds attended to reward and minister to one so favoured by heaven. To complete their wonder, the fakeer disappeared immediately on recovering from his bruises, and sundry solid moveables of his host vanished with him.[132]

It appears that the minarets were climbed time and again not only by the natives but also by the Europeans. Mrs Fanny Parkes too climbed a minaret of this mosque to get a grand view of the city. She writes that the young men prefer climbing the minarets at dawn in the hope of seeing the sleeping ladies on the roofs of houses adjacent to the mosque.[133]

Artist William Hodges has also described this mosque and its minarets, which from the river to their pinnacles were 232 feet.[134] He further mentions having painted the mosque and about it being built by 'the most intolerant and ambitious of human beings, the Emperor Aurangzeb, who destroyed a magnificent temple of the Hindus on this spot, and built the present mosque, said to be of the same extent and height as the building he destroyed.'[135]

The Kashi Vishwanath–Gyanvapi Masjid issue and the Alamgir Masjid, being controversial, are considered unresolved issues that exist between India's two largest communities. Both the communities have taken recourse to litigation in order to resolve the matter, which I believe is a civilized thing to do, instead of murdering each other and affecting millions with the poison of hatred that would be spewed as a result of this.

The Ghats

Having said that, let us walk along the riverbank and visit Banaras's many ghats, starting at the confluence of the Assi with the Ganga and then following the northerly course till Rajghat.

Because of the Assi River (now a narrow drain) emptying itself into the Ganga, the first bathing place on the Ganga is called the Assi Ghat. This ghat is among the five most sacred bathing places in Banaras. As legend states, the river Assi was created by Goddess Mahisasuramardini. Close to the Assi Ghat are three large ponds, called the Kurukshetra Kund, the Durga Kund and the Pushkar Talav.

Walking along the Assi Ghat, one comes to the Tulsi Ghat, which is named after the seventeenth-century saint and poet Tulsidas, the translator of the Sanskrit Ramayana into Awadhi (precursor to Hindi). He is said to have died at the ghat in 1623 CE. Two hundred and twenty-five years before him, in 1398 CE, another saint and poet named Kabir was born in Banaras.

Close to the ghat beside the temple of Durga, I was surprised to see an extremely deep stepwell called the Lolark Kund, which was renovated by Rani Ahalya Bai of Indore (1725–95 CE) and Amrit Rao of the family of the Peshwa.[136] This stepwell is dedicated to Surya and holds great sanctity in the minds of childless women, who take a dip in its water hoping to be blessed with progeny.

After every 50 m there is some ghat or the other, of which the Shivala Ghat is one of the most picturesque because of a fort palace complex above it, which was constructed by Baijnath Mishra.[137] This fortress was the residence of Raja Chait Singh, in the courtyard of which 250 English sepoys, including several officers, were massacred. The riverside wall of the fortress has Raja Chait Singh's name written on it to indicate that this part of the Shivala Ghat has been renamed in his honour. Nevill writes that after the rebellion of Chait Singh, the fortress was taken over by the government and allotted to the descendants of the last Mughal Bahadur Shah.[138] The Nirvani and the Niranjani akhadas (ashrams) of the Naga Sadhus are also on the Shivala Ghat.

An important ghat next to it is the Hanuman Ghat, from where the reformer Vallabacharya fell in the river and died in 1620 CE. This ghat is also known as the South Indian Ghat because of several mathas from the South that are found there. The Juna Akhada of the Naga Sadhus is on this ghat.

After that is the Harishchandra Ghat, which, according to tradition, is one of the oldest in Banaras. The Harishchandra Ghat also has an ancient crematorium, believed to be the one where the mythological king Harishchandra, synonymous with righteousness, worked as a *dom*'s (the untouchable who cremates the dead) slave. To escape the wrath of Sage Vishwamitra, this king had, after giving up his kingdom, sold himself, his wife and his son to slavery in Banaras. The story that unfolds tell us that after the death of his son, he refused to allow his wife to cremate him in that ghat because she could not come up with the burning tax that was to be collected by him on behalf of his master. Unable to stand such a grating situation, the gods, led by Indra, descended from heaven and relieved him of his misery by taking him up to heaven, making him the first human to ascend to the celestial realm without dying. That is the reason why people consider the Harishchandra Ghat crematorium as holy.

Adjacent to the Harishchandra Ghat is the Kedar Ghat. One interesting aspect about this ghat is the tiny Gauri Kund. It is a square tank with steps on both ends. Below this tank are the steps that go into the river. Inside the *kund*, I came across a small stone temple part that had been kept as an object of reverence because of a carved face on it. This piece of sculpture was once a part of a temple, one among the numerous demolished in the city. Above this kund is the Kedareshwar Mandir.

The next ghat is the Chauki Ghat, and adjacent to it are the Manasarovar Ghat and the Narada Ghat. Along the Narada Ghat are seen several impressive palaces, beginning with Amrit Rao's at Raja Ghat. Walking past this mansion, one comes across several other ghats like Chausati, where a modern Chausat Yogini temple exists. Hodges's description of the ruins of a circular temple, which still had some sculptural embellishment on it, makes me conclude that he was referring to a Chausat Yogini temple.[139] Except the Chausat Yogini of Khajuraho, all of them are circular in layout. I did not visit this temple, which is unlike all other Chausat Yogini temples that are found in India.

The next ghats are the Rana Mahal, the Darbhanga and the Munshi, named after Munshi Shridhar, the architect of Rani Ahalya Bai.[140] The ghat adjacent to the Munshi Ghat is the Dashashwamedh Ghat. This ghat was renovated by Rani Ahalya Bai, who spent a considerable fortune reconstructing some demolished temples like the Kashi Vishwanath Mandir in the city, and many other temples in other parts of India. The name Dashashwamedh denotes the ten-horse sacrifice that was done there by Brahma. Due to this, great sanctity is attached to this place, and thousands congregate there to bathe during the eclipses and Sankrantis.

One important structure that is to be found on the Dashashwamedh Ghat is the Man Mandir palace, constructed by Raja Man Singh during the reign of Akbar. On the roof of this palace, Man Singh's descendant Raja Jaisingh II had an observatory constructed, called the Jantar Mantar. This monarch, after whom Jaipur is named, was a savant and had several such observatories constructed in India, namely in Jaipur, Delhi, Mathura, Ujjain and Varanasi. Except the one in Mathura, all his observatories survive. Rev. Heber had found this observatory the most interesting 'object' in Banaras.[141]

Close to the Man Mandir is the Meer Ghat, named after Mir Rustam Ali, who governed Banaras before Balwant Singh became its king. Beside this is the Tripura Bhairavi Ghat, named after Durga, and adjacent to it is the Lalita Gauri Ghat. This ghat is extremely interesting for the pagoda-style Nepalese temple that exists there. Because of this temple, the ghat is also called the Nepalese Ghat. I have dedicated a separate portion to the Nepalese temple and will not delve into it here.

The famous Manikarnika Ghat comes next and is the most important ghat of Banaras, because it is directly connected by a path to the Kashi Vishwanath Mandir, around which the cosmology of Banaras revolves. This ghat is named after the gem that fell from the earring of Sati when Vishnu dismembered her corpse into fifty-one parts. Like the crematorium of the Harishchandra Ghat, Manikarnika's too has perpetually had a pyre or two lit at all times of the day, for several centuries. Recently, a grand access was created from the Kashi Vishwanath Mandir to the ghat that effortlessly allows pilgrims to access the riverbank. While the demolition drive was underway to create this path, called the Kashi Vishwanath Corridor, several later-day ornate temples emerged from the compounds of the buildings that were demolished. At that time, I happened to be in Banaras and carefully documented some of the sculpted structures that emerged.

Going past the Manikarnika Ghat, one comes across some of the best-looking temples of Banaras, some of which are in a state of utter dilapidation, coupled with the black patina of soot from the pyres that has covered their exteriors. The temples in this part of the ghat were constructed by the Bhonsle family of Nagpur and the Scindia family of Gwalior. One of the most ornately carved temples here is the Bala Tripura Sundari Mandir.

A little ahead of these temples is the most handsome structure on the ghats of Banaras: the leaning Ratneshwar Mahadev Mandir, which stands precariously on the lowest portion of the ghats and is presently silted up to its garbhagriha. When the water level rises, half the temple gets inundated. I have on several occasions visited this temple, sometimes by boat and other times by walking.

An elaborate sketch of this temple and another done by James Prinsep in 1825 CE clearly show that the temple existed high over the water.[142] A photo of the temple taken in 1865 CE also shows that the temple's tilt had not yet begun. Another image of the same temple from 1890 CE also shows it as standing erect. The information given by Prinsep about the temples sketched by him mentions that they were constructed by Rani Ahalya Bai.[143]

The ghat adjacent to the precinct of Ratneshwar Mahadev temple is the Scindia Ghat that was constructed by Baija Bai Scindia, the wife of Daulat Rao Scindia.[144] This influential queen was an extremely rich banker and has been written about by Fanny Parkes in her memoir, titled *Wanderings of a Pilgrim in Search of the Picturesque*. Mrs Parkes shares an anecdote about her. In Allahabad, she was made to make her horse wear a fine pink coral necklace that she had purchased for herself, because Baija Bai told her that coral necklaces were only good for horses, with her own horse wearing a necklace of deep red corals.[145]

The ghat next to Scindia is the Sankat, and then there is the Bhonsle Ghat that is surmounted with an impressive fort-like complex. The next ghat in the order of importance is the Ram Ghat, and after a few unimportant ghats is the Panchganga Ghat. Above this ghat is the Alamgiri Masjid, whose height dominates the city.

The ghat next to the Panchganga is the Durga Ghat, and then comes the Brahma Ghat. Next to it is the Bundi Ghat, which has a fort-like residence of the erstwhile king of Bundi. After this are the Sitala, the Lal, the Gaay, the Badrinarayan, the Trilochan and the Tripura Bhairavi ghats. A few ghats after this comes the Rajghat, beside which is the Ravidas Ghat and then the Madan Mohan Malviya Setu (formerly the Dufferin Bridge) that connects Banaras to Mughal Sarai. The Rajghat was not a bathing ghat but the landing of the old pontoon bridge before the Malviya Bridge was constructed. The bridge was renamed after Madan Mohan Malviya, the founder of the BHU.

Going further on the same bank of the river is a modern ghat recently constructed at the initiative of Prime Minister Narendra Modi, which has been named Namo Ghat. Above the Namo Ghat is the archaeological site of Rajghat and the tomb of Lal Khan, constructed in 1773 CE by Raja Chait Singh for his commander. This small tomb is splendidly built and embellished with coloured tiles. It occupies the topmost portion of the Rajghat archaeological site, below the eastern side of which the oldest remains of Banaras have been unearthed. If one goes a kilometre further from there along the river, one comes to the confluence of the Varuna with the Ganga at Adi Keshav Ghat, which is so far the last ghat of Banaras.

Sati on the Ghats

The ghats were used not only for ritual bathing but for ritual murder as well. Innumerable sati ceremonies have taken place on them. The occurrence of such a heinous crime was celebrated by those performing the horrendous act on an innocent widow, sometimes as young as twelve, which Bernier witnessed at Lahore.[146]

The artist Hodges's eyewitness account of a sati ceremony in Banaras is a tale of such morbidity that reading it chokes one's throat with welled-up emotion. He vividly describes one such ritual taking place in a ghat in Banaras—which one, he specifies not.

The husband's body, brought by some ten to fifteen people, was laid on a pyre. After some time, the widow appeared along with some Brahmins, her relations, and musicians:

> The procession was slow and solemn; the victim moved with a steady and firm step; and, apparently with perfect composure of countenance, approached close to the body of her husband, where for some time they halted. She then addressed those who were near her with composure, and without the least trepidation of voice or change of countenance. She held in her left hand a cocoa nut, in which was a red colour mixed up, and dipping in it the fore-finger of her right hand, she marked those near her, to whom she wished to [show] the last act of attention.[147]

Hodges, being in the crowd, was also given the *tika* on the forehead by her. This is when he saw her face clearly and discerned that the lady was not more than twenty-five years old. She was a small woman, and beautiful, draped in the widow's white sari. The pyre was higher up on the ghat, about 100 yards from where they stood. It was piled high with dry branches, leaves and hay that were stacked like an arched gate, beside which stood a man with a lit torch. The body of her husband was brought and laid on it, and after bowing to all those around, she entered the pile through the gate of hay, which was immediately closed. Not a word was spoken by the lady or a cry heard from her; only the stoic passivity of following an age-old diktat that glorified the memory of its victim. Immediately, the man with the torch lit the pyre, which instantaneously went up in roaring flames. Meanwhile, the crowd had multiplied around the flames and was clamorous with rejoicings. The memory of this scarred Hodges who, unlike those celebrating, was overcome with sadness, which after abating caused him to draw the scene in imitation of characters from the canvases of Renaissance artists.

Perhaps due to the presence of British administrators in Banaras, Sati rituals had reduced by the time Rev. Heber visited the city. He tells us that Sati was less common there than in other parts of India, but ritual suicide by drowning was a frequent occurrence. The pilgrims who visited Shiva's city also came there to die. The manner in which they carried out their last wish was that they bought a large pot and tied it to their necks, then swam to the middle of the river using it as a float, and filled it with water.[148] The administration had tried to prevent this but failed to do so, as the person determined to die would only swim further into the river and carry out the act. Five years after the reverend's visit, Sati was abolished in India in 1829 CE.

The Samrajeshwar Mahadev Temple

Of the innumerable temples of Banaras, the most interesting according to me are two small structures. The first is situated on the banks of the Ganga on the Lalita Ghat and is known as the Samrajeshwar Mahadev temple, commonly called Nepali Mandir. The second is the Kardameshwar Mahadev Mandir, found far from the riverbank at a place called Kanchanpur, 9 km away.

The history behind the fantastic Nepali temple is fascinating. The construction of this sculptured, single-spired, pagoda-style structure was started in 1800 CE by the king of Nepal, Rana Bahadur Shah. He was forced to abdicate in favour of his minor son Girvan Yuddha Bikram Shah in the year 1800 CE. He spent his days in exile as Swami Nirgunanda in Banaras, where the British resident accorded him protection.[149]

After the arrival of the deposed king in Banaras, a commercial treaty was signed on 28 October 1801 between the East India Company and the Nepalese Durbar, which for the first time established the post of an English resident in Kathmandu.[150] While the king was involved in spiritual matters in Banaras, the relationship between the Nepalese and the English was getting worse. The English wanted to reinstall the king while a powerful faction of the Nepalese Durbar was vehemently against it. Here one can state that the threads of the future Anglo-Nepalese relations were being played out in the residence of the king behind the yet-to-be-completed Nepalese temple, and a few years later this erupted into an all-out war.

In 1802 CE, Captain William Knox was sent to Kathmandu to represent the East India Company. At Banaras, Rana Bahadur Shah, financed by the British, accrued a large debt due to his extravagant ways, which the resident forced the Nepalese Durbar, now led by Rajrajeshwari, the chief queen of the *rana*, to pay. Meanwhile, the court in Kathmandu was divided between the rana's first queen and the second, named Subarnaprabha, supported by Resident Knox.

This interference by the resident was unfavourably looked at by Queen Rajrajeshwari who, after dissolving the Durbar, made it amply clear to Knox that his presence was unwelcome in Kathmandu. Knox moved to Makwanpur, south of Kathmandu. This was humiliating for the Company, and Governor-General Richard Wellesley recalled Knox to Kolkata and annulled the treaty of 1801 CE. After this, the rana was reinstalled as the king in 1804 CE, albeit under the control of his queen and her coterie.

With the king shifting back to Kathmandu, work on the temple stopped. In 1807 CE, the rana was murdered by his stepbrother Sher Bahadur Shah,[151] who was, in turn, killed for his crime, and Girvan Yuddha Bikram Shah was reinstalled as the king. It was during his reign that the Anglo-Nepal war broke out with several skirmishes.[152]

The murdered rana's son Girvan Yuddha Bikram Shah Deva completed the shrine twenty years after the death of his father. In 1843 CE, the land around the temple, comprising the Lalita Ghat and a dharmshala, was transferred to the Nepalese royal family by the then king of Banaras. At present, this temple is under the ownership of the Government of Nepal.[153]

The temple is an ambassador of the Nepali style of architecture in a land far away from its place of origin. To be more specific, the rather small shrine is the epitome of the Newari style of temple-building and sculptural embellishment, so freely found in Bhaktapur and Patan in Kathmandu. This pagoda-type shrine is dedicated to Shiva, has fantastic wood carvings, and is a hidden gem of Banaras.

The Luckiest Temple in the World

I had planned to visit the Kardameshwar Mahadev temple on my way out of Banaras, but before that I decided to detour to the BHU. My objective was to see the fantastic sculptures in the Bharat Kala Bhavan Museum, which did not materialize, as the museum was closed due to the Covid-19 pandemic. All I managed to do was click pictures of those sculptures displayed on both sides of the museum's porch. I visited the museum in 2022 and was denied permission to click a few photos inside the building, particularly of the colossal Gupta era Krishna sculpture holding up Govardhan hill, which is kind of ironic, because several photos of these sculptures are available in the public domain.[154]

I guess the underworked staff there perhaps wanted to show their importance by telling the visitor a stern 'no' and that 'permission is needed', and all that red tape poppycock. Strange that inside the ill-lit hall of the museum, I came across more staff than visitors and students from the university. At the ticket counter, I saw five elderly security guards sitting around a table—guarding each other, I guess.

From the BHU campus, the Kardameshwar Mahadev Mandir is about 4 km to the west. This temple is inside a crowded locality called Kanchanpur that has three large water bodies. The Kardameshwar temple is situated on the western banks of the largest pond there and should not be missed by anyone visiting Banaras.

This, according to me, is the most fascinating temple of the age-old city. It is a medium-sized stone-crafted Nagara-style structure about 40 feet in height, embellished with excellent sculptures. When compared with other surviving structures of the same age, this temple appears ordinary, and yet I am compelled to call it a wonder, because I wonder how it survived the iconoclastic onslaughts that time and again befell the city. In that regard, I will also call it the luckiest temple in the world, to have survived intact for nearly 700 years, before the hammers of iconoclasts were snatched away by cancerous decay, resurgent Hindu kingdoms, and the new political dispensation, the British.

Originally constructed in the ninth–tenth centuries, the Kardameshwar temple was later enlarged by the Gahadavalas in the twelfth–thirteenth centuries CE. The evidence of an earlier structure at the site is found in the form of a splendid Surya sculpture kept in a shed beside the structure. There are a few more carvings kept beside the temple that are centuries old. The size of those sculptures fits in with the architecture of the temple niches wherein these were placed, making it apparent that they belonged either to this structure or to some other that exists no more.

Dedicated to Shiva, this temple sits on a platform that juts into a large rectangular tank that was renovated in the eighteenth century by Rani Bhabani, the builder queen of Natore, in present-day Bangladesh. She had also built the tall Durga Mandir and renovated the Durga Kund adjacent to it and the Kurukshetra Kund near the Assi Ghat.

The Kardameshwar Mandir's miraculous existence makes it the oldest surviving temple of Banaras. One possible reason for this is perhaps its location. Being situated some distance away from the ghats where most temples are, this site was hidden, which helped it escape the wrath of every other zealot. Another reason may be the jungle that existed around the place, which deterred even the residents of Banaras from going there.

Yet another reason, which I think the most probable, is the temple's positioning, which is not close to any major artery. The old Mughal road from Allahabad to Banaras took a northerly turn from Mohansarai and headed straight for the heart of the city. Since the temple is situated deep inland, anyone approaching Banaras via the riverine route cannot know the existence of any such structure without prior knowledge of it. The temple must really have been forgotten for it to reemerge in the twentieth century, because Nevill's *Benares: A Gazetteer*, published in 1909, is silent about it, which is somewhat strange due to the great detail given in it about the other temples of Banaras.[155]

Banaras Today

To actually feel the essence of Shiva's city and the frenzy with which the city regenerated itself, one must simply walk its narrow lanes. In doing so one will lose oneself in the labyrinthine maze of the city's 'old' quarters, attached to the Ganga. For this I would recommend beginning from the Assi Ghat like I did, losing myself within the lean alleyways that to me seemed like the impossibly tangled locks of Shiva. It is not for nothing that the city is called the abode of Mahadeva, particularly if one imagines it as Shiva's locks letting the Ganga cascade to the earth.

It takes one several hours to walk through the confined quarters, where one is occasionally embraced by renditions of classical Hindustani music by neophytes practising in some guru's house. After this unusual experience, one passes through parts engulfed with the smoggy smell of frying samosas and kachoris. In trying to escape this opacity, one then crosses several shrines, whose smouldering aromatics waft about like the hair ribbon of a careless girl.

After crossing cows, clanking rickshaws, gossiping old men, and carolling crows, one's mind gets cluttered with all that it has perceived, real and surreal. One then begins to long for succour from the confines of Banaras's intestinal knot and desperately longs to see the wide-open skies. An immediate sense of relief bathes one when one comes out onto the ghats and faces the emptiness ahead, with the river flowing below. This feeling is indescribable, and no number of literary devices used in trying to express it can do justice to it.

At present, under the initiative taken by the government and several NGOs, Banaras is seeing a lot of development in its cleanliness drive. My earlier visits would often be overcome with nauseating revulsion at the apathy with which the residents and worshippers treated this timeless city. The ghats were then littered with garbage and dung. Things are different now. One can sit for long hours on the banks of the Ganga and take in what the city has to offer. Another important aspect in this developmental drive is the creation of the Kashi Vishwanath Corridor, connecting the Manikarnika Ghat with the Kashi Vishwanath Mandir. This corridor is an open space on which a boulevard is built through the otherwise congested localities of the city. The people whose homes were destroyed to build this have been compensated amply, which would otherwise have marred the beauty of this place.

8

The Lost Treasures of Sarnath

Sarnath, situated 10 km to the north of Banaras, is one of the holiest Buddhist sites in the world. According to the *Mahaparinirvana Sutra*, the Buddha himself had told Ananda about the four principal places of pilgrimage for a Buddhist, which began at Lumbini, the place of his birth, followed by Bodh Gaya, the place of his enlightenment, Sarnath, the place of his first preaching, and Kushinagar, the place of his death.[1]

The Buddha, after his enlightenment at Gaya, walked 244 km to preach his first sermon at the Deer Park in Sarnath approximately 2,600 years ago. One interesting point that struck me as odd while I was going around the Dhamek Stupa in Sarnath was that the Buddha, after attaining enlightenment, did not preach his 'eureka' moment' at Bodh Gaya, which was the natural thing to do. Instead, he remained mum for forty-nine days, including the five days he walked to reach Banaras, and delivered his gospel to five people in the Deer Park. This incident happened in about 528 BCE.[2]

Well, the Buddha epitomized stoicism, and perhaps it took him forty-nine days to subdue the ecstasy he felt at discovering the simplest philosophy that requires you not to give birth to desire. Who knows...

A Life for a Life

The name Sarnath is derived from the word Sarang-Nath ('lord of the deer') from a Jataka tale of a deer, who had offered his life to a king of Banaras to save that of a doe's. The king, being overcome with shame and emotion at his intended cruelty, gave up hunting.

He then created a protected enclosure as a sanctuary for innocent herbivores. That deer was the Buddha in one of his previous births.

It is due to this story and the Buddha's delivery of his first sermon that one of the prominent Buddhist icons depicts two seated antelopes facing a spoked wheel, which represents the turning of the wheel of law. This icon can be found extensively used by Tibetan Buddhists in their monasteries as well as in monasteries of Ladakh and Spiti. Another important aspect of this icon is that the Jains too use this symbol in their temples. I have come across one excellently carved red sandstone image of the two-deer-and-wheel icon in the Jain temple complex of Osian, in the Jodhpur district of Rajasthan.

Did the Buddha Deliver His First Sermon at Sarnath?

In the *Mahavamsa*, the great chronicle of Sri Lanka, we learn from Monk Mahanama,[3] the scholar credited with compiling the book, that:

> ...at Uruvela [Bodh Gaya], in the Magadha country, the great sage, sitting at the foot of the Bodhi-tree, reached the supreme enlightenment on the full-moon day of the month Vesakha. Seven weeks he tarried there, mastering his senses, while that he himself knew the high bliss of deliverance and let (others) behold its felicity. Then he went to Baranasi and set rolling the wheel of the law; and while he dwelt there through the rain-months, he brought sixty (hearers) to arahantship.[4]

What I find strange is why Monk Mahanama did not specify the important place where this momentous incident occurred, instead of merely stating it as Varanasi. Sarnath and Banaras were then two distinctive places separated by a gap of 9 km, which during the days of snail-paced transportation was quite a stretch.

Well, this stray passage from the *Mahavamsa* can easily be dismissed as an error on the part of Monk Mahanama in describing the site of the great master's first sermon. The name Varanasi being used instead of Sarnath can also be due to both terms being used interchangeably, which we see Lama Taranatha do in *History of Buddhism in India*.[5] Suffice to say that all the other Buddhist books are unanimous in their agreement that the first Buddhist creed was delivered at Sarnath vis-à-vis Banaras.

Sarnath before the Buddha

The importance of Sarnath dates back to the days before the Buddha's first sermon made it famous. The very reason that the Buddha straightaway went to Sarnath instead of the ghats on the Ganga, which would seem to be the logical thing to do, was probably that Sarnath was a known congregation point of different heretical sects like the early Jains, Charvakas and Ajivikas.

My theory is not supported by any evidence but by conjectures that direct me to conclude that the ghats, being occupied by Brahminical adherents, were avoided to prevent confrontation. Also, the sanctuary of a protected place such as the Deer Park is a metaphorical allusion to helpless creatures, which in this case were the members of the heterodox sects.

From satellite images, it appears that once upon a time a river had flowed past Sarnath and later dried up, forming a natural depression. It is highly likely that like Banaras on the Ganga, ancient Sarnath too was an urban centre accessed by a waterway flowing from the north.

This depression, down the millennia, was most probably excavated for clay to bake bricks for the numerous stupas and other edifices that filled up the place during the Gupta and later periods. The presence of large water bodies to the north (the Kurmadeva Kund/Naya Tal) and east (Sarang Tal) of the Dhamek Stupa archaeological compound testifies to this hypothesis.[6] And because of this excavation of clay for purposes of building, whatever evidence of an urban centre that could have been found underground has been lost to us. This we will see being repeated at Sarnath during the later days of the eighteenth century.

The palaeochannel of the river was probably the Gomti, which, after flowing past Sarnath, emptied into the Ganga, somewhere northeast of Banaras. At present, the Gomti's confluence with the Ganga is at Kaithi, about 20 km away from Sarnath.

From Religious Texts and Travelogues

Having shared my hypothesis above, let me now delve into the tangible past of Sarnath with hard evidence procured from ancient texts, archaeology, epigraphy and the travelogues of ancient pilgrims.

Sarnath is also known by other names like Mrigadaya ('deer park'), Rishipatana ('landing of holy men')[7] and Singhpuri ('city of lions'). There is an interesting legend associated with the name Rishipatana, for it was believed that 500 enlightened beings fell at the spot after attaining nirvana.

For long, Sarnath was also called Dharmeksa, which means 'the expounding of the law'. The name in its shortened form, Dhamek, got attached to the stupa due to its prominent height, which stood out from the then unexcavated mound and acted as a landmark. The Jain manuscript *Vividha Tirtha Kalpa* of Jinaprabhasuri, dated to 1612 CE, notes Banaras as a Jain place of pilgrimage, beside which a locality named Dharmeksa is mentioned as a famous Buddhist sanctuary.[8]

It is also the birthplace of the eleventh Tirthankara of the Jains called Shreyansnatha, because of which this place was known as Singhpuri by the Jains. It is possible that the name Shreyansnatha degenerated into Sarnath. The present Jain temple adjacent to the Dhamek Stupa was reconstructed in 1824.[9] It is dedicated to this Tirthankara.

At what point in time Sarnath gained religious eminence as the second holiest Buddhist site is difficult to say. Lama Taranatha shares a legend that tells us how the first temple marking the spot of the first sermon came about. He writes that a Brahmin named Jaya built the first shrine over the spot at Banaras (referring to Sarnath). This Brahmin had heard the Buddha's doctrine of non-violence from a monk named Uttara and was so filled with reverence that he and his two brothers, Sujaya and Kalyana, decided to build shrines commemorating the major events associated with the life of Buddha. While he built the shrine at Sarnath, Sujaya erected one in Rajgriha, and Kalyana, the most devout of them, built the first temple at Bodh Gaya.[10]

The very presence of the best specimen of an Ashokan Lion Capital that had once surmounted a lofty pillar erected by Ashoka tells us that Sarnath gained an enviable position in Buddhist cosmology during the third century BCE. It is only after the construction of a stupa by the emperor that later kings began to embellish the place with numerous structures.

Fa Hien's Visit

By the time the Guptas came to rule over the region, Sarnath had already developed enough as a prominent pilgrimage spot to attract the attention of Fa Hien, who records the existence of two monasteries there, where resided monks of the lesser vehicle and four stupas.[11] These stupas were erected over the spots where the Buddha delivered his first sermon that expounded the fundamentals of his doctrine to the first five disciples. Some distance from there, another stupa stood where the Buddha had sat facing east, preaching to the public for the first time. The next stupa stood at the place where he prophesied the coming of future Buddhas, and the last was erected to mark the spot where he released Naga Elapatra from his horrid existence.[12] From Sarnath Fa Hien then moves to Kausambi, without telling us who built those stupas in Sarnath.

Hieun Tsang's Visit and Vivid Description

Hieun Tsang fills in the gap of information left by his predecessor. Through him we get a vivid picture of Sarnath as it existed in the seventh century CE. The pilgrim begins his documentation of Sarnath from the north of Banaras. After crossing the Varuna, he goes to the monastery of the 'Stag Deer', whose precinct was divided into eight parts connected by walls. The monastery was multi-storeyed with elaborately carved balconies. Like Fa Hien, he too mentions that the monastery belonged to the Hinayana school of thought. In an enclosure beside the monastery was a 200-foot tall temple/stupa topped with a gilt mango. The lower portion of the structure was built of stone, including its stairs, while the rest was crafted with bricks. The niches on the tower of this temple had several gilt images of the Buddha, and at the centre of the tower there stood a life-sized copper image of the Buddha in the posture of teaching his doctrine.[13] The image that this temple brings to mind is of the Mahabodhi temple of Bodh Gaya. However, some have interpreted this as the imposingly tall Dhamek Stupa, which occupies the eastern portion of the compound.

To the southwest of this temple/stupa was a stupa built by Ashoka whose foundations had sunk, yet that edifice stood 100 feet tall. Beside it there stood a 70-foot-tall stone pillar, whose polish was 'as bright as jade'.[14] This stupa and the pillar marked the spot where the Buddha preached the first sermon.

The identity of this structure was concluded to be the Dharmarajika Stupa after the discovery of the broken Ashokan column and the masterfully crafted lion emblem that was found buried beside it. It is presently a destroyed structure, caused due to the scavenging act of Jagat Singh, a *diwan* of Raja Chait Singh, who had scoured for materials to build a market named after him (Jagatganj) near the British-built Sanskrit University of Banaras (now the Sampurnananda Sanskrit University). This desecration I will come to later...

The Ashokan pillar, now in stumps, is kept inside a glass box in situ. It was topped with four splendidly carved lions standing back to back facing the four cardinal directions. This sculpture is in the Sarnath Museum and is the national emblem of India.

Hieun Tsang continues to note that beside the Dharmarajika Stupa, there existed another stupa that marked the spot where the first five disciples joined the sangha. Beside this were four other stupas, the last of which marked the spot where the Buddha predicted the coming of the Maitreya Buddha. To the south of these stupas was a promenade where the past Buddhas walked for exercise. There he saw a fine sculpture of the Buddha poised to walk. Within the precincts of this enclosure, several hundred sacred vestiges like votive stupas were erected.

To the west of this enclosure there was a lake, the traces of which can now be seen in satellite images in the form of the green patch west of the archaeological complex. And further west of this lake was a large waterbody, which still exists in piecemeal, about a kilometre from there. To the north of this is another lake, which I believe is the Naya Tal, where the pilgrim states that the Buddha used to wash his robes. Looking at the satellite image of the Sarnath archaeological compound, one will find it surrounded by water bodies on three sides, the west portion of which has dried out. This portion extends all the way past the Chaukhandi Stupa till the Prasar Bharati compound.

Beside the lake where the Buddha washed his robes was a large square stone that bore the imprints of his robe. Cunningham has spoken about this stone, which he had seen during his first visit to the site but found missing from there during his second.[15] On the other side of the lake there stood several stupas, each dedicated to the past lives of the Buddha. A small distance south of the Sarnath complex, there stood a stupa about 300 feet in height which was embellished by carved stonework and precious substances. Cunningham has identified this structure as the Chaukhandi Stupa. The pilgrim records that the several other stupas around the main complex were all related to the past lives of the Buddha. After concluding his visit, Hieun Tsang went east along the Ganga to 'Chen-Chu', identified as Ghazipur.[16]

As of now, there exist three large stupas at Sarnath, namely the Dhamek Stupa, the Dharmarajika Stupa (the stupa of Jagat Singh) within the same compound, and the Chaukhandi Stupa, about 600 m south of the compound. Atop the ruins of the Chaukhandi Stupa is an octagonal tower built by Akbar. A Persian inscription on the tower notes the visit of Humayun, who climbed to the top of the stupa, an event commemorated by his son Akbar, who caused the tower to be built and a slab engraved in the year 1587 CE.[17]

Near the Dhamek Stupa, within the exposed portion of an

excavated wall, I came across a paw mark of a dog who had walked on a brick while it was being dried. This I found exciting and very contemporary. My father once owned a brickfield where during the drying process of the raw bricks that were laid out or stacked in the open, several creatures such as dogs, foxes and goats would walk over them, leaving their marks on those bricks. Seeing an innocent millennia-old paw mark there did take me back to my childhood.

The Two Catastrophes at Sarnath

For close to 1,000 years, Sarnath remained an oft-visited site for Buddhists till the regeneration of Hinduism in India around the eighth century CE. Despite this, the place did not lose its religious sanctity until the first catastrophe that befell it. In 1018, Aryavarta was overwhelmed by the bloodthirsty hordes of Mahmud of Ghazni. His sacking of Banaras spelt doom for Sarnath too.

An inscription on the pedestal of a sculpture of a seated Buddha/Bodhisattva informs us about the restoration of building works done at Sarnath in 1026 CE.[18] The sculpture is destroyed, and its only remaining portion is a bit of the leg and the pedestal whose central part depicts the *dharmachakra* between two *vajras*, flanked by two deer, surrounded by two lions, and bordered by two bharbahakas, in that order. Above and below this frieze are two lined inscriptions in Sanskrit. Going by the inscription on the sculpture, one can infer that after the first catastrophe of 1018 CE, the monasteries were renovated with new adornments such as the seated Buddha.

In the intervening period between Ghazni and Ghori, in the last decade of the twelfth century CE, the monasteries in Sarnath were rebuilt and embellished. And then the final knell rang with the fall of Jayachandra and the subsequent conquest of Banaras by Ghori, when the monastery was utterly destroyed.[19]

Scavengers

Sarnath was a forgotten site, whose ruins attracted the attention of those that visited Banaras, as is attested to by the Persian inscription of Akbar found atop the Chaukhandi Stupa. The earliest excavation work that we know of at Sarnath was not out of any historical curiosity but scavenging work done by Diwan Jagat Singh in 1793–94 CE. This person completely stole the stones and bricks from the Dharmarajika Stupa and also removed most of the wonderfully carved stone claddings from the Dhamek Stupa.[20]

While digging for bricks and stones, the workers employed to do so came upon two urns. This discovery was noted by Commissioner of Banaras Jonathan Duncan and published in *Asiatic Researches*, Vol. V. Duncan writes that a stone and a marble vessel (the marble vessel was found inside the stone one) unearthed in January 1794 by the labourers working for Babu Jagat Singh were from the 'vicinity of a temple called Sarnath, at the distance of about four miles to the northward of the present city of Benares.' The innermost casket contained 'a few human bones, that were committed to the Ganges, and some decayed pearls, gold leaves, and other jewels of no value.' Duncan concluded that the bones must have belonged to a worshipper of the Buddha, as an idol of him was found below the urn. He also noted that the ruins belonged to a temple that stood there some 800 years ago.[21]

Duncan was not off the mark in any way, which the excavations conducted by Cunningham forty-one years after Duncan's report would prove in 1835 CE. The inner casket, which Duncan noted as marble, was green schist and was deposited with the Asiatic Society in 1794 CE. The scavenging work of Jagat Singh spurred several English officers posted at the cantonment in Sikraul to attempt digs of their own, which caused Emma Roberts to write in 1834 CE that in 1794 CE, the Dhamek Stupa and the ruins of Sarnath attracted the attention of several gentlemen who searched for antiquities and found cartloads of wax images of the Buddha embossed on clay tablets. Many were deposited in museums, while the rest went into private collections. The lady also noted that these discoveries were not documented, nor any record kept of those finds.[22] Even before Emma Roberts's observation, Col. Mackenzie went about digging at the site in 1815 CE. But there exists no record of his observations.[23]

Cunningham Finds Evidence of the Destruction of Sarnath

Cunningham's excavation of 1835–36 CE was the first scientifically done dig at the site. He had made several enquiries of those embossed images of the Buddha and the whereabouts of the 'marble' casket, which by 1834 CE had disappeared from the Asiatic Society's depository. While beginning the dig in 1835, he further asked around for knowledge on Jagat Singh's dig, and was rewarded when an elderly man named Shankar from Singhpur village volunteered information.

As a young man, Shankar had been involved in Jagat Singh's scavenging act and told Cunningham that such boxes were indeed unearthed. The larger of the two was a round urn of common stone, while the inner piece was green, about 15 inches in height and 6 inches in diameter, containing 40–46 pearls, 14 rubies, 8 silver and 9 gold earrings, and three pieces of human arm bones.[24]

Shankar informed that the inner box was given to Duncan while the larger one was reinterred where it was found. Cunningham immediately asked Shankar to dig up the spot, who did likewise and retrieved the larger box, proving his story true.[25]

Shankar had also told him that a damaged statue of the Buddha was unearthed from below the urns. When the stones were carted away to build Jagatganj, this sculpture too was taken there. Later, during Major Markham Kittoe's excavation of the site in 1851 CE, Cunningham requested him to search for that idol. All he could locate was the statue's pedestal from Jagat Singh's house in Jagatganj,[26] which is now displayed in the Sarnath Museum.

The importance of this mutilated statue is in the inscription carved on it. The engraving reads that the illustrious Sthirpala and his brother Vasantapala were instructed by the monarch of Bengal,

Mahipala, to build the temples of Ishana (Shiva) and Chitraghanta (Durga) and other monuments in the hundreds, and also restore the stupa and the shrine of the wheel of law completely and build the new shrine of Gandhakuti ('the hut of fragrance') out of stone, in 1026 CE.[27]

Another inscription found at Sarnath, dated to 4 October 1058 CE, mentions the name of the Kalachuri ruler Karnadeva, indicating the Sarnath monastery was still flourishing at that date.[28] The last inscription unearthed from the site, known as the Sarnath Inscription of Kumaradevi (the queen of Govindachandra Gahadavala of Kannauj, who ruled from 1114 CE to 1154 CE), informs us about the construction of a large monastery at Sarnath. She had also restored the rest of the structures that had existed there from the time of 'Dharmashoka'.[29] The monastery that she had built was to the north of the Dhamek Stupa, whose east–west-lined foundational remains are the only edifices left of it.

These inscriptions conclusively proved that a few years prior to the rebuilding activity at Sarnath, the city met with a catastrophe. And that, by conjecture, was probably done at the behest of Mahmud of Ghazni after his conquest of Kannauj.

Furthermore, Shankar also informed Cunningham that when they were digging for the stones for Jagat Singh, the labourers stumbled upon a large number of statues collected together in a small space. The workers, after carting away the stones, left the sculptures in their original place and reburied them. Shankar identified the spot as the north room of the temple, which is a few feet north of the Dharmarajika Stupa. This spot is presently named the Mulagandha Kuti. To quote Cunninghan, '...at a depth of about 2 feet below the surface, I found about 60 statues and bas-reliefs in an upright position, all packed closely together within a small space of less than 10 feet square.'[30]

Finding so many sculptures huddled together in such a cloistered space led Cunningham to conclude that this was done to prevent these sculptures from being desecrated by berserkers and iconoclasts. And truly, the presence of so many sculptures in such a state is another indicator of the sudden destruction of the holy complex. Getting wind of the approaching doom, the monks most likely tried to hide away all the holy moveables, such as the statues.

Inexplicably, Cunningham only collected the best specimens from that horde and presented them to the Asiatic Society in Kolkata. One of the bas-reliefs from that collection had an inscription on it that narrowed down their possible time of carving to the third–fourth centuries CE. That inscription mentioned the name of a certain Harigupta, who had gifted the relief sculpture to the monastery.[31]

Regrettably, he left the rest almost forty sculptures of the Buddha and several other carved stones there, which were '…carted away by the late Mr Davidson and thrown into the [Varuna] river under the bridge to check the cutting away of the bed between the arches.'[32] The bridge beneath whose arches those statues were thrown is the present-day Samrat Ashoka Bridge, better known as the Purana Pul ('old bridge'). This was not the end of it. While constructing the second bridge over the Varuna, i.e. the railway bridge, fifty-six cartloads of stones/artefacts were taken from Sarnath and dumped in the river.[33] I don't think that these artefacts can be retrieved, or that anyone has ever tried to retrieve them. Cunningham does not specify the exact number of sculptures that he unearthed during his first dig, but Rev. Sherring informs us that the number was close to a paltry hundred.[34]

Apart from the discovery of the sculptures, Cunningham had also dug down the Dhamek Stupa, which was the most imposing structure there with a staggering height of 43.6 m. It took him fourteen months, and more than 500 rupees spent from his pocket to quarry into the stupa from the top. He found no relic in it apart from an inscription, which was recovered near the top. On palaeographic grounds he has dated this inscription to the sixth century CE, when the Maukharis were ruling the region. The inscription states that everything happens due to a cause, which the Tathagata explains, along with the cause of the cessation of existence. It is perhaps due to this find that many attribute the site of the Dhamek Stupa to be the spot where the Buddha preached his first sermon.[35]

Cunningham then dug down the Chaukhandi Stupa, which did not yield any relic, indicating that unlike the Dharmarajika Stupa, which was first constructed by Ashoka, the other two were merely votive structures. However, later digs at Chaukhandi recovered several sculptures of the Buddha. Before he could conclude his dig, Cunningham was transferred to Calcutta, and Sarnath was forgotten for close to fifteen years.

Kittoe's Excavation Reveals Evidence of Destruction

The government archaeologist and architect Major Markham Kittoe, who was then busy building the Queen's College (the present Sampurnananda Sanskrit University) in Banaras, was asked to start digging at Sarnath in 1851 CE. This architect was a somewhat refined version of Jagat Singh, like whom he used blocks of stones from Sarnath and the destroyed temples of the Bakara Kund to construct the Queen's College building.[36]

His excavation work began where Cunningham had left off and came to some startling results, which were published piecemeal in the *Journal of the Asiatic Society of Bengal*. Before he could conclude his dig, he was compelled to leave India for England in 1853 CE, where he died an untimely death before he could satisfactorily document his findings. However, his correspondence with Cunningham, which happened in 1852, gives us a brief of his findings.

Cunningham informs us that Kittoe had unearthed several small votive stupas, sculptures and other remains, one of which was a hospital, within which were found pestles, mortars and other tools related to the medical discipline. He unearthed two large stone umbrellas (displayed in the Sarnath Museum), one of which bore the distinctive marking of being charred. The most important aspect of Kittoe's discovery was the evidence of the monastery complex's sudden destruction.

Like Cunningham, Kittoe too found charred timber and half-burnt grain. However, Kittoe's documentation was explicit when he wrote to Cunningham that '...*all has been sacked and burnt*, priests, temples, idols altogether. In some places, bones, iron, timber, idols, &c. are all fused into huge heaps; *and this has happened more than once.*[37]

Later Digs Showing Evidence of Destruction

Following up on the dig left unfinished by Kittoe, the work was carried on by Judge E. Thomas in 1853 CE and later by Prof. Fritz Edward Hall. Thomas, like Kittoe, concluded that the destruction of Sarnath was brought about suddenly and quoted Kittoe's findings that stated that the monks were compelled to flee, leaving behind their rotis, which were found in the courtyard.

Thomas, too, discovered several signs of sudden abandonment when the conflagration engulfed the complex. His findings, shared in the *Journal of the Asiatic Society of Bengal*, Vol. XXIII, are vividly detailed, where he notes:

> …the chambers on the eastern side of the square were found filled in with a strange medley of uncooked food, hastily abandoned on their floors—pottery of everyday life, nodes of brass produced apparently by the melting down of the cooking vessels in common use—above these again were the remnants of the charred timbers of the roof—with iron nails still remaining in them—above which again appeared broken bricks mixed with earth and rubbish to the height of the extant wall, some 6 feet from the original flooring—every item here bore evidence of a complete conflagration and so intense seems to have been the heat that in portions of the wall still standing the clay, which formed the substitute for lime in binding the brickwork, is baked to a similar consistency with the bricks themselves. In short, all existing indications lead to a necessary inference that the destruction of the building, by whomsoever caused, was effected by fire applied by the hand of an exterminating adversary, rather than by any ordinary accidental conflagration. Had the latter been the cause of the results now observed, it is

scarcely to be supposed that so well-peopled a convent, so time-hallowed a shrine, should have been so hastily and completely abandoned.[38]

He further adds:

> I can myself assert that on the floor of the cell marked 3,[...] a large quantity of rice was found, together with portions of wheat and other grain, part of which was spread out, or possibly scattered at the moment of the destructive inroad that was brought to a climax in the conflagration of the monastery.
>
> [...]
>
> In the cells to the eastward were found, among other things, considerable masses of brass, melted up into nodules and irregular lumps as chance gave them a receptacle amid the general ruin. Here also were seen, broken or whole, the pottery vessels of everyday requirement, and the iron nails which connected the cross rafters, still fixed in the larger beams that had escaped complete combustion.[39]

The Carnage

The use of the phrase 'exterminating adversary' by Thomas now begs the questions: who, and when exactly? My conjecture vis-à-vis the horde of intact sculptures discovered by Cunningham is that the monks, having got wind of the impending storm, probably managed to hide the most important sculptures first; then some of them possibly waited for the arrival of the berserking army, hoping to persuade them to live and let live, as had happened countless times during conquests by different kingdoms. What those monks could not have expected was the new type of enemy who were devoid of an iota of humanity, bent upon the destruction of everything that did not adhere to the tradition of a barbaric tribe from the Hijaz province of Arabia. So, this can only mean that Sarnath was most likely completely destroyed during Ghori's conquest of Banaras in 1194 CE.

A Series of Post-Mortems at Sarnath and the Loot

The sculptures unearthed by Kittoe, Thomas and Hall were first deposited in Queen's College and later moved to the Lucknow Museum and the Sarnath Museum after it was constructed in 1910. It is strange that all the digs carried out after Kittoe were done by amateurs and treasure hunters.

After Hall, the excavations were carried out by Dr Butler, whose report of the finds is missing. The next dig was commenced in 1865 CE by C. Horn, who deposited his findings with the Indian Museum. In December 1877 CE, A. Rivette Carnac discovered an image of the Buddha from Sarnath, which was pilfered and its whereabouts are presently unknown.[40]

One impediment to the excavations was that the land on which the archaeological mounds were situated belonged to an indigo planter named Fergusson. In 1856 CE, the government bought this piece of land from him, and only in 1900 did they appoint a guard to look after the excavated mounds.[41]

It is precisely because of such carelessness that several sculptures from Sarnath found their way into the British Museum. The sheer number of artefacts unearthed at Sarnath was mindboggling. One can make an estimate of the number when Cunningham, speaking about the Mahabodhi Temple of Bodh Gaya, mentions the countless number of small stupas found by him and Kittoe around the Dhamek Stupa. Apart from this, he also mentions lakhs of smaller stupas, some the size of a walnut, which were discovered at Sarnath.[42]

The question 'Where are they now?' demands an answer. All we have are about 1,000 pieces of sculptures and temple parts including inscription slabs of the teeming number of artefacts Sarnath once hid within its mounds.

Sarnath's Greatest Treasure, the Lion Capital

Between Kittoe's professional excavation and the next systematic dig by F.O. Oertel, nearly fifty years elapsed. The German-born F.O. Oertel, the executive engineer of the Public Works Department of Banaras, was drawn to Sarnath when a splendid sculpture of the Buddha was excavated while building a road from Sarnath to Ghazipur in 1904. That very year, Oertel, with the cooperation of the ASI, began digging at Sarnath under the supervision of District Engineer B.B. Chakravarti. Their dig was amply rewarded when they opened up a yet-to-be-excavated mound to the north of the Dharmarajika Stupa. The next year, i.e. 1905, Sarnath was visited by Alexandra of Denmark, the wife of the then British Emperor Edward VII.

Oertel had inadvertently struck at the heart of the ancient Sarnath monastery when he unearthed the remains of the Ashokan pillar and its Lion Capital, which marked the spot where the Buddha had sat and delivered his first sermon.[43] The capital, about 7 feet in height, was crafted out of Chunar sandstone in the third century BCE on the orders of Emperor Ashoka. He also had a few such capitals sculpted, and several more were copied from the one at Sarnath. Such carvings were attributed to Ashoka due to other similar findings elsewhere in India, of animal figures mounted atop tall smooth pillars with inscriptions on them using the same Brahmi script. The style, method of sculpting, and animal motifs on them all appeared to serve the same purpose, that is, to indicate an association with Buddhism, being found in the vicinity of Buddhist sites.

There is an interesting side to the Lion Capital of Sarnath, the national emblem of India, prominently displayed in the Sarnath Museum. The Sarnath Lion Capital shares several similarities with the style of the lions of the famous Burney Relief sculpture of Goddess Esthar of Babylon, dated between 1800 BCE and 1750 BCE, displayed in the British Museum at present.[44] Being sculpted out of fine sandstone and finished with a mirror-like shine, this artefact betrays the employment of the Achaemenid style of stone craftsmanship, employing the sculptural genre of Zoroastrian Persia. This early artistic connection with Iran has not been studied with serious intent and erudition, thus a great void of knowledge regarding such similarities remains.

The Lion Capital of Sarnath is not the only one of its kind; there are several other similar capitals dating back to antiquity. The ornately carved southern gate of the great stupa at Sanchi depicts two lion capitals inspired by Sarnath. The Archaeological Museum in Sanchi and the Gujari Mahal Archaeological Museum of Gwalior both have copies of the four-faced Lion Capital of Sarnath, executed some years after the original. The Karla Caves of Lonavala in Maharashtra also have a colossal monolithic lion capital inspired by the specimen from Sarnath.

The History of the Turning-of-the-Wheel-of-Law Monastery Sequenced from Archaeological Digs by Oertel

The history of the chief monastery at Sarnath, also known as the Dharmachakra Parivartana Vihara (turning of the wheel of law), can be put in sequence by the study of the sculptures unearthed therein.

Beginning with the Ashokan pieces, including the polished Chunar sandstone pillar remains with three inscriptions on them, the Lion Capital, and the monolithic railing found in situ, all are dated to the third century BCE. The first and the earliest inscription on the pillar, also called the schism edict, noted the name of Ashoka as King Priyadasi of Pataliputra, commanding all to care for the nuns and monks and spread the message around among the lay worshippers and not cause any schism in the sangha.[45] The second inscription on the pillar was engraved during the Kushan period. It is fragmentary. It mentions the name of a certain king called Ashwaghosha, who was in his fortieth regnal year at the time of the engraving. The third inscription on the pillar was engraved during the Gupta period and mentions paying homage to the masters of the Sammatiya sect.[46]

The next age of the site will take us to the Sunga period, in the second century BCE. Two fragments of male heads belong to this period.

We then have sculptures belonging to the first century BCE. The Kushan period of Indian history is also well represented in the form of two colossal sculptures unearthed at Sarnath, and several other sculptures of the Buddha. The first of these statues, the earliest of its kind depicting Bodhisattvas, was carved out of spotted red sandstone from Mathura and transported to Sarnath. An inscription on it mentions that the sculpture was the gift of Monk Bala, who caused the image to be crafted during the third regnal year of Emperor Kanishka. The name of Monk Bala had appeared for the first time as a donor on an image excavated in Shravasti, which would reappear twice more on the pedestal of two more Buddhist sculptures, first at Mathura[47] and then at Sarnath.[48]

The next set of sculptures, the largest cache, numbering 300 pieces, belonged to the Gupta period. The best example from this period is the image of the seated Buddha in the act of delivering the first sermon. This sculpture, crafted out of fine Chunar sandstone, is sublime and a masterpiece. The sculpture, measuring about 5 feet 3 inches from its base to the exquisitely carved halo, was discovered by Oertel from the southern side of the ill-fated Dharmarajika Stupa. It was during the Gupta era that Sarnath was thoroughly embellished with beautiful sculptures and was given the name Mula Gandhakuti, i.e. 'the primary shrine of the Buddha'.[49]

Images recovered between the seventh and the thirteenth centuries CE were also numerous, but distinctively broken with deliberate effort. In this group was found one of the most important sculptures of the Buddha, albeit in a destroyed condition, which is important for the historical information it provides about Mahipala, the Pala ruler of Bengal. This period also yielded several images of Jain Tirthankaras and Brahminical sculptures, implying that the monastery complex was being gradually taken over by adherents of Brahminical and Jain persuasions.

Apart from these important finds, Oertel's dig yielded 476 sculptures (complete and in parts) and forty-one inscriptions. Despite such great success, he could not complete his work at Sarnath due to his transfer to Agra.[50]

Sarnath Yields Even More Treasures

The numerous stupas unearthed by Kittoe to the north of the Dhamek had all been destroyed before the dig of 1907–08 began, under the supervision of John Marshall, the director general of ASI. He was assisted by Daya Ram Sahni, Sten Konow, W.H. Nicholls and B.B. Chakravarti.

Adding to the earlier finds, the excavation of 1907–08 yielded several sculptures and bits of the Buddha, Bodhisattvas and Hindu deities, of which one colossus is of particular interest. This bas-relief sculpture is of Shiva in the pose of the slayer of Andhaka, with the named demon pierced by his trident raised high over his head. The massive twelve-foot-tall sculpture is unfinished and exhibits chisel marks on the lower portion of its body. This image was found near monastery no. 4 along with two other roughly hewn stones, one of which was intended to be used as a pedestal. Another image of Shiva recovered from the site depicted the deity as performing the Tandava wearing a garland of skulls.[51]

One very interesting sculpture recovered from the dig at monastery no. 2 of the complex is a hollow terracotta head of a person wearing a distinctive conical cap of the Sakas of Central Asia, assigned to the first century CE.[52] The face is a portrait of some Saka person or a satrap. These Sakas were contemporaries of the Kushans in India, and had ruled the western part of the subcontinent. Unlike the Kushans, the Sakas did not have Mongoloid features and were prominently Iranian-looking. The Mathura Museum has two such cap-wearing Saka heads.

The team went deeper than Kittoe's last level to uncover the undisturbed remains of a monastery that belonged to the Gupta era.[53] From there, several lavishly sculpted steles of the Buddha's image along with other deities, some intact and the rest in parts, were brought out.

Re-excavating other parts of the site, like the ill-fated Dharmarajika Stupa, the eastern side of the Gandhakuti temple, and the hospital, yielded several more sculptures, numbering in hundreds, and twenty-three new inscriptions. Of the lot, an inscription belonging to the ninth century CE mentions the name of Amritpala, who had built ten *chaitya*s (temples). The engraving also mentions the names of Visvapala and Jayapala, who we know was the father of Pala monarch Vigrahapala I.[54]

This dig proved beyond doubt that Sarnath, whose genesis as an important Buddhist site took place under Ashoka, continued to be patronized by the Sungas and the Kushans, and reached its pinnacle under the Guptas, lasting for about seven centuries till the twelfth century CE, meeting its end like Nalanda and Odantapuri... for Nalanda too has traces of an intense conflagration that fused its bricks together, seen on the walls of the monk cells and other parts.

The Sarnath and the Banaras of My Imagination

What if Muhammad Ghori had not completely destroyed such a fabulous place? How would it have come down to us? As I wonder about this, my mind fleetingly conjures up the vision of tall monasteries amidst stupas, temples and pillars; painted walls flourishing like a living gallery, where each renovation would add a new element to the previous; a crucible where the old would amalgamate with the new in a continuous process of churning, like building a ship for Theseus. Perhaps the monuments that come closest to such a description are the monasteries in Tabo, Ladakh or Lhasa, but I imagine them on a scale greater than any conceived.

Not limiting itself there, the mind goes steps ahead and visualizes the ghats of Banaras re-lined with the ghosts of those innumerable temples that were destroyed, their sculpted shikharas jutting into the sky, each one embellished with thousands of sculptures and taller than the other... Envision a world where the likes of Mahmud of Ghazni, Ghori, Sikandar Lodhi and Aurangzeb never existed, and then imagine Sarnath and Banaras.

Acknowledgements

During my rides to historical places across all the states of India, several motorcycling clubs accorded their hospitality by arranging hotel rooms or having me put up in the homes of some of their members. Those evenings would be party-time in my honour, when riders would congregate around a bottle, plus accompaniments, and exchange stories. For such enjoyable moments I must thank the Born to Ride Motorcycling Club of Bhopal and its moderator Prateek Vats, the tallest biker in India. I must thank the founder of Unido Biking Club of Nagpur, the legendary Sachin Brahme, and his lovely wife Rani Brahme for opening the doors of their home to me, several times. Rider Anand Gedam—thanks are due to him for guiding me to the historic sites of Mansar and Ramtek, north of Nagpur. I must not forget to thank the riders of Aurangabad Throttlers and the Cruising Gods of Nashik, and the fun-loving Harley rider Vijay Tiwari of Nashik. I must thank the young history enthusiast Subham Jain for arranging for my stay in Sagar in Madhya Pradesh. Thanks are also due to the young archaeologist Shivam Dubey for opening the ASI guest-house door for me in Jabalpur. Deviba Wala, an artist friend of mine, accommodated me for several days in her art residency during my second ride to Gujarat. For her hospitality, I am indebted to her.

It would be ungrateful of me to not thank my wife's cousin Rajiv Kumar, for the trouble he took to arrange places of stay for my rides to the southern states, particularly while sojourning through Telangana and Karnataka. Also, tons of thanks to my sister-in-law Guncha Agarwal for arranging hotel bookings, whenever I couldn't find an accommodation on my own in some town or city. I must not forget my friend Chinnadurai Pandian who, in Madurai, hosted this bug-spattered rider, showed me around the Meenakshi temple, and gate-crashed a birthday party of his colleague in the American College of Madurai with me.

Also, I should not forget the hospitality laid out by my family friends, the Sanils of Thrissur, who called me 'Santa come early' when I reached their place a day before Christmas in 2017, during my ride to Kanyakumari. Here I was given a great compliment (rather, my bike received it): 'Of all the bikes manufactured by Royal Enfield, this one has gone to the most places.'

Special thanks go to my very close friend from old times, Tshering Bodh, for always having me put up in one of his several hotels in Kaza, during my several rides to the cold desert heaven of the Upper Himalayas. I am grateful to my childhood friend Sunil Prasad for his hospitality in Siliguri during my ride to the northeast, and to Masood Hashmi and Khurshid Bhabhi for theirs at Guwahati. And to my close friend Sandip Majumdar, for lending me his bike twice to visit some places in Bengal when mine was in the garage, and also for accompanying me to a few sites.

To my old friend Supratim who hosted me in his residence at the Doon School during my rides to the lesser-known destinations of Uttarakhand, I owe a feeling of gratitude (we are now colleagues also). Thanks are accorded to rider and cyclist Shekhoo Raja of Gwalior who, without knowing me well enough, accommodated me in his house during my first ride to the Gupta era site of Deogarh in the Lalitpur district of Uttar Pradesh. Post that, he has also joined me on some rides to ancient sites in Rajasthan and Madhya Pradesh.

In such regards, I must say that I am a lucky rider to have so many people who, over the course of my journey, have become friends. Luckiest I am to have Richa, my wife, who accompanied me on several rides in the Himalayas, and permits me to brave the risks of such long-distance solo rides.

Notes

Introduction

1. I-Tsing, *A Record of the Buddhist Religion as Practiced in India and the Malay Archipelago*, J. Takakusu (trans.), Oxford at the Clarendon Press, 1896, p. LII.
2. Ibid., LII.
3. McCrindle, J.W. (trans.), *Ancient India as Described by Megasthenes and Arrian*, Trubner and Co., London, 1877, p. 35.
4. Shamasastry, R. (trans.), *Kautilya's Arthashastra*, https://tinyurl.com/mrx5bm6f. Accessed on 4 October 2024.
5. A tirtha is a ford, chasm or a difficult terrain one crosses to achieve salvation. It can also be metaphorically taken as any difficult situation or as overcoming desire, thus the word Tirthankara, used for the twenty-four Jain teachers who have conquered their desires.
6. Nath, Amarendra, *Excavations at Rakhigarhi [1997-98 to 1999-2000]*, Archaeological Survey of India, p. 10.
7. Most trees that are worshipped do have certain peculiarities, where people find some imagery.
8. Such worldly knowledge was limited in the sense that they believed the earth was carried on the back of an elephant, and other such fantastical imaginations as the eclipses of the sun and the moon being caused by Rahu and Ketu when they swallowed these two celestial bodies.
9. Pargiter, F. Eden (trans.), *The Markandeya Purana*, Indological Book House, 1969, p. 275.
10. Ibid., 284.
11. Jaiswal, Anuja, '4,000-Year-Old Copper Weapons, Some Close to 4 Feet, Found in Mainpuri', *The Times of India*, 24 June 2022, https://tinyurl.com/3azxr4a4. Accessed on 9 September 2024.
12. Sharma, D.V., et al., 'Sanauli: A Late Harappan Burial Site in the Yamuna-Hindon Doab', *Puratattva: Bulletin of the Indian Archaeological Society*, No. 34, 2003-4, p. 35.
13. Kumar, Manoj, 'The Neolithic Cultures of Northern India: An Ethno-Archaeological Study', *Puratattva: Bulletin of the Indian Archaeological Society*, No. 34, 2003-4, pp. 5, 8.
14. Ibid., 10.
15. Dikshit, K.N., 'Origin of Early Harappan Cultures in the Saraswati Valley: Recent Archaeological Evidence and Radiometric Dates', *Journal of Indian Ocean Archaeology*, No. 9, 2013, p. 132.
16. 'Indo-Iranian Mythology', *Attalus*, https://tinyurl.com/e53a2hwv. Accessed on 10 September 2024.
17. McCrindle, J.W. (trans.), *The Invasion of India by Alexander the Great: As*

Described by Arrian, Q. Curtius, Diodoros, Plutarch and Justin, Archibald Constable and Co., 1893, p. 311.
18. Ibid., 311.
19. Hinduism is also called the Brahminical religion.
20. Baugh, Albert C., *A History of the English Language*, Meredith Publishing Company, New York, 1963.
21. Menon, Sunil, 'We Are All Harappans', *Outlook*, 9 August 2018, https://tinyurl.com/37zsrh6a. Accessed on 10 September 2024.
22. Debortoli, Guilherme, 'Novel Insights on Demographic History of Tribal and Caste Groups from West Maharashtra (India) Using Genome-Wide Data', *Scientific Reports*, Vol. 10, 2020, https://tinyurl.com/2p8p998b. Accessed on 4 October 2024.
23. Lal, B.B., 'The Rigvedic Flora and Fauna: What Light Do These Throw on the "Aryan Invasion" Debate?', *Puratattva: Bulletin of the Indian Archaeological Society*, No. 34, 2003-4, pp. 16-18.
24. Ibid.
25. Cowell, E.B., and F.W. Thomas (trans.), *The Harsa-Carita of Bana*, The Royal Asiatic Society, London, 1897, p. 35.
26. Kumar, Vijay, 'A Note on Chariot Burials Found at Sinauli District Baghpat U.P.', *Indian Journal of Archaeology*, Vol. 3, No. 2, 2018, p. 754.
27. Ibid., 754.
28. Lamb, Evelyn, 'Ancient Babylonian Number System Had No Zero', *Scientific American*, 31 August 2014, https://tinyurl.com/mz3fmxma. Accessed on 10 September 2024.
29. Das Gupta, Paresh Chandra, *The Excavations at Pandu Rajar Dhibi*, Directorate of Archaeology, 1964, p. 20.
30. 'Indigenous Aryans', *Encyclopedia*, https://tinyurl.com/4vty2u4j. Accessed on 11 September 2024.
31. McCrindle, J.W. (trans.), *The Invasion of India by Alexander the Great: As Described by Arrian, Q. Curtius, Diodoros, Plutarch and Justin*, Archibald Constable and Co., 1893, p. 101.
32. Ibid., 109-110.
33. Kuropolis is possibly the city of the Kurus.
34. McCrindle, J.W. (trans.), *Ancient India as Described by Megasthenes and Arrian*, Trubner and Co., 1877, p. 160. Claudius Aelianus, the third century CE Roman natural historian, reports from Megasthenes' *Indica*.
35. Anwar, Zameer, 'Roma Community: Lost Children of the Great Indian Family', *The Sunday Guardian*, 16 July 2023, https://tinyurl.com/4rnnzwwx. Accessed on 4 October 2024.
36. The Mandkila Tal inscription, dating back to 3 April 987 CE, was discovered in the Mandkila Lake of Nagar in the Tonk district of Rajasthan. It was composed by a descendant of Banabhatta named Vimalamati, the son of Durlabhraja from Rohetaka (Rohtak in Haryana), the fifth descendant of Banabhatta, and engraved by the sculptor Vahila, the son of Vahari of Dulavasa. See: Chhabra, B. Ch., 'Mandkila Tal Inscription, V.S. 1043', *Epigraphia Indica*, Vol. 34, 1961-62, p. 79.
37. Cowell, E.B., and F.W. Thomas (trans.), *The Harsa-Carita of Bana*, The Royal Asiatic Society, London, 1897, pp. 33-34.
38. Turner, Paula J., *Roman Coins from India*, Royal Numismatic Society, London, 1989.

39. S. Suresh, *Symbols of Trade: Roman and Pseudo-Roman Objects Found in India*, Manohar Publishers, 2004.
40. MacDowall, D.W., 'The Evidence of the Gazetteer of Roman Artefacts in India', *Tradition and Archaeology: Early Maritime Contacts in the Indian Ocean*, H.P. Ray and Jean-Francois Salles (eds.), Manohar Publishers, 2012.
41. The Barwada mosque was built sometime between 622 CE and 624 CE. The mosque's *mihrab* is oriented in the direction of Jerusalem, when Muhammad had not yet directed Muslims to face Mecca and pray. The Cheraman Mosque was constructed in 629 CE.
42. Fredunbeg, Mirza Kalichbeg (trans.), *The Chachnamah, an Ancient History of Sind*, The Commissioner's Press, Karachi, 1900.
43. Elliot, Henry Miers, *The History of India, as Told by Its Own Historians: The Muhammadan Period*, Vol. 1, John Dowson (ed.), Kitab Mahal Pvt Ltd, p. 2.
44. Ibid., 12.
45. Ibid., 26.
46. Sachau, Dr Edward C. (trans.), *Alberuni's India*, Rupa Publications, 2002.
47. Reynolds, James (trans.), *The Kitab-i-Yamini: Historical Memoirs of Amir Sabaktagin and the Sultan Mahmud of Ghazna*, Oriental Translation Fund of Great Britain and Ireland, London, 1758, p. 328.
48. Sachau, Dr Edward C. (trans.), *Alberuni's India*, Rupa Publications, 2002, p. 328.
49. Reynolds, James (trans.), *The Kitab-i-Yamini: Historical Memoirs of Amir Sabaktagin and the Sultan Mahmud of Ghazna*, The Oriental Translation Fund of Great Britain and Ireland, London, 1858, p. 451.
50. Cunningham, Alexander, *Four Reports Made During the Years 1862-63-64-65*, Archaeological Survey of India, 2000, p. 257.
51. Ibid., 257.
52. Raverty, H.G. (trans.), *The Tabakat-i-Nasiri of Minhaj-i-Saraj*, The Asiatic Society of Bengal, London, 1873, pp. 459–68.
53. Cunningham, Alexander, *Four Reports Made During the Years 1862-63-64-65*, Archaeological Survey of India, 2000, p. 261. Aibak had entrusted a certain Akbar, the son of Ahmed, with overseeing the construction by using the remains of several temples.
54. Abu'l-Fazl, *The History of Akbar, Volume 4*, Wheeler M. Thackston (trans.), Murty Classical Library, p. 371.
55. Pandit, R.S. (trans.), *Rajatarangini: The Saga of the Kings of Kasmir*, Sahitya Akademi, New Delhi, 1935, p. 135.
56. Elias, N. (ed.), *The Tarikh-i-Rashidi by Mirza Muhammad Haidar, Dughlat*, E. Denison Ross (trans.), Sampson Low, Marston and Company, London, p. 426.
57. Lal, K.S., *The Legacy of Muslim Rule in India*, Aditya Prakashan, New Delhi, 1992.
58. Saikumar, Rajgopal, 'The Rise of the Liberal-Right Intellectual', *The Hindu*, 4 December 2021, https://tinyurl.com/385v45jj. Accessed on 11 September 2024.
59. Gulbadan Begum, *The History of Humayun: Humayun-Nama*, Annette Susannah Beveridge (trans.), Atlantic Publishers, 1902, p. 105.
60. Babur, Zahiru'd-din Muhammad, *Babur-Nama: Memoirs of Babur*, Annette Susannah Beveridge (trans.), Oriental Books Reprint Corporation, p. 612.
61. The reports of the archaeological tours by Cunningham are voluminous works

that can be found in university libraries. As an example, see: Cunningham, Alexander, *Four Reports Made During the Years 1862-63-64-65*, Vol. 2, Archaeological Survey of India, 1871.
62. Beglar too has several volumes to his credit; see: Beglar, J.D., and A.C.L. Carlleyle, *Archaeological Survey of India: Report for the Year 1871-72*, Vol. 4, Office of the Superintendent of Govt. Printing, Calcutta, 1874.

Chapter 1: Ravages of Kashmir

1. Other such horse-and-rider sculptures have been found in Chitral in the Khyber Pakhtunkhwa province of present-day Pakistan, documented in 1929.
2. Dutt, Jogesh Chunder (trans.), *The Rajatarangini of Jonaraja*, Gyan Publishing House, Delhi, pp. 57-58.
3. Pandit, R.S. (trans.), *Rajatarangini: The Saga of the Kings of Kasmir*, Sahitya Akademi, New Delhi, p. 49.
4. Ibid., 690; Dutt, Jogesh Chunder (trans.), *The Rajatarangini of Jonaraja*, Gyan Publishing House, Delhi, p. 1.
5. Ibid., 1.
6. Ibid., 98.
7. Ibid., 99.
8. Ibid., 337-38.
9. Kumari, Ved, *The Nilamata Purana, Vol. 1: A Cultural and Literary Study of a Kasmiri Purana*, J&K Academy of Art, Culture and Languages, p. 22.
10. Ibid., 22.
11. Scharfe, Hartmut, *A History of Indian Literature, Vol. 5: Grammatical Literature*, Otto Harrassowitz, Wiesbaden, 1977, p. 88.
12. Kak, Ram Chandra, *Ancient Monuments of Kashmir*, The India Society, Victoria Street, London, 1933, pp. 10-11.
13. Iyer, N. Chidambaram (trans.), *The Brihat Samhita by Varaha Mihira*, Vol. 1, Divine Books, pp. 34-35.
14. Kumari, Ved, *The Nilamata Purana, Vol. 1: A Cultural and Literary Study of a Kasmiri Purana*, J&K Academy of Art, Culture and Languages, p. 15.
15. Ibid., 16.
16. Watters, Thomas, *On Yuan Chwang's Travels in India (A.D. 629-645)*, Royal Asiatic Society, London, 1904, p. 258.
17. Beal, Samuel (trans.), *Si-Yu-Ki: Buddhist Records of the Western World*, Vol. 1, Trubner and Co., London, 1884, p. 149.
18. Kak, Ram Chandra, *Ancient Monuments of Kashmir*, The India Society, Victoria Street, London, 1933, p. 7.
19. Sachau, Dr Edward C. (trans.), *Alberuni's India*, Rupa Publications, 2003, p. 160.
20. Ibid., 101.
21. Ibid., 193.
22. Ibid., 194.
23. Ibid., 195.
24. Ibid., 6.
25. Dutt, Jogesh Chunder (trans.), *The Rajatarangini of Jonaraja*, Gyan Publishing House, Delhi, p. 59.

26. Pandit, R.S. (trans.), *Rajatarangini: The Saga of the Kings of Kasmir*, Sahitya Akademi, New Delhi, pp. 352-53.
27. Ibid., 352.
28. Dutt, Jogesh Chunder (trans.), *The Rajatarangini of Jonaraja*, Gyan Publishing House, Delhi, p. 13.
29. Ibid., 13-14.
30. Ibid., 16.
31. Kaul, Gwasha Lal, *Kashmir through the Ages*, Chronicle Publishing House, Srinagar, p. 47.
32. Ibid., 47.
33. Ibid., 48.
34. Dutt, Jogesh Chunder (trans.), *The Rajatarangini of Jonaraja*, Gyan Publishing House, Delhi, p. 16.
35. Ibid., 18.
36. Ibid., 18.
37. Ibid., 15.
38. Ibid., 21.
39. Ibid., 23.
40. Ibid., 24.
41. Ibid., 24.
42. Ibid., 24.
43. Ibid., 25.
44. Ibid., 26.
45. Ibid., 26.
46. Ibid., 27-28.
47. Ibid., 28.
48. Ibid., 29.
49. Ibid., 31.
50. Ibid., 31.
51. Ibid., 32.
52. Ibid., 60.
53. Ibid., 56.
54. Ibid., 57.
55. Ibid., 60.
56. Ibid., 60.
57. Mir Syyed Ali Hamdani, a religious preacher from Iran, who lived in Kashmir for some years and was instrumental to the mass murder and conversion of Kashmiri Pandits.
58. Dutt, Jogesh Chunder (trans.), *The Rajatarangini of Jonaraja*, Gyan Publishing House, Delhi, pp. 57-58.
59. Elias, N. (ed.), *The Tarikh-i-Rashidi by Mirza Muhammad Haidar, Dughlat*, E. Denison Ross (trans.), Sampson Low, Marston and Company, London, 1895, p. 477. Sher Shah Suri defeated Humayun, the second Mughal emperor, on 17 May 1540 CE at Kannauj. Mirza Muhammad Haidar Dughlat, a cousin of Babur, was an eyewitness to this rout and has written a candid account of the defeat in the *Tarikh-i-Rashidi*.
60. A vast area of land north of Ladakh and west of China in Kashgarh, containing parts of the erstwhile Soviet Union and northern Afghanistan.

61. Elias, N. (ed.), *The Tarikh-i-Rashidi by Mirza Muhammad Haidar, Dughlat*, E. Denison Ross (trans.), Sampson Low, Marston and Company, London, p. 432.
62. Ibid., 433.
63. Ibid., 434.
64. Ibid., 428.
65. Ibid., 427-29.
66. Kak, Ram Chandra, *Ancient Monuments of Kashmir*, The India Society, Victoria Street, London, 1933, p. 141.
67. Kumari, Ved, *The Nilamata Purana, Vol. 1: A Cultural and Literary Study of a Kasmiri Purana*, J&K Academy of Art, Culture and Languages, p. 37.
68. Pandit, R.S. (trans.), *Rajatarangini: The Saga of the Kings of Kasmir*, Sahitya Akademi, New Delhi, p. 135.
69. Ibid., 319.
70. Ibid., 322-23.
71. Dutt, Jogesh Chunder (trans.), *The Rajatarangini of Jonaraja*, Gyan Publishing House, Delhi, p. 60.
72. Ibid., 372.
73. Elias, N. (ed.), *The Tarikh-i-Rashidi by Mirza Muhammad Haidar, Dughlat*, E. Denison Ross (trans.), Sampson Low, Marston and Company, London, pp. 424, 430. Dughlat's narration of Kashmir's geography, its people and their culture includes direct quotes from an earlier book named *Zafar Nama* by Sharfuddin Ali Yazdi. Dughlat states that unlike the description of Kashmir given by Sharfuddin, who never visited the valley, his is more accurate.
74. Ibid., 425-26.
75. Ibid., 426.
76. Dutt, Jogesh Chunder (trans.), *The Rajatarangini of Jonaraja*, Gyan Publishing House, Delhi, p. 417.
77. Jarrett, H.S. (trans.), *The Ain i Akbari by Abul Fazl 'Allami*, Vol. 2, The Asiatic Society of Bengal, Calcutta, 1891, pp. 359-60.
78. Thackston, Wheeler M. (ed.), *The Jahangirnama: Memoirs of Jahangir, Emperor of India*, Oxford University Press, New York, p. 335.
79. Vigne, Godfrey Thomas, *Travels in Kashmir, Ladak, Iskardo*, Vol. 1, Henry Colburn, London, 1842, p. 405.
80. Ibid., 404.
81. Kak, Ram Chandra, *Ancient Monuments of Kashmir*, The India Society, Victoria Street, London, 1933, p. 135.
82. Pandit, R.S. (trans.), *Rajatarangini: The Saga of the Kings of Kasmir*, Sahitya Akademi, New Delhi, p. 109.

Chapter 2: Haridwar: The Spiritual Gateway

1. Cautley, P.T., *Report on the Ganges Canal Works*, Vol. 1, Smith, Elder and Co., London, 1860, pp. 330-31.
2. It is a common practice to repair old graves, mosques and temples with ceramic tiles, among the locals who care for them.
3. Cautley, P.T., *Report on the Ganges Canal Works*, Vol. 1, Smith, Elder and Co., London, 1860, p. 387.

4. Sachau, Dr Edward C. (trans.), *Alberuni's India*, Rupa Publications, 2002, p. 187.
5. Elliot, Henry Miers, 'Malfuzat-i Timuri, or Tuzak-i Timuri: The Autobiography of Timur', *The History of India, as Told by Its Own Historians: The Muhammadan Period*, Vol. 3, John Dowson (ed.), Trubner and Co., London, p. 457.
6. Agarwala, V.S., *India as Known to Panini*, University of Lucknow, 1953, p. 59.
7. Cunningham, Alexander, *The Ancient Geography of India: The Buddhist Period*, Trubner & Co., London, p. 352.
8. *The Skanda-Purana: Part I*, Motilal Banarsidass, Delhi, 1950, p. 8.
9. Beal, Samuel (trans.), *Si-Yu-Ki: Buddhist Records of the Western World*, Vol. 1, Trubner and Co., London, 1884, p. 197.
10. Cunningham, Alexander, *The Ancient Geography of India: The Buddhist Period*, Trubner & Co., London, p. 352.
11. Chimpa, Lama, and Alaka Chattopadhyaya (trans.), *Taranatha's History of Buddhism in India*, Motilal Banarsidass, Delhi, p. 179.
12. Beal, Samuel (trans.), *Si-Yu-Ki: Buddhist Records of the Western World*, Vol. 1, Trubner and Co., London, 1884, p. 198.
13. Ibid., 198.
14. Cunningham, Alexander, *The Ancient Geography of India: The Buddhist Period*, Trubner & Co., London, p. 355.
15. Chimpa, Lama, and Alaka Chattopadhyaya (trans.), *Taranatha's History of Buddhism in India*, Motilal Banarsidass, Delhi, p. 224.
16. Mitra, Sisir Kumar, *The Early Rulers of Khajuraho*, Motilal Banarsidass, Delhi, 1977, p. 77.
17. Elliot, Henry Miers, 'Taju-l Ma-asir of Hasan Nizami', *The History of India, as Told by Its Own Historians*, Vol. 2, John Dowson (ed.), Trubner and Co., London, 1869, p. 2.
18. Elliot, Henry Miers, 'Tabakat-i Nasiri of Minhaju-s Siraj', *The History of India, as Told by Its Own Historians: The Muhammadan Period*, Vol. 2, John Dowson (ed.), Trubner and Co., London, 1869, p. 353.
19. Raverty, H.G. (trans.), *The Tabakat-i-Nasiri of Minhaj-i-Saraj*, The Asiatic Society of Bengal, London, 1873, p. 696.
20. Elliot, Henry Miers, 'Malfuzat-i Timuri, or Tuzak-i Timuri: The Autobiography of Timur', *The History of India, as Told by Its Own Historians: The Muhammadan Period*, Vol. 3, John Dowson (ed.), Trubner and Co., London, pp. 450–52.
21. Ibid., 452–53.
22. Ibid., 454.
23. Ibid., 455.
24. Ibid., 455.
25. Ibid., 456.
26. Ibid., 458.
27. Ibid., 459–60.
28. Ibid., 461.
29. Kukreti, Bhishma, 'History of Uttarakhand (Garhwal, Kumaon, Haridwar)–Part 139', *E-Magazine of Uttarakhand*, 10 September 2013, https://tinyurl.com/3hmsxunw. Accessed on 5 October 2024.
30. Jarrett, H.S. (trans.), *The Ain i Akbari by Abul Fazl-i-Allami*, Vol. 3, The Asiatic Society of Bengal, Calcutta, 1894, p. 306.
31. Blochmann, H. (trans.), *The Ain i Akbari by Abul Fazl 'Allami*, Vol. 1, The Asiatic Society of Bengal, Calcutta, 1873, p. 55.

32. Thackston, Wheeler M. (ed.), *The Jahangirnama: Memoirs of Jahangir, Emperor of India*, Oxford University Press, New York, p. 371.
33. Wessels, C., *Early Jesuit Travellers in Central Asia: 1603-1721*, Low Price Publications, Delhi, 1999, p. 47.
34. Foster, William (ed.), *Early Travels in India: 1583-1619*, Humphrey Milford Oxford University Press, England, 1921, p. 239.
35. Terry was another Englishman in India who had joined the service of the English ambassador to the court of Jahangir, Sir Thomas Roe, as his chaplain at Ujjain in 1616 CE.
36. Foster, William (ed.), *Early Travels in India: 1583-1619*, Humphrey Milford Oxford University Press, England, 1921, p. 238.
37. Cunningham, Alexander, *The Ancient Geography of India: The Buddhist Period*, Trubner & Co., London, p. 354.
38. Elliot, Henry Miers, 'Shah Jahan-nama, of Inayat Khan', *The History of India, as Told by Its Own Historians: The Muhammadan Period*, Vol. 7, John Dowson (ed.), Trubner and Co., London, 1877, p. 107.
39. Elliot, Henry Miers, 'Muntakhabu-l Lubab, of Khafi Khan', *The History of India, as Told by Its Own Historians: The Muhammadan Period*, Vol. 7, John Dowson (ed.) Trubner and Co., London, 1877, p. 230.
40. Walton, H.G., *Dehra Dun: A Gazetteer, Being Volume I of the District Gazetteers of the United Provinces of Agra and Oudh*, Government Press, Allahabad, 1911, p. 176.
41. Sarkar, Jadunath, *The History of Dasnami Naga Sanyasis*, Sri Panchayatri Akhara Mahanirvani, Allahabad, p. 102.
42. Atkinson, Edwin T., *The Himalayan Gazetteer: Vol. II Part II*, Cosmo Publications, New Delhi, 1981, p. 620.
43. Raper, Capt. F.V., *Narrative of a Survey for the Purpose of Discovering the Sources of the Ganges*, p. 459.
44. Cunningham, Alexander, *Archaeological Survey of India: Four Reports Made During the Years 1862-63-64-65*, Vol. 2, The Government Central Press, Simla, 1871, opposite p. 231.
45. Thackston, Wheeler M. (ed.), *The Jahangirnama: Memoirs of Jahangir, Emperor of India*, Oxford University Press, New York, p. 371.
46. Cunningham, Alexander, *Archaeological Survey of India: Four Reports Made During the Years 1862-63-64-65*, Vol. 2, The Government Central Press, Simla, 1871, p. 233.
47. Ibid., 235.
48. Sarkar, Jadunath, *The History of Dasnami Naga Sanyasis*, Sri Panchayatri Akhara Mahanirvani, Allahabad, pp. 98-99.
49. Corresponds to the month of January when the Sun enters Capricorn.
50. Sarkar, Jadunath, *The History of Dasnami Naga Sanyasis*, Sri Panchayatri Akhara Mahanirvani, Allahabad, p. 86.
51. Ibid., 86.
52. Raper, Capt. F.V., *Narrative of a Survey for the Purpose of Discovering the Sources of the Ganges*, p. 455.
53. Ibid., 102.

Chapter 3: In Krishna's Cradle

1. Vaidya, Parashuram Lakshman (ed.), *The Harivamsa*, Vol. 1, Bhandarkar Oriental Research Institute, Poona, 1969, p. xxix.
2. Ibid., xxvi.
3. Dutt, Manmatha Nath (ed.), *A Prose English Translation of Harivamsha*, H.C. Dass, Calcutta, 1897, p. 141.
4. Growse, F.S., *Mathura: A District Memoir*, Asian Educational Services, New Delhi, 1979, p. 21.
5. Cunningham, Alexander, *Report of a Tour in Eastern Rajputana in 1882-83*, Vol. 20, Archaeological Survey of India, New Delhi, 2000, p. 31.
6. Ball, V. (trans.), *Travels in India by Jean-Baptiste Tavernier*, Vol. 1, Oxford University Press, London, 1925, p. 105.
7. Griffith, Ralph (trans.), *The Hymns of the Rigveda*, Book 7, p. 18, https://tinyurl.com/mr42pcpf. Accessed on 5 October 2024.
8. One school of Indian historians conjectures that the Vedic Battle of the Ten Kings was the embryonic story that inspired the composition of the Mahabharata, while another school believes that they were events that took place independently of each other.
9. Dutt, Manmatha Nath (ed.), *A Prose English Translation of Harivamsha*, H.C. Dass, Calcutta, 1897, pp. 382-83.
10. Ibid., 348-60.
11. Ibid., 261.
12. Ibid., 280.
13. Ibid., 438.
14. Ibid., 146.
15. Ibid., 485-86. Dwarka, the city of Krishna in Gujarat, is believed to have been engulfed by the sea immediately after the death of Krishna. Out in the sea some distance from modern-day Dwarka, the ancient remains of a once-bustling metropolis have been found submerged. Archaeologists speculate based on dating the artefacts exhumed from there that the city was lost to the sea around 200 BCE.
16. Mitchiner, John E. (trans.), *The Yuga Purana*, The Asiatic Society, Calcutta, 1986, pp. 11, 55. The *Yuga Purana* is a chapter from the manuscript on Jyotisha authored by Vriddha Garga, who has been quoted in the Mahabharata, and by various authors like Varahamihira in his *Brihat Samhita*. Vriddha (the elder) Garga has mentioned the Indo-Greek incursions in the *Yuga Purana* and his existence can be dated to the first century BCE.
17. Jayaswal, K.P., and R.D. Banerji, 'The Hathigumpha Inscription of Kharavela', *Epigraphia Indica*, Vol. 20, 1929-30, p. 87.
18. Cowell, E.B., and F.W. Thomas (trans.), *The Harsa-Carita of Bana*, The Royal Asiatic Society, London, 1897, pp. 192-93.
19. Sachau, Dr Edward C. (trans.), *Alberuni's India*, Rupa Publications, 2002, p. 408.
20. Ibid., 187, 556.
21. McCrindle, J.W. (trans.), *Ancient India as Described by Megasthenes and Arrian*, Trubner and Co., London, 1877, p. 139.
22. Cunningham, Alexander, *The Ancient Geography of India: The Buddhist Period*, Trubner and Co., London, 1871, p. 375.

23. McCrindle, J.W. (trans.), *Ancient India as Described by Megasthenes and Arrian*, Trubner and Co., London, 1877, p. 201.
24. McCrindle, J.W. (ed.), *Ancient India as Described by Ptolemy*, Trubner and Co., London, 1885, p. 129.
25. Strong, J.S. (trans.), *The Legend of King Asoka: A Study and Translation of the Asokavadana*, Motilal Banarsidass, New Delhi, p. 174.
26. Chimpa, Lama, and Alaka Chattopadhyaya (trans.), *Taranatha's History of Buddhism in India*, Motilal Banarsidass, Delhi, p. 34.
27. Ibid., 34; Strong, J.S. (trans.), *The Legend of King Asoka: A Study and Translation of the Asokavadana*, Motilal Banarsidass, New Delhi, p. 174.
28. Ibid., 180.
29. Ibid., 183.
30. Mukhopadhyaya, Sujitkumar (ed.), *The Asokavadana*, Sahitya Akademi, New Delhi, 1963, p. xviii.
31. Chakraberti, Kanchan, *Society, Religion and Art of the Kushan India*, K.P. Bagchi and Co., Calcutta, 1981, p. 25.
32. Sharma, V.K., *History of Jainism with Special Reference to Mathura*, D.K. Printworld Pvt Ltd, New Delhi, 2002, p. 123.
33. Sastri, K.A. Nilakanta, *A Comprehensive History of India*, Vol. 2, Orient Longmans, Calcutta, 1957, p. 5.
34. McCrindle, J.W. (trans.), *Ancient India as Described by Megasthenes and Arrian*, Trubner and Co., London, 1877, p. 10.
35. Ibid., 68, 139.
36. Ibid., 30.
37. Beal, Samuel (trans.), *Si-Yu-Ki: Buddhist Records of the Western World*, Vol. 1, Trubner and Co., London, 1884, p. 180.
38. Interestingly, the Ramayana gives us an instance in which the Yaksha Manibhadra, a powerful demigod under the command of Kubera, was ordered to battle Ravana, when the king of Lanka had besieged the capital of Kubera, his half-brother. In the ensuing duel, Manibhadra was defeated by Ravana when the king of Lanka struck the Yaksha on the chest and deprived him of his protective diadem. Since then, Yaksha Manibhadra came to be known as Parshavamauli. See: Shastri, Hari Prasad (trans.), *The Ramayana of Valmiki*, Vol. 3, Shanti Sadan, London, 1952, p. 415.
39. Luders, Heinrich, *Mathura Inscriptions*, Klaus L. Janert (ed.), Vandenhoeck & Ruprecht, Gottingen, 1961, p. 178.
40. Davids, T.W. Rhys, *The Questions of King Milinda*, Oxford at the Clarendon Press, 1890, p. 15.
41. Quintanilla, Sonya Rhie, *History of Early Stone Sculpture at Mathura*, Brill, 2007, p. 9.
42. Joshi, Esha Basanti (ed.), *Uttar Pradesh District Gazetteers: Mathura*, Government of Uttar Pradesh, Lucknow, 1968, p. 29.
43. Ibid., 30.
44. Puri, B.N., *India in the Time of Patanjali*, Bhartiya Vidya Bhavan, Bombay, 1957, p. 181.
45. Ibid., 86–87.
46. Quintanilla, Sonya Rhie, *History of Early Stone Sculpture at Mathura*, Brill, 2007, p. 255.

47. Thomas, F.W, 'Inscriptions on the Mathura Lion-Capital', *Epigraphia Indica*, Vol. 9, 1907–08, p. 140.
48. Joshi, Esha Basanti (ed.), *Uttar Pradesh District Gazetteers: Mathura*, Government of Uttar Pradesh, Lucknow, 1968, p. 33.
49. Thomas, F.W, 'Inscriptions on the Mathura Lion-Capital', *Epigraphia Indica*, Vol. 9, 1907–08, p. 135.
50. The Hathibada Inscription from Chittor also mentions the worship of Krishna and Balarama. The inscription was discovered in 1934 CE by Dr Niranjan Prasad Chakravarti. Engraved on a large slab, the Sanskrit inscription was deciphered by Dr Bhandarkar and dated to the first century BCE. It recorded the construction of a stone enclosure around a temple dedicated to Balarama and Krishna by King Gajayana Sarvatata, the son of a lady from the Parasara Gotra. See: Bhandarkar, D.R., 'Hathi-Bada Brahmi Inscription at Nagari', *Epigraphia Indica*, Vol. 22, 1933–34, p. 198.
51. Joshi, Esha Basanti (ed.), *Uttar Pradesh District Gazetteers: Mathura*, Government of Uttar Pradesh, Lucknow, 1968, p. 34.
52. Buhler, G., 'Further Jaina Inscriptions from Mathura', *Epigraphia Indica*, Vol. 2, 1892, p. 199.
53. Joshi, Esha Basanti (ed.), *Uttar Pradesh District Gazetteers: Mathura*, Government of Uttar Pradesh, Lucknow, 1968, p. 34.
54. Ibid., 35.
55. Reinjang, Wannaporn, and Peter Stewart (ed.), *Problems of Chronology in Gandharan Art*, Archaeopress Publishing, Oxford, 2018, p. 9, https://tinyurl.com/3cjpcyfz. Accessed on 3 December 2024.
56. Luders, Heinrich, *Mathura Inscriptions*, Klaus L. Janert (ed.), Vandenhoeck & Ruprecht, Gottingen, 1961, p. 135.
57. Mukherjee, B.N., *The Rise and Fall of the Kushan Empire*, Firma KLM Pvt Ltd, Calcutta, 1988, p. 44.
58. Luders, Heinrich, *Mathura Inscriptions*, Klaus L. Janert (ed.), Vandenhoeck & Ruprecht, Gottingen, 1961, p. 134.
59. Ibid., 140
60. Bloch, T., 'Two Inscriptions on Buddhist Images', *Epigraphia Indica*, Vol. 8, 1905–06, p. 182.
61. Ibid., 176, 180.
62. Beal, Samuel (trans.), *Si-Yu-Ki: Buddhist Records of the Western World*, Vol. 1, Trubner and Co., London, 1884, pp. 150, 156.
63. Pandit, R.S. (trans.), *Rajatarangini: The Saga of the Kings of Kasmir*, Sahitya Akademi, New Delhi, p. 28.
64. Ibid., 28.
65. Kak, Ram Chandra, *Ancient Monuments of Kashmir*, The India Society, Victoria Street, London, 1933, p. 105.
66. Chimpa, Lama, and Alaka Chattopadhyaya (trans.), *Taranatha's History of Buddhism in India*, Motilal Banarsidass, New Delhi, pp. 92–93.
67. Mukherjee, B.N., *The Rise and Fall of the Kushan Empire*, Firma KLM Pvt Ltd, Calcutta, 1988, p. 92.
68. Pandit, R.S. (trans.), *Rajatarangini: The Saga of the Kings of Kasmir*, Sahitya Akademi, New Delhi, p. 28.

69. Mukherjee, B.N., *The Rise and Fall of the Kushan Empire*, Firma KLM Pvt Ltd, Calcutta, 1988, p. 98.
70. Ibid., 93.
71. Ibid., 155.
72. This capital in the Gujari Mahal is kept in Gallery No. 2. This gallery has another Ashokan capital of four lions facing the cardinal directions, and a single lion capital datable to the second century BCE.
73. Archaeological Survey of India, *Annual Report: 1908–9*, 1912, pp. 159–60.
74. Ibid., 160.
75. Dutt, Manmatha Nath (ed.), *A Prose English Translation of Harivamsha*, H.C. Dass, Calcutta, 1897, p. 721.
76. Archaeological Survey of India, *Annual Report: 1908–9*, 1912, pp. 160–61.
77. Sastri, K.A. Nilakanta, *A Comprehensive History of India*, Vol. 2, Orient Longmans, Calcutta, 1957, p. 257.
78. Fleet, John Faithfull, *Corpus Inscriptionum Indicarum, Vol. III: Inscriptions of the Early Gupta Kings and Their Successors*, Superintendent of Government Printing, Calcutta, 1888, p. 13.
79. Ibid., 25–28.
80. Legge, James (trans.), *A Record of Buddhistic Kingdoms: Being an Account by the Chinese Monk Fa Hien*, Oxford at the Clarendon Press, 1886, p. 4.
81. Ibid., 43.
82. Ibid., 43.
83. Beal, Samuel (trans.), *Si-Yu-Ki: Buddhist Records of the Western World*, Vol. 1, Trubner and Co., London, 1884, p. 168.
84. Pandit, R.S. (trans.), *Rajatarangini: The Saga of the Kings of Kasmir*, Sahitya Akademi, New Delhi, p. 40.
85. Ibid., 40–42.
86. Fuhrer, A., *The Monumental Antiquities and Inscriptions, in the North-Western Province and Oudh*, Superintendent, Government Press, N.W.P. and Oudh, Allahabad, 1891, p. 107.
87. Ibid., 107.
88. Beal, Samuel (trans.), *Si-Yu-Ki: Buddhist Records of the Western World*, Vol. 1, Trubner and Co., London, 1884, pp. 179–80.
89. Strong, J.S. (trans.), *The Legend of King Asoka: A Study and Translation of the Asokavadana*, Motilal Banarsidass, New Delhi, p. 197.
90. Beal, Samuel (trans.), *Si-Yu-Ki: Buddhist Records of the Western World*, Vol. 1, Trubner and Co., London, 1884, p. 182.
91. Cunningham, Alexander, *Report of a Tour in Eastern Rajputana in 1882-83*, Vol. 20, Archaeological Survey of India, New Delhi, 2000, p. 32.
92. Joshi, Esha Basanti (ed.), *Uttar Pradesh District Gazetteers: Mathura*, Government of Uttar Pradesh, Lucknow, 1968, p. 48.
93. Pandit, Bhagwanlal Indraji, 'Inscription from Kama or Kamavana', *The Indian Antiquary*, Jas. Burgess (ed.), Vol. 10, Swati Publications, Delhi, 1984, pp. 34, 36.
94. Archaeological Survey of India, *Progress Report of the Archaeological Survey of India: Western Circle: For the year ending 31st March 1919*, 1920, p. 64.
95. Pandit, R.S. (trans.), *Rajatarangini: The Saga of the Kings of Kasmir*, Sahitya Akademi, New Delhi, pp. 128–30.

96. Cowell, E.B., and F.W. Thomas (trans.), *The Harsa-Carita of Bana*, The Royal Asiatic Society, London, 1897, p. 175.
97. Majumdar, R.C. (ed.), *The History and Culture of the Indian People: The Age of Imperial Kannauj*, Bharatiya Vidya Bhavan, Mumbai, 2009, pp. 22–23.
98. Joshi, Esha Basanti (ed.), *Uttar Pradesh District Gazetteers: Mathura*, Government of Uttar Pradesh, Lucknow, 1968, p. 49.
99. Cunningham, Alexander, *Report of a Tour in Eastern Rajputana in 1882-83*, Vol. 20, Archaeological Survey of India, New Delhi, 2000, p. 6.
100. Ibid., 6–7.
101. Jain, Kailash Chand, *Ancient Cities and Towns of Rajasthan: A Study of Culture and Civilization*, Motilal Banarsidass, 1972, p. 269.
102. Elliot, Henry Miers, 'Tarikh Yamini of 'Utbi', *The History of India, as Told by Its Own Historians: The Muhammadan Period*, Vol. 2, John Downson (ed.), Trubner and Co., London, p. 42.
103. Reynolds, James (trans.), *The Kitab-i-Yamini: Historical Memoirs of Amir Sabaktagin and the Sultan Mahmud of Ghazna*, The Oriental Translation Fund of Great Britain and Ireland, 1858, p. 455.
104. Ibid., 454.
105. Elliot, Henry Miers, 'Tarikh Yamini of 'Utbi', *The History of India, as Told by Its Own Historians: The Muhammadan Period*, Vol. 2, John Downson (ed.), Trubner and Co., London, p. 43.
106. Reynolds, James (trans.), *The Kitab-i-Yamini: Historical Memoirs of Amir Sabaktagin and the Sultan Mahmud of Ghazna*, The Oriental Translation Fund of Great Britain and Ireland, 1858, pp. 454–6.
107. Joshi, Esha Basanti (ed.), *Uttar Pradesh District Gazetteers: Mathura*, Government of Uttar Pradesh, Lucknow, 1968, p. 51.
108. Elliot, Henry Miers, 'Tarikh Yamini of 'Utbi', *The History of India, as Told by Its Own Historians: The Muhammadan Period*, Vol. 2, John Downson (ed.), Trubner and Co., London, p. 44.
109. Majumdar, R.C. (ed.), *The History and Culture of the Indian People: The Struggle for Empire*, Bharatiya Vidya Bhavan, Mumbai, 2001, p. 14.
110. Elliot, Henry Miers, 'Tarikh Yamini of 'Utbi', *The History of India, as Told by Its Own Historians: The Muhammadan Period*, Vol. 2, John Dowson (ed.), Trubner and Co., London, p. 45.
111. Joshi, Esha Basanti (ed.), *Uttar Pradesh District Gazetteers: Mathura*, Government of Uttar Pradesh, Lucknow, 1968, p. 53.
112. Cunningham, Alexander, *Report of a Tour in Eastern Rajputana in 1882-83*, Vol. 20, Archaeological Survey of India, New Delhi, 2000, p. 6; Joshi, Esha Basanti (ed.), *Uttar Pradesh District Gazetteers: Mathura*, Government of Uttar Pradesh, Lucknow, 1968, p. 53.
113. Buhler, G., 'The Mathura Prasasti of the Reign of Vijayapala', *Epigraphia Indica*, Vol. 1, 1892, pp. 287–88.
114. Raverty, H.G. (trans.), *The Tabakat-i-Nasiri, Minhaj-i-Saraj*, The Asiatic Society of Bengal, London, 1873, p. 545.
115. Ibid., 608.
116. Joshi, Esha Basanti (ed.), *Uttar Pradesh District Gazetteers: Mathura*, Government of Uttar Pradesh, Lucknow, 1968, p. 55.
117. Ibid., 55.

118. Elliot, Henry Miers, 'Tarikh-i Daudi, of 'Abdu-lla', *The History of India, as Told by Its Own Historians: The Muhammadan Period*, Vol. 4, John Dowson (ed.), Trubner and Co., London, p. 447.
119. Beveridge, H. (trans.), *The Akbarnama of Abu'l Fazl*, Vol. 2, The Asiatic Society, Calcutta, pp. 294–95.
120. Fuhrer, A., *The Monumental Antiquities and Inscriptions, in the North-Western Provinces and Oudh*, Superintendent, Government Press, N.W.P. and Oudh, Allahabad, 1891, p. 108.
121. Ibid., 128–31.
122. Hoyland, J.S. (trans.), *The Commentary of Father Monserrate, S.J.: On his Journey to the Court of Akbar*, Humphrey Milford, 1922, p. 90.
123. Ibid., 90–91.
124. Ibid., 93.
125. Thackston, Wheeler M. (ed.), *The Jahangirnama: Memoirs of Jahangir, Emperor of India*, Oxford University Press, New York, p. 313.
126. Ibid., 412.
127. Ball, V. (trans.), *Travels in India by Jean-Baptiste Tavernier*, Vol. 1, Oxford University Press, London, 1925, p. 104; Bernier, Francois, *Travels in the Mogul Empire: A.D. 1656–1668*, Archibald Constable (trans.), Humphrey Milford Oxford University Press, 1916, p. 284.
128. Manucci, Niccolao, *Storia Do Mogor or Mogul India: 1653–1708*, Vol. 1, William Irvine (trans.), John Murray, London, 1907, p. 299.
129. Elliot, Henry Miers, 'Badshah-nama, of 'Abdu-l Hamid Lahori', *The History of India, as Told by Its Own Historians: The Muhammadan Period*, Vol. 7, John Dowson (ed.), Trubner and Co., London, p. 36.
130. Growse, F.S., *Mathura: A District Memoir*, Asian Educational Services, New Delhi, 1979, p. 35.
131. Manucci, Niccolao, *Storia Do Mogor or Mogul India: 1653–1708*, Vol. 1, William Irvine (trans.), John Murray, London, 1907, pp. 298–99.
132. Ibid., 304.
133. Fuhrer, A., *The Monumental Antiquities and Inscriptions, in the North-Western Provinces and Oudh*, Superintendent, Government Press, N.W.P. and Oudh, Allahabad, 1891, p. 131.
134. Manucci, Niccolao, *Storia Do Mogor or Mogul India: 1653–1708*, Vol. 2, William Irvine (trans.), John Murray, London, 1907, p. 140.
135. Kincaid, Dennis, *The History of Shivaji: the Grand Rebel*, Karan Publications, Delhi, 1955, pp. 233, 235.
136. Elliot, Henry Miers, 'Ma-usir-i 'Alamgiri, of Muhammad Saki Musta'idd Khan', *The History of India, as Told by Its Own Historians: The Muhammadan Period*, Vol. 7, John Dowson (ed.), Trubner and Co., London, p. 184.
137. Ibid., 184–85.
138. Ibid., 185.
139. Joshi, Esha Basanti (ed.), *Uttar Pradesh District Gazetteers: Mathura*, Government of Uttar Pradesh, Lucknow, 1968, p. 62.
140. Manucci, Niccolao, *Storia Do Mogor or Mogul India: 1653–1708*, Vol. 3, William Irvine (trans.), John Murray, London, 1987, p. 245.
141. Fuhrer, A., *The Monumental Antiquities and Inscriptions, in the North-Western Provinces and Oudh*, Superintendent, Government Press, N.W.P. and Oudh, Allahabad, 1891, p. 107.

142. Sarkar, Jadunath, *Fall of the Mughal Empire*, Vol. 2, M.C. Sarkar and Sons, Calcutta, 1934, p. 382.
143. Ibid., 115.
144. Ibid., 117.
145. Ibid., 88.
146. Ibid., 88.
147. Ibid., 118.
148. Ibid., 119.
149. Ibid., 117, 120–21.
150. Ibid., 121.
151. Sarkar, Jadunath, *The History of Dasnami Naga Sanyasis*, Sri Panchayatri Akhara Mahanirvani, Allahabad, p. 154.
152. Sarkar, Jadunath, *Fall of the Mughal Empire*, Vol. 2, M.C. Sarkar and Sons, Calcutta, 1934, p. 122.
153. Ibid., 125.
154. Ibid., 124–26.
155. Ibid., 126–30.
156. Ibid., 381.
157. Ibid., 451.
158. Ibid., 480.
159. Joshi, Esha Basanti (ed.), *Uttar Pradesh District Gazetteers: Mathura*, Government of Uttar Pradesh, Lucknow, 1968, p. 68.
160. Ibid., 69.
161. Elliot, Henry Meirs, "Ibrat-Nama of Fakir Khairu-d Din Muhammad", *The History of India, as Told by Its Own Historians: The Muhammadan Period*, Vol. 8, John Dowson (ed.), Trubner and Co., London, p. 253.
162. Ibid., 254.
163. Growse, F.S., *Mathura: A District Memoir*, Asian Educational Services, New Delhi, 1979, p. 46.
164. Ibid., 46.
165. Dutt, Manmatha Nath (ed.), *A Prose English Translation of Harivamsha*, H.C. Dass, Calcutta, 1897, pp. 269–70.
166. Ibid., 271.
167. Ibid., 438.
168. Ibid., 280.
169. Ibid., 284.
170. Ibid., 699.
171. Joshi, Esha Basanti (ed.), *Uttar Pradesh District Gazetteers: Mathura*, Government of Uttar Pradesh, Lucknow, 1968, p. 322.
172. Growse, F.S., *Mathura: A District Memoir*, Asian Educational Services, New Delhi, 1979, p. 61.
173. Jadrup also met Akbar near Ujjain, when the latter was on his way back to Agra after his campaign of Khandesh in the Deccan. See: Thackston, Wheeler M. (ed.), *The Jahangirnama: Memoirs of Jahangir*, Oxford University Press, New York, p. 209.
174. Ibid., 285.
175. Ibid., 313.
176. Growse, F.S., *Mathura: A District Memoir*, Asian Educational Services, New Delhi, 1979, p. 250.

177. A round stone ring stylistically carved in the shape of an amla, which is used to top the spires of temples built after the Gupta period.
178. Ibid., 251.
179. Ibid., 250.
180. Ibid., 243.
181. Ibid., 250.
182. Ibid., 244.
183. Thackston, Wheeler M. (ed.), *The Jahangirnama: Memoirs of Jahangir, Emperor of India*, Oxford University Press, New York, p. 311.
184. Growse, F.S., *Mathura: A District Memoir*, Asian Educational Services, New Delhi, 1979, p. 245.
185. Ibid., 243.
186. Ibid., 246.
187. Eden, Emily, *'Up the Country'*, Richard Bentley, London, 1867, p. 350.
188. Ibid., 349.

Chapter 4: The Ruins of Kannauj

1. The Gypsies derived their name from Egypt but were originally from India. The Gypsies of Europe and America are largely known as Roma, a term that potentially has its root in the word Dom, a low caste of India. These people were first enslaved and taken to Ghazni by Mahmud after his conquest of Kannauj.
2. Panchala is an ancient kingdom that predated the founding of Kannauj. However, the Khalimpur Copper Plate Inscription of Dharmapala of the Pala Dynasty of Bengal mentions that Kannauj was the capital of Panchala. See: Kielhorn, F., 'Khalimpur Plate of Dharmapaladeva', *Epigraphia Indica*, Vol. 4, 1896–97, p. 252.
3. Mukherji, Ramaranjan, and Sachindra Kumar Maity, *Corpus of Bengal Inscriptions: Bearing on History and Civilization of Bengal*, Firma K.L. Mukhopadhyay, Calcutta, p. 171.
4. Kielhorn, F., 'Dubkund Stone Inscription of the Kachchhapaghata', *Epigraphia Indica*, Vol. 2, p. 233.
5. Shastri, Hari Prasad (trans.), *The Ramayana of Valmiki*, Vol. 1, Shanti Sadan, London, 1952, p. 68.
6. Pandit, R.S. (trans.), *Rajatarangini: The Saga of the Kings of Kasmir*, Sahitya Akademi, New Delhi, p. 129.
7. Dutt, Manmatha Nath (ed.), *A Prose English Translation of Harivamsha*, H.C. Dass, Calcutta, 1897, p. 108.
8. Beal, Samuel (trans.), *Si-Yu-Ki: Buddhist Records of the Western World*, Vol. 1, Trubner and Co., London, 1884, pp. 208–09.
9. McCrindle, J.W. (ed.), *Ancient India as Described by Ptolemy*, Trubner and Co., London, 1885, p. 134.
10. Department of Archaeology, Government of India, *Indian Archaeology 1955-56—A Review*, A. Ghosh (ed.), 1956, pp. 19–20.
11. Legge, James (trans.), *A Record of Buddhistic Kingdoms: Being an Account by the Chinese Monk Fa Hien*, Oxford at the Clarendon Press, 1886, pp. 53–54.
12. Sastri, Pandit Hirananda, 'Haraha Inscription of the Reign of Isanavarman [Vikram Samvat] 611', *Epigraphia Indica*, Vol. 14, 1917–18, p. 112.

13. Ibid., 111.
14. Altekar, A.S., 'Three Maukhari Inscriptions on Yupas: Krita Year 295', *Epigraphia Indica*, Vol. 23, 1935–36, p. 52.
15. Majumdar, R.C. (ed.), *The History and Culture of the Indian People: The Classical Age*, Bharatiya Vidya Bhavan, Mumbai, 2018, p. 67; Altekar, A.S., 'Three Maukhari Inscriptions on Yupas: Krita Year 295', *Epigraphia Indica*, Vol. 23, 1935–36, p. 52.
16. The Later Guptas were a dynasty that established themselves in Magadha and ruled the tract in the sixth–seventh centuries CE; maybe connected to the Imperial Guptas or maybe an independent family merely adopting the suffix of Gupta to emulate an imperial aura.
17. Fleet, John Faithfull, *Corpus Inscriptionum Indicarum, Vol. III: Inscriptions of the Early Gupta Kings and Their Successors*, Indological Book House, Varanasi, 1960, p. 206.
18. An inscription of Iswaravarman has been found by Alexander Cunningham in the Shahi Jama Masjid of Jaunpur. The inscription mentions the prowess of Iswaravarman, who had defeated an invading army from Malwa and the south. See: Fleet, John Faithfull, *Corpus Inscriptionum Indicarum, Vol. III: Inscriptions of the Early Gupta Kings and Their Successors*, Indological Book House, Varanasi, 1960, pp. 228–30.
19. Sastri, Pandit Hirananda, 'Haraha Inscription of the Reign of Isanavarman [Vikram Samvat] 611', *Epigraphia Indica*, Vol. 14, 1917–18, p. 119.
20. The identity of this king has not been established. He ruled in the area adjacent to the sea, north of Odisha, in the intervening period after the end of the Gupta reign and the beginning of Shashank's.
21. Majumdar, R.C. (ed.), *The History and Culture of the Indian People: The Classical Age*, Bharatiya Vidya Bhavan, Mumbai, 2018, p. 69.
22. Fleet, John Faithfull, *Corpus Inscriptionum Indicarum, Vol. III: Inscriptions of the Early Gupta Kings and Their Successors*, Indological Book House, Varanasi, 1960, p. 221.
23. Cowell, E.B., and F.W. Thomas (trans.), *The Harsa-Carita of Bana*, The Royal Asiatic Society, London, 1897, p. 122.
24. Ibid., 128.
25. Ibid., 155.
26. Ibid., 165.
27. Ibid., 173, 175.
28. Beal, Samuel (trans.), *Si-Yu-Ki: Buddhist Records of the Western World*, Vol. 1, Trubner and Co., London, 1884, p. 210.
29. Cowell, E.B., and F.W. Thomas (trans.), *The Harsa-Carita of Bana*, The Royal Asiatic Society, London, 1897, p. 178.
30. The 'seven *dwipas*' is a hyperbolic term denoting the realms within India. See: Cowell, E.B., and F.W. Thomas (trans.), *The Harsa-Carita of Bana*, The Royal Asiatic Society, London, 1897, p. 260.
31. The first Maratha king of Tanjore, Venkoji, was the half-brother of Shivaji.
32. Fleet, John Faithfull, *Corpus Inscriptionum Indicarum, Vol. III: Inscriptions of the Early Gupta Kings and Their Successors*, Indological Book House, Varanasi, 1960, pp. 91, 142.
33. Kielhorn, F., 'Aihole Inscription of Pulikesin II.; Saka-Samvat 556', *Epigraphia Indica*, Vol. 6, 1900–01. p. 10.

34. Beal, Samuel (trans.), *Si-Yu-Ki: Buddhist Records of the Western World*, Vol. 1, Trubner and Co., London, 1884, p. 213.
35. Ibid., 210.
36. Fleet, John Faithfull, *Corpus Inscriptionum Indicarum, Vol. III: Inscriptions of the Early Gupta Kings and Their Successors*, Indological Book House, Varanasi, 1960, p. 232.
37. Buhler, G., 'Banskhera Plate of Harsha', *Epigraphia Indica*, Vol. 4, 1896–97, p. 208.
38. Buhler, G., 'The Madhuban Copper-Plate of Harsha, Dated Samvat 25', *Epigraphia Indica*, Vol. 1, p. 67.
39. Ibid., 74.
40. Sastri, Hirananda, 'The Clay Seals of Nalanda', *Epigraphia Indica*, Vol. 21, 1931–32, pp. 74–76.
41. Cowell, E.B., and F.W. Thomas (trans.), *The Harsacharita by Banabhatta*, Global Vision Publishing House, p. 251.
42. Beal, Samuel (trans.), *Si-Yu-Ki: Buddhist Records of the Western World*, Vol. 1, Trubner and Co., London, 1884, pp. 206–23.
43. Beal, Samuel (ed.), *The Life of Hieun Tsiang by the Shaman Hwui Li*, Kegan Paul, Trench, Trubner and Co., London, 1911, p. 183.
44. Beal, Samuel (trans.), *Si-Yu-Ki: Buddhist Records of the Western World*, Vol. 1, Trubner and Co., London, 1884, pp. 206–23.
45. Cunningham, Alexander, *The Ancient Geography of India: The Buddhist Period*, Vol. 1, Trubner and Co., London, p. 478.
46. Beal, Samuel (ed.), *The Life of Hieun Tsiang by the Shaman Hwui Li*, Kegan Paul, Trench, Trubner and Co., London, 1911, p. 181.
47. Manitara on the Rapti (the river should be Ghaghara as the Rapti is one of its tributaries) is unidentified. From Bana's village of Pritikuta on the banks of the Son River, it took him three days of walk to reach the camp, which included crossing the Ganga at a place called Mallakuta (village of the Malla/boatmen caste); one night was spent in a forest village of Yastighrika and the next day he arrived at the camp. See: Cowell, E.B., and F.W. Thomas (trans.), *The Harsa-Carita of Bana*, The Royal Asiatic Society, London, pp. 45–46.
48. Beal, Samuel (ed.), *The Life of Hieun Tsiang by the Shaman Hwui Li*, Kegan Paul, Trench, Trubner and Co., London, 1911, p. 181.
49. Ibid., 184.
50. Ibid., 189.
51. Chimpa, Lama, and Alaka Chattopadhyaya (trans.), *Taranatha's History of Buddhism in India*, Motilal Banarsidass, Delhi, p. 178.
52. Kale, M.R. (trans.), *The Priyadarsika of Sri Harsha-Deva*, Messrs Gopal Narayan and Co., Bombay, 1928, p. xiv. All three plays have been translated by M.R. Kale. The *Nagananda* was published in 1919 by Standard Publishing Co., Bombay, The *Ratnavali* in 1921, and *Priyadarshika* in 1928 by Messrs Gopal Narayan and Co., Bombay.
53. It was King Songtsen Gampo who introduced Buddhism to Tibet and was the founder of the unified Tibetan Empire.
54. Majumdar, R.C. (ed.), *The History and Culture of the Indian People: The Classical Age*, Vol. 3, Bharatiya Vidya Bhavan, Mumbai, 2009, pp. 124–25.
55. Fredunbeg, Mirza Kalichbeg (trans.), *The Chachnamah, an Ancient History of Sind*, The Commissioner's Press, Karachi, 1900, p. 33.

56. Ibid., 39–40.
57. Vakpati, *The Gaudavaho: A Prakrit Historical Poem*, Shankar Pandurang Pandit and Narayan Bapuji Utgikar (eds.), Bhandarkar Oriental Research Institute, 1927, pp. xx–xxii.
58. Gaudavaho in Prakrit means 'the slaying of the king of Gauda'.
59. The carpet manufacturing town of Mirzapur is sandwiched between the Vindhyas and the Ganga near Chunar in Uttar Pradesh. This town has an ancient temple dedicated to Goddess Vindhyavasini. The present temple is a rebuilt structure after its destruction by Islamic forces.
60. Vakpati, *The Gaudavaho: A Prakrit Historical Poem*, Shankar Pandurang Pandit and Narayan Bapuji Utgikar (eds.), Bhandarkar Oriental Research Institute, 1927, pp. xx–xxii.
61. Sastri, Hirananda, 'Nalanda Stone Inscription of the Reign of Yasovarmmadeva', *Epigraphia Indica*, Vol. 20, 1929-30, pp. 39–40.
62. Pandit, R.S. (trans.), *Rajatarangini: The Saga of the Kings of Kasmir*, Sahitya Akademi, New Delhi, pp. 128–30.
63. Lakshmanavati is the original name of Lakhnauti/Maldah, which was established by Lakshmana Sen of the Sena Dynasty towards the end of the twelfth century CE.
64. Tripathi, Rama Shankar, *History of Kanauj to the Muslim Conquest*, Motilal Banarsidass, 1959, p. 211.
65. Ibid., 212–13.
66. Mukherji, Ramaranjan, and Sachindra Kumaer Maity, *Corpus of Bengal Inscriptions: Bearing on History and Civilization of Bengal*, Firma K.L. Mukhopadhyay, Calcutta, p. 171.
67. Kielhorn, F., 'Khamlimpur Plate of Dharmapaladeva', *Epigraphia Indica*, Vol. 4, 1896–97, p. 252.
68. Puri, Baij Nath, 'The History of the Gurjara-Pratiharas', 1957, University of Oxford, PhD thesis, p. 43.
69. Majumdar, R.C. (ed.), *The History and Culture of the Indian People: The Age of Imperial Kannauj*, Vol. 4, Bharatiya Vidya Bhavan, Mumbai, 2009, forward p. X.
70. Sastri, Hiramanda, 'Barah Copper-Plate of Bhojadeva, Vikrama-Samvat 893', *Epigraphia Indica*, Vol. 19, 1927-28, pp. 18–19.
71. Phewa was once an ancient religious centre on the banks of the Saraswati.
72. Buhler, G., 'The Peheva Inscription from the Temple of Garibnath', *Epigraphia Indica*, Vol. 1, p. 185.
73. Ghosh, Manomohan (ed.), *Karpuramanjari (The Prakrit Play of Rajasekhara)*, University of Calcutta, 1939, p. LXV.
74. Buhler, G., 'The Peheva Inscription from the Temple of Garibnath', *Epigraphia Indica*, Vol. 1, p. 189.
75. So far, a total of fourteen inscriptions discovered from far-flung regions of India like Gujarat, Bengal, Bihar and Haryana, among other places, mention the name of the Gurjara-Pratihara ruler Mahendrapala.
76. Puri, Baij Nath, 'The History of the Gurjara-Pratiharas', 1957, University of Oxford, PhD thesis, p. 77.
77. Ghosh, Manomohan (ed.), *Karpuramanjari (The Prakrit Play of Rajasekhara)*, University of Calcutta, 1939, p. LXV.
78. Puri, Baij Nath, 'The History of the Gurjara-Pratiharas', 1957, University of Oxford, PhD thesis, p. 77.

79. Trivedi, Harihar Vitthal (ed.), *Corpus Inscriptionum Indicarum, Vol. VII: Inscriptions of the Paramaras, Chandellas, Kachhapaghatas and Two Minor Dynasties*, Part 2, Archaeological Survey of India, 1991, p. 92.
80. Kielhorn, F., 'Dubkund Stone Inscription of the Kachchhapaghata Vikramasimha', *Epigraphia Indica*, Vol. 2, p. 232.
81. Sachau, Dr Edward C. (trans.), *Alberuni's India*, Rupa and Co., 2002, p. 186.
82. Ibid., 186. Bari is possibly Bangarmau, situated about 45 km across the river from Kannauj.
83. Mitra, Sisir Kumar, *The Early Rulers of Khajuraho*, Motilal Banarsidass, 1958, p. 73.
84. Reynolds, James (trans.), *The Kitab-i-Yamini: Historical Memoirs of Amir Sabaktagin and the Sultan Mahmud of Ghazna*, The Oriental Translation Fund of Great Britain and Ireland, London, 1858, p. 457.
85. Ibid., 457.
86. Ibid., 462–63.
87. Elliot, Henry Miers, 'Habibu-s Siyar, of Khondamir', *The History of India, as Told by Its Own Historians: The Muhammadan Period*, Vol. 4, John Dowson (ed.), Trubner and Co., London, pp. 179–80.
88. Hultzsch, E., 'A Valabhi Grant of Dhruvasena III. Dated Samvat 334', *Epigraphia Indica*, Vol. 1, p. 85.
89. 'Middle East Gypsies: Dom Research Workshop', *Kirkayak Kultur*, https://tinyurl.com/muccu2n7. Accessed on 20 September 2024.
90. Elliot, Henry Miers, 'Diwan of Salman', *The History of India, as Told by Its Own Historians*, Vol. 4, John Dowson (ed.), Trubner and Co., London, p. 524.
91. Niyogi, Roma, *The History of the Gahadavala Dynasty*, Oriental Book Agency, Calcutta, 1959, p. 26.
92. Konow, Sten, 'Chandravati Plate of Chandradeva. Samvat 1148', *Epigraphia Indica*, Vol. 9, 1907–08, p. 303.
93. Sanyal, N.B., 'The Predecessors of the Gahadavalas of Kanauj', *Journal and Proceedings of the Asiatic Society of Bengal*, Vol. 21, 1925, pp. 103, 106.
94. Kielhorn, F., 'Badaun Stone Inscription of Lakahanapala', *Epigraphia Indica*, Vol. 1, pp. 61–62; Buhler G., 'The Peheva Inscription from the Temple of Garibnath', *Epigraphia Indica*, Vol. 1, p. 185; Buhler, G., 'An Undated Prasasti from the Reign of Mahendrapala of Kanauj', *Epigraphia Indica*, Vol. 1, p. 242.
95. Kielhorn, F., 'Twenty-One Copper-Plates of the Kings of Kanauj', *Epigraphia Indica*, Vol. 4, 1896–97, pp. 97–129.
96. Konow, Sten, 'Chandravati Plate of Chandradeva', *Epigraphia Indica*, Vol. 9, 1907–08, pp. 302–03. Yasovigharaha was the grandfather of Chandradeva.
97. Venis, Arthur, 'Benares Copper-Plate Grants of Govindachandra of Kanauj', *Epigraphia Indica*, Vol. 2, p. 358.
98. Konow, Sten, 'Sarnath Inscription of Kumaradevi', *Epigraphia Indica*, Vol. 9, 1907–08, p. 321.
99. Kielhorn, F., 'Twenty-One Copper-Plates of the Kings of Kanauj', *Epigraphia Indica*, Vol. 4, 1896–97, p. 117.
100. Ibid., 126.
101. So far, sixteen inscriptions issued by Jayachandra have been found, and two bear his name in them. See: Ibid.
102. Ibid., 118.

103. Raverty, H.G. (trans.), *The Tabakat-i-Nasiri of Minhaj-i-Saraj*, The Asiatic Society of Bengal, London, 1873, p. 470.
104. Ibid., 470.
105. Elliot, Henry Miers, 'Taju-l Ma-asir of Hasan Nizami', *The History of India, as Told by Its Own Historians*, Vol. 2, John Dowson (ed.), Trubner and Co., London, p. 223.
106. Raverty, H.G. (trans.), *The Tabakat-i-Nasiri of Minhaj-i-Saraj*, The Asiatic Society of Bengal, London, 1873, p. 491.
107. Cunningham, Alexander, *Report of Tours in the Gangetic Provinces from Badaon to Bihar in 1875-76 and 1877-78*, Indological Book House, Varanasi, 1968, p. 130.
108. Kielhorn, F., 'Twenty-One Copper-Plates of the Kings of Kanauj', *Epigraphia Indica*, Vol. 4, 1896-97, pp. 126-27.
109. Hipananda, Pandit, 'Machhlishahr Copper-Plate of Harishchandradeva of Kanauj [Vikrama-]Samvat 1253', *Epigraphia Indica*, Vol. 10, 1909-10, pp. 93-94.
110. Niyogi, Roma, *The History of the Gahadavala Dynasty*, Oriental Book Agency, Calcutta, 1959, p. 29.
111. Raverty, H.G. (trans.), *The Tabakat-i-Nasiri of Minhaj-i-Saraj*, The Asiatic Society of Bengal, London, 1873, p. 627.
112. Gibb, H.A.R. (trans.), *The Travels of Ibn Battuta, A.D. 1325-1354*, Vol. 4, The Hakluyt Society, 1971, p. 784.
113. Elliot, Henry Miers, 'Tarikh-i Mubarak Shahi, of Yahya bin Ahmed', *The History of India, as Told by Its Own Historians: The Muhammadan Period*, Vol. 4, John Dowson (ed.), Trubner and Co., London, p. 26.
114. Ibid., 39.
115. Elias, N. (ed.), *The Tarikh-i-Rashidi by Mirza Muhammad Haidar, Dughlat*, E. Denison Ross, Sampson Low, Marston and Company, London, p. 477.
116. Elliot, Henry Miers, 'Tarikh-i Sher Shahi; or, Tuhfat-i Akbar Shahi, of 'Abbas Khan Sarwani', *The History of India, as Told by Its Own Historians*, Vol. 4, John Dowson (ed.), Trubner and Co., London, p. 382.
117. Ibid., 382-83.
118. Jarrett, H.S. (trans.), *'Ain-i-Akbari of Abul Fazl-i-'Allami'*, Vol. 2, Royal Asiatic Society of Bengal, Calcutta, 1949, p. 191; Thackston, Wheeler M. (ed.), *The Jahangirnama: Memoirs of Jahangir, Emperor of India*, Oxford University Press, New York, p. 124.
119. Foster, William (ed.), *Early Travels in India: 1583-1619*, Oxford University Press, England, p. 175.
120. Jarrett, H.S. (trans.), *'Ain-i-Akbari of Abul Fazl-i-'Allami*, Vol. 1, Royal Asiatic Society of Bengal, Calcutta, 1949, pp. 73-87.
121. Salima Sultan Begum was the granddaughter of Babur from his daughter Gulrukh Begum and her husband Nuruddin Muhammad Mirza. She was the widow of Bairam Khan well as Akbar, who married her after Bairam Khan's death. The poet Abdur Rahim, the Khan-e-Khana, was her stepson from Bairam Khan's other wife.
122. Thackston, Wheeler M. (ed.), *The Jahangirnama: Memoirs of Jahangir, Emperor of India*, Oxford University Press, New York, p. 163.
123. Cunningham, Alexander, *Archaeological Survey of India: Four Reports Made During the Years 1862-63-64-65*, Vol. 1, The Government Central Press, Simla, 1871, pp. 287-88.

124. Ibid., 284.
125. Ibid., 289, 288.
126. Ibid., 290.
127. Ibid., 288.
128. Ibid., 292.
129. The Kannauj Museum is in the Kutalupur locality beside the main road to Farrukhabad, Etah and Aligarh.
130. Cunningham, Alexander, *Archaeological Survey of India: Four Reports Made During the Years 1862-63-64-65*, Vol. 1, The Government Central Press, Simla, 1871, pp. 290–91.
131. Ibid., 293.
132. Ibid., 286–87.
133. Fergusson, James, *History of Indian and Eastern Architecture*, Vol. 2, John Murray, London, 1910, p. 228.
134. Cunningham, Alexander, *Archaeological Survey of India: Four Reports Made During the Years 1862-63-64-65*, Vol. 1, The Government Central Press, Simla, 1871, p. 288.
135. Beal, Samuel (trans.), *Si-Yu-Ki: Buddhist Records of the Western World*, Vol. 1, Trubner and Co., London, 1884, p. 221.
136. Anand, Deepak, 'In the Search for the Two Ashokan Stupas in Kannauj', *Nalanda – Insatiable in Offering*, 12 January 2023, https://tinyurl.com/272tph4y. Accessed on 20 September 2024.

Chapter 5: Lord Rama's Janmabhoomi

1. Carnegy, P., J. Woodburn, and C.S. Noble, *Historical Sketch of Tahsil Fyzabad, Zillah Fyzabad*, the Oudh Government Press, Lucknow, 1870, p. 1.
2. Ibid., 1.
3. Ibid., 1.
4. Gulbadan Begum, *Humayun Nama*, Annette Susannah Beveridge (trans.), Atlantic Publishers, p. 105.
5. Babur, Zahiru'd-din Muhammad, *Babur-Nama: Memoirs of Babur*, Annette Susannah Beveridge (trans.), Oriental Books Reprint Corporation, p. 612.
6. Oak, P.N., *The Taj Mahal Is a Temple Palace*, Hindi Sahitya Sadan, 2003, pp. 45–46.
7. Sankalia, H.D., *The Ramayana in Historical Perspective*, Macmilliam India Ltd, 1982, p. 28.
8. Law, Bimala Churn, *Historical Geography of Ancient India*, Societe Asiatique de Paris, 1954, p. 67.
9. Sister Vajira, and Francis Story (trans.), *Last Days of the Buddha: The Mahaparinibbana Sutta*, Buddhist Publication Society, Kandy, p. 67.
10. *Journal of the Asiatic Society of Bengal*, Vol. 44, Part 1, C.B. Lewis, Calcutta, 1875, pp. 130–73.
11. Shastri, Hari Prasasd, *The Ramayana of Valmiki*, Vol. 1, Shanti Sadan, London, pp. 17–20.
12. Ibid., 367.
13. Law, Bimala Churn, *Historical Geography of Ancient India*, Societe Asiatique de Paris, 1954, p. 67.
14. McCrindle, J.W. (ed.), *Ancient India as Described by Ptolemy*, Trubner and Co.,

London, 1885, pp. 166, 228.
15. Ibid., 99.
16. Cowell, E.B., and F.W. Thomas (trans.), *The Harsha-Carita of Bana*, The Royal Asiatic Society, London, 1897, p. 193.
17. Pargiter, F.E., *The Purana Text of the Dynasties of the Kali Age*, Humphrey Milford, Oxford University Press, 1913, p. 31.
18. Mitchiner, John E. (trans.), *The Yuga Purana*, The Asiatic Society, Calcutta, 1986, p. 55.
19. Jayaswal, K.P., 'The Hathigumpha Inscription of Kharavela', *Epigraphia Indica*, Vol. 20, 1929–30, p. 87.
20. Sahni, Rai Bahadur Daya Ram, 'A Sunga Inscription from Ayodhya', *Epigraphia Indica*, Vol. 20, 1929–30, p. 55.
21. Ibid., 55.
22. Mitchiner, John E. (trans.), *The Yuga Purana*, The Asiatic Society, Calcutta, 1986, p. 93.
23. Kunal, Kishore, *Ayodhya Revisited*, Ocean Books Pvt Ltd, New Delhi, 2016, p. 24.
24. Konow, Sten, 'Karamdanda Inscription of the Reign of Kumaragupta [Gupta-] Samvat 117', *Epigraphia Indica*, Vol. 10, 1909–10, p. 71.
25. Fleet, John Faithfull, *Corpus Inscriptionum Indicarum, Vol. III: Inscriptions of the Early Gupta Kings and their Successors*, Indological Book House, Varanasi, 1960, p. 257.
26. Carnegy, P., J. Woodburn, and C.S. Noble, *Historical Sketch of Tahsil Fyzabad, Zillah Fyzabad*, the Oudh Government Press, Lucknow, 1870, p. 6.
27. Raychaudhuri, Hemchandra, *Political History of Ancient India: From the Accession of Parikshit to the Extinction of the Gupta Dynasty*, University of Calcutta, 1923, p. 282; Fleet, John Faithfull, 'No. 13; Plate VII', *Corpus Inscriptionum Indicarum, Vol. III: Inscriptions of the Early Gupta Kings and their Successors*, Indological Book House, Varanasi, 1960, p. 56.
28. Raychaudhuri, Hemchandra, *Political History of Ancient India: From the Accession of Parikshit to the Extinction of the Gupta Dynasty*, University of Calcutta, 1923, p. 292.
29. Ibid., 293.
30. Legge, James (trans.), *A Record of Buddhist Kingdoms: Being an Account by the Chinese Monk Fa Hien*, Oxford at the Clarendon Press, 1886, p. 55.
31. Kunal, Kishore, *Ayodhya Revisited*, Ocean Books Pvt Ltd, p. 41.
32. There is no record of their ever meeting each other either in the *Si-Yu-Ki* or in the *Harshacharita*.
33. Cowell, E.B., and F.W. Thomas (trans.), *The Harsa-Carita of Bana*, The Royal Asiatic Society, London, 1897, p. 194.
34. Ibid., 97.
35. Beal, Samuel (trans.), *Si-Yu-Ki: Buddhist Records of the Western World*, Vol. 1, Trubner and Co., London, 1884, pp. 224–26.
36. Ibid., 225–26.
37. To the east of Hanumangarhi at the highest point of the mound of Ramkot was the Babri Masjid, which Cunningham fails to mention.
38. Cunningham, Alexander, *Archaeological Surve of India: Four Reports made During the Years 1862-63-64-65*, Vol. 1, The Government Central Press, Simla, 1871, pp. 322–23.

39. Ibid., 325.
40. Pandit, R.S. (trans.), *Rajatarangini: The Saga of the Kings of Kasmir*, Sahitya Akademi, New Delhi, pp. 128–30.
41. Mirashi, Vasudev Vishnu (ed.), *Corpus Inscriptionum Indicarum, Vol. IV: Inscriptions of the Kalachuri-Chedi Era*, Part 2, Govt. Epigraphist for India, p. 380.
42. Ibid., 451.
43. Ibid., 457.
44. Sachau, Edward C. (trans.), *Alberuni's India*, Trubner and Co., London, 1910, p. 200.
45. Reynolds, James (trans.), *The Kitab-i-Yamini: Historical Memoirs of Amir Sabaktagin and the Sultan Mahmud of Ghazna*, The Oriental Translation Fund of Great Britain and Ireland, London, 1858, p. 457.
46. Nevill, H.R. (ed.), *Lucknow: A Gazetteer*, Vol. 37, Superintendent, Government Press, United Provinces, 1904, p. 139.
47. Jarrett, H.S. (trans.), *'Ain-i-Akbari of Abul Fazl-i-'Allami*, Vol. 2, Royal Asiatic Society of Bengal, Calcutta, 1949, p. 182; Elliot, H.M., 'Extracts from the Mir-at-i Mas'udi', *The History of India, as Told by Its Own Historians*, Vol. 2, John Dowson (ed.), Trubner and Co., London, p. 546.
48. Chandravati, where these plates were found inside a strong stone box, is situated on the west bank of the Ganga, about 20 km to the north of Banaras.
49. Sahni, Daya Ram, 'Chandravati Plates of Chandra-Deva: V.S. 1150 and 1156', *Epigraphia Indica*, Vol. 14, 1917–18, p. 193.
50. Law, Bimala Churn, *Historical Geography of Ancient India*, Societe Asiatique de Paris, 1954, p. 67.
51. Raverty, H.G. (trans.), *The Tabakat-i-Nasiri of Minhaj-i-Saraj*, The Asiatic Society of Bengal, London, 1873, p. 470.
52. Ibid., 491.
53. Kunal, Kishore, *Ayodhya Revisited*, Ocean Books Pvt Ltd, p. xxvi.
54. Raverty, H.G. (trans.), *The Tabakat-i-Nasiri of Minhaj-i-Saraj*, The Asiatic Society of Bengal, London, 1873, p. 549.
55. Ibid., 549–51.
56. Ibid., 628.
57. Ibid., 629.
58. Nevill, H.R., *Fyzabad: A Gazetteer*, Vol. 43, Superintendent, Government Press, Allahabad, 1905, p. 151.
59. Elliot, Henry Miers, 'Makhsan-I Afghani and Tarikh-i Khan-Jahan Lodi, of Ni'amatu-lla', *The History of India, as Told by Its Own Historians*, Vol. 5, John Dowson (ed.), Trubner and Co., London, p. 93.
60. Nevill, H.R., *Fyzabad: A Gazetteer*, Vol. 43, Superintendent, Government Press, Allahabad, 1905, p. 153.
61. Babur, Zahiru'd-din Muhammad, *Babur-Nama: Memoirs of Babur*, Annette Susannah Beveridge (trans.), Oriental Books Reprint Corporation, p. 463.
62. Carnegy, P., J. Woodburn, and C.S. Noble, *Historical Sketch of Tahsil Fyzabad, Zillah Fyzabad*, the Oudh Government Press, Lucknow, 1870, pp. 20–21.
63. Kunal, Kishore, *Ayodhya Revisited*, Ocean Books Pvt Ltd, 2020, pp. 274–75.
64. Babur, Zahiru'd-din Muhammad, *Babur-Nama: Memoirs of Babur*, Annette Susannah Beveridge (trans.), Oriental Books Reprint Corporation, p. 603.

65. Ibid., 463.
66. Ibid., 590.
67. Ibid., 602.
68. Ibid., 684.
69. Nevill, H.R., *Fyzabad: A Gazetteer*, Vol. 43, Superintendent, Government Press, Allahabad, 1905, p. 153.
70. Babur, Zahiru'd-din Muhammad, *Babur-Nama: Memoirs of Babur*, Annette Susannah Beveridge (trans.), Oriental Books Reprint Corporation, p. 685.
71. Jarrett, H.S. (trans.), *'Ain-i-Akbari of Abul Fazl-i-'Allami*, Vol. 2, Royal Asiatic Society of Bengal, Calcutta, 1949, p. 182.
72. Nevill, H.R., *Fyzabad: A Gazetteer*, Vol. 43, Superintendent, Government Press, Allahabad, 1905, p. 172.
73. Foster, William (ed.), *Early Travels in India: 1583–1619*, Humphrey Milford Oxford University Press, England, 1921, p. 176.
74. Ibid., 176.
75. Hoyland, J.S. (trans.), *The Empire of the Great Mogol*, D.B. Taraporevala Sons & Co., Bombay, 1928, pp. 64–65.
76. Elliot, Henry Miers, 'Badshah-nama, of 'Abdu-l Hamid Lahori', *The History of India, as Told by Its Own Historians*, Vol. 7, John Dowson (ed.), Trubner and Co., London, p. 36.
77. Manucci, Niccolao, *Storia Do Mogor or Mogul India: 1653–1708*, Vol. 3, William Irvine (trans.), John Murray, p. 245.
78. Kunal, Kishore, *Ayodhya Revisited*, Ocean Books Pvt Ltd, 2020, p. xvi.
79. Carnegy, P., J. Woodburn, and C.S. Noble, *Historical Sketch of Tahsil Fyzabad, Zillah Fyzabad*, the Oudh Government Press, Lucknow, 1870, p. 13.
80. Bhatnagar, G.D., *Awadh Under Wajid 'Ali Shah*, Bharatiya Vidya Prakashan, Varanasi, 1968, p. 117.
81. Cole, J.R.I., *Roots of North Indian Shi'ism in Iran And Iraq*, University of California Press, 1989, p. 245.
82. Bhatnagar, G.D., *Awadh Under Wajid Ali Shah*, Bharatiya Vidya Prakashan, Varanasi, 1968, p. 119.
83. Nevill, H.R., *Fyzabad: A Gazetteer*, Vol. 43, Superintendent, Government Press, Allahabad, 1905, p. 162.
84. Kunal, Kishore, *Ayodhya Revisited*, Ocean Books Pvt Ltd, pp. 375–76.
85. Gopal, Sarvepalli (ed.), *Anatomy of a Confrontation: Ayodhya and the Rise of Communal Politics in India*, Bloomsbury, 1993, pp. 67–68.
86. Fuhrer, A., *The Sharqi Architecture of Jaunpur: With Notes on Zafarabad, Sahet-Mahet and Other Places in the North-Western Provinces and Oudh*, Superintendent of Government Printing, Calcutta, 1889, p. 67.
87. Ibid., 67–68.
88. Ibid., 68.
89. Ibid., 68.
90. Ibid., 68. Treta Ki Thakur means 'the lord of the Treta Yuga', which stands for Rama.
91. *M. Siddiq (D) Thr Lrs vs Mahant Suresh Das & Ors*, (2019), CA 10866-10867/2010, p. 88.
92. Elst, Koenraad, 'The Ayodhya Debate: Focus on the "No Temple" Evidence: 1.6. A British Concoction?', *Ayodhya: The Case Against the Temple*, https://tinyurl.com/ye268ayu. Accessed on 10 December 2024.

93. Husain, Maulavi M. Ashraf, 'Inscriptions of Emperor Babur', *Epigraphia Indica: Arabic and Persian Supplement (In continuation of Epigraphia Indo-Moslemica) 1964 and 1965*, Archaeological Survey of India, p. 58.
94. Ibid., 61.
95. *M. Siddiq (D) Thr Lrs vs Mahant Suresh Das & Ors*, (2019), CA 10866-10867/2010, pp. 641–42.
96. Mani, B.R., and Hair Manjhi, *Ayodhya 2002-03: Excavations at the Disputed Site*, Vol. 1, Archaeological Survey of India, 2003, pp. 268–72.
97. *M. Siddiq (D) Thr Lrs vs Mahant Suresh Das & Ors*, (2019), CA 10866-10867/2010.
98. Ibid., 7.
99. Ibid., 598.
100. Ibid., 594–96.
101. Chaturvedi, Amit, 'Meet Chandrakant Sompura, Man Who Designed the Ayodhya Ram Temple', *NDTV*, 20 January 2024, https://tinyurl.com/nybmtwm9. Accessed on 24 September 2024.
102. Jeelani, Gulam, 'Lok Sabha Election Results 2024: Shocker from Ayodhya as BJP Leader Loses Faizabad, the Seat that Houses Ram Mandir', *mint*, 7 June 2024, https://tinyurl.com/mszj8xjw. Accessed on 24 September 2024.

Chapter 6: Prayagraj: The Immortal Tree and the Invisible Saraswati of the Sangam

1. The Ganesh Prayag confluence is no more, as it has been inundated by the Tehri reservoir of the Bhagirathi.
2. The confluence of the Saraswati at the Sangam is a metaphorical allusion to the long-lost river flowing underground, emptying itself at Prayag. There is more to it than a mere metaphor, as Niccolao Manucci has elaborated. See: Manucci, Niccolao, *Storia Do Mogor*, Vol. 2, William Irvine (trans.), S. Dey, pp. 75–76.
3. Shastri, Hari Prasad (trans.), *The Ramayana of Valmiki*, Vol. 1, Shanti Sadan, London, 1952, p. 281.
4. Kalidas, S. 'Maha Kumbha Mela 2001: Largest Congregation of Hindus Ever Is Ready to Begin in Allahabad', *India Today*, 15 January 2001, https://tinyurl.com/4erza4vm. Accessed on 26 September 2024.
5. 'Around 2.5 million Pilgrims Take Part in Hajj This Year', *Arab News*, 11 August 2019, https://tinyurl.com/47p3nfy2. Accessed on 26 September 2024.
6. Sahib, C.S. Krishnaswamy Rao, and Amalananda Ghosh, 'A Note on the Allahabad Pillar of Asoka', *The Journal of the Royal Asiatic Society of Great Britian and Ireland for 1935*, London, 1935, p. 703.
7. Shastri, Hari Prasad (trans.), *The Ramayana of Valmiki*, Vol. 1, Shanti Sadan, London, 1952, p. 279.
8. Ibid., 281.
9. Lal, B.B., *Excavations at Bhardwaj Ashram: 1978-83*, Archaeological Survey of India, 2011, p. 179.
10. Ibid., 13.
11. Ibid., 179–80.

12. McCrindle, J.W. (trans.), *Ancient India as Described by Megasthenes and Arrian*, Trubner and Co., London, 1877, p. 129.
13. Nanamoli, Bhikkhu, and Bhikkhu Bodhi (trans.), *The Middle Length Discourse of the Buddha: A New Translation of the Majjhima Nikaya*, Buddhist Publication Society, Kandy, 1995, p. 121.
14. Ibid., 121.
15. Hultzsch, E., *Corpus Inscriptionum Indicarum: Inscriptions of Ashoka*, Vol. 1, Clarendon Press, 1925, p. XX.
16. Sen, Amulyachandra, *Asoka's Edicts*, Institute of Indology, Calcutta, 1956, pp. 127, 130.
17. Horner, I.B. (trans.), *The Collection of the Middle Length Sayings (Majjhima-Nikaya)*, Vol. 1, The Pali Text Society, Lancaster, 2007, p. 383.
18. Hultzsch, E., *Corpus Inscriptionum Indicarum: Inscriptions of Ashoka*, Vol. 1, Clarendon Press, 1925, pp. 155–60.
19. Elliot, Henry Miers, 'Tarikh-i Firoz Shahi, of Shams-i Siraj, 'Afif', *The History of India, as Told by Its Own Historians*, Vol. 3, John Dowson (ed.), Trubner and Co., London, p. 351.
20. Fleet, John Faithfull, *Corpus Inscriptionum Indicarum: Inscriptions of the Early Gupta Kings and their Successors*, Vol. 3, Indological Book House, Varanasi, 1960, p. 16.
21. Krishnaswamy Rao Sahib, C.S., and Amalananda Ghosh, 'A Note on the Allahabad Pillar of Asoka', *The Journal of the Royal Asiatic Society of Great Britian and Ireland for 1935*, London, 1935, p. 703.
22. Ibid., 698.
23. Dutt, Manmatha Nath (ed.), *A Prose English Translation of the Harivamsha*, H.C. Dass, Calcutta, 1897, p. 104.
24. Ibid, 103–04.
25. Ibid, 105.
26. Kielhorn, F., 'Bengal Asiatic Society's Copper-Plate Grant of Trilochanapala. The (Vikrama) Year 1084', *The Indian Antiquary*, Vol. 18, 1889, University of Calcutta, pp. 33–34.
27. Beal, Samuel (trans.), *Si-Yu-Ki: Buddhist Records of the Western World*, Vol. 1, Trubner and Co., London, 1884, pp. 230–31.
28. Chimpa, Lama, and Alaka Chattopadhyaya (trans.), *Taranatha's History of Buddhism in India*, Motilal Banarsidass, Delhi, p. 288.
29. Beal, Samuel (trans.), *Si-Yu-Ki: Buddhist Records of the Western World*, Vol. 1, Trubner and Co., London, 1884, p. 232.
30. Ibid., 232.
31. Pandit, R.S. (trans.), *Rajatarangini: The Saga of the Kings of Kasmir*, Sahitya Akademi, New Delhi, p. 106. Kalhan credits Ranaditya for building the first Martand (sun temple) temple in Kashmir.
32. Beal, Samuel (trans.), *Si-Yu-Ki: Buddhist Records of the Western World*, Vol. 1, Trubner and Co., London, 1884, p. 233.
33. Beal, Samuel (ed.), *The Life of Hieun-Tsiang by the Shaman Hwui Li*, Kegan Paul, Trench, Trubner and Co. Ltd, 1911, p. 187.
34. Ibid., 185.
35. Beal, Samuel (trans.), *Si-Yu-Ki: Buddhist Records of the Western World*, Vol. 1, Trubner and Co., London, 1884, p. 234.

36. Cowell, E.B., and F.W. Thomas (trans.), *The Harsa-Carita of Bana*, The Royal Asiatic Society, London, 1897, p. 61.
37. We know that the playwright Sudraka, a king from the Abhira Dynasty (third–fourth century CE) who succeeded the Satvahanas in the Deccan, had also committed ritualistic suicide. The introduction to his play *Mrichchhakatika* states that after living for a hundred years, this king abdicated in favour of his son and then committed suicide by casting his body in a pyre. We don't know where the act was committed, but it was most likely at Nashik. See: Wilson, Horace Hayman (trans.), 'The Mrichchakati, or the Toy Cart', *Select Specimens of the Theatre of the Hindus*, Vol. 1, Asian Educational Services, p. 5.
38. Fleet, John Faithfull, *Corpus Inscriptionum Indicarum: Inscriptions of the Early Gupta Kings and their Successors*, Vol. 3, Indological Book House, Varanasi, 1960, pp. 202, 206.
39. Kielhorn, F., 'Inscriptions from Khajuraho: IV. Stone Inscription of Dhangadeva of the Year 1059; Renewed by Jayavarmadeva in the Year 1173', *Epigraphia India*, Vol. 1, pp. 138–39.
40. Mirashi, Vasudev Vishnu, *Corpus Inscriptionum Indicarum, Vol. IV: Inscriptions of the Kalachuri-Chedi Era*, Part 1, Govt. Epigraphist for India, 1955, p. 290.
41. Sachau, Dr Edward C. (trans.), *Alberuni's India*, Rupa Publications, 2002, p. 200.
42. Al-Badaoni, *A History of India: Muntakhabu-t-Tawarikh*, George S.A. Ranking (trans.), Vol. 2, Atlantic Publishers & Distributors, New Delhi, p. 179.
43. Kielhorn, F., 'Inscriptions from Khajuraho: IV. Stone Inscription of Dhangadeva of the Year 1059; Renewed by Jayavarmadeva in the Year 1173', *Epigraphia Indica*, Vol. 1, pp. 138–39.
44. Babur, Zahiru'd-din Muhammad, *Babur-Nama: Memoirs of Babur*, Annette Susannah Beveridge (trans.), Oriental Books Reprint Corporation, p. 655.
45. Elliot, Henry Miers, 'Tabakat-i Akbari, of Nizamu-d din Ahmad, Bakshi', *The History of India, as Told by Its Own Historians*, Vol. 5, John Dowson (ed.), Trubner and Co., London, p. 296.
46. Ibid., 320–1. The 25-year-old Akbar had personally led the charge, first on an elephant named Balsundar, and later during the course of the action, had ridden a horse.
47. Al-Badaoni, *A History of India: Muntakhabu-t-Tawarikh*, George S.A. Ranking (trans.), Vol. 2, Atlantic Publishers & Distributors, New Delhi, p. 176.
48. Ibid., 179.
49. Jarrett, H.S. (trans.), *Ain i Akbari of Abul Fazl-i-'Allami*, Vol. 2, Royal Asiatic Society of Bengal, 1949, p. 169.
50. Al-Badaoni, *A History of India: Muntakhabu-t-Tawarikh*, George S.A. Ranking (trans.), Vol. 2, Atlantic Publishers & Distributors, New Delhi, pp. 344–36.
51. Thackston, Wheeler M. (ed.), *The Jahangirnama: Memoirs of Jahangir, Emperor of India*, Oxford University Press, New York, pp. 32–33.
52. Foster, William (ed.), *Early Travels in India: 1583–1619*, Humphrey Milford Oxford University Press, England, 1921, pp. 177–78.
53. Ibid., 178.
54. Ibid., 19.
55. Ibid., 269.
56. Ball, V. (trans.), *Travels in India by Jean-Baptiste Tavernier*, Vol. 1, Oxford University Press, London, 1925, p. 115.

57. Ibid., 116.
58. Manucci, Niccolao, *Storia Do Mogor or Mogul India: 1653–1708*, Vol. 2, William Irvine (trans.), S. Dey, pp. 75–76.
59. Ibid., 76.
60. Sarkar, Jadunath, *Shivaji and His Times*, M.C. Sarkar & Sons, Calcutta, 1952, pp. 389–90.
61. Nevill, H.R., *Allahabad: A Gazetteer*, Vol. 23, Superintendent, Government Press, Allahabad, 1911, p. 174.
62. Krishnaswamy Rao Sahib, C.S., and Amalananda Ghosh, 'A Note on the Allahabad Pillar of Asoka', *The Journal of the Royal Asiatic Society of Great Britian and Ireland for 1935*, London, 1935, p. 705.
63. Nevill, H.R., *Allahabad: A Gazetteer*, Vol. 23, Superintendent, Government Press, Allahabad, 1911, p. 175.
64. Sarkar, Jadunath, *The History of Dasnami Naga Sanyasis*, Sri Panchayatri Akhara Mahanirvani, Allahabad, pp. 126–27.
65. Nevill, H.R., *Allahabad: A Gazetteer*, Vol. 23, Superintendent, Government Press, Allahabad, 1911, p. 176.
66. Sarkar, Jadunath, *The History of Dasnami Naga Sanyasis*, Sri Panchayatri Akhara Mahanirvani, Allahabad, p. 127.
67. Nevill, H.R., *Allahabad: A Gazetteer*, Vol. 23, Superintendent, Government Press, Allahabad, 1911, p. 178.
68. Hodges, William, *Travels in India, During the Years 1780, 1781, 1782, and 1783*, J. Edwards, London, 1794, pp. 98–99.
69. Ibid., 99.
70. Ibid., 99.
71. Heber, Right Rev. Reginald, *Narrative of a Journey Through the Upper Provinces of India: From Calcutta to Bombay, 1824–1825*, Vol. 1, Carey, Lea & Carey, Philadelphia, 1829, pp. 292, 294–95.
72. Ibid., 290.
73. Heber, Right Rev. Reginald, *Narrative of a Journey through the Upper Provinces of India: From Calcutta to Bombay, 1824–1825*, Vol. 1, Carey, Lea & Carey, Philadelphia, 1829, p. 290.
74. Ibid., 291.
75. Parkes, Fanny, *Wanderings of a Pilgrim, in Search of the Picturesque*, Vol. 1, Pelham Richardson, London, 1850, p. 86.
76. Ibid., 86.
77. Ibid., 86.
78. Chunder, Bholanauth, *The Travels of a Hindoo to Various Parts of Bengal and Upper India*, Vol. 1, Trubner and Co., London, 1869, p. 324.
79. Cunningham, Alexander, *Archaeological Survey of India: Four Reports Made During the Years 1862-63-64-65*, Vol. 1, The Government Central Press, Simla, 1871, pp. 299–300.

Chapter 7: Eternal Banaras

1. Gupta Emperor Skandagupta defeated a Huna invasion near Bhitari to the east of Banaras about 50 km away from the city, around 455 CE. See: Fleet,

John Faithfull, *Corpus Inscriptionum Indicarum: Inscriptions of the Early Gupta Kings and their Successors*, Vol. 3, Indological Book House, Varanasi, 1960, p. 56.
2. Elliot, Henry Miers, 'Tarikhu-s Subuktigin of Baihaki', *The History of India, as Told by Its Own Historians*, Vol. 2, John Dowson (ed.), Trubner and Co., London, p. 123; Majumdar, R.C., *Ancient India*, University of Calcutta, 1952, p. 344.
3. Elliot, Henry Miers, 'Extracts from the Mir-at-i Mas'udi', *The History of India, as Told by Its Own Historians*, Vol. 2, John Dowson (ed.), Trubner and Co., London, p. 535.
4. Elliot, Henry Miers, 'Taju-l Ma-asir of Hasan Nizami', *The History of India, as Told by Its Own Historians*, Vol. 2, John Dowson (ed.), Trubner and Co., London, pp. 223–24.
5. Reynolds, James (trans.), *The Kitab-i-Yamini: Historical Memoirs of Amir Sabaktagin and the Sultan Mahmud of Ghazna*, Oriental Translation Fund of Great Britain and Ireland, London, 1858, p. 627.
6. Elliot, Henry Miers, 'Tarikh-i Daudi, of 'Abdu-lla', *The History of India, as Told by Its Own Historians*, Vol. 4, John Dowson (ed.), Trubner and Co., London, p. 447.
7. Elliot, Henry Miers, 'Badshah-nama, of 'Abdu-l Hamid Lahori', *The History of India, as Told by Its Own Historians*, Vol. 7, John Dowson (ed.), Trubner and Co., London, p. 36.
8. Nevill, H.R., *Benares: A District Gazetteer*, Vol. 26, Superintendent, Government Press, United Provinces, 1909, p. 183.
9. Cunningham, Alexander, *The Ancient Geography of India*, Vol. 1, Trubner and Co., London, 1871, p. 438.
10. Dutt, Manmatha Nath (ed.), *A Prose English Translation of the Harivamsha*, H.C. Dass, Calcutta, 1897, p. 117.
11. Ibid., 117.
12. Ibid., 119.
13. Ibid., 119.
14. Shastri, J.L. (ed.), *The Linga-Purana*, Part 1, Motilal Banarsidass, New Delhi, 1951, p. 382.
15. Chakrabarti, Dilip K., *The Archaeology of Ancient Indian Cities*, Oxford University Press, Delhi, 1997, p. 200.
16. Jayaswal, Vidula, and Manoj Kumar, 'Excavations at Ramnagar: Discovery of a Supporting Settlement of Ancient Varanasi', *Puratattva*, No. 36, 2005–06, p. 85.
17. Ibid., 86.
18. The Ganga at Banaras is also called Uttaravahini (northerly course).
19. Mani, B.R., and Arundhati Banerji, *Catalogue of Terracotta Figurines from Rajghat Excavations (1940)*, Archaeological Survey of India, 2012, p. XII.
20. Ibid., XII.
21. Ibid., XIII–IV.
22. Ibid., XIII–XIV.
23. Narain, A.K., and T.N. Roy, *Excavations at Rajghat*, Banaras Hindu University, pp. 5–21.
24. Sinha, N.K. (ed.), 'Tomb of Lal Khan and Excavated Site, Rajghat', ASI Sarnath Circle. Pamphlet.

25. Elliot, Henry Miers, 'Taju-l Ma-asir of Hasan Nizami', *The History of India, as Told by Its Own Historians*, Vol. 2, John Dowson (ed.), Trubner and Co., London, pp. 223-4.
26. Legge, James (trans.), *A Record of Buddhistic Kingdoms: Being an Account by the Chinese Monk Fa Hien*, Oxford at the Clarendon Press, 1886, p. 94.
27. Fleet, John Faithfull, *Corpus Inscriptionum Indicarum: Inscriptions of the Early Gupta Kings and their Successors*, Vol. 3, Indological Book House, Varanasi, 1960, p. 56.
28. Beal, Samuel (trans.), *Si-Yu-Ki: Buddhist Records of the Western World*, Vol. 2, Trubner and Co., London, 1884, p. 44.
29. Ibid., 44-45.
30. Ibid., 45.
31. Ibid., 45.
32. Ball, V. (trans.), *Travels in India by Jean-Baptiste Tavernier*, Vol. 1, Oxford University Press, London, 1925, pp. 118-19.
33. Nevill, H.R., *Benares: A Gazetteer*, Vol. 26, Superintendent, Government Press, United Provinces, 1909, p. 207.
34. Ibid., 208.
35. Ibid., 208.
36. Sherring, Rev., M.A., *The Sacred Cities of the Hindus: An Account of Benares*, Trubner and Co. London, 1868, p. 331.
37. Fleet, John Faithfull, *Corpus Inscriptionum Indicarum: Inscriptions of the Early Gupta Kings and their Successors*, Vol. 3, Indological Book House, Varanasi, 1960, p. 251.
38. Ibid., 250.
39. Sarkar, Jadunath, *The History of Dasnami Naga Sanyasis*, Sri Panchayatri Akhara Mahanirvani, Allahabad, pp. 7-8.
40. Chimpa, Lama, and Alaka Chattopadhyaya (trans.), *Taranatha's History of Buddhism in India*, Motilal Banarsidass, Delhi, p. 233.
41. Ibid., 26.
42. Ibid., 31.
43. Sachau, Edward C. (trans.), *Alberuni's India*, Vol. 1, Trubner and Co., 1910, p. 22.
44. Ibid., 22.
45. Ibid., 22.
46. Reynolds, James (trans.), *The Kitab-i-Yamini: Historical Memoirs of the Amir Sabaktagin and the Sultan Mahmud of Ghazna*, The Oriental Translation Fund of Great Britain and Ireland, London, 1858, p. 458. I have identified Manaj and Astar as Jaunpur and Jafarabad respectively, which existed to the south of the Gomti.
47. Ibid., 459.
48. Ibid., 462.
49. Jarrett, H.S. (trans.), *'Ain-i-Akbari of Abul Fazl-i-'Allami*, Vol. 2, Royal Asiatic Society of Bengal, Calcutta, 1949, p. 170.
50. Majumdar, R.C., *Ancient India*, University of Calcutta, 1952, p. 344; Elliot, Henry Miers, 'Tarikhu-s Subuktigin of Baihaki', *The History of India, as Told by Its Own Historians*, Vol. 2, John Dowson (ed.), Trubner and Co., London, p. 123.

51. Elliot, Henry Miers, 'Extracts from the Mir-at-i Mas'udi', *The History of India, as Told by Its Own Historians*, Vol. 2, John Dowson (ed.), Trubner and Co., London, p. 535.
52. Elliot, Henry Miers, 'Taju-l Ma-asir of Hasan Nizami', *The History of India, as Told by its Own Historians*, Vol. 2, John Dowson (ed.), Trubner and Co., London, pp. 223–24.
53. Raverty, H.G. (trans.), *The Tabakat-i-Nasiri of Minhaj-i-Saraj*, The Asiatic Society of Bengal, London, 1873, pp. 470, 627.
54. Chimpa, Lama, and Alaka Chattopadhyaya (trans.), *Taranatha's History of Buddhism in India*, Motilal Banarsidass, Delhi, p. 138.
55. Ferishta, Mahomed Kasim, *History of the Rise of the Mahomedan Power in India: Till the Year A.D. 1612*, John Briggs (trans.), Vol. 1, Low Price Publications, Delhi, p. 101.
56. Nevill, H.R., *Benares: A District Gazetteer*, Vol. 26, Superintendent, Government Press, United Provinces, 1909, p. 257.
57. Elliot, Henry Miers, 'Futhat-i Firoz Shahi, of Sultan Firoz Shah', *The History of India, as Told by Its Own Historians*, Vol. 3, John Dowson (ed.), Trubner and Co., London, pp. 381–82.
58. Elliot, Henry Miers, 'Tarikh-i Mubarak Shahi, of Yahya bin Ahmed', *The History of India, as Told by Its Own Historians*, Vol. 4, John Dowson (ed.), Trubner and Co., London, p. 11.
59. Fuhrer, A., *The Sharqi Architecture of Jaunpur: With Notes on Zafarabad, Sahet-Mahet and Other Places in the North-Western Provinces and Oudh*, Superintendent of Government Printing, Calcutta, 1889, p. 51.
60. Elliot, Henry Miers, 'Makhzan-i Afghani and Tarikh-i Khan-Jahan Lodi, of Ni'amatu-lla', *The History of India, as Told by Its Own Historians*, Vol. 5, John Dowson (ed.), Trubner and Co., London, p. 95.
61. Elliot, Henry Miers, 'Tarikh-i Daudi, of 'Abdu-lla', *The History of India, as Told by Its Own Historians*, Vol. 4, John Dowson (ed.), Trubner and Co., London, p. 447.
62. The Ramnagar Fort was not yet built. However, some speculate that the Rajghat mound was the fort of Banaras.
63. Babur, Zahiru'd-din Muhammad, *Babur-Nama: Memoirs of Babur*, Annette Susannah Beveridge (trans.), Oriental Books Reprint Corporation, p. 652.
64. Ibid., 658.
65. Nevill, H.R., *Benares: A District Gazetteer*, Vol. 26, Superintendent, Government Press, United Provinces, 1909, p. 193.
66. Jarrett, H.S. (trans.), *'Ain-i-Akbari of Abul Fazl-i-'Allami*, Vol. 2, Royal Asiatic Society of Bengal, Calcutta, 1949, p. 169.
67. Ibid., 169–70.
68. Thackston, Wheeler M. (ed.), *The Jahangirnama: Memoirs of Jahangir, Emperor of India*, Oxford University Press, New York, p. 362.
69. Elliot, Henry Miers, 'Badshah-nama, of 'Abdu-l Hamid Lahori', *The History of India, as Told by Its Own Historians*, Vol. 7, John Dowson (ed.), Trubner and Co., London, p. 36.
70. Ibid., 36.
71. Elliot, Henry Miers, 'Ma-a'sir-I 'Alamgiri, of Muhammad Saki Musta'idd Khan', *The History of India, as Told by Its Own Historians*, Vol. 7, John Dowson (ed.), Trubner and Co., London, p. 184.

72. Khan, Saqi Must'ad, *Maasir-i-'Alamgiri*, Jadunath Sarkar (trans.), Bibliotheca Indica, Royal Asiatic Society of Bengal, Calcutta, 1947, p. 55.
73. Nevill, H.R., *Benares: A District Gazetteer*, Vol. 26, Superintendent, Government Press, United Provinces, 1909, p. 197.
74. Sarkar, Jadunath, *The History of Dasnami Naga Sanyasis*, Sri Panchayatri Akhara Mahanirvani, Allahabad, p. 87.
75. Sherring, Rev., M.A., *The Sacred Cities of the Hindus: An Account of Banaras*, Trubner and Co., London, 1868, pp. 30-31.
76. Foster, William (ed.), *Early Travels in India: 1583-1619*, Humphrey Milford Oxford University Press, England, 1921, p. 18.
77. Ibid., 20.
78. Ibid., 22.
79. Ibid., 176.
80. Ball, V. (trans.), *Travels in India by Jean-Baptiste Tavernier*, Vol. 1, Oxford University Press, London, 1925, p. 118.
81. Parkes, Fanny, *Wanderings of a Pilgrim, in Search of the Picturesque*, Vol. 1, Pelham Richardson, London, 1850, p. 67.
82. Eden, Emily, *'Up the Country'*, Richard Bentley, London, 1867, p. 21.
83. Ibid., 28.
84. Ibid., 30.
85. Davids, T.W. Rhys, *The Questions of King Milinda*, Oxford at the Clarendon Press, 1890, p. 69.
86. Strong, J.S. (trans.), *The Legend of King Asoka: A Study and Translation of the Asokavadana*, Motilal Banarsidass, New Delhi, p. 248.
87. Ball, V. (trans.), *Travels in India by Jean-Baptiste Tavernier*, Vol. 2, Oxford University Press, London, 1925, p. 231.
88. Ibid., 231-32.
89. Ibid., 235.
90. Bernier, Francois, *Travels in the Mogul Empire: A.D. 1656-1668*, Archibald Constable (trans.), Humphrey Milford Oxford University Press, 1916, p. 334.
91. Ibid., 336.
92. Manucci, Niccolao, *Storia Do Mogor or Mogul India: 1653-1708*, Vol. 2, William Irvine (trans.), John Murray, London, 1907, p. 83.
93. Nevill, H.R., *Benares: A District Gazetteer*, Vol. 26, Superintendent, Government Press, United Provinces, 1909, p. 198.
94. Ibid., 202.
95. Nevill, H.R., *Benares: A District Gazetteer*, Vol. 26, Superintendent, Government Press, United Provinces, 1909, p. 203.
96. Hodges, William, *Travels in India, During the Years 1780, 1781, 1782, and 1783*, J. Edwards, London, 1794, p. 48.
97. Ibid., 49; Nevill, H.R., *Benares: A District Gazetteer*, Vol. 26, Superintendent, Government Press, United Provinces, 1909, p. 204.
98. Hodges, William, *Travels in India, During the Years 1780, 1781, 1782, and 1783*, J. Edwards, London, 1794, p. 52.
99. Ibid., 53.
100. Ibid., 55.
101. Drake-Brockman, D.L., *Mirzapur: A District Gazetteer*, Vol. 27, Superintendent, Government Press, Allahabad, 1911, p. 237; Hodges, William, *Travels in India During the Years 1780, 1781, 1782, and 1783*, J. Edwards, London, 1794, p. 84.

102. Ibid., 85.
103. Drake-Brockman, D.L., *Mirzapur: A District Gazetteer*, Vol. 27, Superintendent, Government Press, Allahabad, 1911, p. 237.
104. Nevill, H.R., *Benares: A District Gazetteer*, Vol. 26, Superintendent, Government Press, United Provinces, 1909, p. 205.
105. Ibid., 207.
106. Ibid., 208.
107. Ibid., 212.
108. Sherring, Rev. M.A., *The Sacred Cities of the Hindus: An Account of Benares*, Trubner and Co., London, 1868, pp. 39–40.
109. Hodges, William, *Travels in India During the Years 1780, 1781, 1782, and 1783*, J. Edwards, London, 1794, pp. 61–62.
110. Heber, Right Rev. Reginald, *Narrative of a Journey Through the Upper Provinces of India: From Calcutta to Bombay, 1824–1825*, Vol. 1, Carey, Lea & Carey, Philadelphia, 1829, p. 263.
111. Ibid., 252.
112. Ibid., 257.
113. Ibid., 251–52.
114. Ibid., 266.
115. Ibid., 286–87.
116. Ibid., 287.
117. Pandit, R.S. (trans.), *Rajatarangini: The Saga of the Kings of Kasmir*, Sahitya Akademi, New Delhi, pp. 16, 123–5, 358; Dutt, Jogesh Chunder (trans.), *The Rajatarangini of Jonaraja*, Gyan Publishing House, Delhi, p. 16.
118. Heber, Right Rev. Reginald, *Narrative of a Journey Through the Upper Provinces of India: From Calcutta to Bombay, 1824–1825*, Vol. 1, Carey, Lea & Carey, Philadelphia, 1829, p. 288.
119. Ibid., 252.
120. Prinsep, James, *Benares Illustrated, in a Series of Drawings*, Baptist Mission Press, Calcutta, 1831, p. 13.
121. Sherring, Rev., M.A., *The Sacred Cities of the Hindus: An Account of Benares*, Trubner and Co., London, 1868, p. 42.
122. Nevill, H.R., *Benares: A District Gazetteer*, Vol. 26, Superintendent, Government Press, United Provinces, 1909, p. 250.
123. Ibid., 251.
124. Prinsep, James, *Benares Illustrated, in a Series of Drawings*, Baptist Mission Press, Calcutta, 1831, Old Temple of Visheswar information page, opposite the sketch of the Gyanvapi Masjid.
125. Ibid., Old Temple of Visheswar information page, opposite the sketch of the Gyanvapi Masjid.
126. IANS, "'Shivling' Found in Gyanvapi Well, Claim Hindu Lawyers', The Times of India, 16 May 2022, https://tinyurl.com/45f28ab6. Accessed on 27 September 2024.
127. Ghose, Loke Nath, *The Modern History of the Indian Chiefs, Rajas, Zamindars, &c.*, Vol. 2, J.N. Ghose and Co., Calcutta, 1881, p. 362.
128. Heber, Right Rev. Reginald, *Narrative of a Journey Through the Upper Provinces of India: From Calcutta to Bombay, 1824–1825*, Vol. 1, Carey, Lea & Carey, Philadelphia, 1829, pp. 257–58.

129. Ibid. 257-58.
130. Ball, V. (trans.), *Travels in India by Jean-Baptiste Tavernier*, Vol. 2, Oxford University Press, London, 1925, p. 235.
131. Prinsep, James, *Benares Illustrated, in a Series of Drawings*, Baptist Mission Press, Calcutta, 1831, Madhoyray Ghat and the Minarets information page, opposite the sketch of Alamgir's Mosque.
132. Ibid.
133. Parkes, Fanny, *Wanderings of a Pilgrim, in Search of the Picturesque*, Vol. 1, Pelham Richardson, London, 1850, p. 67.
134. Hodges, William, *Travels in India During the Years 1780, 1781, 1782, and 1783*, J. Edwards, London, 1794, p. 61.
135. Ibid., 61.
136. Nevill, H.R., *Benares: A District Gazetteer*, Vol. 26, Superintendent, Government Press, United Provinces, 1909, p. 240.
137. Ibid., 240.
138. Ibid., 241.
139. Hodges, William, *Travels in India During the Years 1780, 1781, 1782, and 1783*, J. Edwards, London, 1794, p. 62.
140. Nevill, H.R., *Benares: A District Gazetteer*, Vol. 26, Superintendent, Government Press, United Provinces, 1909, p. 242.
141. Heber, Right Rev. Reginald, *Narrative of a Journey Through the Upper Provinces of India: From Calcutta to Bombay, 1824-1825*, Vol. 1, Carey, Lea & Carey, Philadelphia, 1829, p. 258.
142. Prinsep, James, *Benares Illustrated, in a Series of Drawings*, Baptist Mission Press, Calcutta, 1831, Sketch of the Manikarnika Ghat.
143. Ibid., Manikarnika Ghat information matter, opposite the image of the sketch.
144. Nevill, H.R., *Benares: A District Gazetteer*, Vol. 26, Superintendent, Government Press, United Provinces, 1909, p. 244.
145. Parkes, Fanny, *Wanderings of a Pilgrim, in Search of the Picturesque*, Vol. 1, Pelham Richardson, London, 1850, p. 254.
146. Bernier, Francois, *Travels in the Mogul Empire: A.D. 1656-1668*, Archibald Constable (trans.), Humphrey Milford Oxford University Press, 1916, p. 314.
147. Hodges, William, *Travels in India During the Years 1780, 1781, 1782, and 1783*, J. Edwards, London, 1794, pp. 82-83.
148. Heber, Right Rev. Reginald, *Narrative of a Journey Through the Upper Provinces of India: From Calcutta to Bombay, 1824-1825*, Vol. 1, Carey, Lea & Carey, Philadelphia, 1829, p. 261.
149. Atkinson, Edwin T., *The Himalayan Gazetteer*, Vol.2, Part 2, Cosmo Publications, New Delhi, 1981, p. 615.
150. Amatya, Shaphalya, 'The Failure of Captain Knox's Mission in Nepal', *Ancient Nepal*, No. 82, June-July 1984, p. 9.
151. Ibid., 618.
152. Ibid., 630.
153. Mishra, Manjari, 'A Piece of Nepal in Varanasi', The Times of India, 17 May 2010, https://tinyurl.com/yy9wkz5t. Accessed on 27 September 2024.
154. 'File: Krishna Govardhana. Bharat Kala Bhavan, ni03-24.jpg', *Wikimedia Commons*, https://tinyurl.com/yc6dbpfm. Accessed on 5 October 2024.

155. I have come across several such 'lucky' temples that survived destruction. Near Chitrakoot, in an 'inaccessible' place called Dadhwa Manpur, close to the destroyed Madfa Fort is a small temple called Bileriya Math. Unlike every other temple around Chitrakoot, including the ones in the Madfa Fort, this temple has survived intact. And just like the Kardameshwar Mahadev Mandir of Banaras, I would also call the Bileriya Math a lucky temple.

Chapter 8: The Lost Treasures of Sarnath

1. Vajira, Sister, and Francis Story (trans.), *Last Days of the Buddha: The Mahaparinibbana Sutta*, Buddhist Publication Society, Kandy, pp. 62–63.
2. Sahni, Daya Ram, *Catalogue of the Museum of Archaeology at Sarnath*, Superintendent Government Printing, Calcutta, 1914, p. 1.
3. Geiger, Wilhelm, and Mabel Haynes Bode (trans.), *The Mahavamsa: Or the Great Chronicle of Ceylon*, Oxford University Press, 1912, p. ix.
4. Ibid., 2.
5. Chimpa, Lama, and Alaka Chattopadhyaya (trans.), *Taranatha's History of Buddhism in India*, Motilal Banarsidass, Delhi, p. 41.
6. The several waterbodies around Nalanda were also excavated for a similar purpose, a parallel with which can be drawn here.
7. Mitra, Debala, *Buddhist Monuments*, Sahitya Samsad, Calcutta, 1971, p. 66.
8. Archaeological Survey of India, *Annual Report: 1904–5*, 1908, p. 60.
9. Ibid., 60.
10. Chimpa, Lama, and Alaka Chattopadhyaya (trans.), *Taranatha's History of Buddhism in India*, Motilal Banarsidass, Delhi, p. 41.
11. Legge, James (trans.), *A Record of Buddhistic Kingdoms; Being an Account by the Chinese Monk Fa Hien*, Oxford at the Clarandon Press, 1886, pp. 95–96.
12. Ibid., 96.
13. Beal, Samuel (trans.), *Si-Yu-Ki: Buddhist Records of the Western World*, Vol.2, Trubner and Co., London, 1884, pp. 45–46.
14. Ibid., 46.
15. Cunningham, Alexander, *Archaeological Survey of India: Four Reports Made During the Years 1862-63-64-65*, Vol. 1, The Government Central Press, Simla, 1871, p. 124.
16. Beal, Samuel (trans.), *Si-Yu-Ki: Buddhist Records of the Western World*, Vol. 2, Trubner and Co., London, 1884, p. 61.
17. Archaeological Survey of India, *Annual Report: 1904–5*, 1908, plate xi.
18. Sahni, Daya Ram, *Catalogue of the Museum of Archaeology at Sarnath*, Superintendent Government Printing, Calcutta, 1914, p. 1.
19. Cunningham, Alexander, *Archaeological Survey of India: Four Reports Made During the Years 1862-63-64-65*, Vol. 1, The Government Central Press, Simla, 1871, p. 126.
20. Archaeological Survey of India, *Annual Report: 1904–5*, 1908, p. 64.
21. Duncan, Jonathan, 'An Account of the Discovery of Two Urns in the Vicinity of Benares', *Asiatic Researches*, Vol. 5, 1799, pp. 131–32.
22. Cunningham, Alexander, *Archaeological Survey of India: Four Reports Made During the Years 1862-63-64-65*, Vol. 1, The Government Central Press, Simla, 1871, p. 119.

23. Sahni, Daya Ram, *Catalogue of the Museum of Archaeology at Sarnath*, Superintendent Government Printing, Calcutta, 1914, p. 11.
24. Cunningham, Alexander, *Archaeological Survey of India: Four Reports Made During the Years 1862-63-64-65*, Vol. 1, The Government Central Press, Simla, 1871, p. 115.
25. This box is presently in the Indian Museum, Kolkata.
26. Archaeological Survey of India, *Annual Report: 1904-5*, 1908, p. 62.
27. Sahni, Daya Ram, *Catalogue of the Museum of Archaeology at Sarnath*, Superintendent Government Printing, Calcutta, 1914, pp. 88-89.
28. Ibid., 7.
29. Konow, Sten, 'Sarnath Inscription of Kumaradevi', *Epigraphia* Indica, Vol. 9, 1907-08, pp. 321, 327-28.
30. Cunningham, Alexander, *Archaeological Survey of India: Four Reports Made During the Years 1862-63-64-65*, Vol. 1, The Government Central Press, Simla, 1871, p. 122.
31. Ibid., 123.
32. Ibid., 123.
33. Archaeological Survey of India, *Annual Report: 1904-5*, 1908, p. 64.
34. Sherring, Rev., M.A., *The Sacred Cities of the Hindus: An Account of Benares*, Trubner and Co., London, 1868, p. 235.
35. Cunningham, Alexander, *Four Reports Made During the Years 1862-63-64-65*, Vol. 1, Archaeological Survey of India, 2000, pp. 111-12.
36. Archaeological Survey of India, *Annual Report: 1904-5*, 1908, p. 63.
37. Cunningham, Alexander, *Archaeological Survey of India: Four Reports Made During the Years 1862-63-64-65*, Vol. 1, Government Central Press, Simla, 1871, p. 126.
38. Thomas, E., 'Note on the Present State of the Excavations at Sarnath', *Journal of the Asiatic Society of Bengal*, Vol. 23, No. 1-7, 1854, p. 472.
39. Ibid., 476.
40. Sahni, Daya Ram, *Catalogue of the Museum of Archaeology at Sarnath*, Superintendent Government Printing, Calcutta, 1914, p. 13.
41. Archaeological Survey of India, *Annual Report: 1904-5*, 1908, p. 63.
42. Ibid., 64.
43. Sahni, Daya Ram, *Catalogue of the Museum of Archaeology at Sarnath*, Superintendent Government Printing, Calcutta, 1914, p. 14.
44. 'Plaque', *The British Museum*, https://tinyurl.com/z3v6yxxw. Accessed on 28 September 2024.
45. Vogel, J. Ph., 'Epigraphical Discoveries at Sarnath: I. Inscriptions on the Asoka Pillar', *Epigraphia Indica*, Vol. 8, 1905-06, p. 169.
46. Sahni, Daya Ram, *Catalogue of the Museum of Archaeology at Sarnath*, Superintendent Government Printing, Calcutta, 1914, pp. 30-31.
47. Bloch, T., 'Two Inscriptions on Buddhist Images: B. Mathura Image Inscription of the Year 33 of Huvishka', *Epigraphia Indica*, Vol. 8, 1905-06, p. 182. Only the portion above the pedestal depicting the feet of the Buddha in the lotus posture remains of the idol. The pedestal has the inscription which notes that a female disciple of Monk Bala had donated the sculpture.
48. Vogel, J. Ph., 'Epigraphical Discoveries at Sarnath: III. Inscriptions of the Third Year of Kanishka', *Epigraphia Indica*, Vol. 8, 1905-06, p. 176. The colossus from

Shravasti is lodged in the Indian Museum in Kolkata, the Bodhisattva sculpture of Mathura on which Monk Bala's name features is in the Lucknow Museum, and the colossus Bodhisattva donated by Monk Bala is in the Sarnath Museum.

49. Mitra, Debala, *Buddhist Monuments*, Sahitya Samsad, Calcutta, 1971, p. 67.
50. Sahni, Daya Ram, *Catalogue of the Museum of Archaeology at Sarnath*, Superintendent Government Printing, Calcutta, 1914, p. 14.
51. Archaeological Survey of India, *Annual Report: 1907-08*, 1911, p. 52.
52. Ibid., 52.
53. Ibid., 59–61.
54. Ibid., 75.

www.ingramcontent.com/pod-product-compliance
Lightning Source LLC
Chambersburg PA
CBHW030517230426
43665CB00010B/658